PRISONERS
OF
POLITICS

PRISONERS
OF
POLITICS

Breaking the Cycle
of Mass Incarceration

RACHEL ELISE BARKOW

THE BELKNAP PRESS OF
HARVARD UNIVERSITY PRESS
Cambridge, Massachusetts
London, England
2019

First printing

Library of Congress Cataloging-in-Publication Data
Names: Barkow, Rachel E., author.
Title: Prisoners of politics : breaking the cycle of mass incarceration /
Rachel Elise Barkow.
Description: Cambridge, Massachusetts : The Belknap Press of
Harvard University Press, 2019. | Includes bibliographical references and index.
Identifiers: LCCN 2018032017 | ISBN 9780674919235 (alk. paper)
Subjects: LCSH: Criminal justice, Administration of—United States. |
Criminal justice, Administration of—Planning—United States.
Classification: LCC HV9950 .B358 2019 | DDC 365/.70973—dc23
LC record available at https://lccn.loc.gov/2018032017

For Nate,
whose love and encouragement
are behind every word in this book
and whose kind and generous
heart keeps me hopeful
for a better future

Contents

PRISONERS
OF
POLITICS

INTRODUCTION

FEW PEOPLE WOULD want to establish air pollutant limits or workplace safety conditions by popular vote. Instead, most people prefer to trust experts with specialized knowledge to set policies based on studies of what maximizes public safety and an analysis of the costs and benefits of different courses of action. This is now the well-established path for just about every public health and safety area in American life because we recognize that the typical voter lacks the requisite data and knowledge to make the best decisions in these areas. We understand that we would get inferior outcomes if instead we relied upon the emotional preferences of the body politic or politicians' intuitive guesses about what is likely to work.

Yet that is precisely what we do when it comes to decisions about public safety and crime control. We do not rely on experts or use studies and rational assessment to minimize crime. Instead, criminal justice policy in the United States is set largely based on emotions and the gut reactions of laypeople. We have been doing this for decades, with the public and politicians reacting to stories or panics about crime with ill-informed laws and punitive policies that extend far beyond the high-profile event that sparked them and without much thought about whether the response will promote public safety. Donald Trump's rise to the presidency follows this tradition and provides a vivid example of how public fear based on misinformation translates into policy. Trump campaigned on the false idea that we have record-high homicide rates and that crime is rampant throughout America, with violent gangs of illegal immigrants roaming the streets and torturing innocent citizens. He misleadingly described inner-city neighborhoods in places like Chicago as areas where people cannot walk down the street without being shot. This rhetoric, with its racist overtones, appeals to voters who are already prone to punitive approaches, and it primes others to support harsh punishments and tactics—and the candidates who endorse them—because the public is ill-informed about actual crime rates or what works to prevent crime. Voters assume incorrectly that violent crime is rising, even as it has plummeted. Politicians eager for votes therefore pursue ever-tougher policies.[1]

We have seen this kind of tough-on-crime rhetoric for decades, by both Republicans and Democrats. Bill Clinton spoke in similarly sweeping and ill-informed tones about drug dealers and sought to create a tough-on-crime image for himself, going out of his way to return to Arkansas from the campaign trail to be present in the state for the execution of an intellectually impaired man. Every recent president has spoken of the need to take a harsh approach to violent crime and criminals. The story has been largely the same at the local level.

The result is that jurisdictions throughout America have produced the highest incarceration rate in the world among major nations, with more than 2.2 million people incarcerated in prisons and jails, and with 1 in 3 adults in America possessing a criminal record.[2] Millions more are on probation or parole and living with onerous supervision conditions.[3] Our policies are unquestionably tough on budgets, tough on individuals, and tough on communities, but are they really tough on crime itself? Is our current approach the best way to reduce crime and improve public safety? Politicians and members of the public who support the most punitive approaches intuitively think that they work and make us safer, thus justifying their human and economic costs.

In fact, many of America's criminal justice policies have little to no effect on crime.[4] They take limited public funds that could be better spent on more effective measures for improving public safety. Even worse, many of our crime policies *increase* the risk of crime instead of fighting it—all while producing racially discriminatory outcomes and devaluing individual liberty. Unfortunately, counterproductive policies like these are not rare; they abound in every jurisdiction in the United States.

If we want better outcomes that will improve public safety, we need to change the institutional framework we currently use to make criminal justice policy. Instead of policies designed to appeal to the emotions of voters who lack basic information about crime, we need to create an institutional structure that creates a space for experts who look at facts and data to set policies that will improve public safety outcomes, even if they are not easily reduced to sound bites or fail to provide emotional appeal.

This institutional model is a well-traveled path for better outcomes. Indeed, this is the model we use in most other areas of governance, from fiscal policy to environmental regulation. We do not have our elected officials set policies based on their intuitive reactions to outlier stories that make the news and arouse the public. We do not, for instance, jettison a therapeutic drug based on one bad outcome. We do not abolish all air travel because of one accident. Instead, we rely on expert agencies to set policies based on the best data available to minimize risks and achieve the greatest benefits at the lowest costs. But all too often crime policy in America is based on a reaction to a single crime without any evaluation of overall programs or approaches. People who care about reducing mass incarceration and want to improve criminal justice thus need to push for a model of criminal justice decision-making that looks more like the way we make policy in other regulatory areas where expertise plays a more significant role.

This is not to say that a shift from policy by populism to expertise will be easy or completely transformative. There is an anti-elite, anti-expert sentiment in America, and large segments of the public are likely to be particularly resistant to the idea that crime policy is something for experts instead of the regular man or woman on the street.[5] If criminal justice were just a matter of achieving retributive justice—of determining what someone morally deserves as punishment for a crime—then a model that relies on the public's emotional reaction might make more sense. But that is not the only goal of criminal punishment. The public and policy-makers often emphasize that the aim of criminal justice policy is the utilitarian goal of maximizing public safety and making the most of limited resources; to the extent that is the goal, we could be doing much better. We have data and evidence about better approaches that would give us better safety outcomes with our limited resources and that would result in less human suffering by individuals currently facing excess punishments. We know that policies that satiate punitive desires in the short term sometimes come with longer-term hits to public safety. If that is the trade-off we want to make as a society, we should be doing so explicitly, instead of often incorrectly assuming that the toughest responses that feel good in the here and now are also the best strategies for long-term public safety. If it turns out that the harsh collateral consequences of convictions or longer terms of confinement make reentry too difficult, thus prompting people to commit more crimes when they finish serving their sentences, we should decide openly whether it is worth paying that price in exchange for whatever retributive impulse those policies are serving. But we cannot evaluate that trade-off if we do not even know that we are making it. And that is often the case right now, because no one is paying attention to the costs and benefits of different policy options. The key to making better decisions about public safety and the use of our limited resources is to create a decision-making structure where we no longer ignore evidence about what does and does not work and at what cost.

To be sure, a new institutional model for making decisions about criminal justice policies will not be the answer to everything that ails criminal justice policy-making in America. Experts do not have all the answers about criminal justice and sometimes disagree among themselves about the best approach. There are limits to what data can tell us about reducing crime and promoting public safety, so policy calls sometimes have to be made on the best evidence available, even if it is incomplete. Any effort at crime control must also be cabined not only by rational analysis of the data but also by what would be retributively just. No one should get more than their just deserts no matter what the data says. And there will be times, perhaps not infrequently, when the public's moral and retributive desires will outweigh utilitarian goals and lead to longer sentences or harsher policies than the utilitarian framework would yield. That is, even if a particular punishment is likely to produce long-term negative effects on public safety, and that is made clear to the public, the public may nevertheless prefer it because of the immediate emotional satisfaction it brings. Sometimes public emotions will be so strong that they will overcome whatever institutional architecture is in place for expert judgment. And of course many of the worst policies in criminal law stem from racism and bias, and it would require sweeping changes in cultural attitudes to get at those root causes.[6] Experts cannot lead a cultural revolution. Moreover, criminal law itself can only do so much to prevent and minimize crime. Other social policies, from education to health care to employment programs, may do more to prevent crime than crime policies themselves. As author James Forman Jr. puts it in his terrific book, *Locking Up Our Own*, we should adopt an all-of-the-above approach to crime prevention and not just rely on a criminal justice response.[7] These are important caveats to what a model grounded in rational decision-making can achieve.

But change must always start somewhere, and there is no more important place to start when it comes to criminal justice reform than with the flawed institutional architecture for making criminal justice policy decisions that got us to where we are today. If the definition of insanity is doing the same thing over and over again but expecting different results, it would seem to be insane to rely on our current political system and institutional structures to meaningfully address problems with criminal justice and mass incarceration in America. Laypeople will always have a visceral reaction to particular high-profile crimes that will prompt them to support an ever-more-punitive response without sufficient attention to details. Politicians, for their part, will consistently seek to gain an electoral advantage by catering to these instincts and pandering to public anxiety and intuitions with ever-more-severe policies instead of pursuing policies that would be more effective at maximizing public safety.[8] Criminologists have labeled this setting of policy based on the emotional response of the public "penal populism," and it is an embedded feature of U.S. politics.[9] Penal populism, like populism more broadly, rests on the "disenchantment and disillusionment" with established experts.[10] The public is moved by "feelings and intuitions" rather than evidence, and "the authority and influence of the criminal justice expert has been decried and reduced."[11] The unfortunate result of a process fueled by ignorance of data and analysis is an excessive reliance on incarceration that is counterproductive instead of employing better strategies for reducing crime and protecting the public.

Indeed, it is one of the great tragedies of American domestic policy that many of our strategies for combating crime ruin lives but are not necessary to improve public safety, and in many cases, we adopt policies that actually increase the risk of crime instead of fighting it. We are wasting billions of dollars on too many practices that achieve the worst of both worlds: they do not protect victims or increase public safety, while at the same time they have catastrophic effects on millions of individuals and entire communities, especially poor people of color. One could say our approach to crime is a failed government program on an epic scale, except for the fact it is not a program at all. It is the cumulative effect of many isolated decisions to pursue tough policies without analyzing them to consider whether they work or, even worse, are harmful.

We have these ill-considered policies because we have a pathological political process that caters to the public's fears and emotions without any institutional safeguards or checks for rationality to make sure these policies work or are the best approach to combating crime.[12] Although one might think the public is attuned to public safety outcomes and not simply rhetoric about being tough, the reality is different. Voters are susceptible to symbolic gestures that yield less than optimal results because the public is not well informed about crime in America. Voters tend to hear only about the worst crimes, priming them emotionally for responses that sound as tough as possible because they want to satiate their desire for vengeance and justice in the here and now. The public often has little if any knowledge of crime rates or the sentences attached to different crimes. Indeed, many people in America are completely unaware that almost every person in prison is ultimately released and that roughly ten thousand people return to society from a term of incarceration every week in the United States. But because this regular return of citizens is not news, the public has little interest in whether or how these individuals have been prepared to reenter society or whether their time in prison has made them more likely to commit crimes.

The political process is also not equipped to discuss these issues in a reasoned way. Any discussion about overall strategies or long-term responses and results can be derailed with a single story. All it takes to kill a reform proposal's chances is one example of an individual convicted of a violent crime who would benefit from the proposed change. That one person ends up being the public's image of the reform, and if it looks like the law is going to coddle that individual, the public will resist, no matter what the overall benefits are.

Politicians know this dynamic well, at least since George H. W. Bush ran a successful campaign ad against former Massachusetts governor Michael Dukakis featuring Willie Horton, an individual on a furlough program in Massachusetts who committed a brutal rape and assault. Even though the furlough program in Massachusetts had a success rate greater than 99%, the public focused only on Horton's case. Bush defeated Dukakis, and no politician since has wanted to risk having their own Willie Horton moment. So even if a reform will bring more benefits than costs, including benefits in violent-crime reduction, politicians won't risk supporting it if their opponents can trot out a story of an individual who previously committed a violent act who would be let out early as a result of the change in policy.[13] We saw this dynamic play out in Arkansas where the populist response to a single crime upended their entire parole program without any consideration of the program's overall costs and benefits. After a high-profile murder by a man with a history of parole violations, the state made sweeping changes to its parole practices, including revoking parole for technical violations. Predictably, the state's incarceration rates ballooned in the wake of the changes, but they did nothing to lower crime in the state and instead funneled tens of millions of dollars into incarceration costs when that money could have been spent on more valuable crime-fighting measures.

We unfortunately lack experts in our system who can keep an eye on decisions like these to make sure we are making the right calls to maximize public safety and are spending our limited resources most effectively. On the contrary, those responsible for law enforcement—the people who should be among the leading experts on public safety—often fail to advocate for policies that would benefit the overall public interest because their professional self-interest clouds their judgment. Soft-on-crime charges leveled at would-be reformers often come from those inside the law enforcement community—particularly prosecutors—because they benefit from the existing set of laws and practices and are all too willing to use high-profile cases to advance their agenda, even if it is not tied to proven public safety outcomes. Prosecutors control the vast architecture of criminal law administration in the United States, and they benefit from the existing stable of broad laws with severe sentences because of the leverage it gives them to process their cases.[14] They are often the first to complain about efforts to reform the system in ways that undermine their power, even if those reforms would better allocate limited resources and not increase crime. Nebraska prosecutors, for instance, ardently opposed a Nebraska law enacted in 2015 that reduced many maximum sentences for both violent and nonviolent crimes. "It's nothing but being soft on crime," said one career prosecutor, angry about losing the leverage that "will help you wrap up a case."[15] In Louisiana, local prosecutors soundly defeated a 2014 bill that would have reduced Louisiana's draconian marijuana possession laws, under which a second possession charge is a felony and the third can land an individual up to 20 years in prison.[16] A few years later, Louisiana passed criminal justice reforms with bipartisan support, but with one notable exception: the Louisiana District Attorneys Association.[17] The organization actively lobbied against almost every suggestion.[18] To take another example, the Indiana Prosecuting Attorneys Council lobbied against a bill that reduced the radius of drug-free school zones from 1,000 to 500 feet, despite evidence that the current law disproportionately impacted minorities living in urban areas by essentially encompassing entire regions of large cities like Indianapolis under the sentence enhancement.[19] One prosecuting attorney argued that the 1,000-foot buffer was an "important tool" that makes prosecutors' cases "easier to prove."[20] At the national level, the National Association of Assistant United States Attorneys (NAAUSA), a group that represents federal prosecutors, sent an open letter to Attorney General Eric Holder expressing opposition to the 2013 Smarter Sentencing Act, which would have, among other things, reduced mandatory minimums for those convicted of nonviolent drug offenses.[21] NAAUSA was explicit that its opposition was based on the fact the law would make their jobs more difficult because it would "prevent[] the government from obtaining benefits gained through concessions during bargaining."[22]

Prosecutors typically claim they are the guardians of public safety when they advocate for longer sentences to stay on the books, even though longer sentences are not always best for public safety.[23] If prosecutors cared mainly about public safety instead of what made their professional life easier, they would be just as vocal about other issues that affect the successful reentry or reform of individuals who have committed crimes. But with the exception of a small cluster of prosecutors elected since 2016 who ran on a reform agenda, most prosecutors have instead been silent on these issues and have spoken out only on those issues that would affect the ease with which they do their day-to-day jobs. NAAUSA, for example, has repeatedly provided congressional testimony and issued myriad press releases, open letters, and policy statements resisting even modest reductions in federal sentences, but it has not weighed in on the debate on collateral consequences or prisoner rehabilitation programming despite the importance of those issues for public safety.[24] In 2015, for example, the Obama administration announced the creation of the Second Chance Pell pilot program, which allowed some prisoners to obtain grants for postsecondary education. There was widespread and diverse support for the program, as well as for legislation that would reverse a 1994 law that made prisoners ineligible for Pell Grant funding (a law, it should be noted, that was itself the product of irrational tough-on-crime politics and was spearheaded by congressional Democrats and President Bill Clinton). The American Bar Association passed a formal resolution encouraging Congress to restore Pell funding.[25] Yet neither NAAUSA nor the National District Attorneys Association, the two leading prosecutor organizations in the country, released press reports or made any type of public showing in support of the policy.

Why are most prosecutors vocal about maintaining longer sentences even though studies show they fail to deter crime and at a certain point could even promote crime by making it more difficult for individuals to reenter society after serving their sentences? And why are prosecutors silent when it comes to a range of other policies that have been proven to promote public safety? A big part of the answer to these questions is that keeping sentences long and mandatory makes prosecutors' jobs easier because it gives them the leverage they need to get guilty pleas and avoid trials, and they believe they are achieving better outcomes with this power because they do not necessarily know about the trade-offs to their approach. Prosecutors may be unaware of other measures that have been shown to reduce recidivism, and they lack the incentives to focus on them because they do not get credit for doing so in the current political environment. Elected prosecutors have also resisted reforms that would lower sentences to forestall having political opponents attack them for being soft on crime. The result is that we lack influential forces to lobby for measured approaches that balance both the costs and the benefits of longer sentences, and we have a powerful prosecutor and law enforcement lobby that stands in the way of all but the most modest sentencing reforms.

This, in a nutshell, is the political dynamic that brought us to the state of mass incarceration and criminalization that we have now, which leaves so much human misery and racial injustice in its wake. Elected leaders fear being labeled as soft on crime, so they aim to appear as tough as possible, even if there is no empirical grounding for the approaches they endorse.

Members of the public respond positively to this posture because they do not understand the ways in which these various policies can backfire in the long run and make us less safe. And law enforcement officials stand ready to fight any significant changes that would undermine their almost complete discretion to operate this system to their own advantage. No one, it seems, is minding the store in the name of tangible public safety results and less costly options, so we have countless policies that undermine them.

If there is any good news in this grim picture, it is that a sizable number of people are finally paying attention to the fact that our approach to crime is misguided, and engaged and active citizens are fighting for change. Politicians across the political spectrum are also beginning to see that we need to do something to address the mass incarceration of Americans and the expansive reach of the criminal justice system.[26] This is thus the ideal time to pursue the kind of lasting institutional change that will produce better outcomes, and this book outlines the key institutional shifts that are necessary.

One key pillar of reform is to institute greater checks on prosecutors. Prosecutors have taken over large swaths of criminal justice decision-making even though they are not well suited to make policies across a range of issues because of their professional conflict of interest. They should not be in charge of policies related to forensics or prisons or clemency because prosecutors have a stake in those decisions that is not in line with the public interest. Prosecutors also need to face a check on their decisions related to charging and sentencing, which means judges must have the discretion to make sentencing decisions without having prosecutors tie their hands. Mandatory sentencing guidelines and mandatory minimum laws create an imbalance of power in favor of prosecutors that leads to unchecked abuses. It is also important for prosecutors' decisions to be reevaluated because our knowledge about individuals and criminal behaviors grows over time, and our criminal justice policies should account for new information. That means it is important to take second looks at sentences, whether through parole or a robust clemency process. It is also important to give prosecutors the right incentives to make the most of limited resources. We need to put in place caps on the resources prosecutors can use so that they do not overuse state prisons when cheaper options would produce the same or better results. We can use a variety of other checking mechanisms as well, from the elimination of cash bail (to avoid having prosecutors seek excessive pretrial detention) to organizational changes within prosecutors' offices that will ensure greater compliance with ethical rules. We can also employ better metrics for assessing prosecutors than simply looking at conviction rates or outcomes in high-profile cases. Instead, we should be asking prosecutors to find ways to lower crime and incarceration rates (which we know can be done together because jurisdictions have done it), to minimize pretrial detention, to adopt better reentry practices so that people leaving prisons are less likely to recidivate, and to divert cases from the criminal justice realm when there are better options. As highly-mobilized and better informed voters in some communities are paying closer attention to prosecutor elections, these metrics can help them identify prosecutors who are truly committed to results and distinguish them from those who speak the rhetoric of reform but continue with the same failed policies of their predecessors.

While demanding more from prosecutors is a necessary step in achieving greater public safety and real reform, it is not sufficient. Prosecutors are powerful, but they do not control all criminal justice policies. The second critical avenue of institutional reform is to create expert agencies and commissions that are charged with using data and facts to make and recommend policies that maximize public safety. Critically, we need to design these agencies so they do not become tools of politicians and end up being used as just another avenue for instituting harsh policies that are not based on data or rational assessment. There are ways to set up agencies so that they can better withstand political pressures if they adopt policies that, on the surface, do not seem sufficiently tough. For example, these agencies should be subject to statutory requirements to stay within certain prison population caps and expenditure limits, which in turn will give these agencies the ability to produce better outcomes and push back against ill-informed populist impulses when those impulses would balloon the prison population or cost too much. These agencies should also be required to have diverse members who are attuned to all the relevant interests in criminal justice administration and who are well connected to key legislators so that their policies will have political support. Of course agencies will still be susceptible to some populist pressures, but these design traits will maximize their ability to resist them. Indeed, we know from the experience of expert criminal justice agencies that already exist that they can and have been successful in making fundamental changes to criminal justice policies that have resulted in better public safety outcomes, lower incarceration rates, cost savings, and far less human misery. The U.S. Sentencing Commission, for example, is not particularly well designed to resist political pressures and has often been used by Congress as just another avenue for increasing punishments. But even that agency was able to reduce more than 30,000 drug sentences retroactively based on its evaluation of data and recidivism studies. Those sentencing reductions caused the federal prison population to drop considerably and freed up resources for other public safety initiatives. And it was possible because the Sentencing Commission is at least somewhat insulated from political pressures and is designed to rely on data and studies. It could have been even more effective with a better design, as we have seen in states that have more successful sentencing commissions. We need to empower more agencies to make important criminal policy decisions and design them so that their expertise, not ill-informed emotional responses, guides their policy-making.

The use of commissions and so-called managerial justice has a bad reputation in some circles because it has been associated with more punitive sentences, but the use of the agency model per se has not been the problem; the problem has been the politics that have overwhelmed these agencies. All too often agencies have been poorly designed to withstand political pressure, and politics overpowered them. It is possible to create better models and achieve better results. We can require agencies to demonstrate that their policies are cost-benefit justified and represent the best options for achieving public safety. And we can and should insist that the agencies responsible for criminal justice policy-making, like other regulatory agencies, face judicial review of their decisions to make sure they are consistent with a statutory mandate to promote public safety and are not arbitrary and capricious. This is the standard model for other regulatory agencies, and it should be used for criminal justice agencies as well. Indeed, it is all the more important to use it in an area where so much is at stake.

That brings us to the third key avenue of reform: the courts. Courts are critical checks on criminal law excess. Judges should be policing prosecutors and criminal justice agencies to make sure they are complying with their statutory mandates and the Constitution. It is critical to have a bench up to the task. If you care about criminal justice reform, you must pay attention to who occupies the bench, and you must support the election and appointment of judges who are committed to reinvigorating constitutional protections that have largely been ignored. The biggest drop in incarceration at the state level—California's reduction in prison population—came about because of a Supreme Court decision that finally put some teeth into the Eighth Amendment in a context outside of the death penalty, where the Court has devoted almost all its Eighth Amendment oversight. Supreme Court appointments matter greatly for the fate of criminal justice reform, but all too often voters and criminal justice groups concerned about those issues have ignored those appointments and what they mean for mass incarceration. Other judges—federal and state—matter, too, because they are guardians of constitutional protections and because their discretionary decisions (especially on sentencing) affect millions of cases and lives.

If we are serious about achieving better criminal justice policies and addressing mass incarceration, we must pay attention to these key aspects of institutional change. If we keep the existing decision-making structure in place—with traditional tough-on-crime politicians and prosecutors setting our policies—we will achieve little more than token reforms that only tinker around the edges of bad policies. At most, the existing political process is capable of producing only modest changes, focused predominantly on the harshest punishments for nonviolent drug and property offenders who do not have much in the way of a criminal record. These are the types of reforms we have seen thus far. For example, jurisdictions have repealed certain mandatory minimum sentences for nonviolent offenses, as South Carolina did in 2010 when it eliminated mandatory minimums for first-time drug convictions, including the 10-year minimum for selling drugs within a half-mile radius of a school, park, or playground.[27] Only Alabama had defined "school zone" more broadly, so curbing this mandatory minimum in South Carolina was hardly revolutionary.[28] Other jurisdictions have reduced sentences for low-level felonies, such as Missouri, which changed its maximum for low-level felonies from 5 years to 4 years, or Iowa, which reduced sentences for burglaries of cars and boats.[29] Some states have touted alternatives to incarceration, such as drug treatment programs for nonviolent drug offenders or those convicted of DUIs.[30] States that passed tough three-strikes laws have modified them to allow those whose strikes consisted of property and drug crimes to earn good-time credits in prison for earlier release, but the core of those three-strikes laws otherwise remained unchanged. For example, in response to some high-profile examples of egregiously long sentences for minor misconduct—one man received a sentence of 25 years to life for stealing videotapes worth $150, and another received the same sentence for stealing one pair of socks—California passed a law to remove the mandatory 25-year sentence for those whose third strike is not deemed "serious or violent."[31] But even while it made that change, California still permitted the 25-years-to-life penalty if the third strike was for "certain non-serious, non-violent sex or drug offenses or involved firearm possession."[32]

Reforms like these are laudable and important, and I do not mean to suggest we should not keep striving to achieve more like them. But efforts like these, which are representative of the kinds of changes we are seeing in the name of criminal justice reform these days, will not make much of a dent in the overall sweep of incarceration or criminal punishment in the United States. As the Sentencing Project recently documented, at our current pace of reform and decarceration, it will take 75 years to cut the prison population in half.[33]

   This is largely the state of criminal justice reform right now, to the extent it exists at all: modest efforts that improve the status quo, mostly focused on drug sentencing and minor property crimes. Individuals serving time for drug convictions make up only 15% of those in prison.[34] Even if reformers expanded their efforts to include a rollback of sentence lengths for additional nonviolent offenses, that still would cover a fraction of the people who are incarcerated.[35] And the reforms we have seen thus far for even these groups of people are incremental, not sweeping. Jurisdictions still impose substantial punishments on these offenses, typically resulting in time in jail and prison. Very few people are diverted outright from the criminal justice system. Instead, many churn in and out of the system repeatedly, such that even when incarceration rates fall, prison admission rates in many places are rising.[36] None of these reforms should be mistaken for reforms that will address mass incarceration and criminalization in any meaningful way or that represent a wholesale evaluation of policies to maximize public safety and make the best use of limited resources. But these are the only kinds of reforms that will pass, given the populist politics of criminal law. If anyone suggested rolling back the punishment or collateral consequences for offenses involving violence, for example, they would likely be voted out of office. So the reform proposals remain modest because that is, at best, all the current system is capable of producing.

   Even more discouraging is that, even as this process gives modestly with one hand, it takes away with the other. Despite the rhetoric of bipartisan agreement to roll back mass incarceration, we continue to see the proposal and passage of new criminal laws and the extension of criminal sentences to address whatever the latest public panic happens to be, whether it is campus rape, sex offenses against children, the scourge of opioids and fentanyl, a new fraudulent scheme or practice, or crimes committed by undocumented immigrants. Prison populations have been growing in about half the states, even while they have declined in the other half.[37] If we continue to pursue substantive policy changes directly from elected officials, the results will continue to disappoint because populist political dynamics will take hold once anything moves beyond the most modest of changes.

   Some politicians have tried to shift the rhetoric from "tough on crime" to "smart on crime," but that rhetoric often means only minor changes to a small subset of crimes involving no violence or risk of violence. If these elected officials really want to get smart on crime, they need to create a space for the people who have actual knowledge and expertise to make key policy decisions. Put another way, if we want to be smart about public safety, we need to seek changes to the decision-making structure responsible for getting us to the sorry state we are in now—with emotional responses to high-profile crime stories all too often setting policy instead of data and studies about what works best. If we are serious about tackling mass incarceration and preserving public safety, we need to minimize the direct role of politics in crime policy and create incentives for key decision-makers to be accountable for real results and not simply high-profile stories.

The path to better results requires us first to identify those policies that need to be fixed and would be changed if we had a better institutional architecture for making decisions. Part One thus begins by providing a range of specific illustrations to prove the point that many laws and policies generated by the current approach to crime are not achieving better public safety outcomes, use limited resources inefficiently, lead to unnecessary confinement, and produce gross disparities and disproportionate punishments that are not tied to culpability or risk. While the list is lengthy, it is not exhaustive. But it should provide enough of a flavor of the kinds of policies produced by populist pressures instead of rational reflection. These are the kinds of policies we can and should change and that would both lower incarceration rates and make us safer. They include, for example, our tendency to group together people of different culpability for the same punishment because we define a crime based on an outlier case that received media attention and did not focus on who would actually be affected by a change in the law. It also includes our reliance on long sentences without recognizing the trade-offs of this approach, and the fact that people coming out of prison from lengthy terms of incarceration have a much harder time adjusting, thus increasing their risks of recidivism. We make the same mistake with pretrial detention, holding people unnecessarily before their trials, even though doing so often means they lose jobs, child care, and other support mechanisms, which in turn places them at a greater risk of committing crime. We fail to pay attention to what happens to people while they are incarcerated, which often means they come out worse off than when they came in because they received no programming, even though we know that cognitive behavior therapy, vocational training, drug treatment, and educational offerings in prison all reduce crime later. We often fail to reevaluate sentencing and policy decisions, leading us to continue on ill-considered paths even when evidence becomes clear that we should be pursuing different sentences for individuals and types of crimes. And we impose harsh collateral consequences on people with criminal records that make it harder for them to successfully reenter society, again increasing the risk they will commit more crimes.

Part Two explains in greater detail the dysfunctional political and institutional dynamics that produce the failed policies outlined in Part One.

These political forces explain why state after state, along with the federal government, all end up reaching the same irrational decisions, even though jurisdictions have vastly different cultures and ideologies. It also explains the persistence of these policies, even when better approaches exist. It is critical to understand the mechanisms that create irrational policies because better policy-making will require us to move away from this failed paradigm.

Part Three outlines the institutional changes for prosecutors, expert agencies, and courts that will help break the hold of populism and this cycle of irrationality. The key is to create and foster an institutional framework that prioritizes data, not stories, to drive decision-making. The actors responsible for making criminal justice decisions must be held accountable for improving public safety and not simply using tough rhetoric. More attention needs to be paid to the costs and benefits of different policy approaches to find the approaches that minimize risk overall, and courts must insist on reasoned decision-making and actively police constitutional boundaries.

Change will not be easy because criminal justice policy-making cannot be completely removed from politics and the populist desire for severe responses to high-profile crimes. But there is a growing bipartisan consensus that we have gone off the rails in criminal law, and more and more people are focusing on criminal justice reform, so this is the best opportunity we have had in decades for real change. We have so many policies that are lose-lose for everyone: policies that are not necessary for and often undermine public safety and that lead to grave individual injustice and discriminatory effects. Rational reflection will lead to the conclusion that these approaches need to change, so we just need to get the institutional architecture in place that allows for that rational reflection to take hold instead of continually getting swept away by populist emotions that ultimately lead to decisions that undermine the very public safety goals that the public so urgently wants to achieve. We have recognized the need to defer to experts in other areas. We live longer and more productive lives because we recognize experts can set better policies than we could using our own gut instincts. This model is consistent with democracy because these experts are pursuing the goals set by the public. They are just using their expertise to identify the best strategies for achieving those goals. It is long past the time we recognized this same model is preferable when it comes to criminal law and policy. Here, too, we can get better outcomes if we think about the long-term goal of public safety, instead of short-term emotional catharsis, and if we let experts look at the entire set of crimes and people committing them, instead of just focusing on the grisliest crimes that make headlines. We can get better results if we consider costs and benefits of different options and balance the risks of different strategies. This is that rare policy public space where we can achieve better outcomes across the board—those that make us safer, save money, reduce racial disparities, and bring families and communities closer together instead of tearing them apart. It is thus in all of our interest to demand more out of our criminal justice policies. One of the government's primary functions is keeping us safe, and we should make sure we are getting results and not rhetoric from our leaders. If we demand real accountability, the need for institutional reform will necessarily follow because that is the only way it will be achieved.

PART ONE

ALL TOO OFTEN, people discussing criminal justice policies in the United States speak in general terms: we are too tough or not smart enough on crime. We hear vague calls to end mass incarceration but get no specifics on who should be released from prison or what sentences should change. Or we might get anecdotes about particularly egregious cases. But real reform requires specifics. That might not be as interesting as emotional stories or rhetorical flourishes, but one of the reasons we have so many ill-functioning criminal justice policies is lack of attention to detail.

In the next five chapters, I will explore some of the most important criminal justice policies and approaches that fail to promote public safety and lead to unnecessary confinement, the misallocation of resources, and have a disproportionate impact on poor and minority communities.

Chapter 1 begins as any criminal case has to begin: with how we define crimes in the first place. All too often, criminal laws sweep far more broadly than the target problems that prompted their passage, or they lump together offenders of widely varying culpability. These laws then place misleading labels on the people who violate them, which in turn causes the public to believe they are far more dangerous or blameworthy than their actual criminal behavior warrants. The problem with these misleading labels is exacerbated by the fact that laws often mandate punishments designed for the very worst offender in a category.

Chapter 2 turns to sentencing and highlights the ways in which criminal punishments undermine public safety. The criminology research is clear that would-be offenders are deterred when they believe they will be caught, and the odds of detection matter far more than possible prison sentences in the decision whether to commit a crime. We also know that the more time an individual spends in prison, the harder his or her reentry will be and therefore the more likely he or she is to reoffend upon release. A rational approach to criminal justice would therefore recognize the costs related to long sentences and would make sure the public safety benefits associated with the time the individual spends in prison and off the streets—the time he or she is incapacitated—are worth the costs to reentry later. In fact, however, Chapter 2 shows that politicians almost never recognize the downsides to longer sentences and therefore rely excessively on them, to the detriment of deterrence and public safety.

The problems outlined in Chapters 1 and 2 are exacerbated by the fact that American jails and prisons do almost nothing to rehabilitate offenders, as Chapter 3 explains. Most correctional facilities offer minimal to no programming; instead, their primary function is to warehouse offenders until their release date. Without programming to counterbalance the negative effects of being housed with other individuals struggling with a range of problems, the psychological damage from social isolation, and the inability to receive treatment for a variety of mental and physical needs, our jails and prisons release individuals who are often more damaged at the end of their sentences than when they went in.

Chapter 4 explores the disuse of so-called second-look mechanisms to correct errors in the system and to adapt sentences as more information about individuals and crimes becomes available over time. Specifically, although people and social conditions can change dramatically over time, our criminal justice process in the United States all too often takes the view that a punishment determination is a one-time event, never to be reconsidered with new knowledge or updated data. Increasingly, jurisdictions have abandoned parole or other second-look mechanisms that would allow them to recalibrate their approaches based on new knowledge. The result is that bad initial decisions remain in place, and decisions that may have made sense at one point but no longer do similarly stay entrenched.

Unfortunately, irrationality in policy-making does not end when a person's sentence does. The same political imbalances and lack of adequate checks in the system that corrupt decisions about how to define and punish crime also infect the process for deciding what should happen to people after they have served their time. Chapter 5 explores the legions of collateral consequences that attach to felony and other convictions that undermine an individual's ability to reenter society and therefore increase the risk that he or she will reoffend. All too often, policies are set in angry response to a caricature of who an offender is or as a reflexive reaction to a particularly heinous offense. But these consequences end up applying automatically to almost everyone with a felony conviction. No actor in the system has the ability to make exceptions once the collateral consequences are triggered by a charge, and few avenues exist to get these consequences lifted even after it is clear they are undermining reentry and thus public safety.

It is a sad irony that a political process that obsessively uses the rhetoric of public safety ends up producing so many policies that in fact undermine it. But that is the outgrowth of the institutional arrangement we have now, as these chapters will document.

1

MISLEADING MONIKERS

"Do the crime, do the time." Read any news story about efforts to reform criminal justice policy in the United States, and it is almost guaranteed you will see someone offering a comment along these lines as the basis for opposing whatever reform is on the table. This populist rallying cry assumes that we have a rational system for defining crimes and assigning punishment for them and that if people would just avoid criminal behavior, we would not have a mass incarceration problem. But the central premise of this line of argument is false, because we do not have a rational system of defining crimes and assigning punishments to them. What a layperson may think "the crime" is turns out in many cases to be different from the law on the books. The popular discussion around a given crime tends to focus on the worst category of offenders, while the statute defining the elements of the crime often sweeps far more broadly, bringing in cases that no rational voter would have ever imagined belonged to that category. Even the terms "crime" and "criminal" suffer from this problem, with the public tending to think immediately of the most violent crimes when they think about crimes and the people who commit them. When you look closer at how the law defines different categories, it immediately becomes clear that we take an excessive approach to punishment because those categories are set with the worst offenders in mind but end up covering conduct that is far less culpable.

Thus "the time" one receives for committing a crime is often excessive by any measure in large part because the definition of the crime ended up being too expansive and lumped together cases of vastly different levels of culpability. The voting public tends to have almost no idea about the complexity behind the various labels they hear—"criminal," "felon," "drug trafficker," "sex offender"—and so the result is that they support the harshest punishments offered based on their view that these words are describing the worst of the worst. Add to that impression the fact that many voters have racial biases that trigger an image of the people in these categories as black or brown, and you can see how the political process ends up creating an irrational collection of criminal laws that fail to group people together in terms of their risk to public safety and culpability, which in turn results in a misallocation of limited resources and unnecessary confinement for many who are assumed to have engaged in much worse behaviors than they actually did.

The Crime

Let's start off by looking at some examples of crimes that are defined far more expansively than a voter might assume. A prime illustration comes from laws dealing with "sex offenders," a category one might think is populated only by the worst kind of offender who deserves the most severe punishment. After all, there are not many people more reviled than sex offenders. But when you hear that term, what kind of offender comes to mind? It is almost guaranteed that you are thinking of rapists and child molesters.

That is certainly the category of "sex offender" that politicians discuss when they speak about sex offenders.[1] When, for example, the New York State Legislature debated a civil commitment statute for sex offenders, one of its supporters asked, "Are we supposed to wait and see if they go back and molest another child and then put them back in prison?"[2] Similarly, when Jeanine Pirro emphasized her work pursuing sex offenders while running for New York State attorney general in 2006, she claimed it led to the arrests of "over 100 pedophiles—with a 100 percent conviction rate."[3] Following the passage of an updated Louisiana sex offender law in 2011, then-governor Bobby Jindal expressed approval of the state's "strong measures to put a stop to these monsters' brutal acts."[4]

It is commonplace for laws addressing the problem of sex offenses to be named after specific victims of horrific, tragic crimes, often involving the sexual assault and murder of children. The Jacob Wetterling Crimes against Children and Sexually Violent Offender Registration Act was named in memory of 11-year-old Jacob Wetterling from Minnesota, who was abducted while riding his bike to his house.[5] When a former sex offender raped and murdered his 6-year-old neighbor, Megan Kanka, Congress amended the Wetterling Act with Megan's Law, which required sex registries to be made public.[6] After Jessica Lunsford, a 9-year-old girl, was raped and murdered by a convicted sex offender who lived nearby, Florida passed Jessica's Law, which imposes a 25-year mandatory minimum sentence and lifetime monitoring for those convicted of molesting children younger than 12.[7] Other states have followed suit and have passed their own versions of Jessica's Law. Other examples of laws named after victims of particularly horrible crimes include the Adam Walsh Act, named for a 6-year-old boy kidnapped and sexually assaulted while shopping at the mall with his mother, the Amber Alert, named after Amber Hagerman, a 9-year-old girl abducted and killed while riding her bike in Texas, and Robby's Rule, named after a 6-year-old boy molested by his T-ball coach.[8] If the public thinks of the people who harmed these children when they consider who a "sex offender" is, it is no wonder there is broad support for tough sentences, for laws that require sex offenders to register, or for restrictions on where they can live or whether they can associate with young people.

Take a closer look at how some laws actually define a sex offender, however, and it is clear that these laws go far beyond the cases of child molestations and brutal rapes that prompted their enactment.[9] A Human Rights Watch report found that at least five states required men to register if they were caught visiting prostitutes. At least 13 required registration for urinating in public, and 32 states registered flashers and streakers.[10] Twenty-nine states required registration for teenagers who had consensual sex with other teenagers. In one case, a teen who had consensual sex with his high school sweetheart is still on the sex offender registry even though he and the girl in question are now married to each other and have several children together.[11] Now a man in his late thirties, he has found it difficult to get jobs, leave the state, or even live with his own children because of his spot on the registry.[12] Sex is not required for a teenager to end up on a registry. A high school senior in Tulsa, Oklahoma, who flashed a group of freshman girls on his way to the bathroom pleaded guilty to indecent exposure and had to register under Oklahoma law as a sex offender.[13] Modern technology has only compounded the problem. In some cases, teen couples have ended up on sex offender registries after engaging in consensual sexting shared only with each other.[14] Even young children can end up on registries. In one instance, a 9-year-old who played "doctor" with a 6-year-old had to register as a sex offender, and in another, a girl who pulled down the pants of an elementary school classmate as a prank ended up as a registered sex offender.[15]

So while it may make sense to tell a child molester that if he does the crime, he should do the time that was set with a child molester in mind, it does not follow that the same amount of prison time (or the same collateral consequences of conviction) should be given to someone who urinates in public after having too much to drink, to teens who engage in consensual sex with each other, or to elementary school children at play. Once these kinds of incidents are included, the sentences and required residency and registration requirements set with rapists and child molesters in mind seem absurd. What makes sense for a child molester hardly applies to young children playing doctor.

This phenomenon of "lumpy" laws is not limited to the panic over sex offenses. Drug trafficking provides another example with widespread consequences. More than a quarter of a million people have been convicted of drug trafficking offenses, making up roughly 16.9% of our incarcerated population.[16] They are a whopping 50% of the federal prison population.[17] They are a huge part of the "mass" that is mass incarceration in the United States. Needless to say, a group that large consists of many different levels of offenders, from low-level mules who carry drugs across the border or street corner sellers who sell to support their own drug habits, to high-level organizers who receive most of the profits from drug transactions and are in control of the entire drug operation. The bulk, however, are at the low end of the distribution totem pole. In the federal system, 23% of all drug trafficking offenders are couriers, or people who transport drugs using a vehicle or other equipment, and 17.2% are street-level dealers, who generally distribute less than one ounce to users.[18] By contrast, only about 10% of offenders were high-level importers, and managers and supervisors each made up about 1.1% of offenders.[19] The same phenomenon exists in the state system, where only about 5% of those convicted of trafficking offenses are high-level importers; instead, a plurality (39.3%) are relatively low-level retail sellers.[20]

But in popular discussion, when there is a call for a war on drugs or some tough response to the drug problem, the target discussed is almost always the high-level trafficker. In popular parlance, drug traffickers are "ingenious" criminals who are always seeking out new ways to hurt children and other innocent victims.[21] These drug-dealing masterminds have even been put on equal footing with terrorists and international criminals in terms of the threat they pose to the nation.[22] Popular discussion does not bother with the reality that many people who sell drugs are doing so to support a drug habit of their own. Indeed, addicts are often mentioned as the *victims* of these crimes, without any recognition that addicts may be trafficking to support their own drug use and simultaneously fall in both the offender and victim categories.

Even if the discourse lacks nuance, one might think the laws themselves would differentiate among the different types of drug offenders because they span a wide range of culpability. In fact, most drug laws in the United States do not. To be sure, the law typically makes a distinction between those who merely possess drugs for personal use and those who traffic or possess sufficiently large quantities that the inference must be that the defendant is distributing and not just using the drugs himself or herself. But once a person passes the quantity threshold from personal use to distribution, critical culpability differences disappear.

Just about every federal and state drug distribution law bases an individual's punishment on the type and quantity of drugs involved in the transaction, not on the individual's role in the offense. Quantity is obviously a relevant consideration. But quantity only tells part of the story; among drug sellers, there is a huge variation in culpability that laws usually fail to address.[23] Laws that rely only or predominantly on quantity treat a drug kingpin who runs an operation and reaps most of its profits on par with a courier who is paid very little to transport the drugs across the border.[24] Many laws lump all traffickers together as long as they are involved in equivalent quantities of the same type of drug, and those laws tend to round up, to focus on the right punishment for the kingpin, instead of rounding down, to focus on the right punishment for the corner seller or mule bringing drugs over the border. Senator Robert Byrd, the cosponsor of the Anti-Drug Abuse Act of 1986, which attached stiff mandatory sentences to drug trafficking, made clear that the purpose behind the law was to punish "the kingpins—the masterminds who are really running these operations."[25] So just as sex offender laws are set with the most heinous offenses in mind, so, too, are our drug trafficking laws.

Theft laws also often lump together disparate categories of people. At the federal level, fraud offenses are grouped together by the amount of loss caused by the fraud, with the higher the loss, the higher the sentence. Certainly, loss amount, like drug quantity, is a relevant factor. But the law does not distinguish among those who intentionally cause these losses and those who have no idea that they will be causing such a loss.[26] Many state sentencing schemes similarly focus on loss amount without taking notice of other relevant distinctions.[27] So an individual who refuses to return a watch worth $1,000 that he finds in the back of a cab with the name of the millionaire who owns it engraved on the back is in the same box as someone who intentionally engages in fraud to bilk a widow out of her last $1,000. Individuals are similarly grouped together even when they have different motives, so someone stealing out of pure greed is equated with someone stealing to meet the basic necessity to survive.

Another illustration of laws that lump together disparate individuals with a single label involves so-called career criminals, or individuals who commit multiple separate offenses over a period of time. If one is thinking about deterrence, it makes sense to give longer sentences to individuals who continue to commit crimes after being convicted and serving sentences, because the first sanction obviously did not deter the individual. Recidivism studies show that prior criminal behavior is the greatest risk factor for future criminal behavior.[28] These individuals may also deserve longer punishments because they are more blameworthy for having blown the chance they were given to start anew.[29] But while it is rational to single out repeat offenders from first-time offenders for longer punishments, it does not make sense to treat all criminal "careers" the same. Someone who commits multiple rapes or robberies is not on par with someone who deals drugs or commits petty thefts repeatedly. Yet many jurisdictions lump disparate offenders together as "career" offenders for the same harsh treatment.

Consider the federal approach. Congress often puts drug offenders in the same category as individuals who commit the most violent offenses. For instance, the Violent Crime Control and Law Enforcement Act of 1994 mandates life imprisonment for defendants with two prior violent felonies or serious drug offenses.[30] So someone with three drug trafficking convictions gets the same sentence as someone who committed three murders. Congress similarly instructed the U.S. Sentencing Commission to ensure that federal sentencing guidelines "specify a sentence to a term of imprisonment at or near the maximum term" for defendants convicted of either "crimes of violence" or drug trafficking offenses who also have two or more prior felony convictions for drug trafficking or crimes of violence.[31] And federal drug penalty maximums are on par with the maximum sentences for violent crimes.[32]

The flaw is not unique to federal law; many state jurisdictions take the same tack. Rhode Island provides for a 25-year discretionary enhancement for any third felony conviction.[33] One Rhode Island defendant was charged with a felony for driving his car into a flock of seagulls.[34] Another Rhode Island offender was given the habitual offender 25-year sentence enhancement for his third felony—throwing a cup containing his feces and urine at a corrections officer.[35] West Virginia takes a similar approach, providing for a life sentence for any third felony conviction, even if the felony is shoplifting videocassette tapes or a DUI offense.[36] Even when jurisdictions provide more specific lists, one can question whether all the crimes listed are really in the same category. Indiana, for example, imposes special enhancements only for "serious" felonies, which it defines to include murder, rape, burglary with a deadly weapon, and dealing in cocaine.[37] One would be hard-pressed to find many people who would put someone selling cocaine on par with someone who murders, rapes, or commits armed burglary.

California provides perhaps the most extreme example of how widely these recidivist laws can sweep. California's initial law dealing with repeat offenders—colloquially known as the three-strikes law—passed after 12-year-old Polly Klaus was abducted from a slumber party in her home and killed by Richard Allen Davis, who had a long and violent past but had been released early from his most recent term of confinement. Davis was thus the kind of person California voters had in mind when it passed its three-strikes law. Indeed, the Klaus family helped mobilize voters for the law, using Davis as the prototype of the kind of repeat violent offender who needed to remain behind bars for a long time.

But once again the rhetoric of the law and the reality of its content did not match up. To qualify for the lengthy sentence provided under the original three-strikes law in California, one did not have to be someone like Davis, whose third strike was a horrific, violent act. Instead, the law initially passed in California imposed no requirement that the third strike even be serious, much less violent. The third strike could apply to a misdemeanor offense, as long as it was what California calls a "wobbler," which is a crime that would otherwise be a misdemeanor but becomes a felony because of the defendant's prior record.[38]

So the law motivated by a child abduction and killing by someone with a long criminal record of violence ended up being applied to an individual whose third strike was stealing a slice of pizza from four children, to another person whose third strike was stealing about $150 worth of videotapes, and to a third person whose third strike was absconding with three golf clubs from a pro shop.[39] The golf club thief was sentenced to at least 25 years in prison, more than typical California sentences for first-time first-degree murderers (from 1945 to 1981, less than 20 years in 90% of cases), arsonists (maximum of 9 years), and offenders who committed voluntary manslaughter (maximum of 11 years).[40] It is hard to come up with any reasoned argument that treats someone who steals a slice of pizza on par with Richard Allen Davis. Yet that is how California approached recidivist offenders for almost two decades, from 1994 until 2012, when it finally amended its three-strikes law to require that the third strike also be violent or serious.[41]

A similar dynamic is at play with what are called felony murder laws. Forty-six jurisdictions have laws that enable prosecutors to charge someone with murder if he or she commits a felony and someone dies during the course of that felony instead of bringing a charge under one of the state's unintentional homicide laws, which would carry a lesser penalty.[42] While that approach may make sense with inherently violent felonies, where the commission of the felony itself demonstrates extreme indifference to human life that is comparable to intentional killings, there are many places that impose no requirement that the felony itself be violent or dangerous for the murder charge to follow. So, for example, prosecutors charged a man with first-degree murder in California after he placed a stolen stove on the back of his truck and it fell off, resulting in the death of another motorist who ran into the stove.[43] Because the theft of the stove was a felony, they opted to charge him under the same first-degree murder law that covers premeditated killings—and he was sentenced to 26 years to life.

In West Virginia, an oxycodone addict gave a pill to his 14-year-old son who suffered from cystic fibrosis. The son died from the pill because his metabolism could not process oxycodone. Because the father committed the felony of delivering a controlled substance to his son, the father was charged and convicted of felony murder and sentenced to life in prison. It did not matter whether the father intended to kill his son or even knew of his son's inability to process oxycodone because the father killed his son in the process of committing a felony.[44]

Or consider the prosecution in Indiana of four teenagers who, along with their 21-year-old friend, decided to burglarize a house that they all thought was empty. The homeowner awoke to the sound of the break-in and ended up shooting and killing the 21-year-old. Prosecutors decided to charge the four teenagers, none of whom were armed, under the state's felony murder law, because a death resulted from their commission of a felony burglary. That is because Indiana, like most states, does not provide a defense for felony murder charges even if the defendant was not the killer, was not armed, and had no reason to believe that any of the accomplices were armed or planned to commit a fatal act.[45] The teenagers—who became known as the Elkhart Four—received sentences ranging from 45 years to 55 years.[46] Of course, individuals who commit felonies should be punished, but the question is what punishment is proportionate. In the case of felony murder, all too often, sentences are not proportional because defendants are getting sentences for accidental and unplanned deaths that are treated the same as intentional killings.[47]

The example of the Elkhart Four illustrates another problem with how felony murder (and other) laws lump disparate categories of people together. In that case, the defendants were all teenagers but were treated like adults, so they received the same sentence an adult would have received under the same circumstances. This is not unusual, and it often applies to the most serious sentences. Human Rights Watch and Amnesty International issued a report showing that, of the more than 2,500 juveniles sentenced to life without parole in the United States, 26% were sentenced under felony murder laws in cases where the juvenile offender did not kill or intend to kill the victim.[48] In one case, a teen, acting on the instructions of his older brother, stole a van with some friends as part of a plan to reclaim stolen goods. When they reached the home with the stolen goods and went inside, a scuffle ensued and two people were shot to death. Because the car theft was a felony, the teen was convicted and sentenced to life without parole even though he did not kill or intend to kill the victims.[49] In another case, a young man agreed with some friends to participate in a theft by deception. The young man had no idea his friends were going to kill anyone and was not present when they did; he was nonetheless charged with and convicted of felony murder and sentenced to life without parole.[50]

The problem with lumping together children and adults is that it is contrary to all that we know about adolescent brain development. We know, for instance, that until around age 25, the parts of the brain involved in critical decision-making are not fully developed.[51] Science also suggests that adolescent brains are more inclined to enter into uncertain situations in search of a thrill or some other reward without adequately assessing risks.[52] Because juveniles possess poor abilities to assess risk as compared to adults, the rationale behind felony murder is particularly ill-suited to them because it is based on the idea that knowingly committing the felony puts the defendant on notice about all the risks posed by that felony. Juveniles should be accountable, but they should be accountable for their own actions, not the "results of their actions that they, as adolescents with poor risk-assessment skills, are unlikely to foresee."[53]

The Supreme Court has already recognized the need to treat juveniles differently from adults because to do otherwise would violate the Eighth Amendment prohibition against cruel and unusual punishment, but its rulings do not apply to most laws affecting juveniles because the Court has thus far only dealt with the most extreme cases. The Court has determined that imposing the death penalty or mandatory life without parole (LWOP) sentences on juveniles would be disproportionate to their culpability.[54] It has also determined that juveniles cannot receive LWOP sentences for crimes other than homicides.[55] But those are the only limits, so jurisdictions can and do lump juveniles in with adults in many other contexts that raise precisely the same concerns as these cases. For example, juveniles can receive mandatory life sentences for their crimes as long as they are eligible for parole at some point.[56] There is no requirement that juveniles actually receive parole. And if the sentence is short of life, there is no requirement that parole even be made available. There are countless cases of juveniles being treated as adults and receiving the same mandatory sentence without any consideration of their age.[57] It is possible that a long sentence is appropriate for a juvenile in a given case, but the laws that lump them together with adults without any consideration of their different brain development present the same problems of disproportionate punishment that the Court recognized in capital and LWOP cases.

Another area in criminal law where actors of varying levels of culpability get lumped together involves group crime, where the commission of a crime is by more than one person, each playing a different role. In criminal law, if someone helps another person commit a crime, the helper can be liable just as if she committed the crime herself. So if person A gives person B a gun and person A has the intent that person B will kill someone, person A is liable as if he or she were the shooter. A and B stand on equal footing. Under traditional doctrines of accomplice liability, however, the government had to show that the accomplice intended to aid the specific crime that was committed. But some jurisdictions have expanded this concept so that individuals become responsible not just for the specific crimes they agree to assist, but for any other crime that ultimately gets committed as long as it was reasonably foreseeable—even if the particular helper had no idea it would happen. So, for example, a man who intends to help his friend beat up an acquaintance can end up being charged with murder even if the man did not realize the friend was going to escalate the situation.[58] Individuals involved in a large-scale drug transaction could be held responsible for murder even if they did not participate in the killing because courts have found that murder is a reasonably foreseeable consequence of selling large amounts of cocaine.[59] In cases such as these, defendants who are negligent— they fail to appreciate the risk of more serious conduct that a reasonable person would anticipate—are treated as if they intended the additional crimes.

The law on group criminality is problematic because it fails to draw distinctions among the different mental states offenders have when committing crimes, or what is known as their mens rea. Few people would disagree that an actor who intentionally causes harm is more culpable—and thus deserves a greater punishment—than one who accidentally causes harm. Yet our laws often fail to make that fundamental distinction. In the conspiracy context, an individual is on the hook for crimes a reasonable person would have anticipated, even if the particular individual had no idea they would occur. Essentially, then, the individual is being criminalized for exercising poor judgment—and held to the same standard as someone who intends the crime.

The federal sentencing guidelines offer another illustration of this problem. These guidelines specify the sentences people should receive for committing federal offenses based on various harms associated with their cases. For instance, if one is engaged in a fraud, the guidelines specify that the sentence should increase based on the amount of the loss, the number of victims involved, and the effect the fraud had on the victims.[60] There is no denying these are relevant factors. The problem is that the guidelines do not draw distinctions between defendants whose very purpose is to achieve the harm and those who never intended or even foresaw that harm. The unlucky are placed in the same box as the malevolent. An individual who intends to bilk an elderly victim out of her life savings gets the same sentence as someone who has no idea that his fraudulent scheme would even cause losses, let alone that there might be identifiable victims. To take another example, two men who participate in a drug transaction will both receive a greater sentence if the police find a firearm at the scene, even if the first person did not know that the second person had a gun.[61] In other words, the law lumps the person who carried a dangerous weapon in with the person who merely chose his partner unwisely.

This turn away from individualized consideration is relatively recent. A defendant's mens rea was a central focus for how crimes were defined for most of the nation's history. An intentional actor would rarely be lumped in with a negligent one. As an initial matter, criminal punishment for negligent conduct was a rarity for most of U.S. history, except for conduct that caused the most serious harms—that is, death—so the issue did not arise at all for most offenses. And even when the law imposed criminal punishment for negligent actions, it carefully distinguished those cases from cases with intentional conduct.[62]

Attention to proportionality started to fall away when U.S. society got more complicated. In particular, the Industrial Revolution brought about sweeping changes in the ordering of society with the mass distribution of food and other products that could cause widespread harm and destruction if done improperly. Desperate for some way to curb those risks, public officials turned to criminal law as a possible answer. Instead of focusing only on malum in se crimes—actions that were inherently wrong— legislators started to criminalize actions that gave actors no notice that they were wrongful except by virtue of the law making it so. So-called strict liability laws targeted outcomes instead of intent. If an actor put an adulterated or misbranded drug in commerce, for instance, that was enough to trigger criminal penalties, without any requirement that the government show that the actor did anything wrong or had any culpability at all.[63]

At the same time, the number of criminal laws exploded. There are now more than 4,000 federal criminal laws alone, most coming after the Industrial Revolution.[64] A huge chunk of federal laws are even more recent than that, with nearly 50% of the laws passed after the Civil War dating from between 1970 and 2014, and over 400 new offenses added between 2008 and 2013 alone.[65] The same dynamic exists at the state level. Between 1943 and 2011, for example, the number of sections in the North Carolina criminal code nearly doubled, and the Virginia criminal code has grown from 170 offenses to 495 offenses in the last 150 years.[66] In Michigan, the legislature has created an average of 45 new criminal offenses each year since 2008.[67]

In addition, there are upwards of 300,000 federal regulations that subject someone who violates them to criminal penalties.[68] Many of these thousands of laws and regulations impose strict liability and therefore make no distinction between intentional violations and accidents that could not be prevented even with due care. In one case, Lawrence Lewis, a military retirement home engineer, diverted backed-up sewage into a storm drain in an effort to protect the elderly residents from health problems associated with sewage overflow at the facility.[69] Unbeknownst to Lewis, however, the backup drain fed into the Potomac River. Lewis was charged with felony violations of the Clean Water Act.[70] Another man, Wade Martin, was convicted of a felony for selling a sea otter to a non-native Alaskan. A federal law criminalizes the sale of sea otters to non-native Alaskans, and Martin's mistake was incorrectly believing his customer was an Alaskan native.[71]

With almost no one in the political process pushing back on the rush to criminalize in recent decades, legislation has been sloppily drafted and sweeping in its coverage.[72] Attention to mens rea fell by the wayside and instead gave way to a greater concern that no one fall through a loophole.[73] Prosecutors grew accustomed to using powerful conspiracy laws to take down criminal organizations and therefore resist any effort to limit the scope of laws addressing group crime.

The American Law Institute, an independent law reform organization of practicing lawyers, judges, and academics, created a Model Penal Code in 1962 that aimed to bring some proportionality to the growing disorder in criminal law and fix some of the problems outlined here. It paid great attention to mens rea, group crime, proportionality, and how to define and categorize offenders. Although the Model Penal Code proved influential in many states, no state adopted it in its entirety. Even those states that did adopt large chunks of the code later came to ignore its fundamental principles and grew more punitive as crime rates went up.[74]

The federal government did not adopt the Model Penal Code at all, so the federal criminal code is among the worst in creating excessively lumpy laws. Congress itself realized as much, prompting it in the late 1960s to create a commission, known as the Brown Commission, to study federal criminal law and sentencing and make recommendations for reform. The commission issued its report in 1971 and included many suggestions that are in the Model Penal Code, including renewed attention to mens rea and a narrowing of the expansive federal conspiracy law.[75] Congress did not act on its recommendations, however, and instead created a sentencing commission charged with creating federal sentencing guidelines in an effort to put a bandage on some of the problems.

Unfortunately, those guidelines ended up replicating the problems they were supposed to help solve. For starters, the guidelines are based on federal statutes, so if the statutes are flawed, the guidelines reflect the same problems. For instance, because statutory drug offenses focus on quantity in setting sentences, so, too, do the guidelines, with only small adjustments for an individual's role in the offense. The guidelines also hold all the individuals engaged in jointly undertaken criminal activity responsible for all the reasonably foreseeable activities of the group, even if someone had no idea about those activities. And they take almost no account of an individual's mens rea, treating those who intentionally cause harm the same as those who accidentally cause it.

The result is that the federal system is perhaps the worst in creating overbroad categories without sufficient attention to culpability. But while it may be the worst, state criminal laws suffer from plenty of the same flaws, particularly with respect to laws passed in the 1970s and thereafter.

Not all the problems are as recent as that. Felony murder is an outlier in that it has a longer history, and thus its overbreadth problems have been around for some time. But it, too, grew considerably more problematic in recent decades because of the expansion in the number of felonies that can trigger its application. Traditionally, felonies were crimes that we would recognize as serious: murder, rape, robbery, and the like. Today, however, the distinction between a misdemeanor and a felony is "minor and often arbitrary," and many crimes that used to be classified as misdemeanors are now felonies.[76]

Whereas having the status of "felon" was once a rarity, today it has become commonplace because of how far criminal law has expanded in every U.S. jurisdiction. Indeed, at least 7.5% of all adults in America are either currently serving a felony sentence or have completed one, and some estimates place the figure closer to 23 million people (or more than 10% of the adult population), which is roughly the population of Florida.[77] And that status matters not only for purposes of whether felony-murder laws kick in. There are multitudes of laws that impose severe collateral consequences on anyone who has committed a felony, as Chapter 5 will explain in greater detail. For instance, those convicted of felonies cannot vote, serve on a jury, own firearms, hold certain types of jobs, or serve in the military.[78] It makes no sense to create categorical bans and penalties on all those with

felony convictions because the category of felon has become almost meaningless given its breadth.

That is the problem with all of the categories created by the laws discussed here: their potential for treating dissimilar cases similarly, which is
a form of disparity as pernicious as treating like cases differently. In other
words, this "excessive uniformity" between dissimilar cases leads to the misleading labeling of hundreds of thousands of people and their arbitrarily
harsh punishment.[79] This is not to say that punishment should not apply
in the scenarios discussed. But it is to say that all too often that punishment is excessive because it is set with a different, much more serious offender in mind. The result is disproportionate punishment and a waste of
limited resources that should be targeting more serious crimes and threats
to public safety.

The Time

While the stigma attached to labels like "felon" and "sex offender" and
"drug trafficker" is problematic in its own right, the misleading nature of
these terms would not be as pernicious if distinctions among offenders could
be drawn at some other point in the process so that they all did not suffer
the same consequences. For most of America's history, judges played that
key role by making the necessary distinctions at sentencing. Until the late
1970s and early 1980s, judges had discretion to sentence an offender within
a broad statutory range, thus allowing them to draw individual distinctions
that the laws failed to make.

To be sure, even with this check, there are significant concerns. For
starters, each judge may have a different conception of what facts are relevant to culpability and how they should be weighed for purposes of assigning a specific sentence. In addition, broad judicial discretion allows for
conscious and unconscious biases to seep into the sentencing decision, thus
creating unwarranted disparities among similarly situated offenders based
on the views of the judge making the decision. And because these determinations are made at sentencing, the due process protections that apply to offense elements do not apply. The relevant facts do not need to be proved by
the government beyond a reasonable doubt, but instead must meet the lower
preponderance of the evidence standard. Nor is there a jury trial right that
attaches to these discretionary facts; juries need only find the elements
that make up the statutory offense. Traditional rules of evidence also do
not apply at sentencing, so hearsay and unreliable evidence may be used to
support the judge's decision.

So even in a world where judges have discretion to sentence individuals within a broad range to account for differences, lumpy laws raise fundamental questions of due process and equal treatment. Fundamental differences— such as mens rea or the role someone plays in a conspiracy or as an accomplice—are the kinds of decisions that should not be left to the discretion of a judge to find by a mere preponderance without sufficient process. This is especially true when so much is at stake in terms of long terms of confinement and devastating collateral consequences.

But whatever the problems with a scheme that uses judicial discretion as a check, our current regime is unfortunately far worse than that. Beginning in the 1970s, and really taking off in the 1980s, jurisdictions decided to limit judicial discretion at sentencing. Thus whatever work judges were doing at sentencing to account for important individual differences that the laws ignored came to an abrupt halt.

Jurisdiction after jurisdiction turned to mandatory minimum sentences, particularly in areas where elected officials believed judges had been too lenient and also in response to high-profile crimes that garnered public attention. Mandatory sentences thus exploded for drug crimes, weapon offenses, and sex offenses.[80] Jurisdictions also turned to mandatory minimums to address repeat offenders, with 40 states adopting a recidivism mandatory minimum regime between 1970 and 1996, and 24 states and the federal government adopting three-strikes versions of these mandatory laws between 1993 and 1995.[81] Whereas previously in American history, Congress had passed mandatory minimum sentencing laws only sporadically, the total number of these laws skyrocketed from 77 in 1980 to 284 in 2000.[82]

Many jurisdictions also turned to sentencing guidelines that similarly restricted judges in their ability to sentence outside a predetermined range and that often failed to take account of individual differences in culpability. The goal was to create uniformity and iron out disparities among judges. But as the Supreme Court stated in the line of cases rejecting statutes that mandated the death penalty under specified circumstances and that limited the facts a jury could consider, "a consistency produced by ignoring individual differences is a false consistency."[83]

Drug laws provide a paradigmatic example of the problems with mandatory minimum sentencing laws. Previously, most laws set broad statutory ranges for drug offenses that allowed judges wide leeway, when determining the appropriate sentence, to take into account an individual's role in a drug trafficking operation, in addition to considering the quantity and type of drugs involved. But that approach shifted dramatically in the 1980s. In response to escalating drug use and crime rates, Congress passed a comprehensive piece of legislation in 1986 that imposed harsh new penalties and mandatory minimums for drug offenses.[84] The legislative history of the 1986 act makes clear that the new 5-year mandatory minimum sentence it established, which also had a corresponding increase in the maximum sentence from 20 years to 40 years, was "specifically intended for the managers of drug enterprises." It aimed a new 10-year mandatory minimum, with a maximum sentence of life, at "organizers and leaders." Put another way, Congress aimed to create a "two-tiered penalty structure for discrete categories of drug traffickers," with the 5-year mandatory minimum aimed at "serious" traffickers and the 10-year minimum focused on "major" traffickers.[85]

Instead of distinguishing among the different roles individuals play in drug offenses and reserving the mandatory minimums for the managers and high-level traffickers it had in mind, Congress lumped all drug traffickers together so that they would all receive the mandatory minimum sentence. Anyone involved in the sale of drugs, irrespective of where the individual fell in the hierarchy of a drug operation, got the same severe mandatory minimum sentence. Fifty-nine percent of all people in federal prison for a drug offense are sentenced pursuant to a mandatory minimum statutory term, for a total of 55,000 people, and their average sentence is more than 11 years. Only 14% of these individuals were identified as being the manager, leader, or organizer that the law's drafters had in mind.[86]

Quantity's disproportionate impact is especially pronounced in drug conspiracies. Even if a street seller has a relatively small amount of drugs, he will be held accountable for all the drugs distributed by individuals within his drug operation. Thus kingpins, couriers, and street peddlers in a conspiracy are held equally responsible for the same quantity amounts because federal conspiracy law makes them all responsible for the reasonably foreseeable quantities distributed by their organizations. But of course those individuals do not have the same blameworthiness, and their roles are far more important than the quantity in assessing their relative responsibility and culpability. Mandatory minimum laws do not allow those differences to be accounted for. This led a bipartisan task force charged with evaluating federal criminal law to conclude that "the mandatory minimum framework . . . is fundamentally broken" because "judges find their hands tied by an extraordinarily punitive one-size-fits-all structure." The task force recommended maintaining the mandatory minimum only for kingpins but repealing the mandatory minimum penalty for all other drug offenses.[87]

These problems have not escaped the attention of lawmakers. But instead of addressing the root causes—the emphasis on quantity at the expense of all other factors—they have chipped around the edges with minor adjustments. Thus Congress passed what is called a safety valve for nonviolent, low-level drug offenders with minor or no criminal history that allows judges to sentence the individual below the mandatory minimum if the prosecutor agrees that the individual has provided the government with whatever information he or she has about the drug operation.[88] Under these restrictions, offenders who have very minor prior infractions like careless driving or who have a lawfully registered gun in their homes are disqualified from mandatory minimum relief under the safety valve.[89] Indeed, only about 16% of offenders qualify for relief under the safety valve because the exception is so narrow.[90]

Career offender laws or three-strikes laws suffer from the same problems of mandated punishments that do not allow for disaggregating among the many disparate individuals who may qualify for the enhancements. Not only are most of those laws broad in their coverage, as already explained, but they also often provide for mandatory sentences once one meets the statutory criteria. California's broad three-strikes law imposes a mandatory minimum sentence of 25 years to life for three-time repeat offenders. As crime rates escalated and news stories highlighted cases where offenders with prior records went on to commit additional crimes, popular support for these laws grew. But while there was great fervor for the laws in general, few paid attention to the details.

This same dynamic can be seen in the treatment of sex offenders. Media stories of particularly egregious cases prompted legislation broad in scope with mandatory sentences and collateral consequences, but with very little focus on the specifics. As a result, a 19-year-old who had sex with his 16-year-old high school sweetheart and an elementary school student who jokingly pulled down the pants of a classmate now face a lifetime as registered sex offenders.[91]

Mandatory sentences affect juveniles more generally. In the middle of the 1990s, in the wake of highly publicized violent crimes committed by juveniles and the prediction by pundits that America was facing an onslaught of crime by juvenile "superpredators," nearly every state passed laws to increase the treatment of juveniles as adults and to lengthen their sentences.[92] Juveniles in many jurisdictions get treated as adults no matter what their individual circumstances as long as they commit certain types of crimes. And once they are in adult court, they are subject to all the same mandatory sentences that apply to adults for the same offenses, so there is no opportunity for judges to account for their age. The Supreme Court recognized the flaws with this mandatory scheme when it came to laws imposing mandatory life without parole sentences and emphasized that failing to account for a juvenile's age and maturity ignores everything we know as a matter of brain science and common sense.[93] But its ruling applies only to mandatory LWOP sentences, so juveniles can and often do receive other harsh mandatory sentences without anyone having taken account of their age and immaturity.

That is the critical flaw with mandatory sentencing laws. They cut off consideration of relevant facts about culpability. They do not allow a judge to take account of the defendant's motive, age, economic circumstances, family situation, background, or other relevant mitigating circumstances. Everyone is lumped together regardless of individual differences. If the minimum were set with the least culpable offender in mind, this would not matter because it would represent a real minimum—those at the bottom of the range. But the reality is the opposite. The mandatory minimum sentences are almost always set with the worst offenders in mind. Giving individuals of lesser culpability sentences that were set based on the most serious offenders is the very definition of disproportionality—and irrationality.

The only actor with any discretion in the system to account for individual differences in the face of a mandatory sentencing law is the prosecutor, who has the discretion not to bring charges under a statute with a mandatory sentence. But sometimes prosecutors adopt the policy that the most serious charge should be pursued in a given case, thus effectively cutting off their own discretion to temper these laws with charging discretion. This has been the federal policy, for example, under Attorney General John Ashcroft and Attorney General Jeff Sessions. Moreover, even when prosecutors take into account differences in culpability in their charging decisions, they are an imperfect check because of the conflict of interest they face in doing their job. They have an incentive to threaten more serious charges than an individual's culpability may suggest in order to extract a plea. So if a defendant does not want to accept that deal, they may well get lumped in with more serious offenders after a conviction at trial.

Moreover, the lack of meaningful differentiation does not stop with one's charge and sentence. Individuals of widely divergent culpability are lumped together when they are incarcerated. Typically, individuals denied bail or those who cannot afford it are all placed together in the same jail awaiting trial.[94] Those accused of nonviolent crimes are housed with those accused of violent ones, and unfortunately this all too often means that individuals are victimized in jail or suffer extreme mental distress, sometimes leading to suicide.[95] After conviction, prison placement can be similarly insensitive to relative differences. While states classify prisoners by their relative level of risk, these categories are broad and often result in placements that lump together people of different risk profiles; for instance, in California, three-strikes offenders are automatically initially placed in the highest-security facility.[96]

When individuals come out of prison and are placed on probation or supervised release, these same grouping flaws may continue. For example, in some states, all individuals with the sex offender label must receive the same supervision, even if that category ranges from child molesters to someone who urinates in public. The result is that probation officers face crushing dockets and cannot provide sufficient attention to the biggest threats to public safety. Commonly, individuals with felony convictions are often given a laundry list of onerous conditions that set them up for failure, thus sending them back to prison for technical parole violations based on conditions that were doing little to promote public safety in the first place because they were ill-suited to most of the people receiving them.

And the problems do not end once an individual is no longer under the supervision of the criminal justice system. Most collateral consequences of criminal convictions apply automatically to all felonies, thus imposing the same restrictions on petty fraudsters as on murderers. All of these individuals face limits on voting, military service, and jury service, as well as activities that even more profoundly impact an offender's ability to provide for herself and her family, such as access to employment opportunities or public housing.[97] There is often no actor in the system—not the judge, not a probation officer, not even the prosecutor—who can stop these collateral consequences.

This, then, is the problem with any resistance to reform based on the vague notion that our laws reflect sensible punishments and that one who does the crime should do the time. Our laws all too often fail to pay much attention to the crime or the time, which means our resources are misallocated and misspent, and we are giving unnecessarily long terms of incarceration to people because we are assuming they represent something they do not because of the misleading labels we apply to them.

2

SENSELESS SENTENCING

CRIMINAL SENTENCES SHOULD SERVE one of the core purposes of punishment: they should either be meting out retributive justice (giving people their just deserts and imposing a punishment that is proportionate to the seriousness of the crime) or achieving utilitarian goals (that is, preventing crime through deterrence, rehabilitation, or incapacitation). But all too often, criminal sentences in the United States bear little relationship with these aims because legislators and prosecutors reflexively pursue more severe sentences without pausing to consider whether those sentences are retributively just or will promote public safety. Their animating principle has instead been the more severe, the better. Except longer sentences are often not better, whether the goal is justice or public safety.

The Laws on the Books

Let's start with considering whether longer sentences serve the aims of retributive justice. After all, elected officials often use rhetoric that sounds like that is their goal. When politicians speak about murders, rapes, terrorism, and the like, there is a desire to find a punishment that matches what they view as the seriousness of the crime. For example, when speaking in favor of stiffer punishments for those who sexually assault children, a Democratic state senator in Florida said, "There are real monsters and we're going to put monsters away for a real, real long time."[1] An Alabama official proposed castration for sex offenders, saying that sex offenders "have marked these children for life . . . and if they've marked children for life, they need to be marked for life."[2] A Maine state representative supported tougher penalties for drug dealers based on the view that the penalty should be "merciless . . . because these are people who have no regard for the people they hurt."[3] These same retributive arguments are often used to oppose sentencing reform. A former prosecuting attorney in Indiana provides a glimpse into the kind of argument often employed, noting that existing laws give "real sentences handed down for shocking and heinous crimes. . . . Rapists, murderers, child molesters, child abusers—any bill to release them early is a bad bill."[4] A former Milwaukee sheriff similarly warned that recent efforts on sentencing reform are just "cuddling up to criminals" and that rehabilitation "is not something the criminal-justice system should do."[5]

People have different conceptions of what a just punishment for a crime is, and retributive theory cannot settle what the exact amount of punishment should be. One person might think 20 years is appropriate for homicide, while another might argue a life sentence is a just desert for the intentional taking of life. There is no objective way to decide which argument is right as a matter of retributive justice, nor can we say anyone is an expert on the issue, so one cannot say choosing one over the other is an irrational choice. But that does not mean that all judgments grounded in retributive concerns are immune from considered criticism or rational evaluation. While it may not be possible to identify the one correct punishment for a particular crime if the theory is retribution, it is possible to identify disproportionate punishments based on how they stack up against other punishments for crimes where there is a consensus view that they are more or less serious. That is, while one might be hard-pressed to say what the one right sentence is for murder, one could say that the sentence for murder should be greater than the sentence for selling drugs because murder causes more serious harm and an intentional killing is more culpable than selling drugs. So if it turns out the person selling drugs is getting more time than the person who commits murder, there would be broad consensus that this punishment scheme fails as a matter of retributive justice.

There is, in fact, widespread agreement about the relative seriousness of most crimes, so punishments can be assessed to make sure they fall along the same basic hierarchy.[6] Using this as the benchmark, we can see that irrational sentencing abounds even if sentencing was designed to give people their just deserts. For example, the average sentence for federal drug traffickers is 6 years, roughly double the average state sentence for rape, which is less than 3 years for first-time offenders.[7] Individual cases highlight even more egregious disproportionality. While the average federal sentence for murder is 23 years, people who sell drugs often get far longer sentences than that. Tyrone Trader, for example, received a mandatory life sentence for street-level drug dealing, prompting the judge in his case to comment that "it is difficult to see how a sentence of life imprisonment in Trader's case is just."[8] The case of Weldon Angelos raised similar proportionality objections from his sentencing judge. Angelos was required by law to receive a sentence of at least 55 years (660 months) for carrying a gun to two $350 marijuana deals and for having an additional gun in his house. His sentencing judge noted this was more than double the required sentence for a kingpin of a major drug trafficking ring in which death resulted (293 months), an aircraft hijacker (293 months), a terrorist who detonates a bomb in a public place intending to kill a bystander (235 months), a racist who attacks a minority with the intent to kill (210 months), a spy gathering top-secret information (210 months), a second-degree murderer (151 months), a kidnapper (151 months), a saboteur who destroys military materials (151 months), a marijuana dealer who shoots an innocent person during a drug transaction (146 months), the rapist of a 10-year-old child (135 months), and a child pornographer who photographs a 12-year-old in sexual positions (108 months).[9]

It is not just drug sentencing that exhibits this kind of disproportionality. It makes little retributive sense for a woman who forged a $200 check to receive a 20-year sentence.[10] It is similarly inconsistent with retributive notions for a man who lent his car to friends who committed a burglary that resulted in a death to receive a life sentence when intentional killings typically receive less.[11] In Louisiana alone, more than 300 people are serving sentences of life without parole despite never having been convicted of a violent crime.[12]

Or consider the irrationality of treating child pornography more seriously than the actual molestation of a child.[13] Senator Debbie Stabenow of Michigan has pointed out the absurdity of a system where "a defendant with no prior criminal record and no history of abusing children would qualify for a sentence of 15 to 20 years based on a small collection of child pornography and one photo swap, while a 50-year-old man who encountered a 13-year-old girl online and lured her into a sexual relationship would get no more than four years."[14] In Arizona, Morton Berger, a man with no prior criminal record, ended up with a 200-year sentence for child pornography. One of the justices on the Arizona Supreme Court observed the irrationality of the state sentencing scheme, where "the *minimum* sentence for possession of an image of child pornography is longer than the *presumptive* sentence for rape or aggravated assault. A presumptive sentence for possession of two images of child pornography . . . is harsher than the sentences for second degree murder or sexual assault of a child under twelve. . . . For molesting a child, one might receive the same sentence that Berger has received for possessing one picture."[15]

Thus even if our goal were retributive justice, we are falling short in achieving it. We could do far better at getting proportional punishment based on retributive goals than our current approach.

Now consider how we are doing if the main goal of punishment is utilitarian. To the extent that public safety is the main goal in having criminal laws and punishments, we are failing miserably in achieving it.

Public safety can be measured in various ways: by crime rates overall, by violent crime rates (because those are the crimes that most concern the public), by recidivism rates (again, either overall or with a particular emphasis on violence), or by desistance rates (how a person may shift to lesser crimes over time even if still recidivating in general). Progress toward public safety can also be determined by looking at the markers that we know improve crime reduction, such as educational achievement and employment. Whatever the metric we use, however, our current policies are failing to optimize public safety outcomes because they are not set by analyzing the costs and benefits of different strategies. Instead, we are in a rut where politicians gravitate toward longer sentences of incarceration without giving much thought to other options and without taking the time to think about the ways different types of offenses and offenders compare to one another.

At the most general level, when sentences do not reflect culpability, individuals begin to question the legitimacy of the state's use of punishment: "If the legal system imposes more, or less, punishment on some crimes than citizens believe is deserved, the system seems unfair; it loses its credibility and, eventually, its effectiveness."[16] When people do not think the laws are legitimate, it can lead to a decline in compliance with the law.[17] People stop reporting crimes and cooperating with law enforcement, which makes crimes harder to detect and solve.[18] That is a devastating outcome because the likelihood someone will get caught committing a crime is the most important factor driving deterrence.

Moreover, particular policies are often pursued with an assumption that they are the best approach to keeping the public safe from the commission of a given crime, when in fact there are better options or the approach itself can cause more problems than it solves. The most common assumption that politicians make without much thought is the idea that longer sentences will deter crime. For example, a congressman in favor of an amendment to federal law to add a sentencing enhancement for carrying a weapon during certain crimes argued that the increase would "persuade a man tempted to commit a Federal felony to leave his gun at home."[19]

Massachusetts state legislators made the same argument in favor of a similar state law that increased penalties for gun possession, saying that the
"law is designed to remove the temptation to carry guns and therefore
greatly reduce the chance that they will be used."[20] Politicians often credit
tougher sentencing for reducing crime. A New York state senator com-
mented (without any evidence) that "over the past 10 years, the NYS Legislature has enacted over 100 new tough-on-crime laws which have helped
reduce New York's crime rate."[21]

Political officials also emphasize the fact that longer sentences incapacitate people, another perceived benefit to public safety. A New Mexico state
representative, for instance, wanted more predicate felonies added to the
list of habitual offenses that trigger a life sentence because it "provide[s]
legislative solutions to keep this handful of violent criminals off the street. . . .
Our No. 1 job as legislators is to make sure people are safe in their homes."[22]
A Florida state representative advocated for tougher sex offender sentences
by arguing, "We know one certain fact. . . . No one has ever raped a
child while sitting in prison."[23] A member of Congress from Washington
supported the federal Megan's Law in 1994 by saying that "the rate of
recidivism for these crimes is astronomical because these people are com-
pulsive" and thus needed to be incapacitated longer.[24] The Republican
party platform in 2012 stated that "criminals behind bars cannot harm the
general public" and used that logic to support more mandatory prison
sentences for a long list of crimes.[25]

These utilitarian arguments about deterrence and incapacitation are used
not only to support proposed sentencing increases, but also to oppose
decreases to existing punishments. For instance, the head of the National
Association of Assistant United States Attorneys objected to proposed reductions in federal sentences by arguing that "when you put criminals in
jail, crime goes down. . . . That's what incapacitation is designed to do,
and it works."[26] Senator David Perdue of Georgia likewise opposed federal sentencing reform on this basis, arguing that the proposed legislation
"would put thousands of dangerous felons back on the streets early, potentially endangering our families and communities."[27]

While these politicians assume the validity of their public safety arguments, reality is far more complicated. Start with their arguments that longer
sentences deter crime. Research shows that recidivism does not decline for
those spending more time in prison.[28] For example, a study of three states
(Florida, Maryland, and Michigan) found that longer sentences for nonviolent offenders "neither prevented crimes during the period of incarceration nor kept offenders from committing crimes once released from
prison."[29] These states could have reduced sentences by 3 to 24 months

without any effect on public safety, and the money saved from doing so would have been substantial.[30] With results such as these, it is not surprising that a report commissioned by the Department of Justice found that lengthy prison sentences are not the best way to deter crime.[31] A 2016 report by the president's Council of Economic Advisers concurred, concluding that "research on the impact of sentence length has found that longer sentences are unlikely to deter prospective offenders or reduce targeted crime rates."[32] What makes a larger difference on behavior is improving the odds that someone will serve a sentence.[33] That is, certainty of punishment matters more than severity for deterrence.[34]

Consistent with these findings, we have seen state after state reduce sentence lengths without an increase in crime rates or recidivism.[35] Seven states put fewer people in prison while also experiencing *decreases* in their crime rates: California, Maryland, Nevada, New Jersey, South Carolina, Texas, and New York.[36] California is a particularly striking example; from 2006 to 2012, it cut its prison population by 23%, and violent crime fell by 21%.[37] Texas also saw its violent crime, property crime, and recidivism rates fall while shrinking its prison population.[38] Indeed, states that lowered their incarceration rates have seen a greater drop in their crime rates than the states where imprisonment rates have increased.[39] West Virginia, for example, increased its incarceration rate more than any other state but experienced a 6% increase in crime.[40]

The federal system likewise shows that sentences can be lowered without affecting crime rates and recidivism. In 2007, the U.S. Sentencing Commission reduced the sentencing guidelines for crack cocaine offenses by two levels (roughly 20%) and applied the change not only to future cases, but also retroactively so that those in prison for crack offenses could petition to receive the reduction.[41] The commission then studied the recidivism rates of those offenders who received the reduction with a comparable group of crack offenders who were released before the effective date of the amendment, so ended up serving their full sentences. The commission found that, five years after their release, there was no statistically significant difference between the two groups when it came to recidivism rates. The group receiving the shorter sentences had a 43.3% recidivism rate, and those who served the longer sentences had a 47.8% recidivism rate.[42]

A 2010 change in federal statutory law on crack cocaine produced similar results. Congress passed the Fair Sentencing Act in 2010, which eliminated the 5-year mandatory minimum for possession of crack cocaine and increased the quantities of crack cocaine necessary to trigger the mandatory minimums for drug trafficking offenses. A follow-up study by the Sentencing Commission found that these changes cut the number of individuals in federal prison for crack offenses, lowered the number of prosecutions for crack offenses, and reduced the disparity between crack and powder cocaine, and all while crack cocaine use continued to decline.[43] In addition, in 2011, the commission retroactively adjusted crack sentences in the wake of the 2010 law, lowering the sentences of roughly 7,700 people by an average of 30 months. A follow-up study comparing the recidivism rates of those individuals who received the retroactive adjustment with a similar group who served their full sentences before the retroactive adjustment took effect showed no difference in recidivism rates between the two groups. Thus, once again a sentencing reduction did not lead to higher rates of offending.[44]

This is not to say that sentence length does not matter at all for deterrence. But it is assumed that a longer sentence always brings greater public safety benefits, when in fact the evidence shows this is often not true.

In fact, longer sentences can actually threaten public safety.[45] The Charles Colson Task Force on Federal Corrections found that, "absent effective rehabilitative programs, the experience of incarceration can be criminogenic, or likely to cause the very behavior it is punishing."[46] As Chapter 3 shows in greater detail, programming is often nonexistent in prison, so the criminogenic effects of prison are typically not counteracted by affirmative benefits. The longer sentences people serve, the harder it is for them to reenter successfully into society. People who have served long periods of time in prison have a difficult time adjusting to an environment that is not highly controlled because their social skills and ability to make independent decisions atrophy when they are incarcerated.[47] One study using data from Texas found that each additional year of a prison sentence caused a 4–7% increase in an individual's recidivism rate once he or she was released.[48] Another study of juveniles in Chicago found that detaining them increased their likelihood of recidivism after release by 22–26%.[49]

Longer sentences also put a strain on limited prison resources, thus making it less likely that there are enough rehabilitative resources to go around to all those who need them in prison. For instance, a recent study of federal prisons found that the demand exceeded the capacity for many programs found to lower recidivism and assist with reentry. These programs include GED programs, postsecondary education, vocational training, and treatment programs for sex offenders.[50] The overcrowding caused by longer sentences has deleterious effects even apart from the strain it places on rehabilitative resources; overcrowding itself causes behavioral problems in people in prison.[51]

We also know that long sentences bring diminishing returns because most people will age out of crime in any case. For most crimes, the likelihood that someone will continue committing them once they hit 40 is negligible.[52] Most juveniles discontinue their criminal activity after brief experimentation with it.[53] People who commit property crimes tend to stop in their 20s, and people who commit violent crimes typically cease those activities in their early 30s.[54] Drug trafficking also tends to taper off sometime in an individual's thirties.[55] More than half of all people arrested are under 30 for the majority of the crimes the FBI tracks,[56] and research shows that for the eight most serious crimes tracked by the FBI, adults tend to commit them over a 5- to 10-year period and then stop.[57]

There are exceptions. Financial fraud is most likely among those 41 to 50 years old, and more than half of cases involve an individual who is more than 40 years old.[58] That is because "older professionals occupy positions with authority and more access to company resources."[59] While most sex offenders reoffend less frequently as they get older, with the peak years for rape offenders occurring between 25 and 29 and declining thereafter, one exception is extra-familial child molesters, who do not see a decline in offending rates until age 50.[60] Indeed, child molesters actually see their rates of offending increase between ages 20 and 40.[61] Individuals also do not appear to age out of gambling along the traditional lines.[62]

But for most other crimes, especially violent ones, individuals cease the activity in their 30s, if not before. Thus long sentences for most offenses may not be doing anything after the offender reaches a certain age, other than costing the state money that could be better used for other law enforcement purposes.

Given these facts, it is unsurprising that studies analyzing the relationship between crime rates and prison expenditures show that increasing sentences does not always bring a reduction in crime. While the increase in incarceration from the early 1970s to early 1990s may be responsible for between 6% and 25% of the crime reduction in that period, the continued growth in prison expenditures in the 1990s had no statistically significant relationship with a reduction in violent crime.[63] An analysis of the prison population growth studies from before and after the mid-1990s concluded that the reason for the difference is that the increase in prison growth in the latter period was largely driven by an increase in the incarceration rate of people committing drug offenses and low-level crimes.[64] For this group in particular, the crime-increasing effects of incarceration might outweigh any deterrent or incapacitation effect of imprisonment.[65]

These same factors must also be considered when analyzing claims by elected officials that longer sentences promote public safety because they incapacitate offenders. Policy-makers, as noted, frequently rely on this line of argument in their support of longer sentences. As former Virginia governor George Allen put it, "If the violent criminals are locked up . . . they can't come back into our neighborhoods to prey on new victims."[66] All too often, the unstated assumption seems to be that the people who are locked up, stay locked up.

While there is no denying that incapacitating someone prevents them from committing crimes outside the prison, if the person was going to stop committing crimes in any event because they were going to age out of crime (as the studies show), there is no point in incapacitating them beyond the point at which they would otherwise age out of their criminal behavior. To do so is to spend money without a corresponding benefit. Moreover, any incapacitation benefit lasts only as long as the person stays incarcerated. And although politicians often speak as if people get sent away for the rest of their lives, the reality is that more than 95% of the people sent to prison are released.[67] Since 1990, an average of almost 600,000 prisoners have been released to the community each year.[68] So any incapacitation benefit that we get while someone is incarcerated has to be weighed against the likelihood that the person might be a greater danger to society when he or she comes back out because the longer that person spends in prison, the more likely it is that his or her reentry will be a bumpy one. A comprehensive summary of the research concluded that "incarceration certainly reduces crime outside prison as long as it lasts, but appears to cause more crime later."[69]

These downsides explain why there is now a growing body of research showing that increases in incarceration reach a tipping point whereby incarceration is not associated with reductions in crime but is instead correlated with *increases* in crime rates.[70] For example, longer sentences were associated with a 4% increase in recidivism for low-risk offenders, and a 3% increase overall.[71] Daniel Nagin, a professor of public policy and statistics at Carnegie Mellon and an elected fellow of the American Society of Criminology, notes: "Prisons are good for punishing criminals and keeping them off the street, but prison sentences (particularly long sentences) are unlikely to deter future crime. Prisons actually may have the opposite effect: Inmates learn more effective crime strategies from each other, and time spent in prison may desensitize many to the threat of future imprisonment."[72] As one commentator put it, "After a certain point, as prison populations continue to grow, the benefit of incarceration declines and reverses, and you even see crime increase. That seems to me to be where we are now."[73]

A rational approach to setting sentences would thus weigh the incapacitation benefit one gets while the person is incarcerated (plus the retributive benefit of seeing that person punished and any deterrence achieved from the sentence) against the increased risk that the person will commit more crimes when released because of the criminogenic effect of the longer prison term and the reentry difficulties it creates. Inevitably, that would mean shortening many sentences so that people are not locked away beyond the point at which they would age out of their crimes in any case.

A full consideration of the pros and cons would also take into account third-party effects from crime and from incarceration. The costs to third parties from criminal behavior are extensive, including physical injuries and death, pain and suffering, reduced quality of life, and direct monetary losses for health bills or the loss or damage to property, on top of emotional damage. Communities also suffer from crime in the form of lower property values and reduced economic and business development.[74] Estimates place the total costs of crime in the United States at billions of dollars per year.[75] If incarceration deters or prevents crimes, it would thus lower some of these costs. Harm to third parties is usually front and center in the minds of elected officials when they advocate for longer sentences.

But incarceration also brings costs to third parties, especially the families and loved ones of prisoners.[76] The families of incarcerated individuals suffer great economic hardships from incarceration, ranging from lost wages from the incarcerated individual to the costs of prison visits and calls, which can be crushing for families already living on the edge of subsistence. The odds that a family will fall below the poverty line increases by 38% while a father is incarcerated.[77] In more than two-thirds of cases, incarceration caused enough damage to a family's financial stability that it had trouble meeting basic needs, with almost half the families struggling to afford basic food and housing.[78] Married men who are incarcerated are three times more likely to get divorced than men who are not incarcerated—and the rate increases the greater the time served in prison.[79] This is especially concerning for recidivism because recidivism rates are reduced by more than 50% for formerly incarcerated individuals who are married.[80] In addition, incarceration leads to negative health impacts on a family member in about half of all cases, including problems such as post-traumatic stress disorder, depression, anxiety, and nightmares.[81]

Most people in prison are more than 100 miles from their homes, making visits difficult for loved ones. Children who have a parent incarcerated are an average of 100 miles from their fathers and 160 miles from their mothers.[82] In some states, such as Arizona, an incarcerated person's friends and family can be charged just to visit them.[83] Video visitation is also costly. Securus Technologies, for example, provides video visitation in 2,600 correctional facilities at one dollar per minute, and 70% of their contracts mandate that the video visitation replace in-person visitation.[84] In these

facilities, family members thus need to pay for visits that were once free.[85]
The costs associated with the legal process, phone calls, and visitation
often amount to a family's household income for an entire year.[86] Even if
family members do not visit, they still often need to pay for the cost of the
incarcerated family member's room and board since 43 states now authorize
these charges.[87]

The effects are particularly hard on children. More than 2.7 million
children have at least one parent currently incarcerated, and more than 5
million children have had a parent incarcerated at some point in their child-
hood.[88] Fifty-five percent of state prisoners have a child under the age of
18, and most of these children are much younger than 18, with 60% under
the age of ten.[89] Sixty-one percent of women in state prisons have minor
children.[90] One out of every 10 children in America has a parent under the
supervision of the criminal justice system.[91] The effect on children is even
more pronounced among the African American community, where roughly
7% of children have a parent in prison and many more under some form
of criminal justice supervision.[92] These children are at greater risk of living
in poverty,[93] and many end up homeless because a parent is incarcerated.[94]
Nearly one-fifth of children who enter the child welfare system have an incarcerated parent.[95] Children whose mothers are incarcerated are at high
risk developmentally, psychologically, emotionally, and economically.[96]
Children with incarcerated parents have an increased risk of post-traumatic
stress disorder and behavior problems, and they exhibit higher levels of
physical aggression.[97] These children also suffer academically, with grade
point averages falling and the likelihood that a child will drop out of school
rising after a parent is incarcerated.[98] It is hardly surprising, given these difficulties, that the children of incarcerated parents are more likely to end up
in prison themselves.[99]

Longer prison stays also have detrimental effects on communities. Incarceration disrupts family structures and removes a large proportion of
adult males, a dynamic that leads children in those communities (even if
their own parent is not incarcerated) to commit disproportionately more
crimes.[100] After individuals have served their sentences, they return to these
same communities, so if these people have been made worse off from their
time away, these communities bear the brunt of these effects. For instance,
in Maryland, roughly 6 out of every 10 people released from prison go to
Baltimore, and within the city, 30% of these people who were formerly incarcerated go to six smaller community areas.[101] In Texas, 1 out of every 4
people released from prison returns to Houston, with 25% of those people
going to just five of the city's 185 zip codes.[102] Between 2005 and 2009,
there were 851 blocks in Chicago alone with more than $1 million per block

being spent on incarceration for residents of those blocks, and 121 blocks with more than $1 million per block being spent for incarceration for non-violent drug offenders alone.[103] In New York City, 50% of the prison population comes from neighborhoods that are home to only 18% of the adult population.[104] In Brooklyn, there were 35 blocks, each with an incarceration cost of more than $1 million, and one block cost more than $5 million.[105] This clustered incarceration has "affected the ability of residential neighborhoods to perform their traditional social control function."[106] In addition, "incarceration may have spillover effects for entire demographic groups or communities," because prospective employers often report avoiding job candidates from particular neighborhoods rather than looking at each individual candidate's criminal history.[107]

When economists have studied the full range of costs and benefits associated with incarceration, they have concluded that the costs of incarceration and sentencing typically outweigh the benefits.[108] Moreover, when they compare this strategy to others, such as increased spending on police or education, they find alternatives to be more cost-effective.[109] Studies of drug courts also show they can be as effective at reducing recidivism and drug use and cost less than incarceration.[110] Similar studies of low-risk offenders find that shorter terms of incarceration reduce crime more than longer terms, and sentences with no prison time are more effective at reducing crime than sentences of incarceration.[111]

None of this is to say that lower sentences are always better or that all courts should be problem-solving courts. But all too often, there are better options for promoting public safety than long sentences, and politicians and policy-makers just fail to consider them.

Thus we continue to see lawmakers approach criminal law matters with calls to intuition about the deterrent or incapacitative effect of long sentences without considering the downsides. For example, legislators consistently claim that mandatory minimums deter crime when there is empirical evidence to the contrary.[112] Senator Chuck Grassley of Iowa, for example, has stated without any supporting evidence that "the absence of mandatory minimums sentences [for sexual assault and domestic violence] is causing serious problems in deterring these terrible acts."[113] Maine state senator Scott Cyrway sponsored a bill increasing mandatory minimums based on his opinion (again without supporting evidence) that "stiffening our current laws will help to deter those importing . . . drugs from entering our state."[114] Senator Ted Cruz of Texas proposed a law that would have undocumented immigrants face a minimum five-year sentence if they reentered the country after being deported if they were previously convicted of an aggravated felony or had illegally reentered the country previously

on two occasions.[115] Cruz lacked any evidence that this would deter individuals from reentering the United States, but there is an abundance of evidence of what a proposal like this would cost. According to an analysis by
the U.S. Sentencing Commission, this measure would add a whopping
60,000 prisoners, or a 28% increase, over five years to the already overcrowded federal prisons and would cost $2 billion.[116] As Molly Gill from
Families Against Mandatory Minimums stated, "This bill won't stop deported immigrants from reentering the country, but it will force American
taxpayers to pay for half a decade's worth of food, clothing, and housing
for people we supposedly don't want in the country at all."[117]

The recent opioid epidemic in the United States is prompting a panic similar to the one that yielded the severe crack penalties in the 1980s. For example, Maine state representative Catherine Nadeau advocated a bill raising
the maximum prison sentence from 5 to 10 years for importing heroin,
saying "I believe we should provide additional tools to law enforcement to
help them stop drug dealers."[118] Louisiana state representative Joseph
Lopinto sponsored a bill requiring prison time even for first-time offenders
because "people are being found dead with the needle still in their arm."[119]
Indiana state representative Timothy Wesco urged legislation to make
"manufacturing, financing or delivering any amount of heroin that causes
the death of a user a Level 3 felony," despite the fact that law enforcement
officials questioned whether the legislation was needed.[120]

These calls for tough responses have no grounding in any empirical evidence that they will reduce heroin trafficking. Michael Botticelli, a former
White House drug czar in the Obama administration, conceded that "we
can't arrest our way out of the problem, and we really need to focus our
attention on proven public health strategies to make a significant difference.[121] A Pew study of state and federal incarceration practices and health
records found no statistically significant relationship between the rate at
which states imprison drug offenders and drug use, drug overdose deaths,
or drug arrests.[122] The calls for longer sentences for drug dealers also fail
to acknowledge that many of the people who would be targeted for tougher
prosecutions are themselves the very people with addictions that the politicians claim to be wanting to help.[123] The victims and the dealers are often
one and the same.[124] Peers are often scared to report overdoses to first
responders for fear it could land them in prison.[125]

Anyone truly interested in public safety has to pay attention to the relevant
empirical facts and not simply rely on gut instinct. But all too often, legislative judgments rest on nothing more than the notion that a longer sentence will cure everything, even when the evidence shows that longer
sentences often make things worse.

The Role of Prosecutors

Legislative bodies are not the only source of irrational sentencing policies. Prosecutors have enormous power over sentencing policy in the United States. For starters, prosecutors are often key lobbyists for getting laws and guidelines with longer sentences passed. They often share the logic of legislators that the longer the sentence, the better. This was starkly illustrated by Lancaster County, Pennsylvania, district attorney Craig Stedman, who pushed for those selling heroin even one time to get a sentence of 1 year in state prison, and for repeat offenders to get 5 to 10 years because "I'm pissed off and we need to do something about it."[126] For elected prosecutors, that "something" is often long sentences, just as it is for legislators.

Because most prosecutors' offices in the United States are locally funded at the county or district level, whereas most of the costs of imprisonment are borne by the state, prosecutors fail to internalize the costs of asking for long sentences or the trade-offs in using funds for those sentences as opposed to other criminal justice efforts. Prison is essentially a "correctional free lunch" for localities, unlike cheaper alternatives such as treatment and probation, which may not be subsidized by state governments.[127] Prosecutors therefore have an incentive to push for long sentences because it scores them political points, costs them essentially nothing, and gives them leverage when they are bargaining with defendants over pleas and cooperation.

Prosecutors' authority over sentencing goes beyond just getting laws passed. They also have control over sentencing through their discretion over charging, which means they can dictate the punishment or range of punishment that will apply in a case. They frequently threaten long sentences so that individuals will plead guilty or cooperate in making cases against other people—thus saving prosecutors the work of going to trial or spending time investigating and proving a case against someone else.[128] For example, a New Orleans man faced a sentence of 20 years to life in prison if he opted for trial for allegedly stealing about $30 worth of candy bars because of his prior record of theft.[129] That was because he turned down a plea deal of 4 years, prompting the district attorney's office to file a so-called quad offender enhancement that would impose a 20-year mandatory minimum.[130] Or take the case of Gary Costanza, who was one of three men charged with murder and could have received a life sentence but pleaded guilty to conspiracy and was sentenced to three years.[131] As his lawyer explained, "The sole reason for the plea was that he couldn't take a chance on the life sentence. It was almost like a coerced plea."[132] "Coercive plea bargaining tactics abound in state and federal criminal cases," and drug defendants alone face sentences 11 years longer by going to trial than pleading guilty.[133]

When defendants do not accept plea agreements, they often face additional charges. Roy Lee Clay, a heroin dealer who turned down a plea deal for 10 years, ended up receiving a mandatory life sentence after a trial in which federal prosecutors invoked additional sentencing enhancements and won a conviction.[134] When Mary Beth Looney, a woman with no prior convictions, refused a plea deal of 17 years for dealing methamphetamines and for gun possession, prosecutors added more charges against her so that she received a mandatory sentence of more than 45 years after she exercised her constitutional right to take her case to trial.[135] Prosecutors offered Orville Wollard a plea offer of 5 years for firing a registered handgun into his living room wall to scare his daughter's boyfriend, but when he refused the offer, they charged him with an offense that carried a 20-year-mandatory minimum.[136]

Individuals who cooperate with prosecutors can receive large sentencing concessions. Nearly one-fifth of federal criminal convictions were granted downward departures from the sentencing guidelines for providing substantial assistance.[137] Half of all defendants who provided assistance got their sentence reduced by 50% or more.[138] The average sentence reduction for robbery is nearly 4 years, and for drug trafficking, it is more than 5 years.[139] The reductions are not necessarily tied to culpability. Only 1% of those convicted of immigration violations or drug possession received more lenient sentences for providing substantial assistance,[140] whereas much more serious criminal conduct has yielded huge reductions. Andy Fastow, the former CFO of Enron served only 5 years after initially being charged with 78 counts of fraud for agreeing to testify as a government witness.[141] Mafia hit man Salvatore "Sammy the Bull" Gravano received a 5-year sentence for 19 murders in exchange for informing against John Gotti and others in the mafia.[142] In these cases, the sentence is based on the utility one provides to the government, which can often mean that the biggest fish get the best deals. "Defendants who are most in the know, and thus have the most 'substantial assistance' to offer, are often those who are most centrally involved in the conspiratorial crimes."[143]

That is how you end up with cases like Andrew Jones's. Jones was a street-level dealer with limited mental capacity who was sentenced to 30 years, while the kingpin in his operation, Lamond Sykes, received 23 years because Sykes was able to provide information on underlings.[144] That is also how you get sentences like the one for Darlene Eckles, a first-time offender who was sentenced to 19 years and 7 months for involvement in her brother's drug-trafficking business.[145] Her brother, the ringleader of the operation, received 11 years and 8 months.[146] Eckles had permitted her brother to live with her when he was released from prison, and against her wishes, he began operating a drug business out of her home. She occasionally collected and counted money for him,[147] but despite this far less significant role in the operation, she received almost 8 years more than him because he testified against her and another sibling.

It may be that the benefits of successfully pursuing other cases make these steep sentencing concessions worth it as a matter of net public safety. But it is hard to argue that prosecutors are in the best position to make that evaluation. When they make those determinations, their own interests are front and center: how to make things easiest for them. What is less likely to be analyzed is how their cases fit within a grander scheme of criminal justice or long-term public safety goals.

When prosecutors lobby for or against sentencing legislation, that same concern is present: will professional self-interest come at the expense of the broader public interest? Although prosecutors typically claim to speak for the public interest, the fact is the public interest may conflict with their professional interests. They have formed influential professional organizations at all levels of government to advance their interests.[148] For instance, Attorney General Holder concluded that reducing mandatory minimum sentences would promote public safety because it would help free up funds used on prison for other law enforcement needs, but the National Association of Assistant United States Attorneys (NAAUSA), disagreed.[149] They submitted a letter opposing the reductions in mandatory minimum sentences, emphasizing that mandatory minimum sentences are an "indispensable tool" to "secure offender cooperation."[150] They explained that "the leverage, the hammer we have comes in those penalties. . . . It is the one and only tool we have on the other side."[151] The professional organization thus highlighted what made federal prosecutors' jobs easier, while the attorney general sought to balance broader public policy goals. The AG and line prosecutors similarly disagreed about whether federal drug sentencing guidelines should be lowered, with the AG again emphasizing the need to free up limited resources for other public safety efforts and the line prosecutors arguing that longer sentences remained necessary.[152]

At the state level, too, elected prosecutors often oppose reductions in sentences because of how those reductions will affect their ability to do their jobs. The California District Attorneys Association Board of Directors voted to oppose Governor Jerry Brown's sentencing reforms because they took away tools from their arsenal.[153] Some prosecutors have admitted openly that they use drug charges and the long sentences that accompany them to incarcerate people they believe are dangerous for other reasons, even when they lack proof. John DeRosier, the district attorney of Calcasieu Parish, Louisiana, confessed that "we have people all the time that we know have been involved in robberies, rapes and murders. We haven't been able to prove our cases, but we're in court with them for second-offense possession of marijuana. What do you think we're going to do?"[154] One can reasonably ask why these prosecutors can be so sure these individuals are involved in violent offenses when they lack proof and why they should be trusted to go on their gut instincts that the individuals are guilty when we have an established process to protect defendants from someone's hunch.

But with this kind of confidence in their own judgment and gut instincts, it is no wonder that prosecutors typically fight against reductions in sentences. They want to keep them for bargaining purposes and at the same time score tough-on-crime points with their local constituents. Local prosecutors are concerned with only their own local election and not necessary statewide policy. So even if a state could better spend the money it would otherwise use for prison to pay for public safety expenditures, like victim services or drug treatment, local prosecutors may oppose those efforts because they are not footing the bill for incarceration in state prison. Some prosecutors have openly advocated building even more prisons, despite any evidence it would reduce crime. Steven Cook, the NAAUSA president said, "Do I think it would be a good investment to build more [prisons]? Yeah, no question about it!"[155] Honolulu's prosecutor Keith Kaneshiro opposed sentencing reforms and instead said, "I have one solution to that problem that I'm going to recommend to the legislature, and I'd like your support. And that is to build a new prison here."[156] Of course, it is easy for prosecutors to say as much. They do not need to pay for prisons and long sentences out of their budgets, but they get the benefits of having those long sentences on the books because of the bargaining leverage it gives them and because they can appear tough to their constituents.

The result of having legislators and prosecutors push for severe sentences without rational reflection is, predictably, having irrational sentences imposed. While judges can sometimes act as a corrective against the excesses of legislators and prosecutors in individual cases (and they should be given the discretion to do so), the current reality is that they often lack the discretion to act as a check because a punishment is mandatory or a guideline range narrows their options. Even when judges have discretion, they are not well positioned to make sentencing policy writ large because each judge sees only the cases on his or her docket. So to the extent that broader policies are being made, the key actors are legislators and prosecutors, and they are pursuing sentences that neither achieve retributive justice nor maximize public safety. Sensible criminal justice reform in the United States must replace this outmoded and empirically groundless way of thinking about sentencing with an approach that considers the costs and the benefits of longer sentences. And that shift will require an institutional change away from the politicians and elected prosecutors who all too often are happy to get by on the baseless rhetoric and empty symbolism that they are doing something to address crime simply because they are lengthening sentences.

3

COUNTERPRODUCTIVE
CONFINEMENT

IN 1976, PAROLE BOARDS released 65% of the people who appeared before them. Two decades later, that figure plummeted to 24%.[1] And that was in the states that continued to use parole boards; about half the states decided to abandon the model that dominated for most of the 20th century and gave a parole board broad authority to release individuals from prison before the end of their maximum prison term.[2] What happened over the span of those two decades?

The demise of parole was part of a broader shift, beginning in the 1970s, "away from rehabilitation as a dominant philosophy and toward retribution or 'just deserts.'"[3] Prison terms became the tool by which society expressed its displeasure with someone. Prison also served—or at least was intended to serve—a utilitarian function. In addition to deterring future crimes, a term of confinement would incapacitate the person so that he or she could not commit additional crimes outside of the prison while incarcerated. But rehabilitation fell by the wayside as one of the motivating utilitarian purposes of punishment.

This was a landmark shift in penal philosophy. For most of America's history, the stated purpose of incarcerating individuals was to reform them.[4] That is why in most states, the agency responsible for its prisons is known as the department of corrections. Time in prison was supposed to "correct" whatever failings led to an individual's criminal behavior. This was a departure from the early colonial model in which punishment was a blunt instrument and most felonies were punishable by death. Starting in the 19th century and carrying forward for most of the 20th century, "the belief no longer prevail[ed] that every offense in a like legal category calls for an identical punishment without regard to the past life and habits of a particular offender."[5] Instead, punishment became individualized, and judges typically sentenced defendants to a range, with the ultimate release date determined by a parole board or official based on the defendant's rehabilitation.[6] By the middle of the 20th century, every state and the federal government followed this model.[7]

Plenty of problems arose from this individualized approach. Because there was no appellate review of individual decisions or any kind of systematic oversight, this regime hardly amounted to a rational program for addressing crime control or rehabilitation. It produced large disparities based on which judge or probation officer happened to be assigned to a defendant's case. Parole board members were often politicians or political appointees with no expertise or experience in assessing recidivism risks or rehabilitation.[8] The rehabilitative programs offered were often lacking. A highly influential study of rehabilitative programs in prisons in 1974 concluded that they did little to lower recidivism rates.[9] In the face of rising crime rates, these shortcomings led to dissatisfaction with this model and with the dominant idea that punishment was to serve rehabilitative purposes.

But in rejecting rehabilitation outright—instead of putting systemic checks in place or examining particular programs to see how they could be improved—jurisdictions overlooked a crucial fact, what Jeremy Travis, the former director of the National Institute of Justice and president of John Jay College of Criminal Justice, calls "the iron law of imprisonment: they all come back."[10] Just about every individual put in a jail or prison is ultimately released back into the community. A full 95% of people are ultimately released from jail and prison—roughly 600,000 annually—whereas less than 4% of incarcerated individuals receive a sentence of life without parole.[11]

As a matter of public safety, then, one would think policy-makers would carefully consider what interventions during confinement would make these individuals less likely to commit crimes when they return to their communities—or at the very least make sure that the time during which they are incarcerated does not make them more prone to commit crimes when they are inevitably released. Sadly, our political process and institutional setup is so dysfunctional that jurisdictions endorse a multitude of corrections policies that compromise public safety instead of improve it.

Jails and Pretrial Detention

More than 700,000 people—about one-third of the total number of people incarcerated each year—are housed in local jails.[12] While some are there to serve out relatively short sentences after conviction, the bulk of the jail population is being held before trial, so there has been no determination that they are guilty or will ever need to be punished.[13] These people are ostensibly being held either because they are seen as a flight risk before their trial or because they are deemed a risk to public safety.[14] All too often, however, little attention is paid to what kinds of risks people actually pose. Instead, prosecutors and judges reflexively set bail amounts (the amount of money a defendant must pay to be released before trial) with little thought given to risk, and those people who cannot pay bail (regardless of risk) are the ones who get locked up.[15] Wealth is a poor proxy for one's risk to public safety, yet we see defendants accused of serious crimes like murder walk free if they can make bail, while those who cannot afford to post even a few hundred dollars languish in jail for minor offenses.[16] Because the detention proceeding becomes just an unthinking request for various bail amounts, it takes only a couple of minutes.[17]

Aside from the enormous liberty costs to the person being detained, the excessive use of pretrial detention under this model creates public safety risks. Pretrial detention can mean the loss of jobs, housing, and custody of children for those already living on the margins.[18] Facing these consequences, it is not surprising that those detained pretrial are more likely to plead guilty (regardless of their crime or actual guilt).[19] Perhaps more surprising, however, is that pretrial detention also correlates with longer sentences and higher recidivism rates. Low-risk defendants who were detained for their entire pretrial period were 5.41 times more likely to be sentenced to jail and 3.76 times more likely to be sentenced to prison than similarly situated low-risk defendants who were released pending their trial.[20] The numbers are similar for high-risk defendants: those who are detained before trial are three times more likely to be sentenced to a term of incarceration than those who were released.[21] That increased likelihood of incarceration costs money that could be better spent elsewhere.

Even more alarming is that pretrial detention itself—regardless of the underlying crime and holding other factors constant—is criminogenic. A person detained pretrial is, all else being equal, more likely to commit crimes later on. A recent study found that incarcerating individuals before trial was associated with a 30% increase in felonies and a 20% increase in misdemeanors 18 months after their hearing.[22] This is consistent with the findings of an earlier study that likewise found that, controlling for their overall risk score on a state assessment tool, offense type, and whether the offense was a felony or a misdemeanor, defendants who were detained for the entirety of their pretrial period were 1.3 times more likely to recidivate than those who were released.[23]

There is a better way than bail to balance pretrial flight risk or the risk that an individual released before trial might commit additional crimes with the risks and costs of pretrial detention itself. We can use aggregate data to create risk assessment tools that do a better job predicting flight and safety risk than a prosecutor's or judge's gut instinct in setting bail amounts.[24] A risk instrument developed by the Laura and John Arnold Foundation looks to various elements of the current charged offense and an individual's criminal history, including previous failures to appear, to determine risk.[25] Unlike some other risk tools, which have been criticized for perpetuating racial and class bias by incorporating variables correlated with race and poverty, the Arnold risk tool does not consider race, sex, neighborhood, socioeconomic status, or level of education.[26] It uses criminal history and age as the main predictors. While criminal history will itself incorporate certain biases because of the biased nature of policing and the concentrated police presence in particular areas, especially those with large percentages of minority residences, judges and prosecutors who do not use tools also look at criminal history. So the question is whether the tool does a better job of predicting based on that history using masses of aggregate data than the gut instincts of prosecutors or judges who are themselves likely to have biases. The Arnold tool has another virtue, which is that jurisdictions using this measure need not engage in additional interviews with a defendant or spend money on extra personnel or investigation, so it saves time and resources in addition to improving outcomes.[27]

If judges and prosecutors take seriously the data from a tool like the Arnold risk assessment, decisions can improve. The key is to have a tool that is fully transparent about its inputs and that eliminates those factors associated with bias, such as geography, employment history, and education. While using criminal history and age as predictors will not be free from bias, those facts will be part of any decision by a judge or prosecutor, so the tool's value is in assessing their statistical relevance instead of just having judges and prosecutors make their best guesses about what they mean. Using a risk instrument like this will mean that judges and prosecutors will at least be fully informed based on data about risk, as opposed to whatever biases they may have—implicit or otherwise—being the exclusive guide. If prosecutors and judges are going to make these decisions pretrial based on their concern that a defendant will commit a violent crime if released—and we know that is what they do—then it is important to give them the best information we have to make that assessment.

Jurisdictions that have switched to this model have enjoyed great success. New Jersey began to use this risk tool in 2017, after the state voted in 2014 to amend the state constitution to largely eliminate cash bail.[28] Under its previous bail regime, 75% of the state's jail population consisted of people detained pretrial, and they stayed, on average, 10 months.[29] Many of the people detained were only locked up because they were poor, with 40% unable to afford bail amounts of $2,500 or less.[30] At the same time, some individuals charged with the most violent offenses walked free before trial because they were able to make their bail amounts. Six months after using the new risk tool, New Jersey's pretrial detention rates dropped by 20%, and only 8 people during that time period were being held on bail.[31] Meanwhile, crime rates remained steady or dropped slightly.[32] Mecklenburg County, North Carolina, which includes Charlotte, has had similar positive results after adopting this model. It reduced its jail population by 20% when it switched to this risk assessment tool, and it did so with no effect on crime rates.[33]

Moreover, for those worried that this turns what should be an individualized decision into one based on general data and may therefore become dehumanizing or eventually lead to greater severity, it is important to emphasize that any risk assessment tool is just a guide. A judge can still consider individualized factors before deciding whether to rely exclusively on the risk tool itself, so the human element does not need to disappear. Indeed, if anything, the use of these tools might be too flexible, as judges in many jurisdictions ignore the risk tools they are given and continue to detain people even when the tool tells them to release them. In some jurisdictions, such as Cook County (which includes Chicago), judges' failure to follow the risk tool's recommendations undermined the tool's effectiveness and created disparities, leading the chief judge there to replace judges who failed to comply with the tool with other judges who had greater training using a risk assessment process.[34] In Kentucky, initial use of the tool led to increases in release rates coupled with improved public safety outcomes; the rate of those rearrested after being released pretrial *declined* 15% shortly after adoption of the risk tool.[35] But unfortunately, over time, judges reverted to old habits and stopped relying on the tool to guide their decisions.[36] These trends suggest that jurisdictions using these tools have to spend time training judges and prosecutors about their predictive value to achieve the positive results seen in places like New Jersey. The tool itself will not be a panacea, but coupled with training and a commitment to reduce jail populations, the use of risk assessment tools can reduce the unnecessary costs of pretrial detention.

Other jurisdictions are rethinking pretrial detention and bail in other ways. After a federal court in Texas ruled that Harris County violated the Constitution by detaining defendants for their inability to make bail, the district attorney announced a series of reforms, including "cite and release 'for appropriate misdemeanor crimes.'"[37] In June 2017, the Cook County State's Attorney's Office announced that prosecutors would begin to ask judges to release defendants charged with misdemeanors and low-level felonies without bail, as long as they do not have a criminal history or pose a clear risk to public safety.[38] Chicago is also among the growing number of cities that have seen the emergence of community bail funds, which raise money to aid indigent defendants and advocate for broader bail reforms.[39] New York City is home to two other examples of this type of fund, in the Bronx and Brooklyn.[40] Other cities with bail funds include Boston, Minneapolis-St. Paul, Memphis, Nashville, New Haven, Philadelphia, Richmond, and Seattle. The Bronx and Brooklyn funds report appearance rates in excess of 95%, not to mention dramatic increases in the rates that cases are dismissed.[41] Based on this success, the founder of the Bronx bail fund is set to start a nationwide bail fund to help 150,000 individuals obtain release pretrial.[42]

While these changes to pretrial detention are promising advances for saving resources and improving public safety, they are unfortunately still the exception. The majority of jurisdictions continue to rely on cash bail, and hundreds of thousands of individuals languish in jails even before they have had a trial, disrupting their lives and making them more likely to commit crimes later. These people are locked away because they are poor, not because they pose a risk of any kind. Jurisdictions are spending millions to keep them in jail, even though doing so diminishes rather than improves public safety.

Lack of Prison Programming and Treatment

Our flawed policies of incarceration are not limited to the pretrial period. We follow the same counterproductive course when it comes to incarceration after trial. When the rehabilitative ideal fell out of favor, it did so in part because of the view that prison was not successfully reforming prisoners. While some prison programs admittedly do not result in reduced recidivism or otherwise improve the ability of prisoners to successfully reenter society when they are released, that is not true of all programs. Research demonstrates the success of various programs and interventions in reducing recidivism rates. The Washington State Institute for Public Policy, which has tracked the costs and benefits of prison programming for juveniles and adults for decades, lists dozens of programming options found to generate a positive return on investment through reduced recidivism.[43] Many cognitive-behavioral treatment programs have proved quite effective at lowering recidivism and producing benefits well in excess of their costs.[44] A 2007 meta-analysis of 58 studies on cognitive-behavioral therapy programs found that such programs, on average, decreased participant recidivism by 25%, with the most successful of the programs decreasing recidivism by 50%.[45]

Reentry and vocational training programs are also effective. Consider, for instance, EMPLOY, a prisoner reentry employment program run by the Minnesota Department of Corrections, which has been shown to decrease recidivism and increase employment for program participants.[46] The program, which participants begin within the final few months of their prison term and conclude one year after their release, reduced the likelihood of reincarceration for a new crime by 55% and increased the likelihood of securing employment within a year of release by 72%.[47] Or take the case of the Prison Industry Enhancement Certification Program, a federal initiative that allows private industries to employ individuals in prison in realistic work environments and helps them acquire marketable skills, all while being paid prevailing local wages for that line of work. The program not only reduces recidivism but also helps incarcerated individuals accrue savings and pay off any money owed for victim compensation.[48]

Vocational training programs such as these are critical because individuals are more likely to commit new crimes if they remain unemployed upon release, and employment is hard to come by for formerly incarcerated people.[49] One study of post-release employment outcomes among individuals in Indiana found that, of the more than 6,000 people tracked, roughly 94% remained unemployed nine months following their release, and 78% of these same individuals remained unemployed even five years later.[50]

Drug treatment programs have also been found to reduce both recidivism and relapse into drug abuse. A 2012 meta-analysis of 74 studies evaluating incarceration-based drug treatment programs over the past 30 years found that, on average, participants in a treatment program had a 15% to 17% reduced likelihood of both recidivism and relapse.[51] And some incarceration-based treatment programs exceed those average results. Participants in the Forever Free Substance Abuse Treatment Program at the California Institution for Women in Frontera, for example, had a 20% reduced likelihood of recidivating compared to similarly situated nonparticipants, enjoyed a 16% increased likelihood of employment, were 26% less likely to have reported drug use in the year since their release, and had a greater likelihood of living independently and maintaining custody of their children.[52]

Unfortunately, prison programs are woefully underfunded and do not come close to meeting the needs of those who are incarcerated. Indeed, the percentage of individuals participating in vocational, educational, and drug treatment programs declined in the 1990s while incarceration rates were going through the roof, demonstrating that jurisdictions were investing in longer sentences but not the programming that would ultimately bring public safety benefits when these individuals were released.[53] One study of prison programming in seven states found that less than 10% of the people who were incarcerated took part in educational, employment, or vocational programming.[54]

To be sure, many people in prison are participating in a work program, but the majority are performing jobs to support the functioning of the prison, such as food preparation or janitorial work, which impart few marketable skills and do not improve the person's employment prospects upon release.[55] The vocational training that works best to help individuals when they leave prison is in short supply. For example, UNICOR, the vocational program run by the Federal Bureau of Prisons which affords participants experience in carpentry, electronics, automotive repair, and other marketable trades, has a waiting list of 25,000 people and a meager 8% participation rate, despite the fact that participating in UNICOR reduces recidivism by 24%.[56]

Education offerings in prison similarly fall well short of reaching all the needs of those in prison. An estimated 40% of people in state and federal prisons have neither a high school diploma nor a GED, but many of these individuals need more than a GED-prep course, which tends to be the standard offering in facilities.[57] More than 20% of state and federal prisoners and more than 30% of people in jail have at least one "cognitive disability" (examples of which include autism, learning disorders, attention deficit disorder, Down syndrome, and dementia), compared to just 5% of the general population.[58] Few facilities offer any kind of educational programming tailored to the needs of these individuals. Prisons also rarely offer the kind of basic education that many of the people in prison need even when they do not have cognitive disabilities. A recent study of more than 200 individuals in a medium security prison in Alabama, for example, found that among the African American and Latino population in the prison, the average grade level for reading was sixth and third grade, respectively.[59] Yet few facilities offer remedial education for individuals at this reading level. Most pre-GED courses are designed for those who are reading between a sixth- and eighth-grade-level equivalent.[60]

Despite the enormous need for educational programming among the incarcerated population, educational offerings are decreasing. While 41% of all people in state prison participated in some kind of educational programming in 1979, that number dropped to 22% by 1995.[61] Participation in educational programs nationally declined from 45% in 1986 to roughly 27% in 2004.[62] These decreasing participation rates are all the more jarring when one considers that the states and the federal government changed their stated policies to mandate more participation. In 1981, the Federal Bureau of Prisons instituted a mandatory literacy program that required people in prison who scored below a certain score on a standardized test to participate; by 2002, 44 states had implemented similar policies, many of which also offer incentives such as good-time credit or more favorable parole consideration.[63] But these mandates were not coupled with resources for programming. Just the opposite, funding support has dramatically declined. For many years, prison education programs were funded, in part, by so-called Specter Funds, which were federal funds named after prison-reform advocate Senator Arlen Specter. In 2011, Congress failed to renew funding for Specter Funds and has not reallocated funds since.[64] States, too, have lowered their financial support, reducing funding for prison education by an average of 6% between 2009 and 2012.[65] Funding was reduced even more—between 10% and 20%—in states with larger prison populations.[66] A report by the Bureau of Justice Statistics showed that, as a percentage of total state correctional expenditures, spending on education programs was lower in 2010 than in any previous year since 1982, the earliest year for which data was provided.[67]

Yet education is one of the best investments one can make in individuals who are incarcerated. A 2013 RAND Corporation study concluded that investment in educational programs for people in prison had a return on investment of over five to one.[68] For those individuals in prison who are ready for higher education, the studies are similarly clear: participation in college-level courses and programs lowers recidivism rates.[69]

Political officials have ignored this track record of success, however, and instead have sought to cut off those in prison from access to education. In addition to cutting off Specter Funds, Congress eliminated the availability of Pell Grants for people who are incarcerated to use for college tuition.[70] While Senator Pell argued that grants should be available for those in prison precisely because "the more education inmates receive while in prison, the less likely it is they will commit crimes on release," opponents successfully argued that allowing people in prison to get the grants would "put convicts at the head of the line for college financial aid, crowding out law-abiding citizens."[71] This zero sum way of couching educational opportunities— that any programming for people in prison means less funding for those who never break the law in the first place—doomed these investments even though they bring an excellent return in terms of public safety.

If one were to ask instead whether investing in education for people in prison would save us money in the long run—thus freeing up those funds for education for those who do not break the law, not to mention keeping everyone safer—then it would be clear that it is a good investment that benefits society at large. That explains why the Obama administration launched a pilot program to restore access to Pell Grants to people in prison in an attempt to get around the federal legislation. Motivated in part by evidence that incarcerated individuals who participate in correctional education are 43% less likely to recidivate within three years of release than those who do not participate in any such programs, the administration announced the Second Chance Pell pilot program. The administration selected 67 colleges and universities to partner with more than 100 state and federal correctional institutions to allow 12,000 incarcerated individuals in the Second Chance Pell pilot program.[72] But federal offerings cannot go beyond this pilot because the legislation eliminating Pell Grants remains in effect. And the pilot program itself remains vulnerable to unilateral discontinuation or contraction.

The story is the same with respect to drug treatment offerings as it is with respect to vocational and educational programs. Jurisdictions utterly fail to provide drug treatment programs to match the need for them. A large portion of the people in prison and jail have drug and alcohol problems. A full 69% of people who are incarcerated regularly use drugs.[73] Of the 2.3 million people in U.S. prisons and jails, 1.5 million meet the DSM-IV medical criteria for substance abuse or addiction, while an additional 458,000 have a history of substance abuse, were under the influence of alcohol or drugs at the time of their crime, committed their crime to get money to buy drugs, or some combination. Collectively, this accounts for 85% of the U.S. prison population. Yet studies show that only 11% of the people in prison and jail are receiving substance abuse treatment.[74] While a recent survey of correctional programs across the United States found that most provided some type of drug abuse treatment, the percentage of incarcerated people who have access to those services at any given time is low, usually less than 10%.[75]

Moreover, even if a correctional facility does provide treatment, the continuity of treatment post-incarceration, which is essential to recovery, is often lacking once the individual transitions from incarceration to community supervision. Failure to receive treatment after release increases the risk not only of relapse, but also of mortality from drug overdose.[76] More than half the people with addiction histories relapse within a month of release from prison, a testament to the inadequacy of current treatment offerings.[77]

In the federal system, the Residential Drug Abuse Program (RDAP) allows people in federal prison to earn up to one year off their sentence.[78] This program is highly successful at reducing recidivism, and yet there is a long waiting list for eligible individuals who want to participate.[79] The lack of drug treatment is, as Jeremy Travis notes, a "particularly acute policy failure" because research shows that these programs reduce drug use and criminal conduct among participants.[80]

Treatment for mental health problems is also lacking. More than half of the people in prisons and jails suffer from a mental illness.[81] Yet despite the high prevalence of mental illness among the incarcerated population, only one in three people in prison and one in six people in jail receive any form of mental health treatment.[82] Treatment is lacking even for those with the most serious mental illnesses, such as schizophrenia and bipolar disorder, with 40% of those people going without help.[83] Jurisdictions also fail to provide transitional services for people with serious mental illnesses who are released from prison. Recidivism rates dramatically improve when mental health and corrections professionals work together to provide plans and referrals for reentry for people with mental illnesses. In the state of Washington, for example, the Mentally Ill Offender Community Transition Program focuses on the reentry of people with mental illnesses, and those who participate in the program have a 19% recidivism rate for felony convictions, compared to 42% for the control group.[84] But a National Institute of Corrections study found that less than half the corrections departments in their sample had partnerships with public health agencies to assist people with mental illnesses in obtaining treatment and services once they are released from prison.[85]

Prisons fail to provide other needed services as well. At the Bureau of Prisons, for instance, not all facilities offer the cognitive-behavioral approaches that have been shown to reduce recidivism.[86] Corrections facilities also fail to offer sufficient victims' services, even though almost 20% of all people incarcerated and more than 50% of women who are incarcerated were physically or sexually abused before they were imprisoned.[87]

Jurisdictions have also eliminated work-release programs and halfway houses that would place individuals serving their sentences in the community while under correctional custody. Studies have shown that individuals who participate in these so-called conditional release programs have lower recidivism rates than individuals who do not.[88] But even when these programs yield more benefits on net than risk, our political climate does not tolerate risk, no matter what the countervailing benefits.

These programs pose the classic Willie Horton problem: if one individual in the program commits a violent crime, the clamor for the program's abolition overwhelms the facts about its overall success rates. Indeed, the program in which Horton himself participated had a success rate greater than 99%, but it was shut down after Horton committed his crimes.[89] And polls conducted after the Horton commercial aired showed that it had the greatest impact of any ad during the 1988 presidential campaign, further affirming for politicians the risk these programs hold for them.[90]

One can see this dynamic play out across a range of programs. New York had a temporary release program in the 1970s that was dismantled after a series of crimes by four people in the program who had escaped. Even though only 3.7% of the participants in the program absconded while the remainder successfully earned wages that helped their transition upon release, New York nonetheless dramatically curtailed the program.[91] In 1994, Massachusetts suspended an otherwise successful work release program for people who were within 18 months of parole eligibility after one participant escaped and shot a police officer during a high-speed chase.[92] In Illinois, then-governor Pat Quinn nearly lost his 2010 reelection campaign because his opponent criticized his administration's policy of enabling "meritorious good time" credit, which allowed detained individuals early release, to begin accruing upon arrival as opposed to accruing after a 61-day waiting period, which was the prior policy. This minor adjustment, which reduced the average sentence in state prisons by 37 days, was blamed for the crimes— including one murder—of three individuals let out roughly 40 days early. As a result, the 61-day waiting period was not only reinstated, but lengthened, causing a rapid 3,000-person increase in Illinois's already overcrowding prison system.[93]

Lack of Accountability

The tragic irony of our current approach of warehousing individuals without programming is that it is failing miserably as a matter of public safety. Within five years after their release from prison, more than 70% of people had new arrests or convictions, with most of the new offenses occurring within the first year of release.[94] Yet consideration of this failure is lacking in political discussions. The public does not seem to connect the lack of programming with the high rates of reoffending by people who have served time. No one points a finger at the state when someone with a drug problem who receives no drug treatment in prison is released and goes on to commit another crime.

Our existing strategies are not questioned as a state failure the way we question the state's role when individuals commit crimes while under state supervision in a furlough program or after an early release. In the latter situations, the public is angry not only at the individual who commits the crime, but also at the state for allowing the individual back into the community before the custodial sentence was up. When crimes occur under these circumstances, "their stories provide fuel to coalitions of politicians, law enforcement representatives, editorial writers, and other advocates for 'get tough' crime policies."[95] These are the types of cases that disproportionately drive policy irrespective of whether the program overall results in a net reduction in crime and improves public safety. So these programs disappear.

But if our decision-making were rational, we would subject other policies to the same scrutiny that we give programs that allow for "early" release. After all, individuals who are released after no programming or after serving their full, original sentence often go on to commit additional crimes, and it is worth knowing whether that happens because our current approach is deficient. We do not do that because, at a superficial level, the existing approach looks like the state took no affirmative action because the crimes happen when an individual is out of state custody. But of course the length of their sentence and the absence of any programming in prison are just as much state choices as are state furlough programs or decisions for early release. There is no difference in terms of the level of state involvement. In both cases, the state is making a choice about what to do in the name of public safety.

But the political process is not equipped to point out the similarities in those cases because it is not a process that is based on rational reflection. It is based on public emotions and the demands of powerful groups. The public is outraged when the media reports that someone commits a crime after being released early or while participating in a program. That is a story with emotional pull that grabs everyone's attention. The media does not run stories about the 76.6% of offenders who recidivate after serving their full terms of confinement because the state failed to provide programming.[96] Even if there were such stories, few members of the public would pay attention because the statistics would not exert an emotional pull on them, and there are no powerful lobbying forces clamoring for any of this to change.

No one is held accountable for the high rates of recidivism that our current system produces. Prison officials get paid the same and keep their jobs irrespective of the recidivism rates among the individuals they release. They do not have to make any effort to show that their interventions work to lower crime rates or reduce reoffending. It is entirely predictable, then, that prison workers would put their own interests ahead of the public's. Thus, for example, when the federal Bureau of Prisons assesses individuals who are incarcerated, it focuses on the risk that they will engage in institutional misconduct. It does not assess them to determine their recidivism risk or their programming needs. That is why a recent bipartisan task force concluded that it should change its practices and adopt a validated risk/needs assessment tool that is designed to focus on recidivism: "The current approach, utilizing security level as a proxy for risk, may be sufficient for the daily management of prisons, but certainly is not the current state of practice for reentry preparation."[97] Corrections officers also often resist changes that they believe would make their jobs more difficult, even if it would be in the public interest. For example, even though the use of solitary confinement impedes an individual's ability to reenter successfully upon release from prison, prison workers fight to keep its use because they believe it is necessary for their safety.

Corrections officials are not the only ones who are not being held accountable for these poor outcomes. Prosecutors are also not held responsible for high rates of reoffending. They are assessed by the short-term outcomes in cases. So they, too, fail to ask what happens to people once they are sent to prison and then after they are released.

Prison Conditions

This same lack of accountability helps explain other prison policies that have the effect of undermining public safety. Consider the physical location of prisons. Individuals are often locked away far from their homes—with more than 75% of people incarcerated more than 50 miles away from home and the average person 100 miles away.[98] These distances make it difficult for family and friends to visit, particularly those who struggle to afford transportation to the facilities. One study found that fewer than half of all people imprisoned less than 50 miles away receive visits at least once a month, and the number declines as the distances increases, with only about one-quarter of the people incarcerated more than 100 miles away receiving monthly visits.[99] In Florida, for example, the majority of people are never visited while they are in prison; 58% were never visited in the year prior to their release. Those who do receive visits are much less likely to recidivate when they are released. People incarcerated in state prisons in Florida who had visitors had a 30.7% lower incidence of recidivism than those who did not. Significantly, for each additional visit an individual received, the odds of recidivism declined by 3.8%.[100]

It is not just distance that matters for visits. It is up to each state whether it wants to impose restrictions on prison visits, and the states can consider any penological goal, not just the effect on public safety. Courts usually defer to prison administrators in making these determinations.[101] The result is that many correctional facilities have limited visits as disciplinary measures or for other cost-saving or administrative reasons, such as preventing the transfer of contraband.[102] Visitation policies in maximum-security prisons are often the most restrictive, even though the individuals housed there are likely the ones who need the most help and support for successful reentry. In North Carolina, for instance, prisoners in maximum security can have only one visit per week for two hours.[103] In Oklahoma, maximum-security prisoners have up to four hours a week of visitation, while minimum-security prisons allow eight hours.[104] While tightening visitation might aid the administration of the facility, it is a terrible policy if the goal is to reduce crime because maintaining connections with loved ones is critical for an individual's successful reentry. Studies consistently show that visitation reduces and delays recidivism.[105]

Visits should be in-person to have the greatest benefit, but many states are now turning to video visits instead to save administrative costs. To be sure, virtual visitation programs are useful when an individual is incarcerated far from their loved ones or when in-person visitation may be dangerous. But video calls should not replace in-person visits in most cases because virtual visitation does not produce the same strong communal and familial ties that are demonstrated to change individuals' behavior both in and out of prison. Video calls are often interrupted by technical difficulties, and prisoners do not have the same privacy and intimacy that in-person visits afford. Video visitation can also have negative effects on the prisoner's loved ones. Seeing someone on a screen does not provide the same reassurance about his or her well-being as does an in-person visit.[106] Despite these negative effects on reentry and ultimately public safety, some jail and prison administrators are nevertheless replacing in-person visits with video visits because it makes their jobs easier, even if the general public pays the price in terms of inferior reentry outcomes.

Facilities often adopt similarly counterproductive telephone policies. The rates for phone calls are often exorbitant because pay phone companies have a monopoly on calls to and from the facilities, and the fees are split between those companies and the prisons and jails.[107] A 4-minute call costs as much as $56.[108] Prisons and jails go along because they reap revenue from this setup, collectively making around $460 million per year in concession fees from the companies.[109] The people incarcerated and their families bear a crushing burden as a result. A retired nurse who spent $100 per month just to talk to her grandson who was in prison in another state brought a civil rights challenge to this structure and pointed out how hard it was on families and the people in prison, many of whom are living in poverty. In 2015, the FCC implemented rate caps for interstate and intrastate prison calls, but in June 2017, the Court of Appeals for the District of Columbia Circuit struck down the intrastate caps as beyond the agency's legal authority.[110] Roughly 80% of prison phone calls are intrastate, so without FCC regulation, states would have to regulate the rates to keep costs down. But all too often that does not happen, and the result is that calls remain prohibitively expensive. It is not just those in prison and their loved ones who suffer. The public loses out as well because a valuable tool for reentry goes underutilized because the financial interests of the phone companies and the prisons cut against the public interest in getting better post-incarceration outcomes.

There is a similar tension—or at least a perceived tension—in the use of solitary confinement. Many prison administrators believe it is critical to be able to use it to maintain control of difficult individuals in their facilities and to keep their employees and other incarcerated individuals safe. Almost 20% of people in prisons and 18% of people in jails reported spending time in solitary, and the figures are even higher for individuals with a history of mental health problems.[111] President Obama noted that "as many as 100,000 inmates in U.S. prisons are currently held in solitary confinement" and that "as many as 25,000 are in long-term solitary confinement, which involves months if not years with almost no human contact."[112] The effects of solitary confinement on individuals when they are released from prison are devastating. Solitary confinement can produce psychological consequences that outlast the period of confinement and increase the risk of violent recidivism.[113]

Even if separation is necessary to maintain order in some cases, the use of solitary confinement goes well beyond necessity. Many people are placed in solitary because of relatively minor disruptive behavior, such as talking back or failing to obey an order.[114] Before a policy change, corrections officers sent people in South Carolina to solitary confinement for an average of 512 days for violating prison protocol by posting on social-media sites.[115] In 2013, a person was sent to solitary for 37½ years for posting on Facebook 38 times.[116] The conditions of separation also often go far beyond a safety rationale. There is no safety reason, for example, for rules that prevent individuals in solitary confinement from having pictures of their family members or newspapers.[117] Nor is there a prison management reason for facilities to be designed such that individuals in isolation have no access to windows. One former warden of the nation's only supermax facility, ADX Florence, admitted as much in an interview, noting, "This place is not designed for humanity. . . . When it's 23 hours a day in a room with a slit of a window where you can't even see the Rocky Mountains—let's be candid here. It's not designed for rehabilitation. Period. End of story."[118]

Evaluating Incarceration and Prison Programming

A rational system should evaluate prisons based on whether they improve the outcomes for the people who serve time there. That is, prisons should be assessed on the basis of things like recidivism rates, post-release employment rates, and substance abuse desistance. If this type of evaluation were occurring, we would invest in better conditions and prison programs now to get the benefits of lower recidivism—and therefore lower incarceration costs—later. But who is going to demand this? Certainly not prison officials, who would much prefer the current system, which does not even ask whether they are doing a good job at lowering recidivism rates. Prosecutors and legislators pay no attention to these issues because the public does not blame recidivism on the failure to provide programming, but instead tends to view the problem as innate to the individuals committing the crimes. If the issue is personal responsibility, then there is no one to blame but the person committing the crime, and no one asks prisons and jails to do more. The result is that they do not—and public safety and welfare suffer as a result because the issue is not simply one of personal responsibility. We could be getting better outcomes with better programming, and our failure to do so is based on institutional pathologies, not sound practices.

4

OBSOLETE OUTCOMES

THE DECLINE IN PAROLE and the skepticism about rehabilitation had another negative consequence for public safety aside from the lack of programming in prisons: we stopped reevaluating people and policies over time. We would achieve better public safety outcomes if punishment decisions were modified as new information becomes available. As we learn more about what works and does not work to deter crime or about the dangers of particular behaviors, we should be adjusting our responses accordingly. Similarly, if we learn more about the people who commit crimes, we should change approaches based on new information. Why mention something so obvious? This is, after all, the path to better decision-making in just about every area of life—adjusting to new information. But as with so many things in criminal law, this rational approach is often nowhere to be found. We continue on paths started long ago, even as facts and circumstances have changed.

This is true at the individual level and more generally. At the individual level, decisions about someone's criminal sentence are made after conviction and are typically never revisited, even when the person is sentenced to decades in prison or when he or she is a youthful offender whose brain is not yet fully developed. This is not because people and circumstances do not change. The people who commit crimes often undergo dramatic changes—particularly as they mature or if they receive treatment for an underlying addiction or mental illness that prompted their criminal behavior.

Our knowledge about certain criminal behaviors and the effects of punishment on those behaviors also grows over time. For instance, there is a tendency to panic and overreact initially in response to a perceived crime wave or when a new illegal drug hits the market. But as more facts develop over time, it often becomes clear that a threat was exaggerated and thus the punishment attached to that threat also went too far.

The response to crack cocaine provides a perfect illustration. Punishments for crack were set sky-high initially when reports characterized the drug as far more dangerous than anything that came before it. When Congress was setting penalties for crack cocaine in the 1980s, it speedily adopted harsh mandatory minimum sentences for the drug. Speaker of the House Tip O'Neill, the legendary Massachusetts legislator, led the bidding war on crack, in large part because Len Bias, a University of Maryland star basketball player who had been drafted by the Boston Celtics, died from a drug overdose that was presumed to be from crack cocaine.[1] Congress decided that the possession of a mere 5 grams of crack should yield a mandatory minimum sentence of 5 years. Possession of 50 grams of crack (an amount associated with trafficking) yielded a 10-year mandatory minimum. One would need 100 times those quantities to get the same sentence for powder cocaine. This is what came to be known as the 100-to-1 ratio between the two drugs. The differential treatment of the two drugs was based on sensationalized media stories and anecdotes that suggested crack was more addictive than powder and that it made people more prone to violence. Instead of researching the issue, Congress rushed to enact tougher crack laws. As one representative noted of the process: "We initially came out of committee with a 20-to-1 ratio. By the time we finished on the floor, it was 100-to-1. We didn't really have an evidentiary basis for it."[2]

Later it became clear that crack and powder are virtually indistinguishable, except in the way they are sold. The chemical effects of crack and powder cocaine are identical, crack is no more addictive than powder, and crack does not provoke more violent reactions in individuals who use it.[3] In fact, Bias had overdosed on powder, not crack, cocaine. The harsher sentences for crack are all the more disturbing when one looks at the racial composition of those charged with crack offenses versus powder offenses. In 2013, 83% of those charged with crack trafficking offenses were black, but only 5.8% were white.[4] By contrast, blacks made up only 31.5% of power cocaine trafficking offenders, while Hispanics made up 58% and whites made up 9.4%.[5] It took Congress more than 24 years to acknowledge this reality, and even then, it reduced the disparity between the two drugs to an 18-to-1 ratio, not a 1-to-1 ratio.[6] For decades, the response to crack remained the same, even in the face of new information and glaring racial disparities in the law's effects. When changes were finally made to the crack/powder punishment regime, they were prospective only, leaving people sentenced under the prior framework to serve out their excessive sentences despite the fact we knew better.

The reason punishment decisions rarely get reassessed is largely political. Once a sentence is imposed on someone, that sentence is what the public expects that person to serve. There is ample research in cognitive psychology about the endowment effect.[7] People react far worse when they lose something they once had than they do if they do not receive something in the first place, even if the item has the same value. In the context of punishment, the endowment effect helps explain why the public is so much angrier when someone who was released early goes on to commit a crime than it is over the consistently high recidivism rates that exist for people who serve their full sentences.

This dynamic accounts for the resistance to taking a second look at someone's initial sentence. A second look is essentially giving up something that society thinks it owns—the longer sentence or term of supervision—so if something goes wrong, blame will quickly follow the decision-maker who made the call. This is why so many jurisdictions abolished parole and why even those that retain it have such low grant rates. It also accounts for the virtual disappearance of commutations and pardons by governors and the president. It likewise explains the reluctance of jurisdictions to release prisoners who are elderly or who develop serious illnesses. And it accounts for worries about giving anyone retroactive sentencing reductions, even if the law going forward will treat people differently. As Senator Ted Cruz explained his own unwillingness to go along with retroactive adjustments to federal drug laws, "Every one of us who votes to release violent criminals from prison prior to the expiration of their sentence can fully expect to be held accountable by our constituents."[8]

California's three-strikes law is a prime illustration of this phenomenon. When first introduced to the legislature in 1993, it did not make it out of the Assembly Public Safety Committee.[9] Then came the murder of Polly Klaas by Richard Davis, who had been serving a 16-year sentence for kidnapping, assault, and burglary but was released 8 years early for good behavior.[10] The high-profile killing led to passage of the three-strikes law within 4 months of the Klaas murder.[11] In addition to increasing the sentences for individuals with a third offense, the bill set the maximum good-time credits a prisoner could receive at one-fifth of the imposed sentence.[12]

One can see a similar story line when jurisdictions reject parole. In Massachusetts, after a parolee killed a police officer, Governor Deval Patrick obtained resignations from the entire parole board, and he subsequently signed a truth-in-sentencing bill that curtailed parole and was named

"Melissa's Law" for another victim of a parolee.[13] A similar process has been under way in Connecticut, where legislators began calling for an end to the state's early release program for those who committed violent or sexual offenses after a woman was sexually assaulted by a man who had been released 7 months early.[14] When Virginia abolished parole in 1994, the governor used a "cadre" of crime victims to testify in support of its abolition.[15]

Arkansas provides yet another illustration. The state limited parole availability in 2013 in the wake of the senseless murder of an 18-year-old by a man with a lengthy history of arrests and parole violations.[16] As soon as the murder gained widespread publicity, state politicians began calling for "wholesale changes," concluding that "we've known all along that parole doesn't work."[17] The state's board of corrections swiftly enacted sweeping changes aimed at tightening parole. One reform mandated parole revocation hearings for all parolees merely charged—not convicted—of any felony or violent or sex-related misdemeanor, "a policy possibly unique among states with parole."[18] Other reforms included harsher consequences, often including parole revocation, for technical violations like failure to report for meetings or hearings.[19] Predictably, these changes to the state's parole policies led to a 17.7% increase in the state's prison population in just 1 year, the fastest increase among all 50 states and more than 7 times the national average.[20] In 2015, Arkansas housed 70% more people in prison than it did in 2012, with the growth driven almost entirely by probation and parole violators.[21] From 2012 to 2013, the number of parole violators sent back to prison increased approximately 135%.[22] One-third of these violators were returned to prison for an average of 12 to 15 months for technical violations, which costs the state an estimated $20 million annually.[23]

Critically, the huge costs of these parole reforms have not been counterbalanced by public safety benefits. From 2004 to 2014, Arkansas's neighboring states saw violent crime rate reductions averaging 14% over the same period that Arkansas's violent crime rate decreased by only 4%.[24] And whereas these neighboring states saw a slight *decrease* in their incarceration rates, Arkansas witnessed a large *increase*.[25] So Arkansas's neighbors were able to obtain greater public safety benefits while lowering their incarceration rates. Between 2012 and 2014, the years immediately before and after Arkansas's hasty reforms, the prison population nationally grew only 0.2%, whereas in Arkansas, the population grew 22%, by far the largest increase of any state.[26] These reforms carried a hefty price tag. Arkansas currently spends half a billion dollars on corrections annually, and without large-scale reforms (including undoing its parole restrictions), its prison population is projected to climb an additional 35% over the next decade, costing Arkansas $1.3 billion in additional spending.[27] That is money that could be spent on more effective crime-fighting strategies. Given that Arkansas's prison population was actually on the decline in the years immediately preceding the changes to the parole laws, it is no exaggeration to say that one crime and the populist fervor around it upended the state's entire criminal justice system—and without tangible safety benefits.

One can understand the outrage when someone released earlier than expected goes on to commit a violent crime. With hindsight bias, one cannot help but ask how the decision was made and seek to prevent a similar outcome in the future. But all too often, the answer in these instances is a knee-jerk reaction to limit parole or to curtail a second look at anyone's sentence without a careful analysis of the pros and cons or without considering whether other solutions might work better. General policies should not be based on single cases if those cases are outliers. If, in fact, most early release decisions do not result in individuals committing violence upon release and there are benefits to adjusting sentences over time, policies need to account for the overall pattern of cases, not exceptional outliers.

This is how we approach other public policy areas. We do not simply ban a therapeutic drug or vaccine if it causes a harmful reaction in one individual but brings benefits to most others. We do not close down all mines or eliminate an entire industry after one accident. Rather, we do a cost-benefit analysis to decide whether, on net, the activity or policy intervention is worth the risks it presents because the benefits are sufficiently great. With criminal law, however, this type of analysis almost never gets done. There is zero tolerance for any risk, even when the risk is outweighed by public safety benefits. The result is that sentences get set in stone even after it becomes clear they no longer make sense.

It is also critical to keep in mind that there is no evidence that extending the term of someone's confinement stops them from committing crimes. On the contrary, as Chapter 2 explained, the length of time someone serves in prison has no effect on the probability that they will be rearrested.[28] At most, "longer prison stays might only postpone, not prevent, the crimes returning prisoners commit."[29] So a real solution would seek to figure out why the crimes get committed at all—whenever they happen—and emphasize whatever rehabilitative programs might stop them. But because media reports paint the earlier release itself as the cause of the crime and fail to report on the overwhelming majority of people who do not commit any violent acts after an early release, the public lacks full information about policies that take a second look at someone's sentence. The result has been a precipitous decline in second looks, whether through parole, good-time credits, compassionate release mechanisms, retroactive adjustments, or clemency.

The decline in these mechanisms makes sense politically, but it is irrational as a matter of public safety and the wise allocation of resources. As one commentator has noted, "The reason why second look mechanisms are so important is because we can expect, we should expect, first looks to be dysfunctionally harsh."[30] But the politics have overshadowed rationality, making second looks nonexistent or anemic across a range of forms.

Parole / Good Time

Parole emerged on the scene in the 1900s and became a staple of criminal justice policy across America until the 1970s, when tough-on-crime politics sprouted a "truth-in-sentencing" movement to abolish or dramatically curtail parole.[31] Sixteen states and the federal system completely eliminated discretionary parole, and a number of additional states ended its use for certain violent offenders.[32] In 1992, there were 12,453 people serving life sentences without parole; by 2016, there were 53,290.[33] In states that retained some form of parole, its use fell dramatically. Whereas roughly 70% of prison releases were a result of discretionary parole in the late 1970s, that number plummeted to 29% by 1997.[34] In 2011, discretionary parole releases accounted for only 26% of all releases nationwide, a sharp decline from its past.[35] In Massachusetts, for example, the parole grant rate for state sentences dropped from 69.9% in 1990 to 40.5% in 2000.[36] By 2011, Massachusetts's grant rate plummeted still further to 26%.[37]

Parole grant rates vary significantly by state and by crime, and for some crimes, parole has become almost nonexistent, no matter how much the person committing the crime may change over time. In New York, for example, in a 6-month interval in 2014, the grant rates for persons serving time for drug and property crimes were 16.2% and 21.7%, respectively. The rate for people incarcerated for violent felonies was even lower, with only 3.5% of those eligible granted parole.[38] Oklahoma's parole grant rates tell a similar story. In 2015, the state Pardon and Parole Board recommended parole to a total of 28 people serving sentences for violent offenses, and the governor agreed to parole for only 6 of those 28. To put that number in context, Oklahoma could find only 6 people deserving of parole who had committed a violent offense even though it had the second highest incarceration rate of all 50 states in 2014.[39]

Other states have restricted parole by increasing the amount of time a person has to wait before getting a parole hearing. In Georgia, for example, individuals convicted of violent felonies used to be eligible for parole after serving 7 years of their sentence, but today they must serve 30 years before they become eligible for parole. In 1993, Missouri changed the first possible date for a parole hearing from 13 years after sentencing to 23 years.[40]

It is not just the rates of parole that have changed, but the mind-set has as well. Parole boards were initially supposed to be comprised of experts who would "evaluate an individual's rehabilitation and . . . determine whether they could be released."[41] But boards have become political bodies made up largely of people with law enforcement backgrounds.[42] The nature of parole officers—those who supervise people released on parole—has also changed. While parole officers previously received training as social workers to help people reenter society and address their various needs while out on parole, today most parole officials are more likely to be trained as law enforcement officers.[43] Parole thus went from a field that emphasized rehabilitation and reentry to one focused on catching violations and policing behavior, with predictably poor results.[44] A study that examined the relationship between a parole officer's practice orientation and recidivism found that high-risk offenders who were assigned officers with a law enforcement orientation received more technical violations and had higher rates of recidivism than those assigned to officers with a social work orientation.[45]

In addition, one consequence of the decline in discretionary parole is that many states now have people serving out their entire sentences instead of being released earlier with a period of supervised release to follow. From 1990 to 2012, there has been a 119% increase in individuals serving their entire term without supervised release.[46] But shorter terms with supervision (though with far fewer conditions of supervision than are currently employed, because jurisdictions tend to place too many conditions on people that end up being counterproductive) are more effective than maxing out sentences without supervision, both in terms of reducing recidivism and minimizing overall corrections costs.

Good time—the policy of allowing individuals to earn modest time off their sentences if they behave in prison or participate in programming—has also undergone a shift.[47] The truth-in-sentencing movement had a major impact on the amount of good-time credit an individual in prison could accrue.[48] Some states eliminated good-time credits entirely; others still use them but reduced the credits available. In 1998, for example, Michigan enacted truth-in-sentencing laws and eliminated good-time credits. It introduced "disciplinary time," which is a system where individuals in prison are given more time for misbehaving. Additional time is not actually added to a sentence but is instead given to the parole board as a factor to consider when determining parole.[49] Other states have followed the federal system and put a cap on the number of good-time credits an individual can earn.[50]

Even when jurisdictions consider allowing individuals to earn time off their sentences by participating in prison programming, they often place limits on eligibility.[51] For example, Congress was considering legislation that would allow people in federal prison to earn up to 10 days off their sentences if they participated in 30 days of individualized programming to reduce their risks of reoffending if they were categorized as a low-risk reoffender, and up to 5 days off if they were categorized as a medium-/high-risk reoffender.[52] But the proposed legislation suffers from the usual problems of criminal law in this area. It specifically exempts those most in need of the programming, namely those in higher risk categories.[53] The states provide similar examples. In Louisiana and Maine, individuals who commit serious violent crimes or sex offenses are ineligible to earn good-time credits.[54]

Some states have begun to reverse this trend, recognizing that it is in the interest of public safety to encourage individuals in prison to participate in rehabilitative programming and that these reductions save money. Wisconsin, California, Colorado, and Mississippi, for example, have all expanded the number of days off a sentence an individual can accumulate through earned time credits.[55] But in general, states have been unwilling to expand the number of days off a sentence an individual can obtain through programming, particularly if the individual is serving a sentence for a crime that involved violence. As a bipartisan task force recently noted, this policy gets it backward because "it is all the more important for higher-risk individuals to be incentivized to participate in intensive programming, as they are in the greatest need and pose the gravest threat to public safety if they are not rehabilitated before release."[56]

Parole and good time reflect the idea that people change over time— because they get older, because they participate in treatment or other programming, because they show good behavior in prison, because they undergo personal or religious transformations. The longer the amount of time, the more likely it is that people will change. Research shows that the peak age for offending is between 15 and 19 and that, as an individual enters his or her twenties, the likelihood of participating in criminal activity declines.[57] Between 2005 and 2010, for example, 31.6% of people who had been released from federal prison into community supervision returned to prison. By comparison, for those aged 50 years or older, 14.7% returned to prison.[58] Because most people age out of crime, the bipartisan, blue-ribbon Colson Task Force urged Congress to establish a second-look provision that would allow anyone who has served more than 15 years to seek a new sentence before a judge.[59] The American Law Institute's Sentencing Project has likewise recommended a second-look policy for prisoners who have served 15 years. The institute adopted this policy because of a view that, as societal conceptions of crime and appropriate punishment change over time, sentences should be modified to reflect these changes.[60] Bipartisan experts recognize the benefits of these second looks, but recommendations like these are difficult to get passed in a political climate where the fear of any one individual committing a crime after early release is seen to threaten a political career.

Clemency

Clemency, like parole, represents another valuable mechanism for taking a second look at sentences. As Alexander Hamilton explained, clemency is critical because "the criminal code of every country partakes so much of necessary severity that without an easy access to exceptions in favor of unfortunate guilt, justice would wear a countenance too sanguinary and cruel."[61] One of the participants in the debate over the ratification of the Constitution, James Iredell, similarly noted that clemency was vital for checking overbroad criminal laws because "it is impossible for any general law to foresee and provide for all possible cases that may arise."[62] The Framers deemed the clemency power so fundamental that it was placed alongside the commander-in-chief powers of the president in Article II of the Constitution.[63] The majority of state constitutions likewise contain provisions that give governors clemency power.[64]

Before the advent of parole in the 1900s, clemency was the most commonly used mechanism for correcting and mitigating sentences.[65] Governors and presidents granted pardons and sentencing commutations frequently and routinely, recognizing that initial sentencing decisions were often mistaken and that people and circumstances change over time.[66] When clemency rates fell in the 1900s, it was because parole became its substitute, not because policy-makers changed their views on the need for a second-look mechanism to correct initial sentencing judgments.[67] Many states vest parole and clemency power in one institution, such as a state board of pardons and parole, thus demonstrating how the two are viewed interchangeably by many state legislatures.

When parole fell victim to tough-on-crime politics in the 1970s, one might have expected clemency to return to the forefront as the key mechanism for sentence correction.[68] After all, there would still be people who had rehabilitated and changed, some sentences that had proved to be too severe, and improved knowledge would show earlier sentencing policies to be misguided—all calling for a second-look mechanism to lower sentences.

To take just one example of the need for clemency to reemerge, consider that when parole was abolished in the federal system, individuals given a life sentence would die in prison without clemency, no matter how much they may have changed over decades or how much society's views of certain laws may have evolved. Many individuals serving life sentences in federal prison received those sentences simply because they trafficked certain quantities of drugs, even if their own role in a distribution ring was minor and they were not a leader or manager. In fact, drug trafficking is the most common offense for which a life sentence was imposed in the federal system.[69] Because of mandatory minimum drug laws, judges would have had no discretion to give a lesser sentence in these cases, no matter how sympathetic the individual or the facts. As Judge Roger Vinson stated in one such case that required him to impose a life sentence: "The sentence . . . far exceeds whatever punishment would be appropriate. . . . Unfortunately it's my duty to impose a sentence. If I had any discretion at all, I would not impose a life sentence."[70]

Most people have changed their views on drug policy since the height of the drug war in the 1990s when many of these sentences were handed down. Marijuana is now legal for medical use in more than half the states, and seven states and the District of Columbia have legalized marijuana for recreational use.[71] There have been significant changes at the federal level, too, in drug policy, including reductions of almost 20% in guideline ranges for federal drug offenses.[72] But thousands of individuals are serving sentences handed down at the height of the drug war, when the outlook on drug sentencing was very different.

While individuals serving life sentences without parole might provide the starkest example of the need for clemency, individuals serving other lengthy sentences also merit a second look. Without parole, there may be no way other than clemency to correct unjust mandatory-minimum or other sentences.

But clemency has not filled the gap left by the elimination of parole because clemency has been a victim of the same political forces.[73] No president or governor has wanted to take the risk that an individual who received a commutation from him or her would go on to commit a highly publicized crime because any single incident could destroy their prospects for reelection.[74]

A case in point comes from former Arkansas governor Mike Huckabee. In 2000, Huckabee granted clemency to Maurice Clemmons, who had received a sentence of 108 years for robberies and burglaries committed when he was 16 years old.[75] This was an outlier sentence for someone of that age to receive for those crimes, so Huckabee agreed with the recommendation of the board that had reviewed Clemmons's case that the sentence should be reduced. Clemmons had already served 11 years at that point, and Huckabee reduced Clemmons's sentence to 47 years, which made him eligible for parole, which a parole board later granted. Nine years later, Clemmons killed four police officers in Washington, and Huckabee was attacked for his clemency decision.[76] Several commentators saw Clemmons as Huckabee's own version of Michael Dukakis's Willie Horton—with the same negative effects on Huckabee's prospects for the presidency.[77]

Just as the discussion of the Horton furlough lacked all nuance, with no one mentioning the 99% overall success rate of the furlough program, so did the discussion of Clemmons. The media paid little attention to the fact that an independent board made the parole decision, not Huckabee, or that hundreds of other individuals who received commutations from Huckabee never committed another crime.[78] Nor did they focus on whether it was reasonable to adjust a sentence of 108 years given to a 16-year-old after 11 years had passed and when more information about the person became known. Huckabee could not have predicted that Clemmons would go on to commit more crimes, and to criticize his decision to give him a lesser sentence is essentially to say that no individual should get a second look, no matter how young they were when they committed their crime or how much they changed over time.

Governors and presidents in recent decades know this is how their decisions will be judged, and their clemency numbers reflect this fear. At the federal level, President Truman granted more than 2,000 pardons and commutations, and President Nixon was still above 900 grants of clemency. But Presidents Reagan and Clinton granted fewer than 400 petitions for pardons and commutations during their terms in office.[79] The clemency grant rate plummeted from 35.7% with President Nixon to 1.8% for George W. Bush.[80] Governors have been similarly stingy with their clemency powers.[81]

Even President Obama, who expressly sought to reinvigorate the clemency power, nevertheless had a modest grant rate overall. His final clemency grant rate was 5%, which was comparable to the more recent presidencies

of George H. W. Bush (5%) and Clinton (6%), higher than the rate for
George W. Bush (2%), but far lower than Presidents Nixon (36%), Ford
(27%), and Carter (21%).[82] Even more telling, he had a record number of
denials—including leaving behind more than 2,500 people who met his
stated criteria for clemency.[83] And these were criteria that were narrowly
tailored from the outset. His initiative only granted commutations to those
convicted of drug trafficking; individuals guilty of other nonviolent offenses
were not part of the initiative.[84] He also excluded anyone with violence or
significant criminal history. Most fundamentally, he required individuals to
show that they would likely receive a different sentence today because of a
change in the law—so he would not grant clemency to anyone who received
an unjust sentence if existing law would also permit the sentence.

In this era of mandatory minimums and overbroad laws, the need for a
second look is all the more important even when there have not been
changes in the law. But the same pathological process that gives us those
laws has taken away the checks that should be exercised on their application. And that was true even when a self-proclaimed criminal justice reformer like President Obama was in the White House.

Compassionate Release

We see a reluctance to take a second look at sentences even in the cases of
elderly individuals or those with serious illnesses. Most jurisdictions in the
country now have some provision in their legal codes to allow people in
prison to be released early for age- and/or health-related reasons as long
as they are not a danger to public safety.[85] These provisions—sometimes
referred to as medical parole, geriatric release, or compassionate release—
make ample sense as a matter of public safety because this is a population
with a low risk of recidivism. A study of individuals released from federal
prison who were age 50 to 54 upon release between fiscal years 2006 and
2010 found they had a rearrest rate of only 19%, and those age 70 and
older had a 0% recidivism rate.[86] The individuals released pursuant to the
Bureau of Prisons (BOP) compassionate release program during the five-
year period from 2006 to 2011 had a recidivism rate of only 3.5%.[87] Even
in the rare circumstances when these individuals do commit a new crime,
it tends not to be a violent one. The most common crime for which these
individuals were rearrested was a drug offense.[88] This is not a group of
people that pose public safety threats.

Moreover, releasing these individuals saves enormous amounts of money
that can be used for other public safety initiatives. Elderly individuals and

those with serious health ailments are the most expensive group of people to incarcerate because of their increased medical needs.[89] Costs for medical care have exploded, with medical care expenses at the federal level alone reaching $1.1 billion in fiscal year 2014, a 30% increase from the costs five years earlier.[90] It costs on average 8% more to incarcerate someone 50 years or older than a younger person. In fiscal year 2013, a full 19% of the BOP budget was spent on incarcerating aging individuals, and medical expenses ate up 17% of the BOP's budget.[91] North Carolina spent four times as much money on people age 50 and older as it did on younger individuals in prison.[92]

Dollar figures alone do not tell the whole story. These older individuals put excess burdens on the staff, and there are simply not enough individuals working for correctional facilities to care for the aging and infirm individuals who are incarcerated or to take them to outside doctors for care. The Department of Justice Inspector General found that, at the federal level, the average wait time to be seen by outside cardiology, neurosurgery, pulmonology, and urology specialists was 114 days. If the visit was for a routine or additional appointment, this time increased to 256 days. Prisons also often lack programming or activities that are accessible to aging and physically ill individuals. And they lack the necessary number of social workers to handle their unique needs both while they are incarcerated and upon release. The BOP, for example, has only 36 social workers for their entire prison population of more than 200,000 people. Aging and infirm individuals are thus particularly ill-suited to spend time in prison facilities. It makes ample sense as a matter of public safety and cost savings to release them.[93]

Yet compassionate release programs are rarely used.[94] For example, in a seven-year period from 2001 to 2008, Colorado released only three prisoners under its compassionate release policies out of an average prison population during those years of 19,883.[95] Virginia released only four individuals under its geriatric release program during the 6-year period from 2001 to 2007.[96] As of 2012, Oregon had never released more than two people per year under its compassionate release guidelines.[97] With an incarcerated population well over 200,000 in its custody, the BOP released an average of 24 people each year under its compassionate release program between 2006 and 2011.[98]

This is not because prisons lack applicants who are elderly or in poor physical health such that they pose no threat to public safety. The prison population in the United States is increasingly older. For example, the percentage of individuals over 50 years old in Oklahoma rose from 6.46% in 1994 to 14.3% in 2008.[99] Prisoners aged 50 and over are the fastest growing segment of the federal prisoner population, increasing by 25% from 2009 to 2014.[100] And many individuals in prison die from illness while incarcerated. More than 88% of state prisoner deaths in 2013 were caused by illness.[101] In the federal system, 400 prisoners died in 2013 alone.[102]

The reasons these programs lie dormant are largely political and institutional. Jurisdictions often restrict the eligibility criteria so that certain groups of people are categorically barred, such as individuals serving life sentences or those convicted of sex offenses, violent offenses, drug offenses, or certain classes of felonies.[103] Jurisdictions also sometimes impose minimum time served requirements.[104] These categorical bans often sweep far too broadly, particularly when the compassionate release provisions themselves require an individualized public safety determination. When jurisdictions do conduct individualized determinations, they are often unwilling to release individuals no matter how infirm they are if the decision-makers believe the individual's criminal history or offense of conviction is too serious. This does not necessarily mean the individual committed a violent offense. Federal prison officials, for instance, often refuse to grant compassionate release to individuals with white-collar convictions or nonviolent drug charges.[105]

Jurisdictions also put up numerous bureaucratic hurdles to obtaining release that often result in individuals dying from their illnesses before obtaining the necessary approvals. And many states lack a timeline for review to be completed, which means that terminally ill individuals sadly often die before their requests are processed. The federal system is a case in point. An individual seeking compassionate release must first get approval from the warden, and the application must include detailed information to support the claim (including any necessary medical information), as well as the individual's plans upon release, including information about where he or she will reside and how he or she will be supported financially.[106] If there are medical needs, the individual must also document how those needs will be met upon release. The BOP has also insisted that those seeking release because of a terminal illness must show that they have a life expectancy of one year or less, even though most medical professionals will not make such a prediction.[107] After all of this information is filed, the warden must approve the request for it to go to the next layer of review, which takes place in the Office of the General Counsel at the BOP's Central Office.[108] The BOP's medical director will weigh in if the claim is based on a medical need, and an assistant director of the Correctional Programs Division will assess nonmedical claims. The BOP director then makes the final decision.[109] While an individual seeking compassionate release can appeal a warden's decision to deny the request, he or she cannot seek review of the BOP director's denial.[110] The Office of the Inspector General for the Department of

Justice found that an individual seeking compassionate release waits up to 160 days for the entire process with appeals to be completed, and even those applications that were approved took roughly 4 months to process.[111] It is hardly surprising that 11 individuals died in 2015 while their requests were being processed.[112]

The stories are heartbreaking. Consider the case of a federal prisoner who was sentenced to 25 years in prison for crimes related to his operation of an asbestos abatement company. He had already served 12 years when his wife unexpectedly passed away, leaving his three minor children without a parent or family member to care for them. Their 15-year-old son had special needs because he was born with multiple congenital and medical issues. While both his parents were specially trained to care for him, none of the neighbors who offered to take in the children could do so, ultimately leading to the son being placed in foster care and separated from his siblings. Pursuant to federal early release provisions, the lack of a family caregiver qualifies as an extraordinary circumstance for early release, but a year after seeking release, the father still had not heard about the status of his request.[113]

Then there is the case of James Bower. He was 11 years into a 30-year sentence for drug distribution when he was diagnosed with prostate cancer and anticipated he only had 6 months to live. Bower's request for compassionate release was denied because officials believed he could still engage in criminal activity with prostate cancer. Bower died behind bars while his subsequent appeal was pending.[114]

Or take the case of Victoria Blain (a pseudonym), who was sentenced to 75 months for drug-related conspiracy charges, leaving behind two children under the age of two. When the children's father was diagnosed with inoperable pancreatic cancer, Blain requested compassionate release so that she could care for the children. The request was denied, as was the administrative appeal. The regional office concurred, explaining that they found no "compelling reasons to support a reduction [in sentence]." While Blain awaited response from the Central Office of BOP, her husband passed away, leaving the kids with strangers who began to isolate the kids from their mother. Nine months after the death of her husband, Blain got a final answer: request denied.[115]

Risk aversion, coupled with bureaucratic complexity, keeps people like these in prison when it no longer makes sense as a matter of public safety—or basic human decency—for them to be there.

5

COLLATERAL
CALAMITIES

IF THE OVERRIDING GOAL OF criminal punishment is public safety, it is critical that individuals successfully reintegrate into society after their terms of imprisonment are over. That is, after all, the endgame: we are locking people away not only to incapacitate them from committing crimes during their terms of confinement but also to motivate them to live law-abiding lives when they are released. And all but a tiny percentage of the people in prison come out and return to their communities, so it is in the public's interest to get them as ready as possible to succeed when they do. Sadly, though, we are failing miserably in this goal, with 7 out of 10 people rearrested or convicted within 5 years of their release from prison, and most of the offenses occurring within the first year that people step out of prison.[1]

One reason for this dismal outcome is the many obstacles we have imposed to successful reentry. Perversely, instead of seeking to help people coming out of prison find housing, employment, and educational opportunities so that they can avoid returning to crime, we have seemingly gone out of our way as a society to set them up to fail by cutting them off from access to a variety of critical public resources, including public housing, drivers' licenses, student loans, and access to employment. These bars—known as collateral consequences of conviction—may satiate populist desires for revenge against those who commit crimes (or, as Chapter 1 explains, those whom the public believes are committing crimes). But they make no sense if the goal is to prevent crime and improve public safety.

There was a point at which jurisdictions recognized as much. During the 1960s and 1970s, a number of states reformed their laws on the collateral consequences of a conviction because of concerns that those laws impeded the ability of individuals to successfully reintegrate after being released from prison.[2] A 1986 report that reviewed all state laws on the consequences of convictions concluded that "states generally are becoming less restrictive of depriving civil rights of offenders."[3]

But that report was issued just as the states were about to binge on collateral sanctions as part of the populist push to symbolically get tough on crime, while actually undermining public safety. Thus, a decade after that 1986 report, a follow-up report documented increases in the number of jurisdictions denying individuals a panoply of rights once they were convicted of a felony.[4] Current counts place the number of collateral consequences of convictions at more than 45,000.[5] The recent bipartisan push for reforming criminal justice restrictions has prompted some rollbacks in the last few years, but "dozens of new legal and regulatory restrictions were enacted for every new relief measure," leaving individuals released from prison in the same awful bind of being set up to fail.[6]

The federal government has led this ill-fated charge, with Congress imposing several critical bans on individuals who have been convicted of certain felonies, particularly drug offenses.

Some of the most counterproductive restrictions relate to public housing, which is an essential resource for many people who have been incarcerated. Almost a quarter of the people in prison previously lived in public or subsidized housing before they were incarcerated.[7] Roughly 10–15% of those released from prison are homeless, with metropolitan areas showing much higher rates.[8] If one also includes among the homeless those forced to live in temporary, overcrowded, or uninhabitable housing, more than one-third of people released from prison are homeless 6 months after their incarceration.[9]

Instead of seeking ways to find housing for this vulnerable population to decrease their incentives to commit crime, Congress went out of its way to make things worse. It dramatically reduced the ability of these people to return to public housing with the passage of a series of laws in the late 1990s. Congress promulgated laws that allowed public housing authorities to refuse public housing to anyone engaged in "any drug-related or violent criminal activity or other criminal activity which would adversely affect the health, safety, or right to peaceful enjoyment of the premises."[10] Congress further authorized public housing authorities to evict entire households if any one person living there was using drugs, whether or not the other members of the household knew, or should have known, about the person's drug activity.[11] The person suspected of the drug offense did not even need to be convicted or arrested for the housing authority to be able to evict the household, nor did the drug use or sale need to occur in public housing.[12] Take, for instance, the case of 75-year-old Herman Walker, who was evicted from his senior public housing facility because his live-in caretaker allegedly possessed cocaine inside Mr. Walker's apartment. There was no evidence or allegation that Mr. Walker knew about the possession, but it did not matter. This elderly man was thrown out of his apartment under the policy of the Oakland Housing Authority.[13] Or consider what happened to Shelly Anderson, a single mother of three living in subsidized housing in Virginia. She was evicted from her home after her children's father and her mother were arrested for drug use. Neither lived in Ms. Anderson's home, but they babysat her children there while she received dialysis treatment, and that was sufficient for her eviction.[14] A New Orleans woman likewise lost her apartment when she hosted her daughter's casual acquaintance and her apartment became, in her absence, the site of a drug exchange with a confidential informant.[15]

While these laws give discretion to local housing authorities to implement, the federal government has encouraged them to use these powers of eviction broadly. President Bill Clinton went so far as to tell housing authorities in his State of the Union speech in 1996 that they should adopt a "one strike and you're out" policy with respect to drug dealers.[16] In the wake of the speech, the Department of Housing and Urban Development provided financial incentives to the 3,400 public housing authorities to adopt a one-strike program. A follow-up study revealed that the incentives worked as intended, with 75% of the housing authorities adopting a one-strike program.[17] A 2013 study found that bans based on the illegal use of drugs continue to be widespread, with 93% of the housing authorities in its sample banning tenants who engaged in or had family or guests who engaged in illegal drug use, abuse, possession, distribution, and trafficking.[18] Individuals can be evicted on the basis of complaints by neighbors or anonymous tips, without any requirement that the tenant or someone in the tenant's household be arrested or convicted.[19]

Individuals who must register as sex offenders for the rest of their lives are banned completely from federally assisted housing.[20] These individuals cannot live in public housing, no matter how dire their economic circumstances. And because the category of sex offender is so broad and lifetime registry requirements so sweeping, as Chapter 1 explains, that means there are individuals who will be ineligible for government-assisted housing for the rest of their lives because they texted a naked photo as a teenager or urinated in public after having too much to drink. Take, for example, Gabriel, who was found guilty of indecency with a child after a playground incident involving two friends and a younger cousin when Gabriel was 10 years old. Despite his young age at the time of the conviction and the fact that he has never reoffended, his status as a sex offender bars him from public housing and from living in many other areas. After reporting and registration requirements made it difficult for Gabriel to find employment and left him living on the streets, he was repeatedly arrested and convicted for failing to register with a suitable address, which is itself a felony.[21] Or consider the case of Shawna Baldwin, who had consensual sex with a 14-year-old boy when she was 19 and has suffered the collateral consequences for more than a decade. She and her family, like Gabriel, have struggled to find housing.[22] Stories like theirs are commonplace among individuals convicted of sex offenses.

While these bans worked as intended in terms of keeping these people out of public housing, they have not achieved public safety goals. On the contrary, these bans contribute to crime. Criminal history restrictions on public housing access often leave formerly incarcerated people with nowhere to go. Research shows that the resulting housing instability increases the individual's likelihood of reoffending and, as a result, increases crime.[23] One study found that public housing residents perceived a decrease in public safety after the bans went into effect.[24] In contrast, when jurisdictions have opted not to impose harsh public housing bans on formerly incarcerated individuals, public safety has not been compromised. For example, both the New York City and Los Angeles housing authorities decline to consider arrest records, limit the type of offenses that warrant exclusion from housing, and impose time limits on exclusion. Despite limiting the scope of their bans, officials from both authorities report that they combat crime just as effectively as "one-strike" housing authorities.[25]

Congressional interference with reentry did not stop with housing limitations. When Congress "ended welfare as we know it" in 1996, it required states to impose lifetime bans on individuals with drug-related felony convictions to prevent them from receiving federal welfare aid or food stamps.[26] States can take affirmative action to opt out of the lifetime ban, and some have done so, but people with a felony drug conviction are fully or partially excluded from food stamp benefits in 30 states and from welfare assistance in 36 states.[27] Research shows that these bans increase recidivism.[28] These restrictions inhibit individuals from rebuilding their lives after release, and they often impact their spouses and children as well. For example, John Waller Jr. was convicted of a felony drug charge in 1998 and subsequently released in 2001. Waller worked hard to establish a new life, starting his own janitorial business after his drug conviction made it difficult for him to attend college or find a job. When he was forced to take time off in 2007 to care for his toddler son, who had been diagnosed with stomach cancer, he needed assistance. But pursuant to Missouri law, which banned those with felony drug convictions from receiving welfare or food stamps, Waller was denied the help he needed to care for his son.[29] Like Waller, Christine McDonald also found herself struggling in the face of Missouri's food stamp ban. Blind and burdened by her felony drug conviction, she struggled to find work. Despite McDonald's need to care for a newborn son, Missouri law refused to grant her access to food stamps because of her conviction.[30] Even completion of drug treatment and rehabilitation programs does not exempt one from the ban, as Jacquelyn Hardy learned. After completing a program and struggling to find stable work, Hardy found herself relying on food pantries to make ends meet. When she requested temporary help in the form of food stamps, she was turned away because of Alabama's lifetime ban on federal assistance for individuals convicted of drug felonies.[31] Ineligibility for welfare benefits and food stamps is a huge problem for individuals released from prison because so many are below the poverty level with no immediate prospects for employment.[32] Moreover, the ban applies to individuals who are in drug treatment or trying to recover from a drug problem, making it that much harder for them to obtain a stable living arrangement, which in turn makes their successful reintegration into the community and desistance from drug use and crime that much more difficult.[33]

Congress went still further in creating obstacles. It also prevented anyone convicted of a drug offense while they were receiving student loans from continuing to receive those loans or federal assistance for specified periods of times. In the case of individuals with three convictions for drug possession, the ban on student loans is for life.[34] If an individual is convicted of selling drugs on two occasions, he or she is also banned indefinitely from receiving federal loans or aid.[35] Individuals can become eligible for federal assistance again only after completing specific drug-rehabilitation programs and testing clean on two unannounced drug tests.[36] Because of these restrictions, nearly 200,000 students have been denied federal loans or aid since 2001.[37] In addition, college admissions counseling and widespread misinformation about the ban mean that an indeterminate number of students with drug convictions may be deterred from even applying for financial aid in the first place.[38]

As with most collateral consequences, the bans focused on drug offenders disproportionately affect people of color. A Drug Policy Alliance Report notes that African Americans comprise 13% of the U.S. population, but they account for 29% of those arrested for drug law violations, and almost 40% of those incarcerated in both state and federal prisons for drug law crimes.[39] Young black men in particular, already the least likely to attend college, are the most likely to be convicted of drug offenses and to be burdened by these bans.[40]

Congress also sought to entice states to pass their own collateral consequences. It passed a law that would take away 10% of a state's federal highway funds unless the state passed laws to revoke or suspend the driver's licenses of people convicted of drug felonies.[41] While the number of states applying these bans has declined, 10 states plus Washington, DC, continue to enforce the federal mandate as of the middle of 2018.[42] Six are among the states with the largest prison populations.[43] Moreover, these jurisdictions account for a large portion of the country's residents, with populous states like Florida, Pennsylvania, New York, New Jersey, and Texas among them. These states also have huge geographical areas that lack adequate public transportation to allow drivers with revoked or suspended licenses to commute to work. Even within those metropolitan areas with greater public transportation infrastructure, workers in low- and middle-skill industries are likely to struggle without a license because only one quarter of jobs in low- and middle-skill industries are accessible within a 90 minute commute.[44] It is also important to note that many jobs require applicants to have a valid driver's license, whether or not the job actually involves driving.[45] It is no wonder, then, that a study found that 42% of New Jersey drivers lost their jobs when they lost their license and 45% of them could not find new jobs thereafter.[46] Of those who were able to find new jobs, nearly 9 in 10 reported income loss.[47] The combination of burdensome restrictions and lack of public transportation has left individuals like Kenneth Seay, a resident of Tennessee, out of work entirely.[48] John Atkinson, a resident of Oklahoma City, has struggled to maintain employment after a drug possession conviction cost him his license.[49] Facing more than $3,000 in costs to reinstate his license after the revocation and living in a large, sprawling city with limited public transportation, Atkinson is forced to rely on rides from family and friends to get to work and court hearings.[50]

Congress also threatened to take away funding from states that did not pass sex offender registration laws. The Jacob Wetterling Act required states to create sex offender registries or they would lose 10% of their criminal justice funding from the federal government. In response, the number of states with registries grew to include all 50 states and the District of Columbia.[51] Subsequent updates to that act have continued to establish new standards for sex offender registries.[52] States that fail to comply with updated standards, even those states that had already established registries following the Wetterling Act, again face a 10% cut in criminal justice finding from the federal government.[53] Some of the updated requirements are so onerous that many states have opted to take a funding cut rather than comply.[54]

Although Congress has been a key instigator of collateral consequences that impede reentry, states have done similar damage on their own. Even before Congress passed the Jacob Wetterling Act and Megan's Law, 31 states had sex offender registration requirements.[55] States also imposed hundreds of employment bans and licensing restrictions on individuals with convictions, frequently without any discernible nexus between the type of crime committed and the nature of the employment or license sought.[56] In Virginia, for example, there are 146 mandatory consequences affecting employment triggered by a felony conviction, ranging from ineligibility to hold a notary commission to a ban on working for the state lottery.[57] New York bans people with a felony conviction from being barbershop owners, emergency medical technicians, or commercial feed distributors.[58] Individuals who have been convicted of drug possession can never obtain an electrician's license in Iowa or bid on a government contract in Illinois, even decades after their crime.[59] Employment restrictions are far from the only collateral consequences imposed by state law. They also cover access to government housing and participation in civic life, with restrictions on voting and jury service.

States have also often opted to impose even more extensive restrictions than federal mandates. So while public housing restrictions were introduced by federal legislation to limit housing opportunities for individuals convicted of drug felonies and violent crimes, local housing authorities used their screening and eviction powers even more broadly, limiting public housing to a greater sweep of criminal conduct, including misdemeanors.[60] The states went further than federal law required with respect to sex offender registry requirements as well. While the federal laws created stringent, minimum standards by which states were to comply, they were also highly deferential. For example, states were given discretion to determine whether disclosure of registry information was necessary for public safety; the standards and procedures for making such determinations; and how to disseminate information to the public.[61] States were also given leeway to determine the length of time someone would be on a registry and available opportunities for removing themselves from the registry.[62] Some states have used this discretion to make it almost impossible for individuals to get off the registry. South Carolina is one such state: absent the reversal or pardoning of a conviction based on innocence, those on the registry face lifetime registration and community notification requirements, with no right to early removal.[63] This includes juvenile offenders.[64] Where states do provide exit opportunities, petition procedures and criteria differ greatly. Some allow only certain subgroups, such as juvenile offenders or those convicted of less serious offenses, to petition for removal; others, like Virginia and Hawaii, allow removal only after a minimum registration term has passed.[65]

And while the federal laws enumerated offenses that required someone to be put on a registry, many states decided on their own to expand the list.[66] Today, public urination and consensual sex between teenagers will put someone on the registry in several states.[67] Presently, four states require lifetime registration for all offenders, irrespective of the nature of the offense committed, whereas federal law mandates lifetime registration only for those convicted of an aggravated sex offense or repeated registrable offenses.[68] Some states have also determined, without federal prompting, that individuals on sex offender registries cannot live in certain areas. In Miami, for example, residency restriction laws are so severe that the only location where convicted individuals can reside is under a causeway.[69] In addition, some states mandate lifetime GPS monitoring for those on the registry.[70] Still other states prohibit individuals convicted of sex offenses from using the internet, while Louisiana has opted to have the words "Sex Offender" imprinted on their state driver's licenses.[71]

Just as the housing laws affect not only the individual who committed the crime but also his or her family, the sex offender laws also negatively impact families. When the registrants become parents, these laws often impede their ability to interact with their own children. For example, a 2013 Human Rights Watch report tells the story of 10-year-old Cindy who cannot have a birthday party at her house because her father is a registered sex offender. Her father is on the registry because, at the age of 14, he had consensual sex with his then 13-year-old girlfriend. At 28, Cindy's father was still prohibited from having unsupervised contact with children under the age of 18.[72] Other individuals on registries cannot take their own children to public parks.[73]

What is most disturbing about these collateral consequences is how little thought typically goes along with their passage. Consider Congress's decision to exclude people with felony drug convictions from receiving welfare or food stamps. How much thought did Congress give this provision? It passed after two minutes of debate.[74] Congress seemed unconcerned with Senator Kennedy's argument at the time that "under this amendment, if you are a murderer, a rapist, or a robber, you can get Federal funds; but if you are convicted even for possession of marijuana, you cannot."[75]

In addition, these provisions are often codified separately from other criminal sanctions, so it is difficult to know what consequences even apply to a felony conviction.[76] Thus defendants often have no idea that these consequences will follow from their guilty pleas or convictions. Under these circumstances, one can hardly argue that these consequences are serving much of a deterrent value.

Instead, these laws make it hard for people already on the margins to live law-abiding lives because they remove the social safety net that helps people get back on their feet. As Jeremy Travis puts it, "This universe of criminal sanctions has been hidden from public view, ignored in our national debate on punishment policy, and generally excluded from research on the life course of ex-offenders or the costs and benefits of the criminal sanction."[77] These laws are not passed to improve public safety—and all too often they compromise it by hindering people who were formerly incarcerated from reintegrating after their release. Instead, these laws are merely an "exercise in symbolic politics" that makes it appear as if elected officials are tough on crime when in fact these measures are often counterproductive for reducing crime and improving public safety.[78] But with no one asking rational questions about them, they continue to operate unabated and automatically.

These collateral consequences force people with vastly different levels of culpability to face the same draconian consequences. Individuals who use drugs and those who commit homicide are subject to the same public housing bans.[79] State occupational licensing laws often apply not only to specific types of convictions, but more generally to any felony or even misdemeanor. That is why Sonja Blake, a grandmother, had her daycare-owner certification permanently revoked because of a 30-year-old misdemeanor conviction for overpayment of public assistance.[80] Jama'ar Brown had been a licensed barber for 5 years when he was convicted and sentenced for a drug offense. Three years after serving his time, he still could not find steady work because Texas bars drug offenders from obtaining or regaining a barber's license.[81]

Sex offender registry laws similarly fail to draw meaningful distinctions among different types of offenses and offenders. Someone convicted of indecent exposure for streaking across a college campus faces the same collateral consequences as someone convicted of aggravated rape; in many states, the laws governing individuals convicted of sex offenses are age-blind as well, so 10-year-olds who commit crimes face the same collateral consequences as mature adults who commit crimes.[82] Everyone on the registry must navigate the same complex web of legal requirements that often leaves them unable to secure employment, attend school, or even associate with their family.

The immigration consequences of convictions likewise fail to recognize important distinctions among those affected by them. The host of offenses that trigger deportation range from drug offenses to falsification of documents to aggravated felonies.[83] A lawful permanent resident who has lived for decades in the United States and served in the military can be deported for any drug offense other than possession of 30 grams or less of marijuana. If the offense is a possession offense, individuals can seek cancellation of their removal, but they will be permanently barred from ever receiving citizenship and must move for cancellation while detained without bond. And if the drug offense is a trafficking offense, the law is even less forgiving. A lawful permanent resident caught selling cocaine worth $10 will be deported as an "aggravated felon"—a label that also attaches to noncitizens convicted of trafficking illicit firearms or murder—with very little likelihood of successfully fighting the case.[84] The result is a skyrocketing number of people who have been deported because of criminal convictions.[85]

These collateral consequences also often fail to provide for changes in circumstances. Thousands of state and federal collateral consequences automatically attach upon conviction permanently or for an unspecified period of time. While some states have recently lifted lifetime restrictions on food stamps and public welfare benefits for former drug offenders, several still impose a permanent ban.[86] And despite growing concern over the efficacy of national sex offender laws, lifetime registrants are still completely barred from ever living in federally assisted housing.[87]

Some well-meaning advocates have tried to mitigate one of the collateral consequences of a conviction: the inability to obtain a job because employers do not want to hire people with criminal histories. The "ban the box" policy adopted by several states and the federal government prohibits potential employers from inquiring into an applicant's criminal history until later in the hiring process, usually after the interview, so that the applicant has a chance to make a positive impression on the employer and the record can be weighed against the candidate's positive attributes instead of serving as an obstacle to an employer even taking a look at someone.[88] This policy might also encourage more people with convictions to apply for jobs.[89] Unfortunately, empirical studies of ban-the-box efforts show that employers without information about criminal history at the outset often resort to naked racial profiling and discrimination as a substitute.[90] It appears that employers try to "guess" which applicants are more likely to have criminal records—because they are still reluctant to hire ex-offenders—and one of the proxies they use is race.[91] A better course would be for jurisdictions to pass laws that provide for nondiscrimination in employment against citizens with criminal records, as New York has done.[92]

Another course that would ease a person's reentry would be to allow individuals to remove criminal convictions from their records after a certain period of time. Sadly, though, individuals in many if not most cases are unable to restore their eligibility for benefits or remove convictions from their records even if they have decades of good behavior. Relief from collateral consequences may exist in theory in the form of pardons; expungement or record sealing; certificates of recovery or rehabilitation, which can be presented to employers or other third parties as evidence of a person's rehabilitation; or the downgrading of an offense. But in reality, the substantive and procedural requirements are often impossible to meet.[93]

Start with pardons, which offer complete relief from collateral consequences.[94] States vary in terms of who has the authority to pardon and what the requirements are for receiving one. Some states have no set prerequisites for pardons, whereas others have concluded that certain classes of offenders cannot receive a pardon. Georgia, for example, has determined that drug offenders and those who commit crimes of violence are ineligible to apply for relief. But even when individuals are eligible to apply, their odds of getting relief are slim. Only 15 states grant pardons more than 30% of the time, while almost half (23) have rarely, if ever, granted pardons in the past 20 years.[95] And in most jurisdictions, the use of pardons has decreased significantly.[96] Take Massachusetts, which issued 477 pardons in 1970, but only 70 pardons total during the 1990s.[97] While Governor Jane Swift, who served as acting governor between 2001 and 2003, granted seven pardons during her tenure, it wasn't until 2014 that a pardon was again granted.[98] Or consider West Virginia, where only 121 applicants were granted a full and complete pardon over a 36-year period that spanned nine governors' terms.[99]

Executive use of the pardon power at the federal level has also significantly decreased over the past several decades. While Gerald Ford and Jimmy Carter both granted more than 30% of all pardon requests, this number saw a steady drop in the 1980s. Ronald Reagan granted only 19% of pardon requests, and George H. W. Bush's pardon rate fell to 10%. Although pardons saw a slight rise under Bill Clinton—who granted 20% of pardon requests—it fell back down to 8% under his successor, George W. Bush. Pardons fell still further under Barack Obama, who had a grant rate of 6%.[100]

Record expungement and sealing procedures also offer little hope of relief for most individuals. Here, too, practices vary significantly among states.[101] Massachusetts, Washington, Minnesota, and New York have some of the more generous sealing laws.[102] New York, for example, allows individuals with past convictions to apply after 10 years to the court in which they were sentenced to seal their records as long as their crime was not too serious and they had a limited number of convictions. While law enforcement and certain state licensing authorities could still have access to the records, they would no longer be available to the public.[103] Massachusetts and Washington have laws explicitly providing that an applicant is entitled to deny the existence of a sealed conviction if asked on an employment application.[104]

Other jurisdictions have more restrictive sealing or expungement laws, often requiring individuals to remain crime-free for some period of time following sentence completion and imposing additional requirements. For example, many states require applicants to file a petition in court demonstrating that they are rehabilitated. This may include showing that they are employed, are not abusing substances, and are leading a law-abiding life. Given the many bars to educational, licensing, and employment opportunities triggered by a conviction, this can be a high bar to meet.[105]

Individuals also face significant hurdles in many states because of limits on eligibility. Expungement and record sealing may be available only to persons convicted of drug or property offenses, and some states disqualify individuals even with only those offenses if they have multiple charges on their record.[106] Some states reserve the right to seal or expunge the criminal record of first offenders or misdemeanants only, while others limit eligibility based on the age of the individual at the time of the offense.[107] In Indiana, which introduced one of the most generous expungement laws in 2013, all individuals convicted of crimes involving serious violence, corruption, or sexual offenses are still precluded from ever having their records expunged.[108]

Even where expungement opportunities exist, fiscal hurdles in the states may make expungement impossible for many. The application process can be time-consuming and costly. For example, a new law in Kentucky requires a $500 fee for applicants who are eligible to have their records expunged. With full-time employment already difficult for those with criminal records, this cost can be prohibitive.[109] In addition, even when an individual successfully expunges or seals his or her conviction, collateral consequences may still follow because prospective employers and others may nevertheless discover the individual's record. Some states expressly require that individuals report convictions in certain job or license applications even after a record has been sealed, and the internet and widespread background checking often expose convictions even after they have been expunged.[110]

Certificates of rehabilitation, which vary by state, allow individuals to defend themselves against some collateral consequences and provide a means by which individuals can provide evidence of their rehabilitation to third parties, such as employers. However, not all employers may find this sufficient to overcome their biases against hiring someone with a conviction.[111] Moreover, even this limited mechanism for relief is hard to obtain. States often impose wait times upon applicants, and only certain classes of offenders are eligible to apply.[112] Like expungement or sealing remedies, the process may also require a formal court petition, which is a time-consuming, costly, and often confusing process.[113] Applicants bear the burden of demonstrating rehabilitation, which often requires obtaining documentation from multiple agencies, letters of support from community members, and proof of sobriety.[114]

Some states also provide avenues to people to get their offenses downgraded. As of 2014, at least five states had introduced laws allowing eligible individuals to reduce their felony record to a misdemeanor to help minimize collateral sanctions. Eligibility criteria and the petition process vary among states. While some allow individuals to petition for downgrades after completion of their probation or other community-based sentence, others require a court hearing.[115]

A few cities in states that have legalized marijuana are taking the initiative in expunging prior marijuana convictions without requiring action on the part of the individuals with those convictions. When California voters passed Proposition 64 in 2017 and legalized marijuana, they also approved a mechanism that would allow individuals with certain marijuana convictions to have those convictions expunged from their records as long as they were not a threat to public safety. But because relatively few people applied—either because they did not know about the option or did not have the ability or resources to make it through the application process—George Gascón, the district attorney in San Francisco, decided to move on his own to wipe out prior marijuana convictions. This will benefit thousands of people in California, particularly people of color because, as Gascón noted, "African American and Latino communities were the most harmed" by enforcement of the marijuana laws.[116] Gascón is going to expunge 3,000 misdemeanors and examine another 5,000 felonies to see if they can be retroactively reduced to misdemeanors.[117] San Diego is similarly going to expunge or downgrade 4,700 cases without any action needed by the people with those convictions.[118] Seattle is following a similar path. The state of Washington legalized marijuana in 2012, so the mayor and city attorney in Seattle decided to vacate misdemeanor marijuana convictions in cases that were prosecuted before that time without requiring any action by the individuals who were convicted.[119] Although these cities take the view that people should not, in Gascón's words, have to "pay lawyers' fees and jump through a bunch of hoops to get something they should be getting anyway," most other jurisdictions have not shared that opinion.[120]

While each state has at least one mechanism for relieving collateral consequences, the accessibility and effect of these mechanisms vary widely among jurisdictions. The lack of a central clearinghouse of information about state and federal restoration procedures means that authorities have minimal access to information outside their own state. The result is a patchwork set of systems that are often not well understood even by those charged with their administration.[121]

Other countries show that this model need not prevail. Most European countries allow all criminal convictions to become "spent" after a period of time, which means the individual is viewed, for purposes of the law, as they were before the time of the offense.[122] Canada follows a similar approach, allowing individuals convicted of summary and indictable charges to have their rights restored after 5 and 10 years, respectively, of crime-free behavior.[123] While such relief is not available for individuals convicted of multiple serious crimes, even those convicted of sex crimes involving children may apply for relief if they were not in a position of trust or authority with the victim; did not use violence, intimidation, or coercion; and were less than 5 years older than the victim.[124] While the United Kingdom follows a stricter regime for restoration of rights, it, too, provides an avenue for a fresh start that is more generous than the approach in the United States. It allows people who have been convicted of most felonies and sentenced to less than 4 years to get their rights restored after a maximum of 7 years.[125]

Jurisdictions in the United States, in contrast, have been generally content to make a one-time, blanket judgment about what restrictions should apply to a broad swath of individuals and then not allow those decisions to be adjusted or revisited no matter how many years of law-abiding behavior have gone by. That is because the expansive nature of the collateral consequences and the restricted provisions to restore rights are two sides of the same political coin: the political process sets policies based on extreme cases, and it is hard to get a rational debate about how to tailor these policies. That is true even though doing so would improve public safety.

A more sensible model would tailor collateral consequences to the particular person. It makes sense to suspend someone's driver's license when they have been convicted of multiple drunk driving offenses; it does not make sense to suspend the license of everyone convicted of any type of felony. And while it may be rational to prohibit someone who abducted a child from living near a school, it does not make sense to prohibit everyone who meets an overly broad definition of sex offender from living in the area.

The current approach in the United States fails both to allow collateral consequences to be tailored to the individual at the time of sentencing (because charging a particular crime automatically brings the collateral consequences along with it, even if the prosecutor does not believe those sanctions make sense) and to revisit those determinations as time passes and the individual shows that he or she is leading a law-abiding life. This failure not only is unjust but also undermines public safety because it hampers the individual's reentry efforts.

PART TWO

PART ONE SHOWS THAT we have numerous criminal justice policies that make no sense as a matter of public safety, that poorly allocate our limited resources, and that lead to unnecessary confinement. How did we end up with so many counterproductive policies, and why do they remain when we could be pursuing a better course? We have a political environment in which no elected official wants to be labeled "soft on crime," so they have either encouraged more incarceration or sat on the sidelines as America's rate of imprisonment grew to be the world's highest. Little attention is paid to what actually goes on in those prisons and jails to rehabilitate the millions of people who cycle through them and ultimately rejoin society. It is an approach designed to be symbolically harsh but with almost no accountability for achieving real public safety or cost-effective results.

Chapter 6 explains that the public, elected officials, and powerful groups all tend to support harsher laws, while the groups seeking to reduce sentences or to promote other reform efforts that focus on results instead of symbolically tough responses tend to have less power and face an uphill battle. In a political world that focuses on sound bites and in which most of the public gets its information about crime indirectly from the media, it is difficult to get politicians to shift from superficially tough, but ultimately ineffective, responses to crime because of widespread voter ignorance about the issues. Even as a nascent bipartisan movement has emerged to try to shift the balance, we see only modest reforms away from the most punitive approach, and at the same time, we continue to see efforts to increase sentences and maintain a harsh approach, even as the evidence makes it clear those latter strategies undermine public safety.

The public's receptivity to punitive responses to crime is not new: even the Framers recognized how populism could produce harsh outcomes. But there was a noticeable shift in approach in the past 40 years, so something changed to light the spark of punitiveness that prevails today. Chapter 7 explains the institutional factors that allowed penal populism to flourish in recent decades in ways that did not exist previously. Specifically, it describes how critical checks that once existed decayed, allowing populist impulses for severity to take hold without any mediating force focused on rationality or results to rein in the excess. Understanding these political and institutional dynamics is critical to finding solutions because they point the way to the kinds of mediating institutions and public information that is necessary to improve criminal justice policy-making and reverse the ill-fated policies and approaches documented in Chapters 1 through 5.

6

POPULIST POLITICS

THE MODERN PUSH for tougher criminal laws and policies that resulted in the massive number of people incarcerated that we see today can be traced to the 1960s, when America experienced widespread social unrest and violence. Violent crime increased by 126% between 1960 and 1970 and by 64% between 1970 and 1980.[1] In 1968, the United States witnessed the highest property and violent crime rates ever recorded.[2] With news reports dominated by stories of spiking crime rates and riots throughout the country, a large majority of people reported fearing for their safety.[3] Racial prejudice was inextricably linked with this fear, and it is never far from the surface in the political response to crime.[4] That fear ushered in the political dynamics we have today.

With public concerns about order at their peak, elected officials rushed to fill the breach: "Crime policy, once the domain of criminal justice professionals, became dominated by electoral politics."[5] Thus the shift to mass incarceration is directly linked to the shift from leaving judgments to professionals to allowing the masses to set policies directly. Both sides of the political spectrum supported that change. Conservative politicians decried the system's inability to address the spiking rates of crime throughout the United States and criticized existing laws as too lenient. Liberal politicians disliked the existing model because it worked to the disadvantage of poor people and people of color. Everyone seemed to lose faith in the idea of rehabilitation, and no one seemed to trust experts to make criminal justice decisions. The era of mass incarceration was born, unleashing forces that make its demise in any significant respect unlikely under the existing institutional architecture that created it.

The Public

To understand the forces behind this dynamic, it is helpful to start with the sense of the electorate. People fear first and foremost for their safety, and crime threatens their sense of security. Barry Goldwater recognized this fundamental truth when he stated, in accepting his nomination as the Republican candidate for president in 1964, that "security from domestic violence, no less than from foreign aggression, is the most elementary and fundamental purpose of any government."[6] The issue is bipartisan: Democrat Bill Clinton similarly told the country in 1993 that "the first duty of any government is to try to keep its citizens safe."[7]

Goldwater and Clinton both recognized that the instinctual reaction among the public with respect to crime policy tends to be "do what it takes to keep us safe." So when crime rates began to rise in the 1960s, the public was drawn to politicians who focused on public safety as a top priority.[8] But while it makes intuitive sense that the public responds favorably to politicians who emphasize public safety at times of rising crime rates, the harder question is why the public seemingly continued to demand (or at least support) even more severe sentences after crime rates began to drop—and drop precipitously—in the 1990s, plunging nearly 45% between 1990 and 2012.[9] "Whether times were good or bad, whether crime was on the rise or on the decline," America since the late 1960s has "put more people in prison."[10]

One reason the public remained receptive to get-tough crime policies is that the public tends to overestimate the threat of crime because most voters are relatively uninformed, both in general and specifically, about criminal justice issues.[11] They are typically unaware when crime rates are down or how prison resources are used. They overestimate their risk of being victimized by crime.[12] We know from cognitive psychology that voters are prone to think of crimes that are the most salient in their minds.[13] If one has direct experience with crime or the criminal justice system, that experience will tend to shape one's views of an appropriate policy response. As founder and executive director of the Equal Justice Initiative and acclaimed social justice activist Bryan Stevenson emphasizes, "You can't understand most of the important things from a distance. . . . You have to get close."[14] But because most voters have no direct contact with crime, their impressions are formed largely from media accounts of crime. It is estimated that more than 90% of Americans use the news media as their primary source of information about crime.[15]

The media, in turn, are obsessed with crime stories. The lead story on local news outlets is either a crime story or an accident story 77% of the time, and 32% of all local television news stories are about crime.[16] The media does not cover all crimes equally or provide a broad view of criminal justice trends and policies. Instead, the crimes that grab headlines are the most violent offenses, even though the majority of crimes committed do not involve violence.[17] Murder stories dominate the news whether overall homicide rates are up or down. For instance, when the Center for Media and Public Affairs conducted a study of television crime coverage in the 1990s, it discovered that the number of murder stories increased 336% from 1990 to 1995, even though the murder rate during that same period had declined by 13%.[18] Network television news coverage of crime stories increased 83% from 1990 to 1998, even though overall crime in that same period declined by 20%.[19] This dynamic remains true today, with studies consistently showing that media stories about crime do not correspond with crime rates or with the proportion of crimes that are violent.[20] For instance, the homicide rate in New York went from 31 per 100,000 people in 1990 to 4 per 100,000 people in 2013, but the use of the words "homicide" or "murder" in *New York Times* headlines was largely unchanged; there were 129 such mentions in 1990 and 135 in 2013.[21]

Both the national and local media also cover particularly heinous crimes or incidents of violence no matter where they occur. So if there are upticks in violence in certain localities, it may lead the public to think there is an increase in crime everywhere. For example, a recent increase in gun violence in Chicago and a few other large cities might play a role in distorting public perceptions about crime rates.[22] Mass shootings receive widespread coverage no matter where they occur, and they also influence public opinion about overall crime.[23]

If a political leader highlights violence, it also receives extensive coverage. One need look no further than the 2016 presidential election campaign of Donald Trump. Trump frequently appealed to the public's fear of crime during his 2016 campaign, conjuring up images of American "carnage" and "lawlessness."[24] He made Chicago's murder rate a focus of attention throughout 2016, spoke about the dangers of the allegedly increasing crime rate in most of his major speeches, and labeled crime by immigrants and terrorist groups as the biggest threats to Americans' safety.[25] As one journalist noted, "Fear has been a fixture of Trump's oratory since the start of his campaign."[26]

The result of this dominant approach in media coverage is that the public often believes crime rates are up, even when the actual rates are decreasing.[27] As one article put it, "Just as with the case of airplane crashes, the public may see the extraordinary event as representative of the norm when it is not."[28] Indeed, despite the fact that crime rates have been falling consistently since the 1990s, Gallup polls for more than a decade have found that a majority of Americans believe that crime rates are up.[29] A Pew study in November 2016 similarly found that "despite double-digit percentage decreases in U.S. violent and property crime since 2008, most voters say crime has gotten worse during that span."[30] The public also often conflates social unrest and protests with rising crime.[31]

It is hardly surprising, then, that a 2017 study found that the most punitive voters are those who "are White, live in politically conservative areas, and view more hours of local television news programs."[32] More interesting is that the study did not find a relationship between actual exposure to crime and punitiveness.[33] Thus the fact that the authors did not find a statistically significant relationship between punitiveness and living in areas with higher crime rates or being a victim of crime, but did find one between punitiveness and watching more hours of local television news, shows the power of the media to shape attitudes and perceptions.[34] As more people turn to social media, some of these dynamics may change. One study found that news consumption on the internet is not related to punitive attitudes in the same way.[35] It is too soon to tell how much this will shift public attitudes toward criminal justice policies, particularly if social media reflects other biases.

We know, for example, that the media helps shape public perceptions in other ways. Media crime stories are skewed based on race. The media places disproportionate emphasis on crimes with racial minorities as the offenders or suspected offenders and with whites as the crime victims.[36] For instance, media accounts emphasize black male offenders and white female victims in homicide cases, even though homicide is predominantly an intra-racial crime involving male perpetrators and male victims.[37] This racialized presentation of crime affects public opinion about it and feeds existing stereotypes and prejudices that a large number of people may harbor.

Media coverage of crime is also directly influenced by law enforcement because government officials are the media's main sources of information on crime.[38] Law enforcement sources can prompt the media to draw greater attention to an issue they wish to highlight.[39] For instance, when President Reagan declared the war on drugs, members of his administration deliberately engaged the media to devote more attention to drug problems.[40] Similarly, when law enforcement focused on crimes against the elderly, the media followed suit and created the impression there was a crime wave against elderly victims by disproportionately covering those stories, even though police statistics showed there was an overall decrease in crimes against the elderly as compared to the previous year.[41]

The crimes featured in the media become salient to voters when they consider what candidates to support, leading them to favor those candidates who talk about being tough. If a voter thinks that a particular drug is destroying the fabric of society based on media reports, he or she will support a harsh response to those who distribute that drug. If a voter is thinking of "sex offenses," the imagery is likely to be horrific child abductions and sex crimes or brutal rapes featured on the news, and voters will tend to favor those candidates who vow to deal with sex offenders harshly. If they are told cities have become more violent, they will be more likely to support candidates who propose a crackdown on crime to restore order. If a member of the public holds an image of a criminal offender as a black male because of media portrayals, he or she may not be disturbed by the disproportionate number of African Americans who are incarcerated or under supervision because he or she may think the prison population reflects actual rates of offending. If a voter subscribes to the idea that some prisons are insufficiently harsh or even resemble "country clubs," he or she may oppose efforts to make prison more humane.[42]

Rarely does a news story explore the costs and benefits of criminal justice policies, the underlying demographic statistics of offenders or victims, or the individual backgrounds of those who break the law.[43] Instead, the stories tend to focus on the emotional horror of specific violent crimes that may not represent overall trends. The public is left with the misleading impression that there is a constant threat from violent crime without much of an understanding of the full range of what is criminalized. The media also fail to provide them with an understanding of the pros and cons of various approaches to addressing the range of criminal behavior or with the knowledge that most people ultimately get released from prison. Everything in the narrative is simplistically framed as good (innocent victims) versus bad (violent offenders with no redeeming qualities), with the solution being harsher punishments. There is no attention to or coverage of what happens to individuals during those long sentences and whether they come out worse than when they went in. It is no wonder, then, that when asked in surveys how courts deal with criminals, about 85% of those responding said "about right" or "not harshly enough" between 1972 and 2012.[44]

The real world of criminal justice in the United States is obviously more complicated than the media portrayals, and when the public gets exposed to more facts and details, its views sometimes shift. Katherine Beckett has observed that "the more exposure people have to nonsensationalistic accounts of real criminal incidents (from court documents rather than media accounts), the less punitive they become."[45] For example, while a majority of residents in Ohio favored a three-strikes law as a general matter, only a small minority supported the law's mandated life sentence when confronted with specific factual scenarios that would trigger the sentence.[46] In other studies, researchers asked participants what sentences they would impose in particular cases and found the lay sentences to be either less severe or no more severe than the ones handed down by the judge in the actual case.[47] A 2016 study of registered voters asked for their views on mandatory minimum sentences. It found that 79% of those responding preferred to give judges flexibility in drug cases, and 77% preferred to give judges flexibility in all cases, compared with 18% who found giving judges flexibility unacceptable in drug cases and 19% who found it unacceptable in all cases.[48]

When asked about specific reforms that focus on reentry, like alternatives to imprisonment or support for rehabilitation programs, the public supports those efforts.[49] For example, 85% of registered voters responding to a survey would allow people in prison to earn up to 30% off their prison time by participating in prison programs that have been proven to reduce reoffending.[50] Even at the height of tough-on-crime politics in the 1990s, nearly two-thirds of survey respondents were in favor of granting prisoners early release if they participated in work programs and demonstrated good behavior.[51] When asked to imagine themselves as a mayor allocating federal grant money, respondents favored using only 8.4% of the money for prisons, compared with using 36.6% for prevention programs and 21% for drug treatment programs.[52]

So while our democratic process produces harsh responses to crime, that process does not necessarily reflect the actual preferences of voters on specific policies when they are fully informed. When faced with more facts and options, the public might be supportive of different approaches that are more likely to improve public safety because that is their ultimate goal. Unfortunately, in the current design of our system, it is rare that the public gets that kind of information because that is not what the media presents, so it is not possible to know when the public's taste for punitive responses would yield to other measures if doing so would produce better long-term outcomes for public safety or would produce the same safety outcomes at a lower cost.

Elected Officials

Elections and political discourse are ill-suited for fact-specific and nuanced discussion of complicated issues. Politicians need to make clear to voters that they are on the side of public safety—and not on the side of crime—in concise sound bites. The most straightforward way for a politician to demonstrate this is to advocate for longer sentences for criminal conduct. As David Garland has explained, "get-tough" rhetoric allows politicians to create the appearance that they have an immediate, tangible solution to so-cial unrest.[53] It is much harder to discuss strategies for addressing root causes of criminal behavior or to explain why proportional sentences are important. When he was the deputy attorney general during the Clinton administration, Philip Heyman explained that the political climate rewards "toughness more than smartness" because "it takes a little while to explain why one thing's smart and the other thing isn't. It doesn't take any time at all to explain why one thing's tougher than the next."[54] As legal scholar Al Alschuler puts it, "Politicians fear endorsing any position that an opponent can characterize as 'soft on crime' in a 30-second television commercial."[55]

This is why it is politically risky for a politician to push for sentencing reductions; they face easy-to-understand attacks for being insensitive to vio-lence and public safety, but the defense of their proposals may take more time to explain. Moreover, politicians must produce tangible results of some kind before they come up for reelection, so policies that require a long time to yield improved outcomes are not as valuable to them as a new sentencing law that serves as an immediate response to crime. The easy ac-cessibility of criminalization and perceived toughness with voters is not restricted to addressing crimes of violence: "Our society has grown ac-customed to thinking of a criminal response as the solution to just about anything, from the financial breakdown, to massive environmental damage, to juvenile misbehavior, because that is the political model they have seen time and time again."[56]

Because most politicians have no expertise or training in criminal justice policy, they may be unaware of the pitfalls of more punitive policies. They may not know the downsides of punitive approaches or the upsides of al-ternatives, and they may not understand the full range of criminal behavior covered by a law. Because they are setting criminal justice policies as a gen-eral matter and are often responding to particularly heinous cases or press accounts, they may lack "context for assessing and passing judgments on the actual persons who will come to violate various criminal prohibitions; they can really only consider criminal offenders as abstract and nefarious characters."[57]

Thus politicians tend to echo the media's accounts of crime, which in turn exacerbates public misperceptions. The public's concern with crime, as mea-sured by opinion polls, is "largely unrelated to the reported incidence of crime and drug use but [is] strongly associated with the extent to which elites highlight these issues in political discourse."[58]

And just as racial bias permeates media coverage of crime, it is also an issue in elections. The United States elects not only legislators, but also sher-iffs, judges, and prosecutors in most jurisdictions. In the campaigns for all these offices, the issue of crime is often tainted by assumptions about the race of criminals and victims. For example, in 2015, Donald Trump tweeted a graphic of a black man with a gun and statistics falsely stating that black people were responsible for 81% of murders in which the victim was white.[59] Richard Nixon was also well known for using crime to appeal to racial fears without explicitly referring to race while campaigning, and George H. W. Bush was widely criticized for the implicit racial bias in ads and speeches about Willie Horton.[60]

These appeals occur in local as well as national elections. A notorious example is Sheriff Joe Arpaio of Maricopa County, Arizona. During six terms over 24 years, Arpaio easily won races by highlighting his reputation for humiliating and mistreating prisoners and being especially tough on undocumented immigrants—so tough that he provoked multiple lawsuits and was ultimately found guilty of criminal contempt, before being pardoned by President Trump.[61] Though a demographic shift ultimately spelled the end of his tenure, he was able to ride a tide of bias to office for more than two decades.[62]

Several scholars have critically explored the use of "racially divisive appeals" in campaigns that focus on racist or nativist sentiments to woo white voters.[63] The goal of these appeals, according to one ad maker, is to "scare the living shit out of white people" by associating minorities and immigrants with criminality.[64] The level of this bias may vary by locality, with jurisdictions in the South "maximally vulnerable to prejudice."[65]

Interest Groups in Favor of Tougher Criminal Laws

These tendencies toward punitiveness by voters and elected officials are exacerbated by the fact that powerful groups often push for longer sentences and more expansive laws. Chief among those lobbying forces are law enforcement officials. Police chiefs and prosecutors in many places are elected, so they have the same incentives as other elected officials to appear tough on crime; indeed, their incentives are greater because criminal policy is the only issue on which they are being assessed. Prosecutors' associations are often the leading obstacles to reform legislation that would lower sentences, provide diversionary programs, or stop treating juveniles as adults. In Louisiana, for example, the district attorneys' association "is the most formidable obstacle to reform."[66] In California, prosecutors have opposed reforms to lessen sentences or to change cash bail practices. As Udi Ofer of the ACLU notes, "No matter whether it's a red state or blue state, DA associations are guided by the same principles—mainly seeking to maintain their members' unfettered powers."[67]

Even without the political incentive to lobby for tougher laws shared by all elected officials, law enforcement officials have a specific incentive to press for harsher laws to make their jobs easier. This is especially true for prosecutors because a multitude of broad and overlapping criminal laws allows them to pick and choose when they are bargaining with defendants, threatening the more serious charges if defendants do not plead or cooperate. Longer sentences and especially mandatory minimum sentences render prosecutorial threats all the more powerful because they make the risk of trial more costly for defendants.[68] Federal prosecutors have consistently pressed Congress to enact or preserve mandatory minimums because of the leverage those laws give them.[69] For the same reasons, state prosecutors have similarly sought tougher sentencing laws and have opposed reforms that would reduce sentences or lower mandatory minimums.[70]

Because their focus is on leverage and not the ideal sentence for a given crime, prosecutors have an incentive to lobby for higher statutory minimums and maximums than even they themselves believe to be appropriate for the crime in most cases; they need higher minimums and maximums so that they can use them to bargain down to what they consider actually to be an appropriate sentence. They want the ability to get to those sentences through a bargain instead of having to use resources on trials—and the only way that works is for the statutory authorizations to be set higher. So criminal statutes become like sticker prices on cars. No one thinks of them as the real price; they are just there to start the bargaining. But for that dynamic to work, prosecutors need to get legislators to set the initial price high. Prosecutors seek these provisions in good faith: they believe a criminal justice response is often the best answer to social problems and they see themselves as the guardians of that process. These are people, after all, who chose this calling, so they believe in its worth. Thus in their view, giving them greater leverage means they have greater power to fix problems. But this prosecution-centered view ignores the data on how best to maximize public safety. Often the best course is lower sentences, a shift away from mandatory minimums, or diversion from criminal justice altogether.[71] Prosecutors just typically fail to see that bigger picture because they are focused on the narrow framework of the world in which they operate.

Prosecutors are not alone in lobbying for tougher criminal laws. There are typically other interests aligned in favor of harsher and broader criminal laws. Various groups have economic stakes in prison growth, such as rural communities, corrections officer unions, and private prison companies.[72] In New York, for example, state legislators who have prisons in their districts are far less likely to support efforts to reform the state's drug laws—and that is true regardless of the legislator's party affiliation.[73]

Victims' rights groups are often a powerful force for longer sentences or additional collateral consequences, such as sex offender notification laws.[74] They have also successfully blocked efforts to roll back sentences.[75] Although offenders and victims overlap significantly, with many offenders having been victims of crimes, victims' rights groups tend not to represent or focus on the most frequent victims of crime.[76] For example, young black males are the group most likely to be homicide victims. The homicide victimization rate for black people is six times what it is for white people, and black individuals make up half of all homicide victims, even though they are only 13% of the population.[77] These patterns hold for other crimes as well. Studies have shown that black people are 66% more likely than white people to be victims of sexual assault, robbery, aggravated assault, and simple assault.[78] They are also 78% more likely than whites to experience household burglary, and 133% more likely to experience motor vehicle theft.[79]

But victims' rights groups rarely focus on people of color in the victim population or think about the needs of offenders who may also be victims themselves. Instead, victims' groups tend to focus on certain subgroups, such as women and children, and they often highlight cases involving white victims instead of the far more frequently victimized communities of color. As a result, victims' groups ignore the trade-offs associated with longer sentences because of the relatively high rates of both offending and victimization in certain communities. They also avoid the complicated narratives at play when victims are themselves engaged in some criminal activity or are close associates with those engaged in risky behavior.[80] The result is that the victims' rights movement ignores "the race, gender, and class-based realities of repeat victims of petty and violent crime" and instead promotes policy based on outlier cases.[81]

As criminal law has spread beyond violent crimes to cover just about every facet of life, various specialty groups often lobby to get particular issues recognized as criminal or subject to higher penalties. Criminalizing problems, as Jonathan Simon, author of *Governing through Crime*, has persuasively argued, become commonplace.[82] Consumer groups push for more regulatory violations to be criminalized. For example, after major automobile manufacturers came under fire for failing to report defects with their vehicles, auto safety and consumer groups urged legislators to make regulatory violations criminal, and legislators responded by proposing bills that would criminalize any safety violation, providing for a maximum sentence of life should one of those safety violations result in death.[83] To take another example, when animal rights groups videotaped animal cruelty at livestock farms, farming businesses urged state legislators to pass so-called "ag-gag" bills that criminalize taking pictures or videos of livestock farms to defame the facilities or their owners, some even going so far as to place violators on a "terrorist registry."[84]

But in the main, prosecutors and law enforcement officials lead the push for longer sentences, and these other interest groups serve as supporting players. For instance, a survey of staff members of the Senate Judiciary Committee found that "the only area in which . . . paid lobbyists had a limited role was standard criminal law issues," where the "regular player" was the Department of Justice.[85] Prosecutors have thus become entrenched and powerful interests in favor of broad statutes with severe penalties, believing that they should play the critical decision-making role about when to roll back penalties in a given case.

Interest Groups That Push against "Tough-on-Crime" Tactics

Very few powerful groups stand in the way of the push for broader and more severe criminal laws. They tend to be strongest when they are pushing against more criminalization or more severe penalties in the regulatory sphere. At present, for instance, influential libertarian groups such as the Heritage Foundation and Koch Industries have been urging reforms of regulatory crimes to require the government to prove a violator knew that his or her behavior was illegal.[86] Other advocacy groups are pushing back on the passage of quality-of-life crimes, such as laws criminalizing public urination, drunkenness, or sleeping on the sidewalk, because they effectively criminalize homelessness in cities across the nation.[87]

But in the context of crimes involving violence or the perceived potential for violence (which often includes drug crimes, especially for drugs other than marijuana), there are often few influential interests lining up to push against the tide for more severity. The direct targets of these laws—those who will or already are engaged in criminal activity—are poorly positioned to lead a lobbying effort. Those who have not yet committed crimes but eventually will engage in criminal activity might have no idea what their future holds. They may have no sense that they will later commit a crime; even if they have concrete plans to do so, they likely do not plan on getting caught. And even if one anticipated being affected, he or she would be unlikely to want to self-identify in advance in order to help lobby for less severity.

The situation is different for those who have been incarcerated or otherwise entangled with the criminal justice system. They have the greatest knowledge about how the system operates and where its failings are, but they have traditionally stood in a poor position to challenge the status quo. For starters, a criminal conviction means the loss of the right to vote in many places. Prisoners are disenfranchised in 46 states and the District of Columbia, sometimes for life.[88] Roughly 2.5% of the voting population in the United States (about 6 million people) has been temporarily or permanently disenfranchised because of a criminal conviction.[89] Individuals who are banned from voting obviously lack the leverage of threatening to withhold their votes from candidates based on their criminal justice policy stances. Even when individuals with criminal records have the right to vote, their turnout rates are low—even relative to the already low turnout rates among the overall population.[90] People with criminal records also tend to lack the organization and funding that make for a powerful interest group.[91] That is similarly true of their families and friends who may be inclined to support more sensible criminal justice policies.[92] JustLeadership USA is an organization aiming to change this dynamic by empowering formerly incarcerated individuals to lead reform efforts, and its early efforts have been promising at the local level.[93] But it will be a tougher climb to bring about broader legislative changes at the national and state level, particularly when these individuals have to go head-to-head with law enforcement interests.

The communities hit hardest by mass incarceration also suffer from organizational shortcomings.[94] These poverty-stricken neighborhoods are often politically powerless. Even when they do seek to get their voices heard, the voices themselves are not in unison. As author James Forman has persuasively documented, people of color in high-crime neighborhoods, faced with few if any alternatives, often support a strong punitive response to stem the pervasive violence they must endure daily.[95]

Individuals who work in the trenches of criminal law are also limited in their ability to bring about change. While there are many reform-minded members of the defense bar who have identified single issues to tackle (cash bail practices, for example), wholesale change is outside both the mission and expertise of defense lawyers. Overstretched public defender offices barely have the resources to manage the individual representation of their clients, let alone to seek large-scale systemic reform.[96] Bar associations are similarly limited. While a few prominent groups, including the New York City Bar Association and the American Bar Association have called attention to mass incarceration, they have offered few concrete roadmaps for change, nor has anything tangible resulted from their efforts.[97] And these voices are atypical, as in general the private bar has been relatively silent on the issue.[98]

Judges also have direct experience with the shortcomings of criminal law, but they may not want to mobilize for change. At the state level, judges are typically elected, so they face all the same pressures as elected legislators and executives to appear tough on crime. Indeed, there is evidence that their average sentences get harsher the closer they are to reelection, which demonstrates their sensitivity to appearing sufficiently tough in criminal cases.[99]

Appointed judges have more political insulation to speak out, though they may be constrained by ethics rules. Some, however, have been quite vocal on the need for change. Former federal judge John Gleeson, for instance, attracted significant attention for issuing opinions decrying mandatory harsh sentences.[100] He also sought to use his judicial authority creatively to promote reintegration of former offenders into society by establishing a reentry court in his district and urging other districts to follow suit, by seeking to expand expungement of convictions from criminal records, and by offering a novel federal "certificate of rehabilitation" to a former defendant.[101] Other judges have urged change not through their opinions or official judicial actions, but in separate writings. Judge Jed Rakoff has written articles and given speeches broadly criticizing the criminal justice system in an effort to draw greater attention to the issue.[102] Retired federal judge Nancy Gertner has also spoken out against mass incarceration in similar forums.[103] Several state supreme court justices have recently used some form of an annual "state of the judiciary" address to criticize broken justice systems.[104]

But when these judges speak, they speak for themselves and not for a consensus view among judges. Some judges prefer longer sentences and a tougher response to crime. This is especially true given the high numbers of former prosecutors on the bench.[105] Moreover, even if a large group of judges could agree on a course of action—such as more judicial discretion in sentencing—there is very little that judges can offer politicians in return for favorable legislation. They cannot deliver dollars or votes in the same way traditional interest groups can.

Racial justice groups represent one of the most promising sources of reform, but the politics are complicated. For most of the tough-on-crime era, these groups were muted. In large part, this is because they have not been of one view on how to address crime and violence. These groups must also contend with multiple missions that might be compromised if they place too great an emphasis on criminal justice reform, an issue that traditionally was far less popular and did not garner as much sympathy from the

broader public as racial justice issues involving law-abiding citizens.[106] As
Michelle Alexander, author of *The New Jim Crow,* has explained, civil rights
advocates have generally pursued issues of racial justice that evoke sympathy and defy stereotypes, which unfortunately has meant that issues involving individuals entangled with the criminal justice system have been
left out.[107]

This is starting to change, particularly as police shootings of unarmed
individuals have sparked a broader concern with how people of color are
treated by the criminal justice system.[108] Mass incarceration has been en-
veloped in this broader conversation, and some racial justice groups are beginning to give this issue a much greater focus. The NAACP Legal Defense
Fund, for instance, has advocated for federal sentencing reform, citing the
need to "ameliorate the harsh impact of draconian sentencing laws on communities of color."[109] The Leadership Conference on Civil and Human
Rights, a coalition of civil rights groups, has also made sentencing reform
and other criminal justice issues—including alternatives to incarceration
and reducing barriers to prisoner reentry—top legislative priorities.[110]
Grassroots advocates, like the Black Lives Matter movement, secured sit-
down meetings with presidential candidates and have directly influenced
local elections, including the successful defeat of prosecutors who failed to
bring cases against police officers who killed unarmed civilians, as Chapter 8
details.

Racial justice groups are not alone in drawing attention to these issues.
Interest groups across the political spectrum have in recent years started
to push for criminal justice reform. In 2014, the Open Society Foundation
gave $50 million to the American Civil Liberties Union to support state-
based campaigns targeting mass incarceration.[111] The ACLU's push for
state-based reform includes ending the war on drugs, reducing sentences,
and promoting alternatives to incarceration.[112] Individuals motivated by
religious convictions and a belief in redemption are also interested in criminal law reform, as are those with libertarian leanings who believe in
fiscal restraint and smaller government.[113] Right on Crime, for example, is
a conservative group that shares the ACLU's policy goal of reducing over-
incarceration. In fact, the two groups—along with the NAACP, the Center
for American Progress, Americans for Tax Reform, and others—formed a
working alliance in 2015 called the Coalition for Public Safety to pursue a
reduction in incarceration.[114] A similarly diverse group of funders is bank-
rolling the group: the Ford Foundation, the Koch Foundation, the MacAr-
thur Foundation, and the Laura and John Arnold Foundation. While the
groups and funders may have different reasons for coming together—some
focus on the need to rein in ballooning state corrections budgets, whereas

others see the reduction of incarceration as part of broader civil rights goals and structural changes—they share a concern with excessive incarceration and irrational punitive policies. Prominent individual voices across the political spectrum have likewise raised concerns with the fiscal and social costs of criminal justice policies and the need for rationality.[115]

The Limits of Progress under Populism

The rise of these groups pushing against excess criminalization and incarceration has resulted in some progress in turning the tide of ever-harsher criminal justice policies. After a steady rise for decades, the total number of people incarcerated began dipping slightly in 2009. Between 2009 and 2013, the population in prisons and jails dropped 3.4%, amounting to a decline of roughly 77,000 people.[116] Thirty-nine states have seen a decline in their prison populations from their peak populations.[117] One might think that if we just wait long enough, these groups will ultimately succeed in bringing more significant reforms. But that wait will be a long one, even assuming nothing slows down or cuts against the current pace. It will take 75 years to cut our prison population in half at the current pace, and there are reasons to doubt we will even get to that point with the current approach because the lowest-hanging fruit of reform will dissipate before then.[118]

Moreover, most of the drop in population came from two sources. The bulk of the reduction in state prison populations (40%) occurred in California after a Supreme Court decision ordered the state to reduce its population because overcrowded conditions prevented the state from providing adequate medical and mental health care, leading to cruel and unusual conditions in the facilities.[119] The other major reduction came from the U.S. Sentencing Commission, a bipartisan agency located in the judicial branch, where I served as a commissioner from 2013 to 2018. In 2014 the commission reduced the sentencing guidelines for many federal drug trafficking offenders and retroactively applied those reductions.[120] More than 30,000 people ultimately obtained retroactive sentencing reductions, for an average reduction of 25 months off their sentence.[121] Going forward, the changes will help reduce federal prison beds by 80,000.[122] It is notable that both of these large-scale reforms took place outside the normal political process, which relies on elected officials. A federal court and an independent agency took the lead on these efforts, and that is the kind of institutional shift that is needed to get substantial changes, as Part Three will further explain.

If one looks solely at the changes from the regular political process, the achievements have been far more modest, with a much smaller dent being made on the prison population.[123] Almost all the reforms have been to reduce imprisonment for what political scientist Marie Gottschalk calls the "non, non, nons—that is, the nonserious, nonviolent, non-sex related offenders."[124] But those offenders make up only 32.4% of the prison population.[125] To put a strategy that targets only the "non, non, nons" in perspective, even if we legalized all drugs—a highly unlikely prospect given how dangerous some are and the public's view of them—we would still have, by far, the highest incarceration rate among Western nations.

And the actual changes in the law affecting the "non, non, nons" have been far less ambitious. Consider, for instance, Oklahoma's recent sentencing reform efforts. In April 2016, Oklahoma made commonsense, yet minor, adjustments to its sentencing laws: allowing certain nonviolent crimes to be charged as misdemeanors instead of felonies, lowering some drug trafficking mandatory minimums, increasing the use of drug courts, and raising the minimum damage required for something to be charged as a felony property crime from $500 to $1,000.[126] Oklahoma's governor Mary Fallin claimed these sentencing changes would "control costs and reduce incarceration rates," and the conservative advocacy group Right on Crime called them "comprehensive criminal justice reforms" to "right-size [Oklahoma's] prison system."[127] While these reforms are sensible improvements, no one should be fooled into thinking that they will have a meaningful impact on Oklahoma's incarceration rate, which became the highest in the nation in 2018.[128] Oklahoma's prisons are currently operating at 123% capacity, yet staffed at only 60% due to budgetary shortfalls, two statistics that, taken together, earn Oklahoma the distinction of the highest prisoner-to-staff ratio in the country.[129] The April 2016 reforms, however, do little to address the existing incarcerated population. Oklahoma's interim director of the state's department of corrections admitted as much, saying that these four reforms amount to merely "nibbling around the edges" of the problem.[130] He lamented that the prisons are "overcrowded and the criminal justice system keeps cramming [people] into bed space that doesn't exist."[131] "Until we start readjusting our criminal justice code," he warned, "this is going to continue."[132] He also estimated it would take years before such reforms would have any meaningful impact on Oklahoma's overall costs of corrections.[133]

Louisiana provides another example of how reform efforts fall far short of having a significant impact on the overall sweep of criminal law. Its legislature recently passed a criminal justice package that the Executive Director of the ACLU of Louisiana claimed was a "landmark reform to [the state's] broken criminal justice system," including lowering sentences for theft and burglary and eliminating some mandatory minimums, making individuals with drug felonies eligible for food stamps and other welfare benefits, giving judges greater discretion to reduce or waive fines for formerly incarcerated people who cannot afford to pay them, and allowing people in prison to earn good time credits more quickly by participating in educational and drug treatment programs.[134] These reforms, like Oklahoma's, deserve praise. But they should not be mistaken for the kinds of changes that will make a dent in Louisiana's incarceration rate, which is the second highest in the country.[135] Many of the proposed reforms for people convicted of violent crimes were removed from the final legislation package,[136] thus rendering about half of the state's prison population ineligible to benefit from any of the policy changes.[137] In total, these reforms are estimated to reduce the prison population by just 10%, which will still leave Louisiana with an incarceration rate that is higher than just about every state in the country.[138]

Georgia, too, has gained widespread publicity for "leading the nation with meaningful justice reform."[139] The state's many reforms include increased educational programming for prisoner, restoring access to food stamps and other public benefits upon release, and preventing state licensing boards from requiring one to disclose a criminal history.[140] Despite these praiseworthy initiatives, the state's harsh sentencing laws remain largely intact, and the state's prison population decreased only 6.5% over Governor Nathan Deal's first four years in office, leaving Georgia's incarceration rate among the highest in the country.[141] A vivid example of the limited promise of these reforms is Georgia House Bill 328, which took effect in July 2015; one provision aims to give drug dealers originally sentenced to lengthy mandatory minimums under Georgia's harsh habitual offender law an opportunity for parole.[142] The law applies to individuals with an impeccable behavior record after serving at least 12 years of their original sentence.[143] Again, while a notable improvement, the reform itself is actually quite limited in scope.[144] With its current requirements, the reform will apply to approximately 50 people, but there are more than 50,000 currently incarcerated in Georgia.[145]

These examples are emblematic of what we are seeing in states around the country and what is being touted as reform.[146] Some states have eliminated criminal penalties for low-level marijuana offenses, but they retain a harsh approach to other drugs or to the distribution of larger quantities of marijuana.[147] Juvenile offenders have also been the subject of some reform efforts, but here, too, the changes have been incremental, with some states cutting back on the use of life without parole sentences for juveniles, but not changing the approach to juvenile crime more generally.[148] States have also targeted reentry as an area for reform by changing their expungement policies and authorizing "certificates of rehabilitation" for some offenders, but collateral consequences of convictions remain sweeping for most people convicted of a felony.[149]

Federal efforts, apart from the Sentencing Commission's changes, have been even less substantial. Legislative changes to reduce federal sentences have been rare. An exception was when Congress reduced the disparity between crack and powder cocaine sentences in 2010 with passage of the Fair Sentencing Act.[150] That law still maintained a ratio of 18-to-1 between the two drugs, and the change was not made retroactive, so thousands of offenders remain imprisoned under the previous 100-to-1 ratio. And other federal legislative efforts to lower mandatory minimum sentences for drug trafficking stalled, despite some bipartisan support and their modest reach. President Obama's administration was more active with executive action but still cautious in its efforts.[151] Attorney General Eric Holder announced a "Smart on Crime" initiative in 2013 aimed at reducing the federal prison population. The initiative included a new charging policy for federal prosecutors to limit the use of mandatory minimums in drug trafficking cases to those involving gangs or organized entities, or for those who engaged in violence.[152] Obama also restored Pell Grants for some prisoners as part of a pilot program, but correctional institutions themselves must apply to participate in the program and many restrictions apply.[153] The president also granted sentencing commutations to a record number of individuals serving long sentences for drug offenses.[154]

But even under President Obama—who was specifically interested in criminal justice reform and went so far as to pen a law review article documenting his achievements in criminal justice in his last month in office— there was widespread resistance to change.[155] Although he granted commutations to a relatively large number of people compared to his immediate predecessors, his overall grant rate for clemency (including pardons) was not significantly higher than those who came before him.[156] Moreover, he had a record number of denials—including of people who met his stated criteria for clemency.[157] The Obama administration was also reluctant to give compassionate release to federal prisoners, with the result that many people died of terminal illnesses in prison.[158] His administration failed to improve those practices even after scathing reports by the independent Inspector General of the Department of Justice.[159] The Obama administration did not agree with the Sentencing Commission that all federal drug offenders should be eligible for retroactive sentencing relief and would have categorically barred more than half the people who ultimately received sentencing reductions from ever going before a judge to ask for relief.[160] So the biggest achievement at the federal level largely took place in spite of the position of the Obama Department of Justice.

There has been similar political resistance at the state level to calls for broader relief. For instance, a trio of 2015 reforms in Maryland to lessen marijuana penalties, limit civil asset forfeiture, and restore voting rights for ex-felons were all vetoed by Maryland's governor, who cited advocacy by law enforcement unions to justify his opposition.[161] Even when a state manages to pass reform legislation, subsequent budget debates can derail the effort. This was the case in Indiana, which reformed its justice system to provide treatment instead of incarceration for many low-level offenses, only to fail to fund those reforms in later years.[162] And successes are often paired with failures. Texas, for instance, has been held up as a model of bipartisan criminal justice reform, but while a recent legislative session generated some reform victories, several other bills were rejected, including legislation to raise the age of adult criminal culpability from 17 to 18 and to set up a needle exchange program.[163]

More critically, not all the changes to criminal justice policies through the political process in recent years have been to lower sentences or reduce the reach of the penal system. On the contrary, in spite of our record-high levels of incarceration and the unprecedented reach of criminal law, we still see calls for increasing punishment and extending criminal law to new areas. Eleven states saw an increase in their prison populations from 1999 to 2014.[164] Responding to a burgeoning increase in heroin use, several states have increased punishments for crimes involving heroin.[165] The one-way ratchet of increased sentences for sex offenders shows no signs of stopping: a 2014 bill signed by Florida governor Rick Scott imposed a 50-year mandatory minimum sentence for felony sex offenders with a single previous sex offense.[166] In response to high-profile gun violence, states have increased mandatory minimum sentences for certain gun crimes.[167] At the federal level, the Department of Justice under President Obama sought to expand the prosecution of corporate wrongdoers, particularly in the wake of scandals in the automobile industry, and the Trump administration's Department of Justice, along with some congressional Republicans, have sought increases across a range of crimes, including immigration and synthetic opioids.[168]

And it is still the case that a single highly publicized crime can set back broad-scale, well-thought-out reforms. Consider the case of Wendell Callahan, who received a retroactive reduction of his federal drug sentence and upon release was arrested for committing a triple homicide. Senate Republicans have used the case as evidence against federal sentencing reform of drug penalties.[169] Similar phenomena threaten state reform. Following the murder of a police officer in New Mexico, for instance, the state legislature pivoted from a proposal to restrict the state's "three strikes" sentencing policy to one that would expand it.[170] More broadly, some commentators worry that a spike in homicides in some urban areas might derail state and local criminal justice reform efforts.[171]

So although there has been some rollback in imprisonment because of a growing number of forces speaking out against mass incarceration, their achievements have been slight and have come nowhere close to tackling the record high levels of incarceration in the United States. Strong political and psychological forces remain decidedly in favor of long sentences and an expansive criminal state—even when doing so is best characterized as pathological. If reform is sought directly through the political process, it will achieve only so much before running up against these political forces.

7

INSTITUTIONAL
INTRANSIGENCE

ONE MIGHT WONDER why it has only been in the past few decades that the United States has taken a punitive turn far sharper than anything in our history—one that sets us apart from the rest of the world in terms of incarceration rates. After all, the underlying political dynamics that produce excessive punishment have been evident from the nation's early days. The public's concern for security, and the incentives for elected officials to show responsiveness to it, are nothing new.[1] The Framers themselves foresaw that the political process might produce excessive criminal laws. As Alexander Hamilton wrote in *Federalist* No. 74, "The criminal code of every country partakes so much of necessary severity, that without an easy access to exceptions in favor of unfortunate guilt, justice would wear a countenance too sanguinary and cruel."[2] That "necessary severity" comes from the retributive impulses of the population and its representatives responding to the worst crimes without thinking about all the cases the letter of those laws will reach and how mitigating circumstances might call for a different outcome. The English philosopher and utilitarian Jeremy Bentham made similar observations, noting that "legislators and men in general are naturally inclined" toward "undue severity" because of "antipathy, or a want of compassion for individuals who are represented as dangerous and vile." As a result, he argued that greater precautions should be taken against excessive severity, as opposed to leniency, because it is on the side of severity that "there has been shown the greatest disposition to err."[3]

If the political pressures for severity have been present from the country's very beginnings, why has it been only in the past few decades that our incarceration rate has exploded to levels that are orders of magnitude greater than anything that came before? Changes in crime rates and social unrest are part of the story, with the shift to punitiveness and mass incarceration starting in response to a large uptick in violent crime and an upheaval in the social order in the 1960s. But the rates of incarceration continued to climb even as crime leveled off or declined and as riots and social unrest abated. So although crime rates and disorder help explain the initial impetus toward severity in the 1970s, they cannot explain the steady and virtually unending march of increased incarceration that we continue to witness and that seems impervious to actual crime rates or danger.

This chapter focuses on critical institutional shifts from the past few decades that have locked in place tough-on-crime dynamics by removing critical checks that previously existed. The Framers constructed a constitutional architecture to guard against pathological politics, but their design assumed a world of criminal trials and a simpler body of laws that no longer exists. Prosecutors have come to dominate decisions about criminal justice policies, but unlike the rise of other executive actors in the administrative state—where the challenges to traditional constitutional principles were obvious and met head-on with other protections—the rise of the modern criminal state was met with no substitutes to check excess. The result has been a framework commanded by prosecutors and a weakening of other forces to act as a check against them. It is this institutional setup that makes real criminal justice reform almost impossible unless the institutions themselves change.

Traditional Checks on Excessive Government Punishment

The centerpiece of our constitutional government is its system of separated powers and checks and balances. As James Madison stated in *Federalist* No. 47, "The accumulation of all powers legislative, executive and judiciary in the same hands, whether of one, a few or many, and whether hereditary, self appointed, or elective, may justly be pronounced the very definition of tyranny."[4] The concern with consolidated powers is at its apex in criminal cases, where the threat to liberty is greatest.[5]

The Framers thus put in place numerous constitutional protections to prevent government overreaching in criminal matters. Article I is aimed at preventing Congress from exercising judicial or executive powers in addition to its legislative powers. Article I directly prohibits Congress from passing bills of attainder that target specific individuals for punishment.[6] This safeguard, as the Supreme Court has noted, is "an implementation of the separation of powers, a general safeguard against legislative exercise of the judicial function, or more simply—trial by legislature."[7] Article I also prevents Congress from passing ex post facto laws to avoid "arbitrary and potentially vindictive legislation."[8] This, too, "upholds the separation of powers by confining the legislature to penal decisions with prospective effect and the judiciary and executive to applications of existing penal law."[9] Article I further limits Congress from suspending the writ of habeas corpus because of its importance in checking arbitrary imprisonments.[10] This provision checks the legislative branch from encroaching on the judicial function.

The Framers did not simply place limits on legislative powers; they also armed the other branches with powers to check against legislative overreach. Article II gives the president a broad power to grant clemency—either with outright pardons or commutations that reduce sentences—for all federal cases except cases of impeachment.[11] This power, which sits alongside the commander-in-chief power, is one of the cornerstones of executive power. Congress has no authority to control it because it serves as a crucial check on Congress itself.[12] James Iredell argued at the North Carolina ratifying convention that clemency allowed the executive to cabin overbroad general laws because "it is impossible for any general law to foresee and provide for all possible cases that may arise." Clemency allowed a correction for the "many instances where, though a man offends against the letter of the law, . . . peculiar circumstances in his case may entitle him to mercy."[13] The Framers knew this dynamic well because English criminal law in the 18th century "err[ed] on the side of severity," and pardons often served as a crucial corrective.[14] Thus, as Alexander Hamilton emphasized, "the benign prerogative of pardoning should be as little as possible fettered or embarrassed."[15]

Clemency not only checks legislative excess but also allows the president to control his subordinates in the executive branch. As the Supreme Court has explained, clemency "afford[s] relief from undue harshness or evident mistake in the operation or *enforcement* of the criminal law."[16] It allows the president to check prosecutors in the executive branch who overstep. Presidents have used the clemency power to express their disagreement with charging decisions and policies of prior administrations, as well as prosecutors serving during their own time in office.[17]

The Framers' preoccupation with providing safeguards in criminal cases carries over to Article III, which vests the judicial actors—judges and juries—with critical tools to protect defendants from government overreaching. Article III mandates that the trial of all crimes must be by jury, giving the jury a critical role in the Constitution's checks and balances. Juries, as Judge Learned Hand put it, "unlike any official, are in no wise accountable, directly or indirectly, for what they do" and "introduce a slack into the en-forcement of law, tempering its rigor by the mollifying influence of current ethical conventions."[18] Their unreviewable power to acquit allows them to prevent legislative and executive overreach in particular cases.[19] Harvard Law School dean Roscoe Pound called the jury's checking function "the great corrective of law in its actual administration."[20]

Although federal judges are part of the government structure and there-fore not as independent as juries, they are designed to be insulated from the other branches, and they serve a critical checking function as well. They have life tenure and salary protections so that they will not fear reprisal based on their rulings, giving them a degree of independence to protect rights against majoritarian overreach. Justice Antonin Scalia argued that the "most significant role" for judges is "to protect the individual criminal defendant against the occasional excesses of th[e] popular will, and to preserve the checks and balances within our constitutional system that are precisely designed to inhibit swift and complete accomplishment of that popular will."[21] The Constitution vests judges with enforcing the constitu-tional protections for criminal defendants, from the limits on Congress in Article I to the many rights for individuals in criminal cases set out in the Bill of Rights.[22]

Many constitutional protections apply not only to the federal govern-ment, but also to the states. The Supreme Court has gradually applied most of the rights contained in the Bill of Rights against the states through the 14th Amendment's Due Process Clause. The notable exceptions to incor-poration are the Fifth Amendment's right to an indictment by grand jury and the requirement of a unanimous jury.[23] Other constitutional rights apply to the states even without due process incorporation. The prohibi-tions on the passage of bills of attainder and ex post facto laws are expressly directed to the states in Article I.[24] And while the president's pardon power only applies to federal offenses, every state constitution includes a provi-sion calling for some sort of clemency procedure.[25]

While the Constitution provides the cornerstones for checking govern-ment excess in criminal cases, traditionally many other mediating devices operated alongside the constitutional protections. Soon after the nation's founding, the United States shifted to a model of criminal justice that was highly individualized and placed great discretion in judges to formulate ap-propriate sentences for defendants. Parole officials could similarly reduce sentences that proved to be too long.[26]

For much of America's history, these checks worked together to keep the country on par with other democracies in terms of the incarceration rate and the scope of criminal punishments. All of these institutional checks rest on the notion that policy-making at the legislative level requires adjustments to account for important case-level specifics. To put it another way, they embrace the idea that the excesses of populist judgments, which by their nature are general and at a wholesale level, must yield to the consideration of the facts of individual cases.

The Checks Diminish

When the tough-on-crime era began in the late 1960s, this institutional balance broke down. Criminal codes expanded everywhere, giving prosecutors a greater menu of possible charges to bring. Through the 1970s and 1980s, legislators began to take on a greater role in sentencing by imposing mandatory minimum sentences, requiring judges to follow specific guidelines, and eliminating parole.

This created a huge shift in the balance of power in criminal matters. The checks provided by judges and parole officials weakened considerably or disappeared as a result of efforts like these. Prosecutorial power concomitantly increased. As legislators rushed to pass more and more laws to show their symbolic concern with crime, prosecutors could choose from a greater range of possible charges to file or threaten to file. As separation of powers scholar Liz Magill has explained, "Given that the range of possible enforcement actions under criminal laws . . . is extremely broad, it is the prosecutors' pattern of decisions that shape the meaning of law, not the underlying statute itself." As a result, "decisions by prosecutors about how to enforce a statute are indistinguishable from lawmaking."[27] Prosecutors thus effectively started to consolidate both executive and legislative powers.

Prosecutorial power became greater still because prosecutors' charging decisions also often dictated someone's sentence if the sentence was preset in a mandatory guideline regime or with a mandatory minimum statutory sentence, thus vesting them with a form of judicial power. Defendants who thought they were overcharged could no longer count on judges to provide a mediating force at sentencing because judges' hands were tied. Nor was parole available in many places to recognize changes in defendants or their circumstances or to act as a check on excessive sentences by judges. Moreover, the greater severity of punishments gave prosecutors more leverage to extract pleas because the sentences defendants risked at trial became substantial. While plea bargaining existed as a sub-rosa practice for most of the nation's history, the official stamp of approval by the Supreme

Court in 1971, along with the vastly increased leverage the new legislative landscape gave prosecutors, led to astronomical increases in the rates of cases settled outside of trial beginning in the 1970s.[28]

The cumulative result of these shifts is that prosecutors combine legislative, executive, and judicial powers under one roof—the very definition of tyranny that the separation of powers was designed to guard against.

Critically, this state of affairs could not come to pass without acquiescence from the judicial guardians of the separation of powers. In other areas of constitutional law, the Supreme Court has made it clear that the government cannot put a price on an individual's exercise of a constitutional right. Thus one might think that a prosecutor's threat to bring charges that carry a much greater punishment similarly places an unconstitutional condition on a defendant's right to a jury trial. For most of the nation's history, plea bargaining largely took place in the shadows precisely because of concerns that it was not a legitimate practice even if the participants had an interest in supporting it.[29] With crime rates and criminal cases skyrocketing, stretching already limited judicial resources, the Supreme Court explicitly accepted plea bargaining as the new normal, even if it stood in sharp tension with the rest of the Court's unconstitutional conditions jurisprudence and seemed to put an unlawful price on the exercise of the jury trial right.[30] The Court has placed almost no limits on what prosecutors can threaten if a defendant turns down a plea deal, as long as there is evidence to support the threatened charges.

The Supreme Court has also taken a cramped view of the Eighth Amendment outside of death penalty cases, further strengthening prosecutors' hands by allowing them to seek ever harsher sentences.[31] Although the Court has used the Eighth Amendment to strike down a defendant's sentence as disproportionate in a small number of cases, the Court in recent decades has generally taken a far more limited view of what the Eighth Amendment requires.[32] A majority of the Court has embraced the view that the Eighth Amendment imposes only a "narrow" proportionality principle in noncapital cases.[33] In particular, since 1991, the Court has required an individual challenging a particular sentence on Eighth Amendment grounds to make a threshold showing that the sentence is grossly disproportionate to the crime, a test that requires the challenger to show that the state has no "reasonable basis for believing" that the sentence will serve any penological goal.[34] Thus if the state reasonably believes that the sentence serves either deterrent, retributive, rehabilitative, or incapacitative goals, the sentence passes constitutional muster. Commentators have rightly pointed out that this test gives states virtually a free pass to impose whatever punishments they want, because just about any sentence can be justified based on one of these theories of punishment.

Looking at just a few of the sentences the Court has upheld using this test proves the point. The Court condoned a mandatory life sentence for a defendant who committed three separate low-level theft offenses that cumulatively totaled less than $230.[35] It upheld a mandatory life sentence without parole for a first-time offender charged with possessing 672 grams of cocaine.[36] The Court permitted a 25-years-to-life sentence under California's three-strikes law for an individual whose third strike was the theft of three golf clubs worth roughly $1,200 because the defendant had a record of prior offenses, including burglaries and a robbery.[37] In another three-strikes case, the Court allowed a 50-years-to-life sentence for an individual whose criminal history contained no violence and whose three strikes consisted of a petty misdemeanor theft and two separate incidents where he stole a total of nine videotapes worth $150 from Kmart.[38] While the Court has softened its stance somewhat in cases raising categorical challenges to life without parole sentences in cases involving juveniles, it has yet to engage in more scrutiny of the government in other noncapital cases.[39] The result is that the Eighth Amendment fails to act as a check on prosecutors and government overreach.

This one-two punch—legislatures arming prosecutors with a choice of charges and severe mandatory sentences and the judiciary giving them unlimited license to use harsh sentences as leverage to extract pleas—virtually knocked jury trials out of the system. In the federal system, those who go to trial face sentences three times as long as those who plead.[40] It is thus no surprise that 97.1% of convictions in the federal system are the result of pleas.[41] At the state level, 94% of felony convictions are the result of pleas, and those who go to trial similarly face significantly longer sentences, with a mean maximum sentence imposed on state felony convictions after trials of 78 months compared to 29 months after pleas.[42]

With jury trials a rarity, one of the Framers' central checks on government excess lost its mediating influence. Although plea bargaining takes place in the shadow of a jury trial—because the defendant's bargaining chip is his or her ability to threaten to take the case to trial—there are many reasons why the possibility of a jury trial does not exert a large pull on the process. As legal scholar and now judge Stephanos Bibas explains, a variety of factors distort the bargaining process, including attorney competence, compensation, and workloads; information deficits; and a variety of psychological considerations, including "overconfidence, denial, discounting, risk preferences, loss aversion, framing, and anchoring."[43]

The new normal in criminal law administration over the past four decades is thus a regime dominated by prosecutors, with almost no role for judges or juries in policing them. Congress and state legislatures now promulgate criminal statutes for a world in which plea bargaining is the overwhelming default mode of operation. Legislators pass statutes with high statutory maximum penalties and mandatory minimum penalties to give prosecutors the leverage they need to induce guilty pleas—not necessarily because they believe those penalties should be the actual punishments imposed. We now have an endless cycle in which legislators continue to have incentives to pass excessive laws and prosecutors have incentives to ask for them. And no other institutional actor is currently positioned or willing to stop this dynamic.

But it is even worse than that. The decline in the judiciary's role (juries and judges) in criminal cases and the corresponding rise of prosecutorial power has been the most fundamental shift in the balance of powers in criminal law, but it is not the only one. Other checks have atrophied as well. As noted, many jurisdictions eliminated parole, thus removing another important check after someone has been charged and sentenced. Recall that clemency, too, has fallen into desuetude. Clemency relies on elected leaders—the president or a governor—exercising their discretion. But those elected leaders feel the same political pressures as others, so they have become reluctant to give anyone a break out of fear that person might go on to commit another crime.

The result is an institutional arrangement that essentially places prosecutors, with their powers not to charge or to pick from among a range of charges, as the only firewall against excessive legislative judgments. Defendants can argue the merits of their cases before prosecutors in the hopes of convincing them that certain charges, while technically available, would nonetheless be excessive in a particular case.[44] But those pleas will be made to people with a stake in the proceeding and no guarantee that they will take an unbiased view.

Prosecutors are thus an imperfect and incomplete check on legislative excess. In most jurisdictions, head prosecutors are elected, so they will typically have an incentive to bill themselves as tough on crime. And because local jurisdictions do not pay for prisons, which are funded by the state, prosecutors are not internalizing the direct costs of their choices. To the extent that long sentences are themselves criminogenic because they make reentry difficult, prosecutors are unlikely to think about that, either, because the link is too attenuated and hard to explain in an election cycle. Thus their usual incentives are to pursue tough policies with little regard for the downsides of that approach. Economist and legal scholar John Pfaff has recently shown that a significant part of the increase in incarceration in the last few decades comes from an increase in prosecutorial decisions to pursue felony charges.[45]

Even when a lead prosecutor is appointed, instead of elected, they lack the proper incentives to push back against legislative excess because they still work in a highly political environment. The U.S. attorney general is appointed, for instance, and yet for decades the Department of Justice has taken the position that prosecutors either must or typically should charge the most serious readily provable offense.[46] This guidance fails to acknowledge that the executive should exercise discretion when laws go too far.[47]

Whether appointed or elected, prosecutors lack an incentive to push back because they have a vested stake in maintaining things as they now exist—with a wide menu of charges from which to choose, with mandatory sentences that give them leverage to extract pleas, and with almost no oversight. They stand as poor stewards to see whether the overall working of the administration of criminal law furthers public safety and maximizes limited public resources because they have too much to lose if it changes. They possess all the power in the current institutional arrangement and no incentives to let that power go.

No Check on Irrationality

In some ways, the administration of criminal laws in the United States mirrors the administration of any number of other regulatory laws: an executive agency is chiefly responsible for administering broad statutes and giving them content by its enforcement decisions. That describes not only how prosecutors' offices administer criminal laws, but also how we handle environmental law, securities regulation, consumer protection, telecommunications, and a host of other issues. The agency is the adjudicator in these disputes, deciding what sanction is appropriate.[48]

But there are fundamental differences between the administration of criminal law and the administration of civil regulations. As an initial matter, the politics tend to be different in the two spheres. In a typical civil regulatory context, there are powerful interests on both sides of the issue. If anything, in many civil regulatory areas, the regulated entity has disproportionate power to block laws that it views as too sweeping.[49] This is the well-known phenomenon of regulatory capture, and it is arguably present across a range of issues because the interests subject to regulation are well-financed and organized.[50] No one would argue that criminal defendants—the target of criminal regulations or laws—are able to exercise much if any influence. Instead, in the criminal context, the regulators—the prosecutors—hold the power because legislators are only too willing to give them whatever authority they need to fix any instance of under-regulation.[51] If prosecutors want broader laws or longer sentences, they almost always get their way. In contrast, while civil regulators win some battles in other contexts, they often lose or have to settle for watered-down versions of their requests.

Even if the politics were not so lopsided in criminal law, however, there would be significant differences between the administration of criminal laws and the administration of civil regulatory laws. Regulatory agencies expressly recognize that they are performing more than ministerial tasks when they administer the laws. They are often expressly charged with promulgating rules and making policies. And they know that they are also charged with making policy judgments when determining which laws to prioritize and how best to use limited enforcement resources.[52] Prosecutors, in contrast, tend to see their professional role quite differently. They tend not to recognize that they make policies (even though they do) through their charging practices. You will often hear them say their job is simply to enforce the laws on the books, when in fact their exercise of discretion gives shape to that law (and even though prosecutors and their professional associations often lobby legislators directly to shape the content of the law itself).[53]

Another significant difference between regulatory agencies and prosecutors is that there is an entire body of administrative law that exists to police civil regulatory agencies and their decisions. Civil agencies must use impartial adjudicators who are institutionally separated from agency employees responsible for investigation and prosecution.[54] Anyone at the agency who is responsible for adjudicative decisions is prohibited from having ex parte contacts about the merits of a proceeding. The Administrative Procedure Act imposes various process requirements when agencies take actions against individuals, including giving interested parties notice and an opportunity to present evidence and arguments and to log exceptions to tentative agency findings.[55] When an agency proceeds in a formal proceeding, it must issue a decision on the record with a statement of findings and conclusions.[56]

Prosecutors' offices are under no obligation to provide any kind of process to individuals during plea bargaining, even though that is the final adjudication for all but a tiny percentage of cases that go to trial. Misdemeanor cases are run like an assembly line of take it or leave it offers, with defendants lacking any practical ability to challenge prosecutor decisions.[57] Felonies are not much better. The same prosecutor who investigates a case can make the final charging decision and determine what plea to accept.

There is no separation of executive and adjudicative power. Defendants have no right to any formal process within the office. The prosecutor is not obligated to allow a defendant to present evidence in his or her defense or to refute or dispute prosecutorial claims at the bargaining stage. During plea bargaining, prosecutors can engage in ex parte contacts with witnesses or the police or other investigators, and prosecutors do not need to share with the defendant information on which they are relying. Defendants have no right to an internal appeal up the chain of command within a prosecutor's office to dispute a charging decision or plea offer. Prosecutors never need to explain why they offered a particular sentence to one defendant but refused to do so for another similarly situated defendant. Transparency is woefully lacking in prosecutors' offices, so most defendants usually do not even know what other similarly situated defendants have been offered or if prosecutors are diverging from office policies.[58] While the formal trial process is heavily regulated by constitutional provisions, the plea bargaining process—the real site of criminal decision-making for all but a small percentage of cases—is left entirely to the prosecutor's discretion.

The role of reviewing courts is also starkly different in the criminal and civil contexts. Courts review civil regulatory agencies to make sure their policies are rational and not arbitrary and capricious. Agencies must explain why their approaches are consistent with their governing statutes. If they change course from one case to another, they must explain why they are doing so and support their decision in the record.

In contrast, judicial review of prosecutors (and criminal justice policies in general) has been almost nonexistent. "In the ordinary case, 'so long as the prosecutor has probable cause to believe that the accused committed an offense defined by statute, the decision whether or not to prosecute, and what charge to file or bring before a grand jury, generally rests entirely in his discretion.'"[59] Prosecutors rarely need to explain their policy choices or enforcement priorities or decisions. Although prosecutors' offices often change their enforcement policies, those shifts are neither public nor subject to review to make sure there is a reasoned basis for the new approach. When courts evaluate pleas to make sure they are knowing and voluntary, the process is a cursory rubber stamp—a far cry from the hard look courts take at agency decisions.[60] Although it is theoretically possible to bring a claim for vindictive or selective prosecution on "an unjustifiable standard such as race, religion, or other arbitrary classification," the hurdles for doing so are so high that almost no one prevails in even getting discovery, much less succeeding on the underlying claim.[61]

The result is that prosecutors escape scrutiny for their enforcement choices. The judiciary does not review their choices, and the political process takes little interest because the vast majority of the electorate, who are unaffected by prosecutions, pays little attention. And because the Supreme Court has all but abandoned Eighth Amendment oversight of sentencing decisions in noncapital cases, the resulting punishment also escapes scrutiny. "Without judicial oversight to speak of or any internal constraints, the potential for arbitrary enforcement is high."[62]

Other oversight mechanisms fail to pick up the slack. Civil regulatory agencies face oversight from other executive actors.[63] At the federal level, the Office of Information and Regulatory Affairs makes sure that the benefits of agency regulations outweigh the costs and that less expensive alternatives have been considered.[64] No such review is in place for prosecutors. And with parole gone and clemency a nonstarter in many jurisdictions, no other executive actor takes a second look at prosecutorial decision-making in individual cases, much less undertakes an analysis of the way in which the broader policies are operating and interacting.

Legislators cannot be counted on to oversee prosecutors any more than prosecutors can be counted on to check legislators. Because of the politics of criminal law, legislators, like prosecutors, fail to take an interest in or assess the costs and benefits of particular policies. Instead, they focus only on the benefits of long sentences and severity, without recognizing the trade-offs. They do a poor job assessing risk trade-offs, often opting for policies that appear to satiate a short-term retributive impulse (whether it is longer sentences, a lack of programming in prison, or disallowing public benefits on release) but that over the long term increase the risks of crime.

What is needed to check these flaws is a different institutional actor that can assess the bigger policy calls and check them for irrationality. In the civil regulatory field, institutional designers have long recognized the need for this kind of check. The administrative state is based on the idea that legislators are not well suited for making detailed policy calls and that experts in a field can produce better substantive decisions, guided only by the general instructions of the legislature about the basic goals. Congress thus leaves it to the Federal Communications Commission to set the nation's communication policies with only the vague instruction to further the "public interest, convenience, and necessity."[65] While Congress gave the Environmental Protection Agency more details, it nevertheless leaves the specifics of environmental policy to the agency's expertise. These agencies are then policed by the courts and various administrative law doctrines to make sure their judgments are rational and justified.

This model is not completely foreign to criminal law. Starting in the 1980s, many jurisdictions created expert agencies in the hope that they would set criminal punishments based on the best knowledge available instead of the political winds of the moment. Those who designed these agencies, typically known as sentencing commissions, hoped that they would help insulate sentencing policy from the pathologies of the political process. Senator Ted Kennedy, one of the leading backers of the creation of a federal sentencing commission, emphasized that such an agency was necessary because it was not "likely that Congress could avoid politicizing the entire sentencing issue."[66] A key staffer who helped draft the law creating the federal commission echoed this motivation, noting that "a Congress caught up in the politically volatile issues of law enforcement and crime control would be unable or unwilling to avoid the temptation to increase criminal sentences substantially."[67] But more than half of the states have no sentencing agency to temper the political forces in favor of harsher laws.

And even when a sentencing commission is in place, it is only responsible for sentencing. It does not set the policies for other critically important criminal justice issues, including charging decisions, crime definitions, reentry and collateral consequences, prison programming and conditions, or so-called second-look decisions that include parole and clemency and involve the reevaluation of an individual after he or she has served a prison sentence of some length of time.

Just about everywhere in the United States, most critical decisions about criminal justice policy are nothing more than highly politicized gut reactions. Most jurisdictions have collateral consequences of conviction set by statute, so the decisions are made by legislators without input from expert agencies or criminologists. The same is true for crime definitions. Charging decisions are the exclusive province of local prosecutors' offices for the most part, unaided by data or systemic analysis. Prison officials and probation officers might play a role in prison programming and reentry policies, but often these decisions are guided by past practice instead of current data or there is no money to do much of anything.[68]

Even where it still exists, parole is also influenced by political concerns. For most of the 20th century, jurisdictions used parole commissions to determine whether a defendant had been rehabilitated and could therefore be released. From the beginning, politics influenced these boards. Boards were traditionally composed of political appointees. Few standards governed the boards' decisions on whether to grant or deny parole; instead, boards looked primarily to the seriousness of the underlying offense.[69] Because there was no objective determination of "seriousness," decisions "were personal and therefore not subject to debate."[70]

These decisions did not receive much scrutiny until violent crime rates shot up and the public and politicians took greater notice of how the state was addressing crime. As crime in general has become more politicized, so have parole determinations. In the last 40 years, the growth of mass incarceration and heightened public attention to crime policy "have not been lost on parole boards." The resulting political pressure exerted on boards has become "immense," leading to "increas[ed] reluctance to release prisoners before the expiration of their maximum sentences."[71] Indeed, it is "not uncommon" for parole board members to lose their positions for making politically unpopular decisions.[72]

Clemency, too, is a highly political process that is rarely informed by data or part of a framework that relies on dispassionate expert assessments. In the past few decades, clemency rates have plummeted at the state and federal levels, with executive leaders unwilling to take the political chance that someone granted relief will go on to commit a highly publicized criminal act.

In the rare areas where agencies are operating in the criminal justice sphere, they tend to proceed unlike typical regulatory agencies. Just as prosecutors have avoided rationality checks on their policies, so, too have most of these agencies. Sentencing commissions typically escape traditional arbitrary and capricious review by the judiciary. Prison regulators face judicial review, but it is far more deferential than the review given to most agencies for their decisions.[73] In New York, for example, judicial intervention is warranted "only when there is a showing of irrationality bordering on impropriety."[74] Parole boards also receive little oversight. In California, judicial review is limited to determining whether there was "some evidence" supporting the parole decision.[75]

The consequence of this institutional structure is that the political forces described in Chapter 6 face almost no pushback in any area of criminal justice policy-making, either in individual cases or in assessing the overall rationality of any given policy, because critical checks to push against them have atrophied or disappeared. It is no surprise, then, that we have the bloated codes and prisons we have today because there is no one keeping an eye on this Leviathan to make sure it makes any sense. Any reform of criminal justice in America must therefore begin with institutional changes that address these shortcomings.

PART THREE

FOR THOSE AFFECTED BY MASS incarceration and the thousands of criminal laws and long sentences on the books, it is a cruel irony that we arrived at this point almost by accident. No central planner sat down to craft it as a solution to society's many ills. Indeed, we do not have anything remotely close to a central criminal justice system in the United States. We have 51 jurisdictions making criminal laws and more than 2,300 prosecutors' offices making their own decisions about how to enforce them.[1] Yet somehow these different sovereigns and government officials have all more or less coalesced around the same punitive policies.

To be sure, there is wide variation among states in incarceration rates and among localities in enforcement practices. Incarceration rates range from that of Oklahoma, which currently has America's highest incarceration rate of 1,079 persons for every 100,000 residents, to that of Massachusetts, which has the lowest rate of 324 individuals per 100,000 residents.[2] These rates reflect differences in various practices and policies, from how the jurisdiction treats juveniles who commit crimes to the way they charge recidivists. Nor is all the variation at the state level. Within each state, counties and districts differ from one another. For example, all of the executions since the death penalty was reinstated in 1976 have been carried out by only 15% of the counties in the United States.[3] Communities in southern states that have higher income inequality, a larger number of evangelists and fundamentalists, and/or higher crime rates are particularly punitive.[4]

This variation reflects the fact that the politics and institutions in different states diverge. But even Massachusetts would lead most of the rest of the world in incarceration, so American jurisdictions have more in common with one another than with most other countries when it comes to crime policies.[5]

Indeed, most of the various irrational policies described in Part One have sprouted up everywhere in the United States—sometimes with jurisdictions deliberately borrowing the same flawed ideas from other places. Political forces and emotional responses have taken charge throughout the nation, leaving any concern with rational evaluation to the side. Case by case, statute by statute, the carceral state metastasized, without anyone looking to see whether it made any sense overall or even policy by policy.

But it is not enough to point out the flaws. Reformers and critics have been shouting from the rooftops about many of the policies outlined in Part One, begging for reform. They are often shot down by the usual tough-on-crime rhetoric or dismissed as insufficiently attentive to public safety, even when the status quo is doing little to protect the public and often creates greater dangers in the long run.

The problem, as Part Two makes clear, is that the political system is not the right location for debating and addressing the flaws in criminal justice. The politics of fear take charge, and without institutional checks to inject rationality into the process and with prosecutors firmly in charge, we will continue to get the same irrational policies.

To get better outcomes, we need a better institutional structure and process. The Framers knew it. They worried that legislators would tend to excess, so they created significant constitutional checks for individual cases. But those checks are in disrepair. And even if they were working as intended, they would be insufficient because they tend to focus on checking abuses in individual cases and do not provide a safeguard against broader irrational policy decisions.

Because of the politics of criminal law, legislators often fail to assess the costs and benefits of particular policies. They focus only on the benefits of long sentences and severity without recognizing the trade-offs. They do a poor job assessing risk trade-offs, often opting for policies that serve a short-term retributive impulse to deprive offenders of some benefit (whether it is a lower sentence, programming in prison, or the opportunity for public benefits on release) but that over the long term increase the risks of crime.

The traditional checks of individualization do little to address these problems because the problem is at a higher level of policy-making. What are needed to check these flaws are different institutional actors that can assess the bigger policy calls and check them for irrationality.

The solution to the over-politicization of criminal law—and the corresponding lack of rational deliberation it brings—is thus to make sure that there are appropriate checks in individual cases *and* that there is better broadscale decision-making. The next three chapters take up the task of describing a better institutional model for criminal justice decision-making that insulates the worst self-destructive impulses of populism and injects rationality in the system so that public safety is maximized at the lowest cost and on the best available evidence. And it seeks to offer solutions that are feasible in the political environment we live in. Another way of achieving better outcomes would be to remove politics from the equation as much as possible, such as by eliminating elections for prosecutors and judges where they exist. But that kind of sweeping change is simply not feasible, at least in the foreseeable future. The reforms outlined here, in contrast, may also be difficult, but they are within the realm of the possible in the current climate of criminal justice reform. Although changes to policing practices should also be part of any criminal reform package, those issues merit their own book-length treatment, so I leave questions of policing policies and practices for others with the relevant expertise.

Chapter 8 begins by offering an administrative framework to replace the largely unchecked power that prosecutors currently exercise. No solution to criminal law's excesses can ignore the powerful role prosecutors play in the system, so one key is to reconceive that role and recognize its enormous power and scope—and then seek to make sure prosecutors exercise their powers rationally and responsibly. Voters have a big role to play here by electing district attorneys committed to more rational, data-driven decision-making instead of stale rhetoric about long sentences. While the punitive political dynamics discussed in Chapter 6 apply to district attorney elections, these local elections might be more likely to involve voters with more direct knowledge and experience with how crime-fighting strategies are working (or, more to the point, not working) in their communities. Thus a mobilized segment of this electorate can bring about change by electing district attorneys who are focused on real results instead of the usual tough-on-crime rhetoric that often yields poor outcomes for both crime and the people who live in these communities. But elections will only go so far precisely because the politics of fear and misinformation about crime policies is so entrenched, particularly when it comes to violent crime or people believed to be at a risk for violence. So other checks on prosecutors are needed, as well as other institutions to play a mediating role.

Chapter 9 explains the need for using an expert agency model to address criminal justice policy-making and to coordinate policies among key actors. These expert bodies should use empirical data and studies to guide their decisions about criminal justice policy to maximize public safety. At the same time, these agencies must be designed to withstand the political pressures they will inevitably face to adopt superficially tough, but actually ineffective, measures to address crime.

Chapter 10 then turns to the judiciary. The courts are critical checks on criminal law excess. At the federal level, the Supreme Court must reinvigorate the constitutional checks that already exist to police improper practices and to check excessive punishments. And at both the state and federal level, more attention needs to be paid to who occupies the bench. Currently, judges are overwhelmingly former prosecutors, making them particularly ill-suited to provide the meaningful second look of prosecutorial decision-making that is necessary to bring rationality to the system.

8

POLICING PROSECUTORS

MEANINGFUL INSTITUTIONAL REFORM must begin with changing the way prosecutors operate. They have all the powers of traditional civil regulators—and then some—but none of the checks designed to ensure they make rational, nonarbitrary decisions. This chapter explores a variety of needed reforms to improve the operation of prosecutors' offices in the United States. Many of the proposed reforms will sound familiar to anyone who deals with other regulatory and enforcement agencies because they are taken from the administrative law and policy realm. The United States has a long history of checking excess agency behavior, but those institutional safeguards have largely bypassed prosecutors. This chapter outlines how those traditional administrative law checks can be translated to fit the realm of criminal prosecution.

In addition, there is another way to check prosecutors in the United States that is not available in the traditional civil regulatory context: elections. For most of American history, elections have resulted in the failed policies discussed in Part One. Populist fears and impulses among the electorate create pressure on prosecutors to make ill-advised short-term decisions that end up compromising public safety in the long run, and few voters pay attention to anything other than the usual tough-on-crime campaign strategies, even when those policies produce poor results. While there is no denying this dynamic still exists, thus making electoral accountability an imperfect and incomplete institutional constraint on prosecutors, it is also true that in local prosecutor elections, voters tend to have more direct experience and information about how these strategies are playing out in their communities. A significant portion of the electorate—especially people of color, who have borne the brunt of the current policies—has seen the costs of these tough-on-crime strategies directly and knows that these methods are not the best option for addressing crime in their neighborhoods. In these elections, where turnout tends to be low, a mobilized subset of a community interested in a new model of prosecution has the potential to make a big difference. This chapter discusses how voters can better assess candidates for district attorney by focusing on metrics associated with public safety and fiscal responsibility instead of empty rhetoric that ends up being counterproductive. This is not to suggest that elections are the fix, because the political dynamics discussed in Chapter 6 are too strong and in many places will continue to yield the same kind of outcomes in prosecutor elections. But because that will not be the case everywhere if voters can get better information about actual public safety results, it is worth noting this as another possible check on prosecutors that can supplement the institutional changes that should be the first priority.

Bringing Administrative Law and Better Institutional Design to the Prosecutor's Office

Prosecutors' offices in the United States engage in both individualized enforcement actions and the setting of broader criminal justice policies. Unlike just about every other government agency, they face almost no oversight or scrutiny in either of these roles. The result is that they often pursue policies that are in their professional interest but not necessarily in the public interest. Although changing the way these offices have operated for decades will not be an easy task, if the momentum exists for any kind of criminal justice reform, it is ideally channeled to improve prosecutorial decision-making and to check prosecutorial abuses.

Let's start with prosecutorial policy-making. Prosecutors' offices throughout the United States play a key role in setting punishment policy in America. As discussed in Chapter 7, their control over charging and their leverage in plea bargaining effectively give them sentencing power. Their charging policies are thus some of the most important policy calls being made about criminal law in the United States today.

Even when prosecutors do not control sentencing outright—either by charging a statute with a mandatory minimum punishment or working out a plea deal with an agreed-upon sentence—they influence outcomes in cases because of the deference they receive from courts. Judges typically defer to their recommendations on bail and sentencing, thus giving prosecutors' own benchmarks about pretrial release and sentencing key policy influence.

Prosecutors often exercise control over other aspects of criminal law as well. The Department of Justice, for example, is an agency run by prosecutors that also sets policy with respect to forensics, corrections, and clemency, in addition to its policy calls on charging and sentencing. While most states use departments independent of their prosecutors to administer corrections policy and tend not to give prosecutors an official role in clemency, they often allow prosecutors to play a key role in setting forensic policies.[1] Even when prosecutors are not formally in charge, they influence many key policy decisions through their lobbying efforts.

So what can be done to improve the content of those policies, given that prosecutors' positions on criminal justice policies will inevitably be clouded by their self-interest in making their jobs easier, even if that comes at the expense of the broader public interest? One key institutional change is to make sure that prosecutors are not put in charge of areas outside their core law enforcement responsibilities. There is no reason prosecutors should be in charge of criminal justice policies that do not involve charging and prosecuting criminal conduct. Forensics, corrections, clemency, and other criminal justice policies should be made by individuals who do not have a conflict of interest in the substance of those policies, as prosecutors do. Prosecutors will inevitably view these issues through a prism of what would be good for them and their cases and will not be able to assess objectively other interests that conflict with their own. For example, commentators have observed that the Bureau of Prisons "has become captive to the Justice Department's prosecutorial agenda."[2] That explains why so few elderly or terminally ill individuals in federal prison get compassionate release even though they pose low recidivism risks, would ease up pressure on overcrowded prisons, and would save taxpayer dollars. Prosecutorial bias also accounts for various scandals at crime labs throughout the country where scientists had, in the words of one former lab director, too often viewed "their role as members of the state's attorney's team."[3] It also explains why local, state, and federal law enforcement organizations, including the Department of Justice and the National District Attorneys Association, resisted the findings of expert scientific panels on the need to change their practices with respect to forensic science. Prosecutors dismissed without discussion a National Academy of Sciences report documenting the flaws with current practices, urging the creation of an independent federal agency, and encouraging states to use independent administrative units to handle forensics because having forensics controlled by prosecutors and law enforcement could make them "subject to subtle contextual biases" and because "the potential for conflicts of interest between the needs of law enforcement and the broader needs of forensic science are too great."[4]

The broader literature on how agencies handle conflicting missions explains prosecutors' behavior. When agencies have multiple goals and they come into conflict, they adhere to their primary mission.[5] A law enforcement agency like the Department of Justice has a dominant mission of law enforcement and prosecution. Any other mandate—to set forensic policy, to run prisons, to administer a clemency process—will take a back seat to the main goal of pursuing what is in the interests of prosecutors as law enforcers.[6] Policy calls will thus be made with prosecution, and not other interests (including the public's), at the forefront. The solution to this conflict is to remove it by taking these policy decisions about areas other than charging particular cases out of the hands of prosecutors. At the federal level, for example, that means taking the Bureau of Prisons, clemency, and forensic science out of the Department of Justice and allowing independent experts to set those policies.[7] While prosecutors can weigh in on those issues, they should not be in charge of them. To the extent that any state follows a similar model of giving their prosecutors control of any of these policy areas, they, too, could create independent bodies to handle these issues. Indeed, that is why the National Academy of Sciences recommended separating any agency responsible for forensics from those in charge of prosecution and law enforcement. Empirical evidence and data should govern these decisions, and those facts should be evaluated by a neutral decision-maker, not by prosecutors who will be biased because of their desire to defend decisions they have already made or to choose policies that would make their burden of proof easier to meet even if the science says otherwise. Because prosecutors are elected in most places, their positions are likely to be tainted further still by what will hold up in campaigns, thus further corrupting their ability to make decisions objectively.

So a crucial first step in getting better outcomes is to remove all but core prosecutorial decisions from prosecutors. This is the kind of institutional change that is unlikely to garner the same kind of voter fear and opposition that surrounds substantive changes in criminal policy. To say the sentences for drug trafficking will be reduced is to set off the usual alarms about being soft on crime. But to say that a jurisdiction will establish an independent forensics commission to decide matters of science is not nearly as contentious. To be sure, vested interests (namely prosecutors) will object, but if there is enough momentum among reformers, this is the kind of structural shift that can get bipartisan agreement.

That takes care of the tangential policy portfolio that some prosecutors have, but what about those areas that will stay within the hands of prosecutors because they are a core part of their function? Prosecutors will inevitably make charging and sentencing policies. One key institutional check to improve prosecutors' decisions in these areas is for legislatures to allow other actors to check those decisions. That means eliminating mandatory minimum sentences or binding sentencing guidelines so that judges have the discretion to use their authority over sentencing to correct prosecutors that go too far. Just as agencies face judicial review of their decisions, prosecutors need to face judicial review of theirs. But if judges' hands are tied because a sentence is mandatory, they cannot perform their critical role as a check on excessive sentences.

This reform will be tougher to achieve than shifting institutional responsibility for policy decisions from prosecutors to other agencies because eliminating a mandatory sentence allows prosecutors to claim not just that they are losing a turf battle, but that sentences are being reduced and public safety is at risk. Indeed, that has been their playbook when jurisdictions have sought to roll back or eliminate mandatory minimum sentences. Prosecutors attack those proposing such changes as being soft on crime if they remove mandatory minimum floors. So this suggestion is not an easy one to accomplish. But to the extent this is feasible politically—because prisons are overcrowded and costs are too high, thus presenting a need for sentencing reform that is in the interests of legislators—it is a crucial check on and balance to prosecutorial decision-making. This is a substantive change that will have enormous institutional consequences because it will allow judges to check prosecutorial overreach.

Parole and clemency also serve as fundamental back-end checks on prosecutorial decision-making. People change over time, not the least because they age out of criminal behaviors, but also because people learn and develop. But prosecutors make their decisions before they know what the future holds. Without someone else in the system to take a look at how a person may have changed since he or she engaged in criminal conduct, the prosecutor's decision will be set in stone. So even if someone gets a sentence of decades, there will be no opportunity to revisit it. Prosecutors cannot anticipate how much someone will change, so lacking second-look mechanisms places too great a burden on their initial assessment. Having an active back-end review process that takes a look at how people change over time and their progress at rehabilitation is critical. This second look also allows decision-makers to take advantage of new knowledge, such as when we learn more about the relative danger of drugs or the science of juvenile brain development. Administrative agencies typically revisit their own decisions over time, rescinding and changing prior rules as new facts become known or as administrations change their political priorities. Prosecutors, in contrast, decide individual cases and then do not revisit those decisions, thus ossifying prior judgments even when the evidence would point in a different direction as time passes.

While some prosecutors may accept the idea of a back-end review process to assess rehabilitation and changed circumstances, many may object. So this kind of reform will likely face political obstacles in jurisdictions where it does not already exist or, where it does exist, if it is going to be used more robustly. But a system dedicated to promoting public safety has to reconsider sentences and the people who receive them at various points in time to decide what the appropriate course should be. At a certain point, as Chapter 2 explained, long sentences themselves become criminogenic because of the barriers to reentry they create. And while some criminal justice policies are hard to explain to voters, the notion that people change over time is not foreign to the average person. We see it with the people in our own lives, whether it is our children, our siblings, our friends, or anyone else we know over a period of years. To be sure, any one decision to release someone who goes on to commit a violent crime runs the risk of derailing second looks for everyone, and parole where it exists right now is often moribund precisely because of those risks and political pressures. While there is no magic bullet for that problem, Chapter 9 explains that there are better institutional designs for this process that can help improve them, such as the use of cost-benefit analysis to show the value in giving people a second chance, or prison-capacity caps to create the incentive to take those second looks because release is necessary to prevent overcrowding and strains on budgets. But there is no denying that the risk will always be there that one person's early release will create a firestorm that derails an entire second-look program. This fear may mean that parole and robust second-look review do not get off the ground in some jurisdictions. But as more formerly incarcerated people speak out and show through their own example how important it is to recognize the potential in people because of the contributions they can make to society, this may become more viable. It is a critical step worth taking, and those interested in changing the institutional dynamics discussed in Part Two must press for back-end review as a check.

Even with these institutional changes, prosecutors will still be making important policy calls about charging and sentencing. Sometimes an office will do so explicitly with formal guidelines or written rules about how to charge cases (for example, what quantity thresholds will trigger certain drug trafficking charges or requests for cash bail, or what factors make someone eligible or ineligible for diversion). Prosecutors should be held accountable for the costs of these decisions, including the impact those decisions have on jail and prison budgets.

When prosecutors make these judgments, they should be required to use the best available data in setting their policies and should face review. This can be done in a variety of ways. One option would be to place a cap or limit on how many or what share of state resources each local prosecutor's office is allowed to use so they do not "overspend" those resources.[8] Without imposing cost or other constraints, prosecutors will have an incentive to overuse prisons and jails to avoid the risk of being blamed if someone who could have been detained pretrial or given a longer sentence ends up committing another crime after release. Because prosecutors currently do not have to pay for the use of prison or jail resources, they have no incentive to think of them as scarce resources that should be reserved for people who commit the most serious offenses.

Another option for achieving this goal would be to require prosecutors to submit their policies to an oversight body within the government structure that is charged with reviewing those policies to make sure that they represent the most cost-effective option and that the costs of the policies are outweighed by the benefits. This kind of outside check can assure that the prosecutors' decisions are based on empirical evidence and not professionally risk-averse preferences to seek too much cash bail or prison terms that end up creating a greater public safety risk for society. A variant of this model is used in Washington, which has the Washington State Institute for Public Policy analyze its criminal justice policies to make sure they are cost-benefit justified.[9] The federal system also uses this kind of oversight for civil regulatory agencies. The idea behind a check like this is that it will give prosecutors the right incentives to use the best information out there and to maximize limited resources. Reformers should thus push for laws and oversight mechanisms that hold prosecutors accountable for the costs of their policies and to make sure they are choosing policies that maximize public safety given what we know about what works and what does not. Voters are always concerned with costs and public safety, so this is the kind of design change that is more easily accomplished than substantive changes to laws or sentences.

Often, however, prosecutors' offices will have no written policies or general guidelines about a particular issue. They may instead rely on informal advice by supervisors or veterans in the office about how to handle individual cases. To get better outcomes in the inherent policy decisions that guide case-by-case decisions, offices can make some structural changes. Currently, very little thought goes into how prosecutors' offices should be structured or what kind of oversight they should face. If prosecutors engage in poor decision-making, the only real check in most places comes at the ballot box when the head prosecutor faces reelection. Even if individual prosecutors misbehave—by intentionally or negligently violating the law—there are typically few consequences. It is almost impossible to bring a successful civil suit against a prosecutor because of the absolute immunity prosecutors enjoy for any conduct "intimately associated with the judicial phase of the criminal process."[10] Prosecutors are rarely sanctioned by state bars or by their supervisors, even when they engage in intentional misconduct (such as making a deliberate decision not to disclose exculpatory evidence to a defendant), and even when prosecutors repeatedly engage in misconduct.[11] What, if anything, can be done to yield better outcomes and to police prosecutors' individual decisions?

Administrative law again offers some insights. One concern posed by prosecutors is their ability to combine enforcement power with adjudicative power, as Chapter 7 explained. Because prosecutors can typically choose from a range of charges, some of which might have mandatory punishments attached, prosecutors have leverage to extract pleas and cooperation from defendants and thus control the ultimate outcome and sentence in a case. Their power to enforce thus turns into the power to adjudicate. This is a classic concern of separation of powers because it puts law enforcers in the position of judging their own cause. After spending time investigating a case and pursuing a particular defendant, it is too much to ask prosecutors to be impartial in deciding what should happen to that defendant because they develop a "will to win" that clouds their judgment.[12] This was a central concern of the administrative state because Congress was establishing agencies that combined enforcement and adjudicative powers. So Congress put in place internal separations within agencies to guard against bias. Specifically, the Administrative Procedure Act disallows "an employee or agent engaged in the performance of investigative or prosecution functions for an agency" from also participating in formal adjudicatory proceedings.[13]

Translated to the prosecutor's office, this means that a prosecutor who has been involved in the investigation of a case or who has obtained information about a defendant in a proffer session or in discussions with an investigative agent should not have final decision-making authority over what charges to bring or whether to accept or offer a plea deal. Charging and plea decisions are properly viewed as adjudicative because they effectively determine the outcome in cases.[14] It is also important to separate prosecutors who will represent the government in court (either at trial or in pretrial proceedings) from those who make charging and plea decisions because representing the government in court puts prosecutors in an advocacy position that is at odds with their role as impartial adjudicators. This basic framework—where an attorney involved in investigation or advocacy before judges is not involved with adjudicative decisions in a prosecutor's office—can be adopted in most offices because there are enough lawyers to make it work. Ideally, those individuals who make the adjudicative decisions about charging and pleas will be the people in the office with more experience because that longevity of service will give that person perspective on how any one case fits in with the larger caseload before the office and will also make any particular decision about a case less important to that attorney's overall record of decisions.

It is important not to oversell what this model can accomplish. Because everyone involved in these decisions will be a prosecutor and will be part of a larger team of people working for the same office, it can achieve only so much objectivity. Additionally, the prosecutor making the adjudicative decision will likely be getting most of his or her information from the prosecutor doing the investigation, so the setting will not parallel a court in terms of having both sides equally represented before a neutral party. But this setup is still preferable to a model that makes no effort at separating the different roles prosecutors assume in a case. Moreover, this is the kind of reasonable change in practice that should appeal to lead prosecutors. Some offices already do versions of this successfully, so its viability has been established.[15] And it serves the interests of lead prosecutors to exercise greater control of case management to ensure uniformity in how the office treats similar cases and to get unbiased assessments of how cases should be settled.

In the misdemeanor context, there are just too many cases to expect a division of labor or anything more than a few minutes for each case. But if substantive changes are made, such as the elimination of cash bail and limits on the pretrial conditions of release, prosecutors will lose some of the leverage that enables them to seek excessive amounts of confinement and supervision in these cases that end up undermining public safety.

Prosecutors' offices could make other internal improvements to check against abuses and further public safety. While many offices have the most junior attorneys screening cases at the outset to decide which ones should be dismissed and how they might be charged, those lawyers lack the experience to sift through cases as effectively as more experienced prosecutors. A new prosecutor might think everything looks serious or that all cases should be charged because they lack the perspective of having seen the overall caseload of the office for a number of years. Veteran prosecutors can more easily recognize the kinds of minor cases that should be dismissed or if particular defendants would be better served by treatment or diversion.

They also have more credibility and confidence if it is necessary to push back against police officers who might want more serious charges.[16]

Other mechanisms exist to guard against abuse by agencies that could be adapted to prosecutors' offices. Government agencies have long been subject to review by independent monitors to make sure that they are complying with the law and to improve their accountability. These monitors can take different forms, from inspectors general to internal affairs bureaus to civilian oversight boards.

Some prosecutors' offices already have oversight bodies such as these. The Department of Justice (DOJ), for example, is subject to oversight by the independent Inspector General (IG), and DOJ pursued some of its most significant reforms after prompting by critical IG reports. Inspector General Michael Horowitz, in particular, offers a model for how an oversight body like an IG can prompt valuable changes in the name of public safety. Horowitz did not see his role as limited to finding instances of misconduct or fraud, which is the typical IG model. Instead, he audited DOJ practices to find irrational policy decisions that resulted in the wasteful allocation of government resources that could not be justified as a matter of public safety. For instance, Horowitz highlighted the fact that overcrowded federal prisons took up a vast chunk of DOJ's budget and looked for ways to free up funds for corrections to use for other law enforcement needs.[17] He highlighted DOJ's flawed approach to compassionate release as one such example where DOJ could pass needed reforms to free up prison beds without compromising public safety. While DOJ did not adopt all his recommendations, it did change some of its practices and likely would not have done anything without his prompting. DOJ similarly responded with policy changes after critical IG reports on its use of private prisons and on BOP's failure to adequately prepare individuals for reentry.[18] Horowitz's influence shows that an IG charged with auditing policies to point out areas where resources could be more effectively allocated—and where those reports are public so that voters can see the areas that should be changed—can make a difference. To be sure, the right kind of person needs to be appointed IG, so it is helpful to get someone with an excellent reputation, strong investigative experience, a commitment to data and evidence-based evaluations, and the necessary independence from prosecutors to point out where their approach is flawed. But if reformers focus on getting these kind of oversight bodies in place and pay attention to the people who occupy the posts, they can be helpful advocates for reform.

A related model for reforming prosecutors' offices comes from the area of corporate misconduct and compliance. Companies and prosecutors' offices have in common conditions that give individuals incentives to cut corners to make their jobs easier and to show results (in companies because they want raises and in prosecutors' offices because they want to win their cases). Sometimes that means there are incentives to violate the law. Both contexts are also characterized by poor oversight or insufficient resources to monitor employee behavior, making it more likely that negligent violations will occur. Prosecutors have recognized the need to change company structures and incentives to stop misconduct and have used the leverage of criminal charges to get companies to agree to a variety of organizational changes to incentivize future compliance with the law. Those very same techniques could be applied to prosecutors' offices themselves.

The core idea is to "promote an organizational culture that encourages ethical conduct and a commitment to compliance with the law."[19] To achieve that end, organizations must make specific people responsible for compliance and ethics, and those people must report to other individuals at the highest levels of the organization. Thus, in a larger prosecutors' office, one of the attorneys could be put in charge of office ethics and compliance, and that person should report directly to the district attorney or a top deputy. In smaller offices, the district attorney should take charge of ensuring that the attorneys in the office are meeting their obligations.

To ferret out wrongdoing, an organization must monitor and audit activities to detect unlawful or inappropriate conduct. In prosecutors' offices, this means looking for things like compliance with disclosure obligations and monitoring prosecutors to check that they are not asking for excessive bail or threatening excessive charges or sentences to coerce guilty pleas. If the office finds such violations are occurring repeatedly or systemically, it can institute reforms to address the root cause of the problems. For example, if the reason prosecutors are failing to turn over exculpatory information is poor record-keeping within the office, the office can establish new protocols for keeping track of evidence and witnesses. If instead the office discovers that prosecutors are committing violations because they are unaware of their obligations or of office policies, the solution might be improved training, written guidelines distributed to all attorneys, or a staff meeting to discuss their duties.[20] Offices should also make clear to the public what they are doing to address violations and problems. This means publicizing their written standards and manuals and providing the public with information on how they have handled any discovered violation of the law. Offices should also have in place a reporting system so that employees can confidentially or anonymously alert the leaders of the organization when they suspect or know of wrongdoing by others.

A final key is to make sure the organization has the right incentives in place to reward ethical behavior and to sanction noncompliance with the law or misconduct. Office leadership should praise those attorneys who discover errors and disclose them and who pursue policies that promote public safety even when those policies look lenient. One hallmark of a successful conviction integrity program within a prosecutor's office, for example, is the praise it gives to those attorneys who discover and remedy wrongful convictions.[21] Offices cannot expect to promote ethical behavior if the only rewards and accolades go to those who get convictions or long sentences. They must also praise successful diversions from the criminal justice system, efforts to limit the number of people who are detained pretrial, assistance with someone's successful reentry into society, and any other instance of a prosecutor making sure that justice is done and public safety is prioritized.

Prosecutors will need to be pushed to adopt these institutional changes within their offices, as it will be the rare head prosecutor who opts to do this on his or her own. While some prosecutors may see the light on their own, most will need a nudge. Chapter 9 will discuss how another agency in government can help spark and oversee these kinds of changes, and Chapter 10 will discuss how courts can likewise provide such prompts. These will likely be the key sources to promote change. But voters also have the power to push these kinds of reforms by choosing prosecutors who are committed to policies that promote public safety instead of pursuing a tired and failed rhetoric of superficial toughness that locks people away only to release them far worse off than when they went in. The next section discusses how that electoral check could operate to encourage these changes even if doing so is likely to be an uphill battle because of the political forces described in Chapter 6.

Democratic Accountability

Most prosecutors in the United States are elected, so if they are not using their authority to maximize public safety or are otherwise behaving improperly, they can, in theory, be voted out of office. In practice, however, incumbents win a whopping 94–95% of the time when they are up for reelection. Most of the time, they do not even face a challenger. When races are contested, the candidates tend to focus on their own personal attributes or particular high-profile crimes and cases, not overall patterns or policies.[22] And as with most popular elections that touch on criminal justice issues, tough-on-crime rhetoric has been dominant.[23]

But some characteristics about these elections may allow more room for change. The candidates for district attorney are responsible for the single issue of criminal law enforcement. That means that voters do not have to rank various policy preferences in choosing a candidate who may represent a range of views that they like and do not like. They can focus solely on the candidate's approach to criminal law enforcement and criminal justice policies. And because the election is local, voters may have a better sense of actual crime rates and practices and how they affect their lives and communities. Thus if a significant portion of the community is unhappy with how these policies affect them, they could use their votes to get prosecutors who will implement better practices and policies.

In fact, we are starting to see just this dynamic, as decades of tough-on-crime policies are under scrutiny because of the mass incarceration and human misery they bring, particularly in communities of color, and because voters are questioning whether there is a better way. Incumbents are getting voted out of office if they are not sufficiently committed to reform, and when seats open up for new prosecutors, reformers are starting to win. This shift in local elections holds promise, though it is important not to overstate its potential.[24] Higher crime rates or even a single high-profile crime could turn the tide even in places where reformers have won. And while it has been progressive forces that have mobilized thus far to focus on these elections, it is perhaps only a matter of time before more traditional tough-on-crime voices rally on the other side. That said, precisely because so many of the policies prosecutors pursue undermine public safety, there is an opportunity to elect officials with a reform agenda grounded in superior practices when voters are better informed about the shortcomings of an incumbent.

Some criminal justice reformers have made a targeted effort to unseat incumbent district attorneys with troubling records. In many instances, the key triggering event was a prosecutor's deficient performance in addressing a police shooting of an unarmed citizen.[25] For example, in Cuyahoga County, Ohio, which includes Cleveland, the incumbent Timothy McGinty lost after failing to indict the police officer who fatally shot 12-year-old Tamir Rice.[26] The challenger, Michael O'Malley, all but conceded that his main attraction for voters was that "I am not Tim McGinty."[27] O'Malley did not have a broader reform agenda, so all the activism around that election centered on the Rice case.[28]

But in other jurisdictions, interest in the DA's handling of a police shooting served as an entry point to deeper scrutiny into the office's practices and criminal justice reform more broadly. For example, in Cook County, which includes Chicago, Kim Foxx successfully campaigned against the incumbent, Anita Alvarez, who had been widely criticized for her handling of the Laquan McDonald case, which involved an officer shooting a 17-year-old

that was captured on video and discredited the officer's claim that Mc-
Donald was a threat to his safety.[29] Alvarez failed to show the surveillance
video to the public for more than a year and released it only after a judicial
order required her to do so.[30] It was not until the video's public release and
the public outcry that followed that Alvarez finally brought charges against
the officer.[31] The protests surrounding Alvarez suggest that the election was
more about getting her out of office for her treatment of the McDonald
case than it was an affirmative embrace of Foxx. But Foxx ran a campaign
that went much further than distinguishing her approach to cases involving
officers shooting unarmed civilians; Foxx criticized Alvarez for creating a
culture in the office that was "tough on crime, as opposed to thoughtful or
smart on crime" and emphasized the need for reforming the office's approach to juvenile justice and bail.[32] Activists have warned Foxx that they
stand ready to oppose her at the next election and will be watching for her
not only to change the "culture of police impunity" but also to "cut off the
school to prison pipeline, end prosecutions for low-level drug possession
and work with us to create mass expansion of alternatives to incarceration."[33] So while a police shooting triggered an incumbent DA's fall in
Chicago, the activism around it has broader criminal justice goals.

One can see a similar storyline out of Harris County, Texas, which includes Houston. Kim Ogg unseated the incumbent, Devon Anderson, after
Black Lives Matter activists set their sights on defeating Anderson for failing
to hold law enforcement accountable after the death of Sandra Bland. Bland
had been pulled over for allegedly failing to signal when changing lanes.
Because she could not afford the $500 bail bondsmen fee, she was put in
jail, where she was found dead 65 hours later, hanging from a noose made
out of a garbage bag.[34] While Bland's death seemed to spark the initial
movement to remove Anderson from office, other criticisms emerged. Anderson came under fire for her decision to jail a mentally ill rape victim to
ensure her availability for trial, for her comments blaming Black Lives
Matter for the fatal shooting of an off-duty officer, and for the disproportionate number of death sentences sought by her office.[35] Thus, as was the
case in Chicago, the race became as much about the incumbent's broader
criminal justice policies as it was about the handling of law enforcement
misconduct. And Ogg was just as vocal as Foxx in asserting her desire for
broader reforms. Ogg acknowledged the "human toll" misdemeanor criminal convictions take and promised not to prosecute misdemeanor marijuana offenses.[36] She also emphasized the need for bail reform, calling the
current system "an unjust 'plea mill'" and a "tool to oppress the poor."[37]

The reform spirit also triumphed in St. Louis. When incumbent Jennifer
Joyce decided not to run for election, it set the stage for a crowded Demo-

cratic primary that included a challenger who received the endorsement of Joyce and the St. Louis Police Officers Association, which would be the traditional tough-on-crime endorsement that would signal victory.[38] But the primary also included Kim Gardner, who tried to appeal to voters eager for reforms to the justice system in the wake of Michael Brown's killing by a police officer.[39] Gardner won the crowded primary with 47% of the vote and went on to win the general election.

The tragic deaths of unarmed citizens at the hands of law enforcement thus served in these districts as canaries in the coal mine, raising larger issues about the need for reform in these offices. And the successful campaigns of the challengers demonstrate that with the right narrative to grab attention—in these cases, innocent lives lost after interactions with law enforcement—voters can be as moved about overaggressive but ineffective prosecutors who are too friendly to law enforcement as they are to narratives that focus on the fear of violent crime.

Importantly, the narratives that grab public attention about prosecutorial overreach do not have to involve police shootings for incumbents to lose elections. In some instances, incumbent prosecutors have been successfully challenged because of misconduct in their office. Kenneth Thompson, for example, beat incumbent Charles Hynes, who had held his office in Brooklyn for 23 years, in part based on allegations that Hynes failed to adequately investigate cases of wrongful convictions and on other claims of misconduct under Hynes's leadership.[40] Thompson unabashedly ran as a reformer, pledging not only to clean up the alleged misconduct under Hynes, but also work for racial justice and to combat excessive stop-and-frisk tactics by the police.[41] Scott Colom likewise defeated incumbent Forrest Allgood in the Sixteenth District of Mississippi, which encompasses Jackson, both by highlighting Allgood's pattern of aggressive prosecutions and his failure to investigate a wrongful conviction that received significant media attention. Colom also emphasized his own agenda to "find better ways to transition some . . . people out of the criminal justice system, or avoid the criminal justice system altogether."[42] In Nueces County, Texas, which includes Corpus Christi, a career defense attorney beat the long-time incumbent with a similar approach. The challenger, Mark Gonzales, proudly touted the "not guilty" tattoo on his chest and the fact that he has "more in common with my defendants than with my colleagues across the bar."[43] Gonzales's platform emphasized a plan to be smarter about charging decisions and the importance of turning over exculpatory evidence to defense attorneys in a timely manner.[44] Gonzales thus won by explicitly highlighting his reform agenda and by noting several cases of prosecutorial misconduct under the incumbent in which exculpatory evidence had been improperly withheld.[45] One can see the same blueprint in Hillsborough County, which contains Tampa, where Andrew Warren unseated the incumbent, Mark Ober, both by highlighting the incumbent's handling of a sex offense case involving a 17-year-old victim and by running his own progressive campaign that promised "a renewed focus on rehabilitation and reducing recidivism." Warren pointedly criticized Ober's approach as overly punitive and behind the times—or what he called "the rotary phone of criminal justice."[46] Another reform candidate, Aramis Ayala, likewise rode to victory in the wake of a scandal involving the incumbent. In the district that includes Orlando, Florida, the incumbent, Jeff Ashton lost his election after voters discovered he had signed up for the Ashley Madison dating site, which caters to married men and women seeking to have affairs.[47] Ayala's criticisms of the incumbent were broader than his personal moral failings. She criticized Ashton for pursuing racially discriminatory criminal justice policies and advertised herself as a reform candidate who understood the concerns of communities of color.[48] She noted her own husband's criminal record and her background as both a prosecutor and a public defender.[49]

It does not always take misconduct or a high-profile police shooting for prosecutor elections to be about reform. In Henry County, Georgia, Darius Pattillo won his election with the goal of "establish[ing] a pre-trial diversion program, a domestic violence/crimes against children unit, and a community outreach program."[50] In Bernalillo County, New Mexico, which has Albuquerque as its county seat, the two candidates vying for the DA position after the incumbent stepped down presented two different visions for voters: one emphasized his police officer background and pledged to be tough and no-nonsense, whereas the other, who ultimately won, emphasized that "being tough on crime doesn't mean we can't be smart on crime" and argued that "non-violent offenders need treatment and rehabilitation."[51] The primary race for district attorney in Durham County, North Carolina, focused on which candidate could best achieve criminal justice reforms, with Satana Deberry, an outsider with a criminal defense background, beating Roger Echols, the incumbent district attorney, who was a career prosecutor. Echols had instituted reforms in the office, but Deberry won by criticizing Echols for not going far enough.[52]

Larry Krasner represents the biggest win to date for a progressive approach to criminal prosecution. Krasner was a civil rights attorney who represented activist groups, including Black Lives Matter, and had sued the police 75 times. He won a crowded Democratic primary in Philadelphia with almost 40% of the vote on a platform of ending mass incarceration. He emphasized the need for abolishing cash bail, lowering sentences, and diverting individuals with drug problems to treatment instead of incarceration. His opponent in the general election, a career prosecutor, received the endorsement of the police union and chided that the city already had a public defender's office and didn't "need the district attorney to be a second."[53] Yet Krasner emerged victorious, demonstrating the willingness of voters to upend the status quo under the right electoral circumstances. Krasner himself observed that a big part of the reason for his win was that the black voters in Philadelphia "are more likely to have a family member who is a police officer, a family member who is in jail, and a family member who has been killed or severely victimized. They are more likely to have seen this whole thing in three dimensions."[54] These voters, in other words, were informed enough to know that a "tough on crime" campaign was ineffective and that a better approach was needed.

This reform-minded approach does not always work. For example, a well-financed challenger to the incumbent DA in Denver lost after campaigning with a promise to end mass incarceration and to "stop incarcerating non-violent drug users."[55] But the fact that an appeal to reforms and a dismissal of tough-on-crime rhetoric as simplistic and ineffectual has worked in many places of late shows that prosecutors could be accountable through elections for policies that are too harsh, costly, and ineffective.

The key is to identify what made these challenges work. In many cases, the Black Lives Matter movement and affiliated groups have been key ingredients for unseating incumbents in several jurisdictions. Krasner had huge support among movement activists, as did Foxx.[56] Some of the activist groups focused their efforts on negative campaigns against incumbents without endorsing alternative candidates, whereas other groups not only protested against incumbents but also affirmatively supported challengers. The political organizing group Color of Change, for example, supported Foxx and has also focused on helping challengers win races in Columbus, Cincinnati, Tampa, and Houston.[57]

Those interested in reform of prosecution practices would do well to continue to get movement activists interested in problematic prosecutorial practices. While a prosecutor's failure to pursue a police shooting case in many of these instances has correlated with other problematic practices, there are countless jurisdictions with troublesome practices that have not yet been scrutinized because no high-profile police shooting or case of wrongful conviction brought the office into the public's eye in the same way. Those who care about prosecutorial reform thus need to be as focused on practices that needlessly promote mass incarceration as they are on police misconduct, and must encourage prosecutors to follow policies that reduce crime, maximize limited state resources, and pose the least amount of damage to communities and individual liberty interests.

Another critical takeaway from successful reform elections is that they were often fueled by campaign donations by people who are interested in criminal justice reform. The most notable contributor has been liberal billionaire George Soros, who has in many cases contributed millions to races that ordinarily seldom exceed five-figure fund-raising.[58] Krasner, for example, received more than a million dollars of funding from a Soros-backed group. In at least two instances, Soros's injection of financing prompted a competing candidate to drop out of the race.[59] Of the first 10 candidates Soros supported, only two failed to unseat the incumbents.[60] But Soros is not the only one funding challenges. Kim Foxx in Chicago received sizable donations from, among others, the Civic Participation Action Fund, the Service Employees Union International, and a local millionaire known for backing Democratic initiatives.[61] Kim Ogg in Houston received funds not only from Soros, but also from a Democratic trial lawyer.[62] The political action committees Color of Change and Real Justice are also getting involved in district attorney races.[63] Regardless of who supplies the funds, the key is that, with enough financial support to get out their message, challengers have been able to win on progressive agendas.

The Right Metrics

It is not enough to get reform-minded prosecutors elected. Criminal justice reformers and activists must police and monitor these newly elected prosecutors and other prosecutors claiming a more progressive, "smart on crime" agenda to make sure they really are performing well. As Stanford law professor David Sklansky points out, one key to this effort will be to have transparent metrics that allow outside groups and reformers to assess prosecutorial performance.[64] Traditionally, prosecutors have touted guilty verdicts in high-profile cases or their own qualifications in their election campaigns, and the public's focus has largely remained there.[65] But these markers say little about whether a DA's office is working well overall to reduce crime and recidivism.

Other metrics do a better job alerting voters to whether a prosecutor's office is working optimally to serve the public interest.[66] Crime rates would be obvious markers of how well an office is doing to improve public safety. But because crime rates are a factor of many different variables beyond law enforcement—including the overall economic health of a district, the strength of its schools and economic opportunities, and the quality of its medical care—it may not be appropriate to hold prosecutors accountable for factors outside their control. So although crime rates might be considered, they will be a rough measure of prosecutor efforts because so many other factors affect them.

Another key indicator could be the jurisdiction's incarceration rate (both pretrial detention and for those serving sentences after convictions). We know jurisdictions can reduce crime rates or keep rates low and reduce incarceration rates at the same time, which saves taxpayer dollars. Here, too, though, we have the problem that prosecutors in any one district are not solely responsible for the incarceration rate in a state prison because other prosecutors in the state are also contributing to that rate. But prosecutors could be assessed on how much their prosecutions cost voters in terms of the number of prison years served by defendants charged by the office.[67] If those costs are going up, that should be of concern to voters. Moreover, because prosecutors are typically responsible for local jail populations, those incarceration rates are a direct measure of their decisions. Thus, prosecutors seeking reelection can thus be assessed on whether incarceration rates in jails are going up or down. For those seeking office for the first time, prosecutors can explain their plans for decreasing jail admissions, such as through an abandonment of or sharp reduction in requests for cash bail.

There are additional metrics that could be used to assess prosecutors' direct efforts to lower crime rates and incarceration rates. For example, prosecutors could be pressed to explain their strategies for reducing crime rates, and particularly those crimes that cause significant harms and may have low clearance rates within a community. Nationwide, the police solve on average fewer than half of all crimes involving physical violence; while more than 59% of murders are solved, only about 37% of rapes and 30% of robberies are.[68] And those are averages from across the country. In some communities, the rates are even worse. For example, the murder clearance rate in Chicago for the past three years has been less than 30%.[69] These failings are not distributed equally. A Washington Post analysis of the 52 largest cities found that "black victims, who accounted for the majority of homicides, were the least likely of any racial group to have their killings result in an arrest," with someone arrested in 63% of the cases where the victim was white but only in 47% of the cases where the victim was black.[70] While these rates and disparities are largely a measure of policing, prosecutors can help improve those rates by urging police officers to focus on investigating homicides and other more serious cases, regardless of the race of the victim, instead of devoting resources to low-level cases that require little effort. Thus prosecutors can be assessed on their efforts to get police to devote their resources more effectively. If prosecutors stop charging the minor cases police bring in, that will help create more pressure on police departments to focus on bigger cases and problems.

Recidivism rates are another key metric for assessing prosecutors. Like crime rates more generally, this is another variable that is affected by multiple factors outside prosecutors' control. But we know that various prosecution decisions affect recidivism and reentry, so we can use those decisions as metrics that directly capture what prosecutors are doing to improve reentry outcomes.[71]

Prosecutors can first affect reentry at the front end of a case with decisions they make about bail, charging, and diversion. Prosecutors can improve recidivism results by supporting the elimination of cash bail and not seeking bail for those individuals who are not at high risk of flight or of committing a violent crime. All too often, people who pose no risk to the public but cannot afford bail are held because prosecutors reflexively ask for it. Because they are held pending their trials, these individuals lose jobs, child care, educational services, and other connections to their community. This pretrial detention makes them more likely to commit crimes later because their lives have been so disrupted. A prosecutor concerned with public safety should recognize this risk and allow more people to be released pending trial unless a validated risk tool shows they pose a serious risk of violence or of flight. Prosecutors should use a tool that does not rely on factors such as education or employment, which can have a disproportionate impact on the poor and on communities of color. To be sure, criminal history is the key ingredient in any validated risk tool, and it can also have a disproportionate impact on these same communities because of the way they are policed. But it is still preferable to use a validated risk instrument that uses criminal history as a predictor than to use the gut instincts of prosecutors and judges, who also rely on criminal history but do so with implicit biases and without a strong track record of predicting public safety risks. A validated tool such as the one developed by the Arnold Foundation both lessens racial disparities compared to the individualized decisions by judges and prosecutors and improves public safety outcomes.[72] Indeed, for those reasons, prosecutors should push for the use of risk assessments instead of money bail with their state legislatures. New Jersey, for example, switched to this model and now uses risk-assessment tools to make pretrial release determinations so that low-risk and moderate-risk defendants are released with few monitoring conditions, while only high-risk defendants are kept in jail pending disposition.[73] The switch away from money bail and toward risk assessments saves money, reduces recidivism and risks, and maximizes human liberty. It is the kind of policy that makes sense on any measure, and prosecutors have no reason not to support it.

Prosecutors can also be assessed on whether they are seeking to improve safety outcomes by removing more low-level cases from the system entirely by not prosecuting them and by using diversion programs in more serious cases to target underlying problems, such as drug use or mental illnesses, which make individuals more likely to commit crimes. Diversion programs should not be used as a net-widening device, to bring more people into the system who previously might not have been charged at all. Rather, those programs should be used to help get at underlying problems in more serious cases. Because so many individuals who commit crimes are themselves victims of crime, prosecutors can also make sure they are getting the services they need to address trauma. Prosecutors should collect data on these programs to make sure they are using ones that work and can make adjustments if needed.

Prosecutors can also help with reentry outcomes by considering whether their charging decisions will trigger collateral consequences that may later harm an individual's reentry prospects. This consideration may counsel against certain charges because the collateral consequences are too severe and deleterious to public safety.

Prosecutors should also pay more attention to what happens to criminal defendants while they are in prison and when they get out, and voters should assess prosecutors on that basis. If the goal is maximizing public safety, prosecutors need to make sure that prisons are offering the kind of programming that will aid people when they reenter society. This means educational programming, cognitive behavior therapy, job training, and drug treatment. Prosecutors are not finished with cases once an individual is convicted. As the chief law enforcement official in a jurisdiction, they should be on the front lines making sure that defendants have reentry plans and educating the public and relevant members of the community about how important it is for these individuals to get housing, jobs, and educational opportunities. Today, they are often seen lobbying for longer sentences or mandatory minimum terms of imprisonment or opposing anything that seems to reduce sentences. This makes sense if they are only thinking about their professional self-interest because they want greater leverage over defendants to get cooperation and guilty pleas. If prosecutors care more broadly about public safety, they should be lobbying for changes that will improve reentry outcomes.

All these metrics should be front and center for any reformer seeking change through prosecutor elections. They need to support those candidates who want to bring about real change and who possess the management and administrative skills to achieve it. Although a sizable portion of the electorate is likely to be swayed by the most punitive approach being offered, if reform candidates can get enough voters to give them a chance, they may make the best case for themselves by producing real results. That is, because the facts and data are on their side—so many reforms promote public safety as well as racial and social equality—it may be possible to push back against the worst populist impulses that are based on voter misperceptions about what works.

Reformers have the edge right now because they are focused on these elections, and the voices in favor of a more punitive approach have not targeted these elections in the same way. At some point, we may see money getting funneled to tough-on-crime candidates to compete, so it is unclear whether the current model is transitional and we will ultimately go back to the dynamic where the seemingly tougher candidate wins. But district attorney races are local and tend to have a low turnout, so those with the most intense preferences will likely win. Right now, the people who have personally experienced the shortfalls in the system (such as those Philadelphia voters that Krasner described) care the most, and as long as that continues, they can mobilize for significant changes. But the whims of the electorate are no replacements for the structural changes outlined above and in the two chapters that follow.

9

ENGAGING EXPERTS

ONE KEY THEME THAT EMERGES from Chapters 1 through 5 is that we could be doing a better job with criminal justice policy-making if we made better use of empirical studies and if we looked at our existing policies carefully and objectively instead of reacting quickly and emotionally to adopt policies without much thought to their details. The problem, though, is that the political process is not set up to pay that kind of close attention to data and is instead always going to be responsive to whatever hot-button issue is dominating the news cycle. We have recognized this dynamic in countless areas of American life and in many cases opted to take a different approach and allow individuals with expertise to fill in the policy details so that we get better results. That is why we have the administrative state we do. It is long past time to use a similar model for criminal justice policies. We need to establish expert agencies charged with instituting and evaluating criminal justice policies so that we get better outcomes, and those agencies need to be designed smartly so they do not fall victim to populist impulses.

Chapter 8 explained how we can get better outcomes from prosecutors by taking a page from administrative law and policy because changing the way prosecutors operate and are checked is a critical first step. But it is only a first step to real institutional reform because prosecutors, while important, do not cover the entire criminal justice landscape. For starters, they are responsible only for the cases within their jurisdiction. There are more than 2,300 prosecutors' offices throughout the country,[1] and there is very little coordination or oversight of what they do at the state or federal level. So even if progressive prosecutors are installed in some communities, those who operate in a business-as-usual manner in other jurisdictions will be unaffected. Second, prosecutors can only deal with criminal justice policy as it relates to specific cases, except in their role as thought leader or someone who seeks legislative change. While prosecutors are an important lobbying influence, all too often they have used their influence to enhance their own powers and discretion, even at the expense of the system overall. Although Chapter 8 discussed some strategies for changing that—including trying to elect prosecutors who seek out real reforms to improve public safety— inevitably we will have prosecutors (even self-proclaimed progressive ones) who put their professional interests first, which in many cases will mean a continued push for excessively punitive laws. They may agree to more progressive positions in some areas but resist change in any area that would make their jobs harder to perform.[2] Third, prosecutors often lack the necessary expertise to know what does and does not work across a range of criminal justice options. While they often believe they are experts in public safety, they are not criminologists or social scientists who study these issues on a regular basis. When they decide policy questions, it tends to be from their own experience as prosecutors, uninformed by broader data or empirical analysis. So while it is important to change the way prosecutors function to improve how they handle the vast number of cases that fall within their jurisdiction, that will not be enough to address the pathologies we currently see because prosecutors have institutional limitations that prevent them from seeing or implementing all the needed reforms in the system.

No matter how much progress we make with prosecutors, we will still need another institutional actor or actors with the relevant expertise and access to data and empirical information to coordinate and oversee criminal justice policies throughout a state or at the federal level. This body should be charged with analyzing all criminal justice practices to make sure they are promoting public safety and that the state (or federal government) is pursuing the least costly and least liberty-restrictive alternative to achieve a particular end. For example, if a jurisdiction wants to pursue imprisonment but a drug treatment program could achieve the same public safety results at a lower cost and without unnecessary confinement, that treatment program should be used.

There are two crucial premises behind this idea. The first is that criminal justice policy has to be more coordinated than it is now. It makes no sense for a state to spend money on prisons but not subsidize other options that might be more effective and cost less, like drug treatment.[3] Nor does it make sense to allow local actors to decide how state prisons should be filled without oversight, because inevitably the local actors will end up overusing them because they do not pay for them. Economists label this an externality problem, and Franklin Zimring and Gordon Hawkins coined the phrase "the correctional free lunch" to describe the specific externality problem that exists when localities get to use prison resources without paying for them.[4] David Ball has shown that the rate at which localities send people to prison bears no relationship to their violent crime rates.[5] To fix this mismatch, institutional changes must force local decision-makers to internalize all the costs of their choices, including the costs that accrue to the state. Thus some state actor is needed to coordinate decisions by local district attorney offices in order to put pressure on them to make decisions with an eye toward these costs. This could be done in a variety of ways, including by imposing caps or rationing access to the number of prison beds a local jurisdiction can use proportionally based on the locality's violent crime rate; charging localities for their proportional share with adjustments for the levels of crime or violence in their communities; or using some kind of system of block grants to local communities so they could allocate the resources most efficiently and not simply reflexively rely on prisons when other options make more sense.[6] However this is achieved, the need for some kind of coordination is necessary to get better outcomes.

The second premise behind this recommendation for expert oversight is that empirically valuable information on criminal law can lead to better decisions. And by better, I mean decisions that improve public safety and human lives at a lower cost. Part of the reason we have arrived at a point where 8% of Americans have a felony conviction and 1 in 3 people have a criminal record is that no one has paused to consider whether it is good policy to use criminal law this much.[7] We have not subjected our sentencing policies or laws to any kind of expert or rational analysis to determine if we are overspending on punishment or if our resources could be better spent on other measures to improve public safety. Of course we do not know everything about crime control through studies and data, but we can learn quite a bit from data and empirical study. We can learn what is and is not cost-effective and whether there are cheaper and/or less liberty-infringing ways to achieve the same public safety outcomes.

To be sure, expert analysis cannot definitively answer what kind of punishment someone deserves in a retributive justice sense. If all we are doing with criminal law is making gut-level moral determinations about the just deserts for particular crimes, then the model I propose is not as useful. The American people and their representatives may be just as qualified as any expert to decide what seems like a commensurate punishment for any given crime based on their notions of right and wrong and morality. That said, even in a system geared toward retributive goals, there is a role for experts and the courts because the irrationality of the political process often means that universally agreed crimes of greater seriousness end up punished less severely than less serious crimes because of disproportionate media attention to particular issues or a lack of attention to how broadly laws will apply, as Chapters 1 and 2 explained. Some kind of expert oversight could help address those inconsistencies even in a system that concerned itself only with retributive justice. But experts are especially valuable if the goal in using criminal law is to improve public safety, maximize limited public resources, and make sure policies are not being arbitrarily and discriminatorily applied. The average American citizen is not on equal footing with an expert who studies the data in achieving these goals. Put another way, when it comes to public safety and maximizing limited resources, there is such a thing as expertise that can improve decision-making.

Several commentators have noted that criminal law has shifted in recent decades to a system of aggregate regulation designed to prevent future criminal conduct instead of traditional individualized punishment. Berkeley law professors Malcolm Feeley and Jonathan Simon termed the shift "the new penology" and described the transition as one "from a concern with punishing individuals to managing aggregates of dangerous groups."[8] It is a regime designed for "safety management."[9] Harvard law professor Carol Steiker observed a similar dynamic when she called attention to the "preventive state."[10] Other commentators have found this regulatory dynamic working in the mass processing of misdemeanor cases and the use of various risk instruments.[11] And of course politicians, prosecutors, voters, and others involved in the political process emphasize public safety as the main goal of criminal laws.

To the extent that this is what we are doing—seeking to promote public safety and prevent harm in the most cost-effective way—we can do a better job. Part One outlined many areas in need of improvement to better advance public safety, reduce unnecessary confinement, and save limited resources. The problem is that right now we fail to harness the information that is out there on what we can do better because we leave those decisions largely to the political process and populist impulses, which are often self-defeating when it comes to improving safety outcomes. To get better policy outcomes if safety is our goal, we need to change the institutions making the calls.

This chapter explains that the key is to create and employ expert bodies that use empirical data and studies to guide their decisions about criminal justice policy. The specific model of expertise could vary. Jurisdictions could opt to use one umbrella agency that is responsible for all criminal justice policies within the jurisdiction—from bail to sentencing, collateral consequences to prison conditions and programming. Or jurisdictions could use a number of such agencies. Under either approach, jurisdictions must make sure that any agency setting criminal justice policies is held accountable for the costs it imposes on the jurisdiction overall and that it uses the least costly options for addressing a particular issue.

Jurisdictions must also be attuned to how these agencies will operate in a political environment that suffers from all the pathologies already discussed. In other words, these agencies must be designed to withstand the pressures they will face to adopt superficially tough but actually ineffective measures to address crime. Thankfully, we already have enough experience with such agencies and can learn from their failures and successes to develop a blueprint for designing ones that have the best chance to succeed.

The Lessons from Sentencing Commissions

The idea of using experts to improve policy decisions has already been used in criminal law. The rehabilitative model that dominated criminal justice until the past few decades rested on the idea that expert parole officers could assess when someone was sufficiently rehabilitated to be released from prison. But the notion of using experts to set broad policies—not simply weigh in on individual cases—did not really take hold until the 1980s, and even then it was limited to the idea of using expertise to influence sentencing policies as opposed to various other aspects of criminal law. Politicians on the left and the right saw value in moving sentencing policy from the realm of pure politics to more insulated expert agencies vested with the authority to establish guidelines. In addition to the U.S. Sentencing Commission, sentencing commissions now exist in almost half the states.[12] The idea behind these agencies was that a group of experts could figure out what the range of sentences should be for each crime. Legislators embraced the model of a sentencing commission for several reasons. First, an agency is well situated to change policies as new facts and information become available, whereas the legislative process takes much longer and cannot adapt as quickly to changed circumstances. Second, many legislators were drawn to the idea of using experts to set sentences based on data and with an eye to maximizing limited resources and keeping costs down. Third, as noted in Chapter 7, some politicians wanted to insulate decisions about punishment from political pressures because they believed that insulation would produce better policy outcomes. They recognized, in other words, the pathological politics surrounding crime policy and wanted to place decision-making elsewhere to improve it.[13]

The experience of sentencing commissions shows the promise and the pitfalls of using an expert agency model to improve decisions in criminal law. Because jurisdictions followed different institutional models for these agencies, we can compare those models to see which ones were most successful in being able to overcome political pressures to constantly increase sentences based on outlier cases or the news story of the moment and which models failed in that regard and often exacerbated already pathological political dynamics. One common lesson from every jurisdiction with a commission is that it is not possible to completely insulate these agencies from politics. All agencies face political pressures and oversight, and because the politics of crime are so lopsided in favor of powerful interests pushing for severity, agencies responsible for criminal justice policy-making are going to face particularly close scrutiny if they make decisions to lower sentences or take a less punitive approach. The temptation will always be there for a politician to step in and score political points by criticizing a decision of the agency as insufficiently harsh. The actual practice of sentencing commissions bears this out, with these agencies often being overruled by their respective legislatures when they have tried to lower sentences.

Perhaps the most notorious illustration of political control over an agency ostensibly set up to be insulated comes from the federal level, where the U.S. Sentencing Commission has, throughout its existence, been ordered to raise sentences by Congress and has faced tremendous pushback when it has tried to lower them. Two of the more noteworthy examples of this dynamic were the agency's attempt to eliminate the disparity between sentences for crack and powder cocaine and its efforts to eliminate statutory mandatory minimum sentences. Congress and President Bill Clinton rejected the commission's proposed amendments to the guidelines in 1995 that would have treated crack and powder cocaine equally. Federal legislators have similarly ignored the commission's many empirical reports detailing the ineffectiveness and disparities created by mandatory minimum sentences. Congress demonstrated its lack of interest in the commission's views on mandatory minimum sentences at the outset, when it passed mandatory minimum drug sentences before the commission even had a chance to write its first set of guidelines. Congress did not bother to wait to see what the agency discovered by investigating past practices or by studying individual drugs. It simply set its own mandatory floors with no empirical analysis. And in the years since, Congress has—with the backing of the Department of Justice and its prosecutors—continued to ignore the commission's views on mandatory minimums.

Congress has also issued many directives to the commission to raise sentences—whether in child pornography or white-collar crime or any number of other offense types—whether or not empirical evidence supported such increases.[14] The result has been a federal prison population that has exploded since the commission was established in 1984. In 1987, when the commission's first set of guidelines came out, there were fewer than 50,000 people in federal prisons, and today there are more than 185,000.[15] The average time served by people in federal prisons increased dramatically as well, from 17.9 months in 1988 to 37.5 months in 2012.[16]

Many observers have looked at the experience of the U.S. Sentencing Commission as a cautionary tale and have concluded that the lesson is that experts can make things even worse. And that is true, if the model of expertise does not account for the political pressures any given agency will face. The federal Sentencing Commission has rarely been left alone to make policy and Congress has directed just about everything it has done over the years. The Commission has little ability to push back because of the way in which it was designed. So while the experience of the federal commission may be a cautionary tale, the lesson is not that experts inevitably make things worse. Instead, if there is any lesson to be drawn from the experience at the federal level, it is that politics will overcome any agency unless important design features are put in place to guard against those forces taking over. Care must be taken in setting up these agencies to allow experts to do their jobs most effectively.

Moreover, even with what might be the most ineffective design among sentencing commissions, the federal commission has succeeded in pushing some reforms in recent years. While the nascent political movement in support of federal sentencing reform has not been sufficient to overcome the objections of those in Congress or of prosecutors in the Department of Justice to result in significant legislative changes, the Sentencing Commission has been more successful in remedying some excessive federal sentencing policies. Specifically, because the commission's guideline changes go into effect within 180 days unless Congress and the president pass a law to oppose those changes, a smaller group of politicians can protect the commission's proposals than the number that would be needed to enact legislation in the first place.

That gives the agency space to enact some reforms that would never have happened if Congress were left to its own devices. For example, in the last decade, the commission made significant reductions to drug sentences, starting in 2007 with a reduction in sentences for crack offenses and then lowering the sentences for all drug offenses in 2013. The commission made both changes retroactive, allowing tens of thousands of people to obtain shorter sentences. The 2007 adjustment allowed more than 16,000 people to obtain reductions of 17% from their original sentence, or an average of

26 months.[17] The 2013 change allowed more than 30,000 people to obtain sentencing reductions that averaged 25 months.[18] The commission has made other changes that would have been hard to get through Congress but that made it through because the commission is more insulated than Congress from direct political pressures. This includes the removal of burglary of a dwelling from the list of "crimes of violence" and expanding the people who qualify for compassionate release.[19] So even the federal agency responsible for sentencing, flawed as it has been as a matter of institutional design, has managed to achieve some significant success where Congress has stalled because the data supported changes. Indeed, if one looks at the total decline in prison population of roughly 21,000 between 2015 and 2016, a full third of that decline was due to the 7,300 person drop in the number of people in federal prison.[20] That drop, in turn, was driven in large part by the commission's decision to reduce drug sentences retroactively.

The state experience with sentencing commissions is still more promising, as many of those commissions were designed more effectively to work within the politicized environment of criminal punishment. Minnesota's state commission, for example, has been able to push back against many of its legislature's attempts to increase sentences by pointing out that the increases would run afoul of prison capacity and strain the state's budgets.[21] Commissions in Washington and North Carolina have likewise been able to influence their respective legislatures with cost projections and reports that demonstrated what proposals would do to already strained correctional capacity.[22]

A comparison between those commissions that have succeeded in lowering sentences and those that have stalled in such efforts offers clues to what makes agencies more successful. One critical ingredient for the more successful sentencing commissions is having them produce information about how much sentencing increases will cost over time and requiring the agencies to adopt sentencing policies that will not require additional prison resources. Just about every state must balance its budget as a matter of state law, so the more expensive criminal justice policies become, the less money is left for everything else. It is thus not surprising that the states most likely to adopt sentencing commissions in the first place are the ones that are spending an increasing share of their budget on incarceration costs and that have high incarceration rates.[23] States are also more likely to create commissions when they have narrow partisan margins in their state legislatures (thus increasing the likelihood that the parties will vie with each other to appear tougher on crime by increasing sentences) and elected judges (who may also feel the pressure to impose long sentences to improve their reelection prospects).[24] In that kind of climate, the creation of an agency that can rein in costs becomes appealing, and legislators are more likely to see the value in deferring to an agency. Thus, just as politicians have decided that it is better to hand over interest rate policy to the Federal Reserve to get better long-term fiscal policy and to avoid the temptation to alter rates to provide short-term relief that scores political points but harms long-term economic growth, politicians in many jurisdictions have realized that the irrational politics of crime can similarly produce costly and ineffective long-term outcomes unless they do something to stop themselves. Commissions are an ideal brake on this dynamic when they focus on resource constraints and are given a mandate not to exceed existing prison capacity because costs matter to many legislators.

The commissions charged with not exceeding prison capacity have been more effective at holding back legislative pressure for increased sentences than those commissions that operate with no resource constraints.[25] The first director of the Minnesota Sentencing Guidelines Commission observed that the requirement that the Minnesota agency not exceed 95% of the state's prison capacity led those working on the commission and reviewing its work to recognize that imprisonment is "a scarce and expensive resource, which had to be allocated rationally" and allowed the commission to push back against calls for various increases because of what those requests would mean for prison capacity.[26] One legislator succinctly framed it this way: "Whether or not you think everybody in jail deserves to be there, it's another issue when you're weighing that against the stuff that makes you popular, likes roads and schools."[27] Corrections spending has grown faster than any other portion of state budgets except for Medicaid:[28] "Between 1977 and 1999, state and local expenditures for corrections rose by 946 percent, far outpacing the growth in outlays for education (370 percent), hospitals and health care (411 percent), and public welfare (510 percent)."[29] So designing agencies to focus on costs and budget impact is critical to their success because state legislators care about how limited resources are allocated.

The experience with sentencing commissions shows the influence an expert agency can have when it has the necessary expertise and data to forecast how different sentencing policies will affect existing resources and can document what sentencing changes will cost. Sentencing commissions become, in effect, "a de facto interest group for cost concerns and system-wide rationality."[30] Once sentencing guidelines go into effect in a state, we see a decline in the growth of both corrections expenditures and incarceration rates.[31] Even an agency like the U.S. Sentencing Commission, which does not have a mandate to stay within existing prison capacity, can more successfully push for reforms when prison resources are stretched. The

Department of Justice acceded to the 2013 reductions in drug sentences because federal prisons were operating at nearly 40% over capacity and the Bureau of Prisons budget was taking an ever-larger share of the overall DOJ budget, accounting for more than 25% of the DOJ budget in fiscal year 2013, and a third of the budget in 2015.[32]

A second key hallmark among the most successful sentencing commissions is a diverse membership. Diversity enables various viewpoints to be heard and understood, something often lacking in the political process, where the rhetoric of appearing tough on crime can drown out empirical data or those pointing out the human and fiscal costs of such policies. A successfully designed commission guards against this imbalance by including not only law enforcement interests but also those who represent the interests of criminal defendants, academics with deep knowledge of criminal law issues, and those concerned with the costs of sentencing. Just as important, the agency should also include individuals with ties to the legislature, either because they serve on it (where such a structure does not run afoul of the separation of powers) or because they have strong connections to those who do.[33] The most successful interest groups have such connections, and criminal justice agencies are no exception. This gives the agency notice of how politicians will respond to proposals and also gives the agency an opportunity to persuade those individuals with legislative connections about the policy merits of a proposal outside the noise of political rhetoric. Legislators serving on a commission or those with ties to them will often be persuaded that the policies are sound and can become crucial advocates for those policies in the legislative sphere.

This dynamic can be seen in the most successful state commissions. North Carolina's Sentencing and Policy Advisory Commission, for instance, includes members with a broad array of interests, including an academic who specializes in criminal justice and someone who was formerly incarcerated.[34] The agency also has legislators among its members, and those legislators have helped form a bridge between the two bodies, giving notice of legislative concerns and serving as advocates for the agency's position in the state's General Assembly. The balance cannot tilt too heavily toward elected officials, of course, or else the advantage of expertise is lost. But having some connection to key politicians confronts the reality that politics cannot be removed from criminal justice policy, so the key is to figure out how to channel it most effectively.

Commissions that focus on fiscal costs and have a diverse membership that includes political connections are able to harness politicians' concerns with fiscal discipline and pit them against the impulses to lengthen sentences. Politicians thus have to choose whether to pursue symbolic but ineffective strategies even if it means taking limited resources away from other important legislative goals. This kind of institutional design forces the issue that otherwise could be ignored. In the normal political give-and-take, politicians often talk about crime policies as if resources were unlimited. But they are not, and as soon as they become a consideration, many costly proposals that do nothing to promote public safety can be avoided. Agencies can help make those choices clear, as the real-world experience of these sentencing commissions has shown.

Beyond Sentencing Commissions

While the discussion so far has focused on the experience of sentencing commissions, the larger institutional points would apply to all criminal justice agencies whether they are corrections agencies, sentencing commissions, or general criminal justice policy commissions. Any agency responsible for criminal justice policy requires a diverse membership that reflects all of the relevant interests in the given area, and it should be constrained by cost ceilings and required to base its decisions on empirical evidence about what will best promote public safety at the lowest cost.

Currently, jurisdictions do not follow this model across the range of criminal justice issues. They might have a sentencing commission (though most still do not), but even when they do, that agency typically just bears responsibility for sentencing guidelines that apply to judges and does not consider the range of other issues relevant to criminal law, such as the content of the criminal code, prison conditions and programming, bail policies, collateral consequences, or second-look mechanisms. Criminal justice reformers should seek to change this by insisting that expert agencies take the lead on policy calls such as these. This can be accomplished either by expanding the portfolio of an existing agency such as a sentencing commission, by creating a number of expert agencies with specialties in different areas, or by creating a new umbrella agency that is responsible for setting and coordinating policy across the range of issues.

Whichever model is adopted, it is critical for these agencies to set their policies with a focus on how they will improve rehabilitation and reentry outcomes because that is what improves public safety. Oddly, this key metric is all too often ignored, largely because of a skepticism that developed toward rehabilitation in the 1970s and 1980s that has not been revisited. By the early 1980s, an unfortunate and flawed consensus developed that rehabilitation in the criminal justice setting was not working. The Senate issued a report in 1983 stating that "almost everyone involved in the criminal justice system now doubts that rehabilitation can be induced reliably in a prison setting, and it is now quite certain that no one can really detect whether or when a prisoner is rehabilitated."[35] While there is no foolproof way to know whether an individual is rehabilitated (either in prison or outside it), our knowledge of a person's progress and future risk is actually quite extensive. We now know of many interventions that improve rehabilitation and reentry outcomes.

This knowledge should be applied across the range of criminal justice policy issues. It should drive decisions about pretrial release, prison conditions and programming, sentencing length and the use of alternatives to incarceration, victim services, collateral consequences, clemency, parole, and other second-look processes. Agencies must evaluate these policies and choose those that best improve long-term reentry outcomes and thus save the jurisdiction money and hardship later by reducing the need for future criminal justice interventions.

It may seem unbelievable that this is not what we are already doing. Why wouldn't we be setting all of our criminal justice policies with an eye toward improving outcomes for individuals so that they are less likely to commit further crimes? If we were rational and focused primarily on public safety, this is of course what we would do. But we have not let rationality guide our criminal justice decision-making in America. We have let emotions take charge. There is, of course, a place for emotions, and there is no denying the societal need for retribution when horrible crimes occur. And I am not suggesting that experts are any better than the general public at deciding the best punishment as a matter of retribution in an individual case. But much of what the public wants from a criminal justice apparatus is public safety, and when gut-level reactions govern the entire system and lead us to responses that end up making us less safe, we must confront the trade-off we are making. We must decide if we would prefer to prevent future tragedies and be safer in the long run, or if we want to let visceral reactions to outlier cases lead us into making decisions that might feel good in the short term but that actually make us less safe. I think most people would rather adopt a course that maximizes public safety. To do so, we can no longer leave the decisions to a political process that relies on uninformed voters to decide how angry they are about whatever crimes are currently appearing in the news and who assume all crimes and criminals look like the ones highlighted by the media. We need to use professional agencies that take the best available knowledge from careful study of actual cases, data, and facts to put in place those policies that work to improve outcomes across the range of real-world cases, not just those that get attention in the media.

Critically, it is not enough to buy into the idea that agencies with this mandate are a good idea. Any agency responsible for criminal justice policy-making must be designed to withstand the inevitable pressures that will come from an emotional electorate and outraged politicians. Like the most successful sentencing commissions, they need to be created with a diverse membership that is attuned to all the relevant interests and that provides a bridge to politicians to explain agency policies. It may also mean the agency should have a politically balanced membership so that its recommendations are bipartisan and can appeal broadly. Because these agencies should be bringing forth reforms that promote public safety and save money, they should appeal to those across the political spectrum. Having members of both parties support reforms gives political cover for elected officials to accept the proposals.[36] The key to making a bipartisan agency work is to appoint people with expertise who are committed to going where the data leads and who do not enter with a political agenda. That may be easier said than done, but appointing the right people to these agencies is critical to their success. These agencies should also be careful to ground their decisions in facts that matter to those politicians, such as costs. Helpfully, many criminal justice policies that are effective at promoting public safety also reduce unnecessary confinement and save money.

To be sure, that is not always going to be the case. Some policies might be the humane and just thing to do, even if they cannot be supported by data and studies. This agency model may not help much to promote policies like that. That would require cultural shifts beyond the scope of an institutional fix. There are limits to what the expertise model can accomplish, and I do not want to overclaim here. But changing institutions and creating an expanded role for smartly designed expert agencies will make a difference—both to public safety and to the countless lives affected by our criminal justice policies.

Creating Stronger Criminal Justice Policy Agencies

One reason some might resist a turn to an institutional model grounded in expertise is that we have done that in the past, and it has often failed. Indeed, we have seen countless examples in the past of a desire to bring rationality and expertise to criminal justice policy-making only to see those efforts end up leading to the same dysfunctional outcomes of harsher sentences or net-widening so that even more people faced criminal punishment than before. Whether it was a desire for parole reforms, better juvenile justice policies, or an emphasis on rehabilitation, we have seen plenty of examples where expertise fell short. The reason is that experts need an institutional architecture that rewards the use of expertise and insulates them from political pressures and from agency capture by interests in favor of harsher policies. The discussion of sentencing commissions gave some key traits for those agencies to succeed. But a diverse membership, political connections, and a focus on costs may not be enough. Thankfully, there are additional ways to strengthen the hand of agencies responsible for criminal justice policy-making beyond the features that have worked well for state sentencing commissions. These added protections are particularly important because sometimes the politics of the moment will override fiscal concerns (especially if crime rates are rising or there is a budget surplus, which will create added pressures to throw fiscal concerns to the side). The design features discussed so far only serve to highlight the fiscal consequences for legislators; they do not do much more to tie the hands of those who may give in to political symbolism even if it is costly and ineffective. But stronger restraints are possible if criminal justice reformers push for them.

As Chapter 7 noted, most administrative agencies in the federal system and in the states are subject to judicial review to make sure that their rules and regulations are not arbitrary and capricious. Courts take a "hard look" at their decisions to make sure that they ground their decisions in law and evidence, and agencies must explain why they are departing from any previous practices or policies. Many criminal justice agencies, in contrast, are exempt in whole or in part from such obligations. Sentencing commissions, for example, generally have been exempt from the administrative procedure acts that impose this judicial review.[37] States vary in how they treat the regulations adopted by departments of correction. While corrections agencies in some states are bound by the provisions of the state administrative procedure act, including notice-and-comment rule-making procedures, in more than half they are exempt in whole or in part from these requirements.[38]

When criminal justice agencies do not have to comply with state administrative procedure acts, it means these agencies need not explain the basis for their rules and why they are consistent with statutory mandates or other existing guidelines to a court. One way to further insulate criminal justice policy-making agencies from immediate and irrational political pressures would be to require them to establish the empirical basis for their rules and policies, to explain how they are consistent with public safety objectives, and to face judicial review of those decisions. This would keep the agency's focus on data and analysis and help it resist pressure to make decisions based on political factors that have no empirical grounding because doing so would not withstand judicial review.

We already have indications that courts are capable of this kind of assessment because we have seen parallels to this type of inquiry in the context of challenges to collateral consequences on the ground that they are really punishments (and therefore in violation of some constitutional provision like the prohibition on double jeopardy, the Eighth Amendment, or the Ex Post Facto Clause).[39] In defending these collateral consequences, states argue that they are engaged in regulation with these provisions, not punishment.[40] Take the case of *Smith v. Doe,* which involved Alaska's sex offender registration law. The defendant challenged the law as violating the Ex Post Facto Clause. In rejecting the challenge, the Supreme Court concluded that the Alaska legislature did not intend to punish, but rather its intent was "to establish a civil regulatory scheme."[41] In *De Veau v. Braisted,* the Court similarly concluded that a statute that excluded individuals who had been convicted of felonies from working on the waterfront was not punishment but a "much-needed scheme of regulation."[42] For state claims to succeed as being something other than punitive, their claims of regulation must be rational.

A federal court of appeals, for example, had to determine whether various changes under Michigan's Sex Offender Registration Act that were applied retroactively violated the Ex Post Facto Clause of the Constitution. Part of the court's inquiry required it to ask whether the law's changes—prohibiting sex offenders from living within 1,000 feet of a school and creating tiers of dangerousness based solely on the defendant's offense of conviction and not individualized assessments—were rationally related to a nonpunitive purpose. The state grounded retroactive application of its changes on the idea that recidivism rates for sex offenders were "frightening and high" and that these changes would protect the public by allowing them to keep tabs on those individuals with knowledge of their tier ranking and by keeping sex offenders away from vulnerable populations. The court, however, found "scant support" for the state's claims. It noted that empirical studies refuted the state's claims of high recidivism rates among sex offenders, and studies further demonstrated that "offense-based public registration has, at best, no impact on recidivism." Because the state failed to offer any support for the idea that residential restrictions would lower recidivism rates and because the statute did not provide for individualized assessments of dangerousness to target the specific types of offenders—e.g., pedophiles—who should be kept away from schools, the court concluded that the law was punitive and not connected to nonpunitive goals.[43]

This is the same kind of inquiry that arbitrary and capricious review would demand of all criminal justice policies subject to it. While the federal court in Michigan did it in the limited context of an Ex Post Facto Clause inquiry, it is possible to create a broader framework for this kind of court review by passing statutes that require agencies to explain the basis for concluding that their policies will promote public safety.

To be sure, if a court overruled an agency for lacking empirical support but the legislature wanted the policy to move forward anyhow to score political points, legislatures could simply change the governing policies by statute. But note how much more effort and cost that requires. Politicians would have to go on the record opposing both the agency and a court decision finding either that the policy did not promote public safety or that cost constraints supported a different path of action. And those politicians would need to be large enough in number to get legislation through. To be sure, the politics of crime are such that this will happen in some, perhaps many, instances. But it will happen less frequently than in a world where agencies and the courts fail to act as restraining forces. Sometimes, politicians will let those decisions stand. Indeed, in many cases, the politicians might rail against those decisions and hope that their rhetoric criticizing the agencies and the courts suffices to score them the political points they want, without having to actually make an effort to change the outcome. Politicians could, in effect, have their cake and eat it, too. They get the benefits of fiscal discipline because the agency's decision ties their hands from spending money on irrational criminal justice policies. But they also get credit for criticizing the agency on the substance of the policy decision and being perceived as willing to be tougher on crime, if only they had the freedom to do more. We have seen this dynamic play out in the context of many other agencies.[44]

Agency decisions can be strengthened in other ways as well. One fruitful avenue is to have decisions reviewed by other officials outside of the agency to make sure that that the policies are cost-benefit justified and that equally effective but less costly alternatives are considered. This model, as Chapter 7 noted, has been used extensively at the federal level with civil regulatory agencies. Federal regulatory agencies must submit their proposed rules to the federal Office of Information and Regulatory Affairs (OIRA) in the Office of Management and Budget within the executive office of the White House. The agencies must show that the benefits of their proposed rules outweigh the costs and explain why they did not choose less expensive alternatives.[45] When this review process was established, it was defended on the grounds that civil regulatory agencies would "invariably wish to spend 'too much' on [their] goals" because each agency looks only at the goals it seeks to further and does not consider how resources it spends might be used for other benefits in the public interest.[46] Whether or not this is true of all the civil regulatory agencies that must submit rules to OIRA oversight, it is a phenomenon that accurately describes agencies responsible for criminal justice policies. Prosecutors, for example, may wish to score easy political points by appearing tough on an issue, especially when they do not have to pay for it. So to the extent that prosecutors continue to engage in policy-making—for example, by pursuing certain kinds of sentences in categories of cases or because they have control over a related area of policy like forensics or clemency—this kind of oversight would act as a check on them to make sure they are considering other interests besides narrow professional ones.[47]

But the value of this kind of check applies more broadly than prosecutors and extends to any agency responsible for criminal justice policy-making because these agencies will inevitably face pressure from legislators to promulgate seemingly tough penalties for political points when in fact those policies may not stand up to closer scrutiny. The agencies may wish to placate politicians who can slash their budgets or pass legislation limiting their authority, so the temptation to accede to their demands can be great if there is no countervailing pressure to explain why their policies are justified as a matter of cost-benefit analysis and represent the best of the alternatives. Having oversight by a body like OIRA puts in place an institutional check that requires the agency to think about its choices rationally and not simply give a knee-jerk reaction in support of something that appears tougher. Agencies should consider more broadly what works best for victim services and for reentry, and the answer on closer inspection might not always be longer sentences. While states do not currently use OIRA-like review in a manner that mimics the federal system, they do have oversight mechanisms in place for regulations.[48] And organizations like Vera and PEW have been working with states to use cost-benefit analysis to analyze criminal justice policies, so we know this model can be adapted successfully to the criminal law context.[49]

Having a strong inspector general (IG) system may also help promote better criminal justice decision-making. Most federal agencies and many state agencies are subject to oversight by inspectors general who investigate agencies for fraud, waste, and mismanagement. The typical IG model tends to be weak, with the IG looking for egregious examples of fraud and waste but otherwise not scrutinizing how agencies choose to exercise their discretion or asking whether the agency could be performing better.[50] But there are exceptions to this model, and where they exist, they show how an active IG can promote better policies. As Chapter 8 explained, Inspector

General Michael Horowitz has engaged in vigorous oversight of the Department of Justice, its policy-making, and its implementation of policies. For instance, he highlighted how DOJ policy decisions such as a failure to grant compassionate release have led to excessive spending on the Bureau of Prisons at the expense of other law enforcement needs, thus compromising public safety.[51] In response to his reports, which were publicly reported and garnered media attention, the department shifted some of its policy positions.[52] This kind of IG model—where the IG evaluates the agency's substantive policies to make sure they are using limited resources efficiently and where the IG also verifies that policies are being implemented as claimed—can work as a valuable check to keep agencies focused on the mission of promoting public safety with policies that are cost justified.

Another helpful mechanism to promote rationality in the system is the use of sunset provisions in laws and regulations addressing criminal justice issues. Politicians often interfere with agencies through legislation that responds to some immediate high-profile crime, requiring agencies to do something or refrain from doing something in response to that specific case. For example, if the media is focused on financial crimes, a legislative body might order an agency to increase sentences for fraud. The problem with this approach is that the legislature often lacks the full picture of a substantive area or how it relates to other laws already in existence. This is what creates the lumpy laws and excessive sentences highlighted in Chapters 1 and 2. Once these laws are in place, there is little an agency can do to address them. To give the agency the space to adapt to changing circumstances and the accumulation of new information that may suggest a more nuanced or refined approach to an area, reformers should urge legislators to pass criminal justice legislation with sunset provisions. So a law requiring a sentencing increase might expire after three to five years without reauthorization by the legislature and a report by the relevant expert agency on how the law has been working (or not working). Sometimes these laws will be reenacted even when the expert agency concludes they should not be because politics will override expertise. But sometimes the legislature may be content to let a law lapse, particularly if the media fervor that led to its passage has long passed.

Finally, it is helpful to have agencies responsible for criminal justice issues pay particular attention to racial bias in their policies. One model would be to have any agency that is responsible for criminal justice policy contain a unit that monitors decisions for racial and ethnic bias. Regulatory agencies in other substantive fields have specialized units along these lines, such as the Office for Civil Rights and Civil Liberties in the Department of Homeland Security, or the Office of Economic Impact and Diversity in the Department of Energy.[53] The idea behind these subdivisions within a larger agency is that certain interests might otherwise be overlooked by the agency at it goes about its regular tasks, so the unit's responsibility is to make sure those issues do not fall out of view. In the context of a criminal justice policy-making agency, the unit would be on the lookout for racial and ethnic bias through data analysis and should investigate causes for any disproportionate effects. The unit could have the authority to address citizen complaints, to make recommendations for policy changes, or to issue reports highlighting problems it sees.

Another model for checking bias is to require agencies responsible for criminal justice policy-making to produce racial and ethnic impact statements to show not only the fiscal impact of a proposed law or rule, but also how the change in law will affect certain groups. Four states (Iowa, Connecticut, Oregon, and New Jersey) currently have laws requiring such impact statements.[54] This information may not ultimately tip the scales to get politicians to change their minds about a proposal, but it may make the difference in some cases. An analysis of Iowa's experience with racial and ethnic impact statements found that proposed legislation with a disproportionate impact on minorities was twice as likely to fail relative to those bills that were rated as neutral or having no such effect.[55] This is far from a cure-all for the disparities we see in criminal cases in the United States, but having the data available in stark terms may at least give legislators pause in some circumstances, particularly if voters or groups mobilize around the issue.

Coordinating Public Policy across Related Issues

Many criminal justice policies intersect with other substantive areas. The people who commit crimes often have physical and mental illnesses, struggle with substance abuse problems, and lack housing, education, and jobs. If the goal is to improve reentry and to have better public safety outcomes, it is important to tackle these related social problems.

The courts and the participants within them have realized the overlap. The rise of so-called problem-solving courts is a direct response to seeing the intersection between crime and these other problems. Drug courts and mental health courts developed to try to get individuals the treatment they need because in many criminal cases, some underlying problem is what prompts the criminal activity. If you can solve that underlying problem, you can thus prevent or minimize future crimes.[56] Reentry courts seek to assist individuals in finding housing and jobs with the same goal in mind. While problem-solving courts can serve a valuable function, they often operate on an ad hoc basis, and it is unclear how they select which cases qualify for diversionary treatment or whether they are choosing approaches and programs with proven track records of success. They typically serve only a fraction of the overall caseload, thus they barely scratch the surface of addressing the relationship between crime and these other issues.

To tackle these issues more systematically and effectively, jurisdictions need a coordinated approach. This means screening cases at the outset to identify individuals with particular needs, such as mental health and drug treatment, which are better addressed outside the criminal justice context. Promising research by former New Jersey attorney general and NYU School of Law professor of practice Anne Milgram aims to do just that by helping law enforcement officers identify people with mental health needs who should be diverted for treatment. After cases are in the criminal justice system, these needs should be addressed through treatment and programming. Jails and prisons must be more than warehouses. It is critical that they provide the kind of rehabilitative services that will make it less likely that individuals commit crimes when they are released. And when people finish serving terms of incarceration, they need bridges to services to ease their reentry. Jeremy Travis advocates for a "boundary spanning advocate" to help find people the resources they need throughout a jurisdiction. He offers the Vera Institute's Project Greenlight as an example. In that program, a community coordinator meets with people released from state prison to create a profile of each that includes their criminal history and any substance abuse problems, their job skills and abilities, and their family circumstances. The coordinator then seeks to find housing, treatment, and employment opportunities for these individuals.[57] Corrections officers and defense lawyers could also provide this kind of bridge to needed reentry services.[58] The key takeaway is that whatever the source, some kind of coordinated assistance is critical if public safety is the goal because it helps improve reentry outcomes.

Of course the ideal approach tackles these issues before a crime even occurs. But often other societal safeguards are absent or fail, thus leaving it to criminal justice institutions to address the problems. Political scientist Naomi Murakawa notes that "a meager welfare state but a capacious carceral state had led interest groups to rely on criminal justice for social change" because "reformers tend to build on or adapt existing institutional structures."[59] Substantive education policy, mental health treatment, employment training, and the like are well beyond the scope of this book. But because these areas are critical if the goal is maximizing public safety, it is important for the institutions addressing criminal law issues to be attuned to them. That, then, is another key question of institutional design. Jurisdictions must recognize the connections among these issues and seek to coordinate among the relevant agencies and professionals in these areas. Criminal justice professionals must be among those who speak out for reform in other areas, such as education, and raise the connection between the two.

Coordination is necessary among criminal justice professionals as well. A bipartisan expert body created by Congress to address federal criminal justice and corrections issues, the Charles Colson Task Force on Federal Corrections, highlighted the need for interagency oversight bodies that coordinate their efforts at criminal justice reform.[60] Several states, through the Justice Reinvestment Initiative, have created versions of interagency oversight bodies that bring together key actors, including law enforcement officials, defense lawyers, mental health officials, specialists in substance abuse, victims' advocates, corrections officers, parole and probation experts, and court administrators.[61] Working together instead of in silos enables the interagency working groups to recommend where reform is needed, to structure efforts across agencies, and to track results.

For instance, the Georgia Council on Criminal Justice Reform, created by legislation in 2013, has 15 members appointed by the governor. Currently, there is one state senator, one state representative, three judges, one district attorney, one sheriff, one solicitor general, one court administrator, four criminal defense attorneys, one businessperson, and one member of the governor's office.[62] The members serve 5-year terms, which allows them to "expand their expertise while overseeing and guiding system change over time."[63] The Georgia Council helped to create the state's first problem-solving courts and started training programs for people in prison to receive job certifications prior to release.[64] Other states experimenting with these interagency groups have also seen promising results, with most of the states experiencing relative decreases in projected prison population growth and significant cost savings. This, then, is another area where expert focus and coordination can yield better results.

WE MAY HAVE ARRIVED at mass incarceration and excessive criminalization by a variety of ad hoc decisions, but those decisions together have put in place institutions and interests that will resist change unless a new set of institutions is created that shifts the focus to data and rational analysis of what will actually work to promote public safety. We have used expert agencies to improve substantive policies across a range of areas in America, from workplace safety to the environment. It is long past time we use this model to improve our approach to crime and public safety.

10

CATALYZING COURTS

IN CASTING INSTITUTIONAL BLAME for the irrational set of criminal justice policies we have, it is important not to overlook the role of judges. The federal courts in general and the Supreme Court in particular have weakened constitutional protections against government excess in criminal law and have failed to question, much less scrutinize, government punishment practices. State judges, too, have fallen short in policing constitutional bounds and have not used their discretion to curb the worst excesses of the system.

But court oversight practices are not set in stone, and renewed attention to the courts is one of the key institutional pillars for reform. Although it will be an uphill climb to change courts' perspectives on their role in policing government excess in criminal proceedings, the seeds are already there for what this kind of review would look like and the results it could help achieve.

Recall that the decline in California's prison population accounts for a full 40% of the drop in incarceration numbers in the United States.[1] That decline never would have happened but for the Supreme Court holding, in *Brown v. Plata,* that California's prison conditions violated the Eighth Amendment ban on cruel and unusual punishment because overcrowding prevented adequate medical and mental health care. The Court upheld a remedial order that required California to cap its prison population at 137% of design capacity, which meant that California had to reduce its prison population by about 35,000 people within 2 years.[2] It was "the largest court-ordered reduction in prison populations ever in the United States."[3]

California responded by passing the Public Safety Realignment Act, which aimed to place more individuals in local jails instead of state prisons, by curbing the number of people sent to prison for technical parole violations, and by improving rehabilitation and decreasing recidivism.[4] The state provided $7 billion to 58 counties to administer the new regime and imposed few requirements as to how localities were to spend the money.[5] Although the results vary by county, the California prison population has declined more than the local jail population has increased, thus the overall population of people incarcerated has been reduced by roughly 18,000 people.[6] While there was an initial uptick in crime rates in 2012, they dropped in 2013 and 2014, so by 2015, property and violent crime rates were below pre-realignment levels (with the one exception being auto theft).[7] Thus California has achieved a dramatically lower incarcerated population without suffering an increase in crime—and all because the federal courts did their job.

But currently *Brown v. Plata* stands out as the exception, not the rule. The federal courts have largely failed to protect constitutional guarantees across a range of doctrinal areas, thus allowing the government to run amok in criminal cases without a check. Judges stand as the last check against prosecutors to make sure they are not overstepping. They bear the responsibility for calling out their constitutional violations, such as the failure to disclose exculpatory evidence. And when they see unethical conduct, they have an obligation to do something about it. Moreover, they often have the leeway to determine a defendant's punishment. In the absence of a mandatory sentence, judges will have the freedom to sentence a defendant within a range, and how they exercise that discretion matters a great deal to what our overall criminal justice landscape looks like. Indeed, judges (federal and state) have discretion over a range of important criminal justice issues.

This chapter surveys the critical role of judges in any reform effort. First, to highlight those areas best suited for legal challenges, this chapter outlines the areas where federal courts have failed to live up to their constitutional responsibilities. It then notes where the doctrine has started to move, thus paving the way for more significant inroads. It then explains the discretionary responsibilities of judges that are so important for how criminal justice is administered in the United States. Finally, it turns to the critical question of how to change the bench at the federal and state level to improve criminal justice decision-making.

The Constitution in Waiting

The federal courts—led by the Supreme Court—have gutted many constitutional guarantees. Consider first the right to a jury trial. The Constitution guarantees jury trials in Article III and the Sixth Amendment.[8] While the Supreme Court has made clear that the government cannot condition the exercise of other constitutional rights on concessions to the government, it has, as Chapter 7 notes, allowed the government to put a heavy price tag on the exercise of the jury trial right by allowing prosecutors to threaten far more serious charges when a defendant opts to go to trial instead of pleading guilty.[9] It has, for example, upheld a prosecutor's threat (which the prosecutor ultimately carried out) to charge the defendant under a repeat-offender law with a mandatory life sentence if the defendant refused to plead guilty and accept the prosecutor's initial offer to seek a 5-year sentence.[10] The Court likewise allowed a prosecutor to threaten to bring a death penalty charge if a defendant refused a plea deal that would impose a 50-year sentence.[11] Lower courts have followed the Supreme Court's lead and have recognized that prosecutors can threaten sentences orders of magnitude higher than the plea deals they are offering if defendants opt to exercise their jury trial rights. Thus a defendant could lawfully receive a 55-year sentence because he opted to go to trial instead of accepting the prosecutor's offer of a 15-year sentence if he pleaded guilty to a charge of distributing marijuana while possessing a gun.[12]

By allowing the government to threaten severe punishments that are far greater if a defendant exercises his or her right to a jury trial, the Supreme Court has weakened the jury power to the point that it exercises little restraint on the government. The result is that prosecutors operate virtually unchecked when seeking pleas, creating the world we live in now where more than 95% of the cases that reach a disposition get there through a plea instead of a trial.

A second crucial area where the federal courts have effectively ceded their authority to police constitutional rights is the substantive review of punishments. The Eighth Amendment of the Constitution bars cruel and unusual punishments, but as Chapter 7 explains, the Supreme Court has done little to enforce that guarantee outside the context of the death penalty.[13] The lower courts have taken the Supreme Court's cues and have similarly upheld egregiously long sentences. They have, for example, upheld a sentence of 71 years for a driver in four bank robberies who had no prior record and who cooperated with law enforcement.[14] Courts have been just as reluctant to second-guess prison conditions, no matter how abhorrent. *Plata* was the rare case where overcrowding conditions had become so egregious that the federal courts drew a line. But in just about every other instance, no punishment length or condition of confinement is bad enough for a court to intervene.

A third important area where the judiciary has failed to check the government is its interpretation of criminal statutes. The rule of lenity is a ven-

erable canon of statutory construction that holds that ambiguities in statutes should be interpreted in favor of criminal defendants, not the
government.[15] The rule reflects the important separation of powers principle
that legislators, not courts, should be making laws that impose punishment.[16] So if a statute is not clearly applicable to a defendant's conduct, it
should be up to the legislature to specify that it meant to include that
conduct within the statute's ambit. Legislation that results in the loss of
liberty should have to go through the appropriate legislative process. At
the federal level, that means it must make its way through both houses of
Congress and be signed by the president. Because bicameralism and pre-
sentment would be rendered meaningless if the legislation passed is am-
biguous on its face and only receives its content when interpreted by the
judiciary, the rule of lenity insists on resolving any uncertainty in favor of
the defendant. The rule also reflects the reality that it is far easier for the
government to go back to the legislature to fix an interpretation resolved
against its interests than it is for criminal defendants to do so.[17] And of
course the rule of lenity protects the fundamental due process value of notice.[18] But despite lenity's pedigree and importance, it is all too often ignored
by the courts as they stretch to find clarity in favor of the government where
none exists.

Courts have also given shoddy treatment to the related constitutional rule
against vague criminal statutes that fail to give sufficient notice to defendants. One review of cases found that, in the 30-year period from 1960 to
1990, the Supreme Court held only about a dozen statutes to be unconstitutional because of vagueness concerns.[19] The rarity of a successful vagueness challenge continues to the present day, with few statutes falling on that
ground. In the majority of instances, vagueness arguments are given little
weight—as one commentator has noted, "dismissal in one this-contention-
is-without-merit sentence or even footnote."[20]

Federal courts have also made it almost impossible for defendants to
bring actions against prosecutors for violation of their constitutional rights
under the relevant statute, 42 U.S.C. §1983. Although the statute's plain
language contains no bars against lawsuits against prosecutors, the Supreme
Court has concluded that prosecutors should be entitled to absolute immunity from civil suits under §1983 for actions they take in their capacity
as prosecutors (even if prosecutors intentionally violate someone's rights),
and so-called qualified immunity for the actions they take as investigators,
which requires someone challenging the action to show that prosecutors
violated clearly established law.[21] Scholars have debunked the Court's claims
that these immunity doctrines are justified by historical practice and have
persuasively argued that the Court should not have read them into the

statute.[22] Additionally, although the Court allows individuals to sue municipalities for prosecutorial violations of constitutional rights when prosecutors act pursuant to official municipal policy, the Supreme Court rarely finds the requisite deliberate indifference to constitutional rights by the municipality, even in egregious cases.[23] For example, the Court failed to find deliberate indifference in the case of *Connick v. Thompson,* where no fewer than four prosecutors made intentional decisions not to disclose to Thompson exculpatory evidence that demonstrated that his blood type did not match the blood type of the perpetrator of the murder for which Thompson was accused. The district attorney failed to take actions to make sure prosecutors in his office understood their disclosure obligations, and he did not provide any training on those requirements. Thompson was almost executed for a crime he did not commit, and it was only through the chance discovery of the exculpatory evidence that he was taken off death row and finally exonerated after serving 18 years. Yet the Court ruled against Thompson.[24]

Finally, courts have condoned imprisonment for defendants who fail to pay fees and fines that they cannot afford, in violation of due process and equal protection. Municipalities frequently impose fines as punishment for offenses not traditionally thought to merit incarceration, especially traffic offenses. Individuals can also face fees for jail and prison stays, probation supervision, and court costs.[25] Jurisdictions then often detain those defendants who fail to pay those fees and fines.[26] The Supreme Court recognized decades ago that "due process and equal protection converge" in failure-to-pay cases and that imprisoning someone who cannot afford to pay a fee or fine offends both the "fundamental fairness" that is the touchstone of due process and the equal treatment of the poor.[27] Thus, under Supreme Court case law, courts should consider whether a defendant has the ability to pay a fee or fine before incarcerating him or her for failure to pay. Specifically, a court must find that the failure to pay was "willful" or resulted from lack of "bona fide efforts" to avoid "punishing a person for his poverty."[28] However, there is ample evidence that courts are simply not upholding these constitutional touchstones against state and local authorities.[29] This was demonstrated by the Department of Justice's Ferguson report, which found that municipal courts were issuing warrants "without any ability-to-pay determination."[30] This dereliction of constitutional duty is not confined to Ferguson, as the same problem exists in jurisdictions throughout the country.[31] Even when judges do inquire into a defendant's reasons for failing to pay fees or fines, they often have such a weak definition of "willful" or such a demanding definition of "bona fide efforts" as to render the inquiry almost meaningless.[32]

The courts have taken the wrong legal turn in all of these areas, and the policy consequences of failing to uphold the law have been devastating. The net effect of courts failing to police these constitutional protections has been to enlarge government power and to create space for abuses in criminal matters. The courts have thus assisted in creating an irrational scheme that overcriminalizes and imposes excess punishment at a great cost to liberty and government budgets and without any tangible benefits to public safety. The Constitution and the rule of law demand far more of the courts and our government.

Hints of Change

Law is not stagnant, however, and the federal courts, including the Supreme Court, seem to be slowly realizing at least some of their doctrinal missteps. Consider first the Supreme Court's treatment of the jury guarantee, which is starting to get more attention by the Court. Until 2000, it looked as if the Court would permit legislators to write laws to make just about anything that increased a defendant's punishment into a sentencing factor to be decided by a judge by a preponderance of the evidence instead of treating such facts as offense elements that had to be decided by a jury beyond a reasonable doubt. In 2000, the Court began a major shift in course. It held that the Sixth Amendment places limits on the ability of legislators to create mandatory statutory sentencing factors that the government need prove only by a preponderance of the evidence in order for a defendant's maximum punishment to increase. The Court held that any factor (other than a prior conviction) that increases the statutory maximum must be treated as an offense element that the jury must find beyond a reasonable doubt (or to which the defendant must plead guilty).[33] The Court continued down this path, finding that mandatory sentencing guidelines would be treated the same way, first striking down a Kansas state sentencing regime in *Blakely* in 2004 and then ruling that the federal sentencing guidelines ran afoul of this principle in *Booker* in 2005.[34] In 2013, in *Alleyne,* the Court took yet another step, ruling that facts that trigger a mandatory minimum sentence must also be treated as offense elements that must be proven beyond a reasonable doubt to a jury.[35]

It would be hard to overstate the significance of this line of cases. In the federal system, *Booker* made the federal sentencing guidelines advisory instead of mandatory, thus giving judges discretion to take into account individual facts in a case and ultimately resulting in a significant reduction in the length of federal drug sentences.[36] *Alleyne* then paved the way for the Obama Justice Department's shift in its charging policy to bring fewer prosecutions that trigger a mandatory minimum and to reserve them for the most serious cases.[37] Although that policy shifted again under the Trump administration, with federal prosecutors being instructed to charge the most serious readily provable offense and without special instructions to limit charges in cases with mandatory minimums, the underlying Court holding still stands, so now the government will have to prove those facts that trigger a mandatory minimum sentence beyond a reasonable doubt.

This shift in doctrine was thus substantial, and it came about because of a Court that finally recognized that the jury had been unconstitutionally shut out of criminal cases.[38] The majority consisted of a mix of justices sensitive to the separation of powers and the Framers' commitment to the jury and those attuned to defendants' individual rights. Justices Scalia and Thomas represented the conservative flank of this coalition and did so because of their commitment to originalism and the Framers' conception of the jury trial right. Justices Stevens, Souter, and Ginsburg represented the liberal wing of this group because of their commitment to individual rights and the jury's crucial role in protecting defendants.[39] These justices restored the jury to its rightful position as a check on the exercise of government power in individual cases. The Framers recognized the importance of the jury check because they were aware that policy is made in the aggregate in the legislative process and inevitably gets swayed by the most extreme cases.[40] The judicial process, and the jury's role within it, provides a crucial corrective because of its focus on individual facts and circumstances.

This was not the only line of cases in which the Court has recently recognized that it must provide a more robust check against the government to comply with the Constitution. The Court also acknowledged, for the first time, that more checks are needed on the plea bargaining process than simply a defendant's ability to take his or her case to trial. In *Lafler v. Cooper* and *Missouri v. Frye,* the Court held that in cases in which a defendant does not accept a plea offer because of ineffective assistance of counsel, the fact that a defendant receives a fair trial does not remedy the ineffective assistance.[41] The Court noted that the defendant received a more severe sentence as a result of going to trial, so that "far from curing the error, the trial caused the injury from the error."[42] The Court rejected the government's argument that "[a] fair trial wipes clean any deficient performance by defense counsel during plea bargaining," because the government's "position ignores the reality that criminal justice today is for the most part a system of pleas, not a system of trials."[43] The Court concluded that the remedy for this kind of ineffective assistance may be having the district court conduct a hearing to determine whether, but for the error of the defendant's lawyer, the defendant would have accepted the plea. If such a showing is made, the court should then decide whether to give the defendant a new sentence. Another possible remedy may be to require the prosecution to reoffer the plea deal. This was a huge acknowledgment by the Court, and one that could pave the way for future regulation of the plea process.

Indeed, state courts have already taken further steps to level the playing field in plea bargaining negotiations. For example, in 2015, the West Virginia Supreme Court held that prosecutors violate a defendant's due process rights when they do not provide exculpatory evidence during plea negotiations.[44] The defendant, Joseph Buffey, had pleaded guilty to rape and robbery in 2002, though at the time of the plea negotiation, prosecutors already had forensic lab reports concluding that Buffey was not the DNA source from the rape kit.[45] By extending *Brady v. Maryland* to the plea negotiation stage, the court paved the way for future defendants to "seek to withdraw a guilty plea based upon the prosecution's suppression of material, exculpatory evidence."[46]

While these are important steps, complete reinvigoration of the constitutional jury guarantee would require the Court to recognize that allowing the government to impose vastly higher sentences on defendants who exercise their right to a jury trial is an unconstitutional condition on that critical right. While that would be a bold step from where the Court has been, it is consistent with the Court's unconstitutional conditions jurisprudence and would not necessarily mean having to overrule the Court's past decisions accepting plea bargaining, because even those decisions had caveats. In *Brady v. United States,* the Court cautioned:

> We here make no reference to the situation where the prosecutor or judge, or both, deliberately employ their charging and sentencing powers to induce a particular defendant to tender a plea of guilty. In Brady's case there is no claim that the prosecutor threatened prosecution on a charge not justified by the evidence or that the trial judge threatened Brady with a harsher sentence if convicted after trial in order to induce him to plead guilty.[47]

It is thus entirely consistent with existing case law for the Court to start policing prosecutors to make sure they are not threatening defendants with longer sentences just to get them to plead guilty. This could be done, for example, by setting up a limit on the difference between the sentence offered and how much of a sentence the defendant faces if he or she goes to trial to limit the coercion of the plea offer.[48] Or courts could look to see if a sentence threatened is an outlier for the jurisdiction for similar cases. The

Court has not yet shown an interest in doing something like this, but it is the kind of policing that is necessary to make sure that prosecutors are not placing unconstitutional conditions on the exercise of the jury trial right. With the right litigation strategy and enough justices willing to rethink the Court's flawed plea bargaining jurisprudence, it could pose a needed corrective on prosecutorial interference with the jury guarantee, and given the Court's recent recognition of how important it is, it is not inconceivable that the Court will go down this path.

Another doctrinal area where some movement is being made and more could be done is in the Eighth Amendment context. Here, too, we have seen some modest inroads that could eventually pave the way for much more. Until 2010, the Supreme Court reviewed noncapital sentences with great deference to the government. As Chapter 7 explains, a defendant challenging a sentence as cruel and unusual would have to show, as a threshold matter, that the state lacked a reasonable basis for believing that the sentence would achieve any of the traditional purposes of punishment (i.e., deterrence, rehabilitation, incapacitation, or retributive justice).[49] It is almost impossible to meet that standard, because the state can almost always make a credible argument that it believed a sentence would incapacitate an individual from committing more crimes. It is hardly surprising that the Court did not strike down a single sentence under that inquiry. But in 2010, the Court seemed to change the test, at least in some cases. In *Graham v. Florida,* the Court held that life without the opportunity for parole was a disproportionate sentence for all juveniles who do not commit homicide. Instead of applying its usual threshold test, the Court applied a categorical test that had previously been used only in capital cases. Under this approach, the Court "first considers 'objective indicia of society's standards, as expressed in legislative enactments and state practice' to determine if there is a national consensus against the sentencing practice at issue." Then the Court must "exercise its own independent judgment whether the punishment in question violates the Constitution."[50] The Court followed up *Graham* 2 years later with *Miller v. Alabama,* in which the Court determined that *mandatory* life without parole (LWOP) sentences for juveniles are unconstitutional in all cases, including homicides, because a judge must make an individual determination that such a sentence is appropriate in a given case. The majority concluded that mandatory LWOP "prevents those meting out punishment from considering a juvenile's 'lessened culpability' and greater 'capacity for change.'"[51] Thus in *Miller,* the Court borrowed from another line of death penalty cases that prohibited the mandatory imposition of the death penalty without individualized consideration of the defendant's characteristics and the details of the offense. These two decisions were expressly limited to juveniles, but one can imagine broadening them to other noncapital contexts as well, thus paving the way for more categorical challenges and striking down mandatory sentencing schemes in other contexts.

Indeed, if the Court continues to see that its approach to capital cases also should be applied to noncapital cases—as it did in *Graham* and *Miller*—it will see that it has an obligation under the Eighth Amendment to check mandatory sentences not only in capital cases and in LWOP cases involving juveniles, but in all cases. When the Court rejected mandatory death sentences, it noted that "the fundamental respect for humanity underlying the Eighth Amendment requires consideration of the character and record of the individual offender and the circumstances of the particular offense as a constitutionally indispensable part of the process of inflicting the penalty of death."[52] But of course that same "fundamental respect for humanity underlying the Eighth Amendment" applies to noncapital sentences as well and likewise calls for individualized assessment of whether the punishment fits the circumstances of the crime and the individual character and record of the person who commits it.[53] The Court has already acknowledged this when it comes to juveniles receiving LWOP sentences, but the concern cannot be cabined. Logical and doctrinal consistency should lead the Court to see that there is not one Eighth Amendment for death cases and one for everything else. Its principles should apply across the board, thus paving the way for abolition of all mandatory sentences that prohibit judges from taking into account an individual's circumstances.

Recent developments suggest there is an opportunity for progress on the fees and fines front as well. As noted, this is an area in which the doctrine is already clear that failure to pay fees and fines cannot be the basis for imprisonment where defendants are too poor to pay, but courts have weakly policed this area of law. As more attention has been paid to the abuses of criminal justice administration, federal district courts have started taking seriously challenges brought against municipalities for their policies of incarcerating indigent defendants for failure to pay fees and fines with no regard to their ability to pay. For example, claims against both Ferguson and New Orleans have moved past the motion-to-dismiss stage.[54] Despite a 2014 settlement purporting to end practices like these in Montgomery, Alabama, several new cases are currently moving forward there challenging "a series of interwoven policies designed to increase municipal budgets at the expense of members of the community."[55] A federal court has also preliminarily enjoined a Tennessee county's practice of jailing indigent probationers for failure to pay court fees with no regard to their ability to pay their bond.[56] Some state courts have recently moved to police these practices more closely as well.[57] Whether this litigation will ultimately lead the way for even bolder decisions remains to be seen, but the seeds for change have been planted.

There is room for change, too, when it comes to the federal courts' approach to interpreting statutes—whether with respect to applying the rule of lenity or in relation to a constitutional vagueness challenge. Justice Antonin Scalia was a strong advocate for lenity on the Supreme Court and was willing to strike down laws as vague as well, even if meant individuals who committed violent crimes would benefit. His decision for the Court in *Johnson v. United States,* for example, struck down a clause of the Armed Career Criminal Act (ACCA) as vague.[58] Because that decision ultimately applied retroactively, it paved the way for at least several hundred of the estimated 6,000 to 7,000 individuals serving ACCA sentences to be released from prison earlier than their initial sentences.[59] Moreover, in response to *Johnson,* the U.S. Sentencing Commission deleted an identical "residual clause" from the sentencing guidelines, which ought to reduce by 2,000 the number of people receiving that enhancement each year going forward.[60] Although there are fewer signs of change in the area of immunity defenses, it is nonetheless possible that the Court will someday take a new look at those defenses in cases of prosecutorial misconduct, particularly as more and more cases of misconduct pile up.

The key takeaway is that none of these doctrinal doors are slammed shut for all time, and some have already been pried open. It is just a question of how much further the courts might be willing to go to protect constitutional guarantees that have for too long been dormant.

Judicial Discretion

Judges do more than just interpret and pronounce the relevant legal standards. They have tremendous discretion across a range of issues that are of critical importance to criminal law. In most cases, judges choose the sentences defendants will ultimately receive. Unless there is a mandatory sentence—usually a mandatory minimum—the judge will have the freedom to pick a sentence within a wide range. In states without sentencing guidelines, that range can be quite substantial. It is not uncommon, for example, for a judge to have the freedom to choose a sentence anywhere within a range of 0 to 20 years.[61] Judges can even decide whether the automatic imposition of collateral consequences should affect the length of a term of confinement.[62]

Judges make other key decisions as well, from evidentiary rulings to jury instructions. Since most cases get resolved by pleas, it is noteworthy that it is up to judges whether to accept those pleas. Although judges typically accept the deal as long as the plea was knowing and voluntary, some judges push back when they see prosecutorial overreaching. For example, when he was serving as a federal judge, John Gleeson called out what he saw as excessive charging in the Eastern District of New York "in the hope that doing so might eradicate or reduce the number of such abuses."[63] In one such instance, the government agreed to vacate convictions to allow an individual who had already served two decades of a more than 57-year prison sentence to be resentenced.[64] On the heels of broader criticisms by judges (including Judge Gleeson) about how federal prosecutors were charging defendants in drug trafficking cases involving mandatory minimums and enhancements for prior felonies, the Department of Justice (DOJ) altered its policies.[65] To be sure, one cannot know whether the judges' critiques caused the shift, but the timing suggests that DOJ heard the judges' concerns.

When prosecutors engage in misconduct, such as by failing to disclose exculpatory *Brady* material, judges determine the remedy and whether prosecutors should be sanctioned. Some judges have been vocal about what they see as a pattern of prosecutorial misconduct or overreach and have used their position on the bench to seek to address it. Judge Emmet Sullivan, for example, appointed an outside attorney to investigate the failure of federal prosecutors to disclose exculpatory evidence in the prosecution of former Alaska senator Ted Stevens.[66] Alex Kozinski, a former federal appellate judge in California, has argued that judges need to publicly name prosecutors who engage in misconduct.[67] Other judges have likewise issued opinions or orders calling out prosecutorial misconduct. Sometimes they ask the government to conduct an internal investigation, and other times they refer the prosecutor involved for discipline.[68] In some cases, a judicial critique has sparked greater change in office practices.[69] Some judges, including Judge Sullivan, have put in place standing orders placing greater demands on prosecutors to turn over exculpatory evidence in proceedings before them.[70] At times, judges are concerned that prosecutors are not sufficiently vigorous in pursuing criminal activities, particularly when it comes to wealthy corporations. Thus judges have indicated a greater willingness to police settlements that appear too favorable to corporate defendants or that contain illegal or unethical settlement terms.[71]

Judges have also taken the lead in many cases in establishing alternatives to incarceration or treatment models in their courts because of their frustration with the "perceived inadequacies in the conventional criminal law administrative approach."[72] These so-called problem-solving courts seek to address some underlying problem of the defendant that has a nexus to his or her criminal activity (such as drug addiction or mental illness) in a collegial, nonadversarial environment. Judges have similarly used their discretion to create so-called reentry courts, which aim to help defendants transition from terms of incarceration to jobs, educational opportunities, and housing.[73] There are thousands of problem-solving courts at the state level, and in recent years, federal courts have started to create such courts as well.[74] In many if not most cases, judges spearheaded the creation of these courts (with the consent of the parties) as a matter of discretion and took the lead in designing the courts, including setting the eligibility criteria and determining the effect of participation on a defendant's ultimate sentence.

Sometimes judges go beyond using their authority in the courtroom to effect change and use their stature to call attention to broader failings in the system. Justice Anthony Kennedy, for example, has spoken out against solitary confinement and the failure to rethink long sentences, noting in 2003 that "our resources are misspent, our punishments too severe, our sentences too long."[75] Judge Jed Rakoff of the Southern District of New York has called out the disproportionate share of power lodged in prosecutors, has criticized mass incarceration, and has urged other federal judges to speak out against the failings of the criminal justice system.[76] Several state judges have been advocating for bail reform. For example, Chief Justice Tani Cantil-Sakauye of the California Supreme Court publicly announced that she supported an overhaul of the state's pretrial system because it unfairly disadvantages low-income defendants.[77] Timothy Evans, the chief judge of the Circuit Court of Cook County, Illinois, recently issued an order requiring judges to set bail at an amount that the defendant can actually pay.[78]

Even this relatively brief overview of judicial powers and discretion should make it plain that who sits on the bench makes an enormous difference in how criminal law looks in the United States, not only because these judges interpret criminal laws but also because of their vast discretion and the stature they have to urge changes. While it has been obvious to many criminal justice reformers to pursue a litigation strategy as part of their reform efforts, they have largely ignored judicial selection as a key area for pursuing change, but the selection of judges is critical for all the areas outlined here.

Selecting Judges

It is long past time for those interested in criminal justice reform to focus on the composition of the bench as part of their reform efforts. Although there has been a nascent movement focusing on prosecutor elections, judges have thus far escaped attention. Reformers have also failed to pay much attention to the federal bench and appointments made by the president. This relative lack of interest was vividly demonstrated when Justice Scalia passed away, and President Obama had to name a successor to his seat on the Supreme Court. This vacancy should have been of central concern to those interested in criminal law, not only because the Court is responsible for policing constitutional guarantees in criminal cases, but also because Justice Scalia was often a crucial vote for protections for defendants.[79] On the modern Supreme Court, Justice Scalia was the greatest defender of both the rule of lenity and the rule against vagueness.[80] Justice Scalia was also committed to other substantive criminal law issues, including a defendant's right to confront witnesses against him or her and the jury guarantee, which led him to vote with the majority in a host of important sentencing decisions that gave greater discretion to judges and placed a greater check on the government.[81]

Given Justice Scalia's importance to many blockbuster criminal cases that protected defendants' rights, one might have expected criminal justice reform advocates to pay close attention to his replacement by President Obama. Black Lives Matter and other criminal justice reform advocates could have focused on the nomination to ensure that Justice Scalia's replacement would, at a minimum, share his commitment to constitutional rights that protect defendants—and indeed look for someone who would be more protective, as Justice Scalia was not uniformly protective of defendants' interests, all but ignoring the Eighth Amendment, for example.[82]

There were some reports that President Obama had considered people with public defense in their background for the open seat, but there was little advocacy by criminal justice reformers around the issue or any noticeable attention by them to the type of justice who should be selected.[83] When President Obama announced his selection of Judge Merrick Garland, a former career prosecutor with a record of supporting the government in criminal cases, there was hardly a word from the criminal justice advocacy community.[84] If reformers want to achieve real substantive changes in criminal law, this must change, not only by paying attention to Supreme Court appointments but to all federal court appointments and judicial selection at the state level, too. Who serves in the judiciary is critical to the development of criminal law. Ironically, the judge ultimately selected to the open seat left by Justice Scalia, Justice Neil Gorsuch, might in the end be more likely to rule in favor of criminal defendants than Judge Garland because Justice Gorsuch seems to share Justice Scalia's commitment to lenity, textualism, and the separation of powers.[85] But if that occurs, it will largely be fortuity, as groups concerned with criminal justice failed to mobilize around the issue of the Supreme Court appointment. Moreover, if groups had focused on the issue, it might have resulted in getting someone even more attuned to the need for robust protection of rights in criminal cases.

Reformers in other areas have recognized the importance of the courts to their agenda and have actively participated in the politics of judicial selection to make sure their positions are represented. Abortion-rights groups, for instance, were a driving force in the ardent Democratic opposition to the nomination of Justice Gorsuch, urging Democratic senators to filibuster a procedural vote by sending letters to the senators and organizing anti-Gorsuch protests around the country.[86] Liberal groups also strongly opposed President Obama's nomination of Michael Boggs, a conservative Democrat, to the U.S. District Court for the Northern District of Georgia, because of his opposition to same-sex marriage and his record supporting anti-abortion legislation.[87] Labor and environmental groups initially opposed President Obama's consideration of Judge Sri Srinivasan of the D.C. Circuit for a Supreme Court vacancy, voicing concerns over his representation of a mining company and Enron while he was an attorney at O'Melveny & Myers.[88] These other progressive groups have long recognized that judicial appointments are critical to their goals, and they have pushed Democratic politicians to put judges on the bench who will not be hostile to those goals.

Criminal justice reform advocates have been largely silent on judicial selection to this point, but if they want to achieve meaningful change, they, too, must pay attention to judicial appointments and elections. It is critical to change the composition of a bench dominated by prosecutors. Currently, the federal bench is overwhelmingly comprised of individuals with prosecution experience and has very few individuals with a public defense background. Almost half the active judges on the federal bench (43%) have prosecutorial experience, compared with only 10.4% with public defense experience.[89] Even with a president who proclaimed an interest in criminal justice reform, these numbers barely budged. Of President Obama's nominees, a full 41% had prosecution experience, and only 14% had public defense experience.[90] While President Obama appointed five of the current federal appellate judges with public defense backgrounds, that brought the total to just seven.[91]

The state court bench suffers from a similar skew. A survey of state supreme courts found that those with prosecution experience outnumbered those with a public defense background by a 2 to 1 margin.[92] Lower courts often contain a disproportionate number of judges with prosecution backgrounds as well.[93] One county in Florida, for example, has a bench where 3 out of 4 judges has prosecution experience.[94]

Although judicial doctrine is often slow to change, a bench with more diverse perspectives than those of government prosecutors is more likely to shift, both in terms of doctrine and in terms of those critical day-to-day findings of fact and exercises of discretion. Social scientists have long demonstrated that judicial backgrounds affect decisions.[95] One cannot expect much scrutiny of the government with a bench overwhelmingly occupied by prosecutors. Of course, people can and do obtain new perspectives and outlooks as they take on different roles, so some people who become judges with a professional background in prosecution may not simply defer to the government's claims and positions. But "it defies what we know about human nature and experience to think that someone's past experiences have no effect on their outlook. Because real criminal justice reform requires judges to check overreach by prosecutors and other law enforcement officials, it is critical that the bench reflect a range of professional backgrounds."[96]

Thus if criminal justice reform groups want to make real changes in the system, they need to take that commitment to all areas, including the judiciary. That means taking an active role in policing who gets appointed to the federal bench and showing the same zeal they have started to apply to local prosecutor races and using it to address judicial elections in the states.

CONCLUSION

I HAD THREE GOALS in writing this book. The first was to demonstrate that many of our criminal justice policies that are promulgated under the guise of being tough on crime are anything but. In fact, as Part One showed, they often make us less safe while costing a fortune and ruining lives. My second aim was to explain why we ended up with such counterproductive policies. Part Two took on that task and explained how the lopsided politics of crime, which favor superficial severity, put in place an institutional framework that is resistant to change and leaves prosecutors essentially unregulated as they enforce bloated and overly punitive criminal codes. Third and most importantly, for those seeking to reform criminal law in the United States, I wanted to craft a new agenda that sets its sights on dismantling the institutional architecture destined to continue producing excessive criminal laws and policies that do not promote public safety and that replaces it with a framework designed to produce a more rational approach to public safety that will also be more protective of individual liberty and make better use of our limited resources for addressing crime. The three key pillars of this new institutional framework require a system of checks on prosecutors, the creation of expert agencies designed to withstand political pressures for irrationality, and a robust role for courts in policing against government excess.

What remains is the question of how to make these institutional changes in the dysfunctional political environment we operate in. Won't the structural changes proposed in Part Three face the same opposition as movements to lower sentences or divert more people to alternatives to incarceration? I would be lying if I said no without qualification. Institutional reform will be hard.

But there are several reasons why the institutional changes outlined in this book will be easier to get adopted than seeking first to make direct substantive changes to sentences or criminal laws. First, while it is easy for a politician seeking to block a substantive reform to use a Willie Horton–style ad campaign against it, institutional changes are much harder to paint in the same simplistic light. These are good government proposals about getting better results and saving money. To the extent there is opposition, it is going to come from entrenched interests, and they are going to have a harder time getting the public to sympathize because institutional reform is just not as amenable to the same sound-bite politics and scare tactics as substantive changes. The very nature of a structural change is that it is about altering institutional architecture, not dictating an outcome. So while opponents might seek to predict what an institutional change might mean, those are just guesses because none of the institutional shifts promise any given outcome. Institutional changes of the kind advocated here just ensure a process whereby decisions can be made with attention to costs, rationality, constitutional values, and public safety—and it will be harder to oppose those points than substantive shifts.

Second, and relatedly, there is a growing movement of interest groups in favor of reforming criminal law and its administration in the United States, and they have already achieved some modest successes. If these groups start channeling their energy to institutional change—and they already have with respect to local prosecutor elections—they are likely to achieve similar success as they have with modest substantive changes because these are the kinds of sensible reforms people can get behind—or at least not oppose. An interested and engaged group of citizens can achieve tangible results as long as the opposition is not easily mobilized against them, and many of the changes outlined in Part Three are precisely the kinds of proposals that get less attention except by a smaller group of interested parties.

Third, as these institutional changes are made, it is likely the public and powerful interests will grow to support the substantive changes that follow as a result. By definition, these institutions will be set up to produce policies that are cost effective and promote public safety, so they should lead to better outcomes. And as those better outcomes materialize, the case for institutional change and the policies it produces gets stronger. Fiscal conservatives and those looking for budget relief will thus think twice before dismantling an architecture that produces more cost-effective outcomes. And while the politics of fear are always an issue, if enough key thought leaders and politicians stand behind these policies, the public will see their value. Although the public is punitive at the wholesale level and in the abstract—supporting harsh sentences or new criminal laws in the wake of

some high-profile incident of violence or media attention to a particular social problem, such as a new drug wave—people think differently about punishment when faced with the facts of particular cases. Indeed, studies show
that laypeople would impose less severe sentences than the ones actually
imposed by judges in real cases.[1] And because the public has recently been
exposed to stories of excessive sentences and unjustified pretrial detentions
as part of the media's relatively recent attention to the problems of mass incarceration, the public has grown more receptive to reform, including
placing a greater emphasis on rehabilitation and using alternatives to incarceration. So if enough key leaders endorse these models, enough members
of the public could go along as well to keep these policies in place.

One cautionary note is that I am proposing a model that relies on expertise and decisions grounded in empirical evidence at a time when it seems
like the notion of expertise itself is under attack. Whether it is the denial of
climate change or the broader dismissal of science across a range of health
and safety areas, we seem to be witnessing a backlash against elites and
science and expertise.[2] If a sizable portion of the public won't trust scientists to deal with energy policy or the environment or public health, why
would they trust experts who aren't even scientists to handle public safety?
This turn from accumulated knowledge to a broader embrace of populism
across a range of issues may turn out to be the biggest obstacle to the reforms outlined here. "At its core, populism is the fallacious and dangerous
idea that the people's will is absolute, and that what's 'popular' must also
be good or true."[3] In a world where facts and results do not matter but
what is popular does, it is harder to argue for the institutional changes I
propose because tough-on-crime proposals, no matter how wrongheaded,
have always been popular.

That said, more and more people are learning about the failure of our
criminal justice policies firsthand, without the filter of experts having to explain it. Because so many people are now involved in the criminal justice
system—with one in three adults having some kind of criminal record—
they are learning through experience how overbroad our approach is. This
is particularly true in communities of color, where direct interaction with
criminal justice policies is even more widespread. The recently elected district attorney in Philadelphia, Larry Krasner, highlighted this kind of on-
the-ground knowledge as a potential game changer for paving the way for
significant criminal justice reform when he noted:

> The black voters in Philly . . . are more likely to have a family member who is
> a police officer, a family member who is in jail, and a family member who has
> been killed or severely victimized. They are more likely to have seen this whole

thing in three dimensions. Whether or not they have affluence and a fancy degree like the white liberals do in certain parts of town, they know what they are talking about. So I think perhaps we had the advantage that these were issues that were very, very well known to African-American voters, especially women voters.[4]

People with that kind of direct experience already recognize that the current approaches are failing and need to be reformed. They do not need an expert to explain it to them. And those are the kinds of well-informed reformers who will be critical to paving the way for a new institutional model even if traditional elites are not trusted.

But even if skepticism about elitism and expertise can be overcome, there is a second significant hurdle. The arguments in this book are premised on the idea that the public is primarily concerned with public safety as the goal in setting criminal justice policies. It is entirely possible that a significant segment of the public is willing to sacrifice public safety for what it believes to be retributive justice—giving people what they deserve, even if that undermines public safety. These people may not care that long terms of incarceration or collateral consequences of conviction prompt more criminal behavior. They may simply want to inflict pain on people who commit crimes and make them pay. Of course, even if this were one's goal, the current system is ill-designed for achieving it because it lumps so many disparate types of criminal behavior together, as Chapter 1 explained.[5] But there may be enough people out there who simply do not care about that nuance and who view all people who commit crimes as deserving of harsh treatment, no matter what the cost to public safety. This may be particularly true if one views criminal justice issues through a racial prism and all the biases it too often entails. This book makes no attempt to resolve a battle between the utilitarian goal of maximizing public safety and the pursuit of retributive justice, should those two ends come in conflict. To the extent members of the public are out for short-term emotional fulfillment even if it comes at a long-term cost to their own safety, nothing here will overcome that.

Rather, the arguments here are for those who want to make us safer and who recognize that our current approach is fundamentally flawed. For that audience, institutional changes will bring a much-needed shift in tactics that will save money and save lives. There is a win-win to be had in criminal justice policy-making, and if we can loosen the populist grip on our policies, we can achieve it.

Notes

Introduction

1. To be sure, the tactic does not always work, particularly if other electoral concerns are pressing. In the 2017 governor's race in Virginia, for example, Republican Ed Gillespie tried to paint his Democratic opponent, Ralph Northam, as weak on crime committed by immigrant gangs. Northam prevailed, but that victory could have been as much a backlash against Trump as it was disapproval of the soft-on-crime attack. More importantly, Northam responded to the attack by proclaiming that he would be tough on crime and would prosecute anyone who committed a felony, regardless of immigration status. Fenit Nirappil and Laura Vozzella, "Gillespie Rolls Out 'Kill, Rape, Control' Attack Ad against Northam," *Washington Post,* September 29, 2017, https://www.washingtonpost.com/local/virginia-politics /gillespie-quietly-rolls-out-second-kill-rape-control-attack-ad-against -northam/2017/09/28/8540cd24-a46f-11e7-8cfe-d5b912fabc99_story.html. Politicians know better than to try to debate whether one should be tough on crime. Instead, the question is how to prove to voters that they are sufficiently tough.

2. World Prison Brief, Highest-to-Lowest Prison Population Rate, bit. ly/1plWDg3; Sentencing Project, *Americans with Criminal Records* (n.d.), http://www.sentencingproject.org/doc/publications/cc_HiT_CriminalRecords _profile_1.pdf.

3. Julian V. Roberts et al., *Penal Populism and Public Opinion* (New York: Oxford University Press, 2003), 27.

4. Franklin E. Zimring, *The Great American Crime Decline* (New York: Oxford University Press, 2007), 197–199, 205–209.

5. Tom Nichols, *The Death of Expertise: The Campaign Against Knowledge and Why It Matters* (New York: Oxford University Press, 2017).

6. Michelle Alexander, *The New Jim Crow: Mass Incarceration in the Age of Colorblindness* (New York: New Press, 2010); Paul Butler, *Chokehold: Policing Black Men* (New York: New Press, 2017); Angela J. Davis, *Policing the Black Man: Arrest, Prosecution, and Imprisonment* (New York: Pantheon Books, 2017); William J. Stuntz, *The Collapse of American Criminal Justice* (Cambridge, MA: Harvard University Press, 2011).

7. James Forman Jr., *Locking Up Our Own: Crime and Punishment in Black America* (New York: Farrar, Straus, and Giroux, 2017), 12.

8. Roberts et al., *Penal Populism and Public Opinion*, 24.

9. John Pratt, *Penal Populism* (New York: Routledge, 2007); Roberts et al., *Penal Populism and Public Opinion;* Tim Newburn and Trevor Jones, "Symbolic Politics and Penal Populism: The Long Shadow of Willie Horton," *Crime, Media, Culture* 1 (2005): 72–87.

10. Pratt, *Penal Populism*, 12.

11. Pratt, *Penal Populism*, 12, 18–19.

12. Bill Stuntz deserves credit for labeling the political process surrounding criminal justice as pathological. William J. Stuntz, "The Pathological Politics of Criminal Law," *Michigan Law Review* 100 (2001): 505–600.

13. Matthew R. Christiansen and William N. Eskridge Jr., "Congressional Overrides of Supreme Court Statutory Interpretation Decisions, 1967–2011," *Texas Law Review* 92 (2014): 1383.

14. Angela J. Davis, *Arbitrary Justice: The Power of the American Prosecutor* (New York: Oxford University Press, 2007).

15. Deena Winter, "Some Prosecutors Think Nebraska Has Gone Soft on Crime," Watchdog, June 19, 2015, http://watchdog.org/225079/prisons-bill.

16. Martin Kaste, "States Push for Prison Sentence Overhaul; Prosecutors Push Back," NPR, July 9, 2014, http://www.npr.org/2014/07/09/329587949/states-push-for-prison-sentence-reform-and-prosecutors-push-back.

17. Larry Hannan, "Is the 'Incarceration Capital of the World' Finally Ready to Lose Its Title?," *Slate*, April 6, 2017, http://www.slate.com/articles/news_and_politics/trials_and_error/2017/04/is_louisiana_finally_ready_for_criminal_justice_reform.html.

18. Julia Craven, "This Letter from Louisiana Prosecutors Perfectly Explains Why Criminal Justice Reform Is So Hard," *Huffington Post*, September 14, 2016, http://www.huffingtonpost.com/entry/criminal-justice-reform_us_57d87019e4b0aa4b722d3af0.

19. Sentencing Project, *State Criminal Justice Advocacy in a Conservative Environment* (2015), 2–4, http://www.sentencingproject.org/wp-content/uploads/2015/09/inc_Conservative_State_Advocacy.pdf.

20. Legislative Services Agency, *Criminal Law and Sentencing Policy Study Committee: Meeting Minutes* (October 31, 2013), 6, http://www.in.gov/legislative/interim/committee/minutes/CLSPGAV.pdf.

21. Radley Balko, "Federal Prosecutors Cling to Mandatory Minimums," *Washington Post,* February 6, 2014, https://www.washingtonpost.com/news/opinions/wp/2014/02/06/federal-prosecutors-cling-to-mandatory-minimums.

22. Letter from Dennis Boyd, Executive Director, National Association of Assistant U.S. Attorneys, to Patti B. Saris, Chair, U.S. Sentencing Commission, July 2, 2014, https://www.naausa.org/2013/index.php/news/naausa-news/112 -no-retroactive-application.

23. National Association of Assistant United States Attorneys, *Statement on Federal Sentencing Policy* (2014), 2, http://www.naausa.org/site/index.php/resources /policy/75-sep-2014-federal-sentencing-policy; Steve Cook, President of the National Association of Assistant U.S. Attorneys, "Statement on the Sentencing Reform and Corrections Act of 2015," news release, October 1, 2015, http://www.naausa.org/site/index.php/resources/press-releases/89-oct-2015-srca -press-release; Association of Indiana Prosecuting Attorneys, "Protecting Indiana Children and Families: Association of Indiana Prosecuting Attorneys, Inc. Announces 2016 Legislative Goals," news release, December 9, 2015, http://www.in.gov/ipac/files/2016_Association_Legislative_rollout_PR.pdf.

24. *See, e.g.,* "Resources," NAAUSA, http://www.naausa.org/site/index.php /resources.

25. SpearIt, "The Return of Pell Grants for Prisoners?," *Criminal Justice* (2016): 13, https://www.americanbar.org/content/dam/aba/publications/criminal _justice_magazine/v31/SpearIt.authcheckdam.pdf.

26. Charles Colson Task Force on Federal Corrections, *Transforming Prisons, Restoring Lives* (2016), ix.

27. Shane Bauer, "How Conservatives Learned to Love Prison Reform," *Mother Jones,* March/April 2014, http://www.motherjones.com/politics/2014/02 /conservatives-prison-reform-right-on-crime; Sentencing Project, *Drug-Free Zone Laws: An Overview of State Policies* (2013), 6, http://sentencingproject .org/wp-content/uploads/2015/12/Drug-Free-Zone-Laws.pdf. *See also* Judith Greene et al., Justice Policy Institute, *Disparity by Design* (2006), 6, http://www.drugpolicy.org/docUploads/SchoolZonesReport06.pdf.

28. Sentencing Project, *State Criminal Justice Advocacy,* 6–10; S.C. Code Ann. § 44–53–445 (2010).

29. Rachel E. Barkow, "Federalism and the Politics of Sentencing," *Columbia Law Review* 105 (2005): 1285.

30. Barkow, "Federalism," 1285.

31. David Kohn, "Three Strikes: Penal Overkill in California?," *CBS News: 60 Minutes,* October 28, 2002, http://www.cbsnews.com/news/three-strikes -28–10–2002; Matt Taibbi, "Cruel and Unusual Punishment: The Shame of Three Strikes Laws," *RollingStone,* March 27, 2016, http://www.rollingstone .com/politics/news/cruel-and-unusual-punishment-the-shame-of-three-strikes -laws-20130327; California Legislative Analyst's Office, Proposition 36: Three Strikes Law; Sentencing for Repeat Felony Offenders; Initiative Statute (2012), http://www.lao.ca.gov/ballot/2012/36_11_2012.aspx.

32. California Legislative Analyst's Office, Proposition 36. *See also* Marie Gottschalk, *Caught: The Prison State and the Lockdown of American Politics* (Princeton, NJ: Princeton University Press, 2016), 184.

33. Nazgol Ghandnoosh, Sentencing Project, *Can We Wait 75 Years to Cut the Prison Population in Half?* (March 8, 2018), https://www.sentencingproject

.org/publications/can-wait-75-years-cut-prison-population-half/?utm_source
=In+Justice+Today+Newsletter&utm_campaign=a3f47f1a44-&utm_medium
=email&utm_term=0_0331e33901-a3f47f1a44-52937171.

34. Bruce Western, "The Rehabilitation Paradox," *New Yorker,* May 9, 2016,
http://www.newyorker.com/news/news-desk/the-rehabilitation-paradox.

35. E. Ann Carson, Bureau of Justice Statistics, *Prisoners in 2014* (2015), 16–17,
tables 11–12, http://www.bjs.gov/content/pub/pdf/p14.pdf.

36. Max Ehrenfreund, "The Myth That Fewer People Are Going to Prison,"
Washington Post, May 18, 2016, https://www.washingtonpost.com/news
/wonk/wp/2016/05/18/the-myth-that-fewer-people-are-going-to-prison.

37. Gottschalk, *Caught,* 8.

1. Misleading Monikers

1. *See, e.g.,* Dan Gunderson, "Law Based More on Myth Than Fact," *MPR
News,* June 19, 2007, http://www.mprnews.org/story/2007/06/11
/sexoffender2; Dana Williams and Selly Kestin, "Lawmakers File Sex
Predator Legislation," *Sun Sentinel,* December 17, 2013, http://articles.sun
-sentinel.com/2013-12-17/news/fl-sex-predators-legislation-filed-20131217_1
_cherish-perrywinkle-offenders-predator-law.

2. "Critics Look for Alternative to Offender Civil Commitments," *Fox News,*
July 12, 2006, http://www.foxnews.com/story/2006/07/12/critics-look-for
-alternative-to-sex-offender-civil-commitments.html.

3. Serge F. Kovaleski, "In Sex Arrests Hailed by Pirro, Little Jail Time," *New
York Times,* October 13, 2006, http://www.nytimes.com/2006/10/13
/nyregion/13pirro.html?pagewanted=all.

4. "Louisiana Gov. Jindal Authorizes Chemical Castration of Sex Offenders,"
Huffington Post, May 25, 2011, http://www.huffingtonpost.com/2008/06/26
/louisiana-gov-jindal-auth_n_109342.html.

5. *See* Office of Justice Programs, Federal Sex Offender Legislation, http://ojp
.gov/smart/legislation.htm; Parents for Megan's Law, Megan's Law and the
Adam Walsh Child Protection Act, http://www.parentsformeganslaw.org
/public/meganFederal.html#.

6. "Clinton Signs Tougher 'Megan's Law,'" *CNN,* May 17, 1996, http://edition
.cnn.com/ALLPOLITICS/1996/news/9605/17/clinton.sign/index.shtml.

7. *See* Bill O'Reilly, What Is Jessica's Law?, http://www.billoreilly.com
/jessicaslaw; Jessica's Law, Wikipedia, https://en.wikipedia.org/wiki
/Jessica%27s_Law.

8. Emanuella Grinberg, "5 Years Later, States Struggle to Comply with Federal
Sex Offender Law," *CNN,* July 28, 2011, http://www.cnn.com/2011/CRIME
/07/28/sex.offender.adam.walsh.act; Haylee Barber, "The Amber behind
Amber Alert Still Waiting for Justice 20 Years Later," *NBC News,* January 17, 2016, http://www.nbcnews.com/feature/cold-case-spotlight/amber
-behind-amber-alert-still-waiting-justice-20-years-later-n497696; Jon
Leiberman, "Child Molestation Victim Campaigns for Sex Offender Registry

Improvements," *HNGN,* February 16, 2015, http://www.hngn.com/articles /69758/20150216/child-molestation-victim-campaigns-sex-offender-registry -improvements-hngn-true.htm.

9. Catherine L. Carpenter, "A Sign of Hope: Shifting Attitudes on Sex Offense Registration Laws," *Southwestern Law Review* 47 (2017): 6–15.

10. Human Rights Watch, *No Easy Answers: Sex Offender Laws in the US* (2007), 39–40, https://www.hrw.org/sites/default/files/reports /us0907webwcover.pdf.

11. Abigail Pesta, "The Accidental Sex Offender," *Marie Claire,* July 28, 2011, http://www.marieclaire.com/culture/news/a6294/teen-sex-offender.

12. *See* Pesta, "The Accidental Sex Offender."

13. Curtis Killman, "Sex Offenders Struggle to Find Jobs," *Tulsa World,* July 10, 2005.

14. *See* Robby Soave, "These Teens Kept Their Sexting Private, But Cops Found Out. Now They Face Sex Offender Registry, Jail," *Reason: Hit and Run Blog,* September 1, 2015, http://reason.com/blog/2015/09/01/these-teens-kept-their -sexting-private-b; Tamar Lewin, "Rethinking Sex Offender Laws for Youth Texting," *New York Times,* March 20, 2010, http://www.nytimes.com/2010 /03/21/us/21sexting.html?pagewanted=all&_r=0.

15. *See* Pesta, "The Accidental Sex Offender"; *see also* Sarah Stillman, "The List," *New Yorker,* March 14, 2016, http://www.newyorker.com/magazine /2016/03/14/when-kids-are-accused-of-sex-crimes.

16. *See* E. Ann Carson, Bureau of Justice Statistics, *Prisoners in 2014* (2015), 5, 16–17, http://www.bjs.gov/content/pub/pdf/p14.pdf. This estimate is based on the fact that 12.1% of all sentenced prisoners under state jurisdiction have, as their most serious offense, a drug offense other than possession, Carson, *Prisoners,* 16, and that 50.1% of all sentenced prisoners under federal jurisdiction have, as their most serious offense, a drug offense (where 99.5% of those drug offenses in the federal system are for trafficking), Carson, *Prisoners,* 17. Thus, it is a total of 12.1% of those under state jurisdiction (in 2014, there were 1,317,262 prisoners under state authority, so approximately 159,389 for drug offenses), and 50.1% of those in the federal system (in 2014, there were 191,374 prisoners sentenced, so approximately 95,878 prisoners sentenced for drug trafficking).

17. Charles Colson Task Force on Federal Corrections, *Transforming Prisons, Restoring Lives* (2016), 7.

18. U.S. Sentencing Commission, *Report to the Congress: Mandatory Minimum Penalties in the Federal Criminal Justice System* (2011), 167, http://www.ussc .gov/sites/default/files/pdf/news/congressional-testimony-and-reports /mandatory-minimum-penalties/20111031-rtc-pdf/Chapter_08.pdf.

19. *See* U.S. Sentencing Commission, 167.

20. *See* Eric L. Sevigny and Jonathan P. Caulkins, "Kingpins or Mules: An Analysis of Drug Offenders Incarcerated in Federal and State Prisons," *Criminology and Public Policy* 3 (2004): 410.

21. Ronald Reagan, "Campaign against Drug Abuse," PBS, September 14, 1986, http://www.pbs.org/wgbh/americanexperience/features/primary-resources

/reagan-drug-campaign; Brian Mann, "The Drug Laws That Changed How We Punish," NPR, February 14, 2013, http://www.npr.org/2013/02/14 /171822608/the-drug-laws-that-changed-how-we-punish.

22. William J. Clinton, "1998 State of the Union Address," *Washington Post,* January 27, 1998, http://www.washingtonpost.com/wp-srv/politics/special /states/docs/sou98.htm.

23. Stephen J. Schulhofer, Letter to Hon. Patti B. Saris regarding Proposed Amendments to the United States Sentencing Guidelines 10, March 11, 2014, https://www.ussc.gov/sites/default/files/pdf/amendment-process/public -comment/20140326/public-comment-Schulhofer.pdf; United States v. Ysidro Diaz, No. 11-CR-00821-2 (E.D.N.Y. January 28, 2013).

24. Some jurisdictions, like the federal system, allow for relatively small adjustments based on role that "mitigate sentences slightly but still leave low-level offenders facing prison terms suitable for a drug boss." Memorandum Explaining a Policy Disagreement with the Drug Trafficking Offense Guideline, United States v. Ysidro Diaz, 11-CR-00821–2 (JG), 2013 WL 322243, at *7 (E.D.N.Y. January 28, 2013).

25. Alex Stamm, "The Reality of Federal Drug Sentencing," *ACLU,* November 27, 2012, https://www.aclu.org/blog/reality-federal-drug-sentencing.

26. *See* James E. Felman, American Bar Association, Testimony before the U.S. Sentencing Commission for the Hearing on Proposed Amendments to the Federal Sentencing Guidelines regarding Economic Crimes 2, 10, March 12, 2015, http://www.americanbar.org/content/dam/aba/uncategorized/GAO /2015mar12_ussceconcrimetestimony.authcheckdam.pdf.

27. Stuart P. Green, *Thirteen Ways to Steal a Bicycle* (Cambridge, MA: Harvard University Press, 2012), 31.

28. *See, e.g.,* Thomas A. Powell and John C. Holt, "Forensic Psychological Evaluations: The Methods in Our Madness," *Vermont Bar Journal* 31 (2005–2006): 40.

29. *See* Youngjae Lee, "Repeat Offenders and the Question of Desert," in *The Role of Previous Convictions at Sentencing: Theoretical and Applied Perspectives,* ed. Julian V. Roberts and Andrew von Hirsch (Portland, OR: Hart, 2010).

30. 18 U.S.C. § 3559(c) (2000).

31. 28 U.S.C. § 994(h) (2012).

32. *Compare* 21 U.S.C. § 841(b)(1)(A) (2012) (setting a maximum penalty of ten years to life for certain drug offenses), *with* 18 U.S.C. § 1111 (setting a maximum penalty of life in prison for second-degree murder).

33. R.I. Gen. Laws Ann. § 12-19–21 (West 2016).

34. "Man Charged with Felony for Killing 3 Seagulls with Audi," *Providence Journal,* September 14, 2015, http://www.providencejournal.com/article /20150914/NEWS/150919616/-1/breaking_ajax.

35. State v. Lyons, 924 A.2d 756, 759 (R.I. 2007).

36. W. Va. Code Ann. § 61-11–18 (West 2016); State ex rel. Chadwell v. Duncil, 474 S.E.2d 573, 576 (W. Va. 1996); State ex rel. Appleby v. Recht, 583 S.E.2d 800, 805–805 (W. Va. 2002).

37. Ind. Code Ann. § 35-50–2-8 (West 2015).

38. Ewing v. California, 538 U.S. 11, 16 (2003).

39. *See, e.g.,* Jack Leonard, "'Pizza Thief' Walks the Line," *Los Angeles Times,* February 10, 2010, http://articles.latimes.com/2010/feb/10/local/la-me -pizzathief10-2010feb10; Ewing v. California, 16; Lockyer v. Andrade, 538 U.S. 63 (2003).

40. *See* Ewing v. California, 44–45 (Breyer, J., dissenting).

41. Even the new version is broad. Among the "serious" felonies that can trigger the third-strike enhancement is burglary. Cal. Penal Code § 1192.7. *See* People v. O'Conner, E060763, 2015 WL 3542399, at *1–2, 8 n.5 (Cal. Ct. App. June 5, 2015) (defendant's third strike was stealing DVDs from neighbor's apartment to support drug habit).

42. *See* Kevin E. McCarthy, Connecticut General Assembly Office of Legislative Research, Felony Murder, February 13, 2008, https://www.cga.ct.gov/2008 /rpt/2008-r-0087.htm.

43. R. Scott Moxley, "OCDA Seeks to Retry Man for Murder in Bizarre Stove Death," *OC Weekly,* January 20, 2016, http://www.ocweekly.com/news/ocda -seeks-to-retry-man-for-murder-in-bizarre-stove-death-plus-other-local-stories -6910858.

44. State v. Jenkins, 729 S.E.2d 250, 257–258, 261 (W. Va. 2012).

45. There are exceptions to this. Some states do provide such a defense. *See, e.g.,* Colo. Rev. Stat. Ann. § 18–3–102(2) (West 2015); Conn. Gen. Stat. Ann. § 53a–54c (West 2015); Me. Rev. Stat. Ann. tit. 17-a, § 202(2) (2015); N.J. Stat. Ann. § 2C:11–3 (West 2015); N.Y. Penal Law § 125.25(3) (McKinney 2016).

46. Three of the four ended up benefitting from an appellate court ruling overturning their convictions because the court interpreted the law to require that the underlying felony involve "dangerously violent and threatening conduct." Layman v. State, 42 N.E.3d 972, 979–980 (Ind. 2015). But in many jurisdictions, courts have not taken such a limited view, and these convictions would have been upheld.

47. George P. Fletcher, "Reflections on Felony-Murder," *Southwestern University Law Review* 12 (1981): 427.

48. Amnesty International and Human Rights Watch, *The Rest of Their Lives* (2005), 1, https://www.hrw.org/sites/default/files/reports/TheRestofTheirLives .pdf.

49. Amnesty International, 11–12.

50. Amnesty International, 29–30.

51. "Brain Maturity Extends Well beyond Teen Years," *NPR,* October 20, 2011, http://www.npr.org/templates/story/story.php?storyId=141164708.

52. "Brain Maturity Extends."

53. Steve Drizin, "The Elkhart Four and the Unjust Application of the Felony Murder Rule on Teens," *Huffington Post,* January 23, 2014, http://www .huffingtonpost.com/steve-drizin/the-elkhart-four_b_4034052.html.

54. Roper v. Simmons, 543 U.S. 551, 568 (2005); Miller v. Alabama, 567 U.S. 460 (2012).

55. Graham v. Florida, 560 U.S. 48, 74 (2010).

56. *See, e.g.,* State v. Hoeck, 843 N.W.2d 67, 70–71 (Iowa 2014).
57. *See, e.g.,* Clark Merrefield, "Should Juveniles Be Sentenced Like Adults?,"
    Daily Beast, November 26, 2012, http://www.thedailybeast.com/articles/2012
    /11/26/should-juvenile-criminals-be-sentenced-like-adults.html; Trymaine Lee,
    "Juvenile Offenders Sentenced to Life Can Face Harsher Treatment Than
    Adults: Report," *Huffington Post,* May 15, 2012, http://www.huffingtonpost
    .com/2012/05/15/juvenile-offenders-life-sentence-_n_1519298.html; Robert
    Schwartz, "Kids Should Never Be Tried as Adults," CNN, February 18, 2010,
    http://www.cnn.com/2010/OPINION/02/18/schwartz.kids.trials.
58. People v. Robinson, 715 N.W.2d 44 (Mich. 2006).
59. United States v. Alvarez, 755 F.2d 830, 849 (11th Cir. 1985).
60. U.S. Sentencing Commission, *U.S. Sentencing Guidelines Manual* (2011),
    § 2B1.1.
61. United States v. Martinez, 924 F.2d 209, 210 (11th Cir. 1991).
62. Homicide provides the classic illustration. Common law homicide drew
    distinctions between intentional killings without provocation (which
    constituted murder), intentional killings with provocation (which constituted
    voluntary manslaughter), and unintentional (reckless or negligent) killings
    (which constituted involuntary manslaughter). Jurors would make the
    relevant findings of mens rea that would distinguish intentional from
    unintentional actors, and the statutory punishment would then vary
    accordingly.
63. *See* 21 U.S.C. §§ 331, 333(a)(1) (2012).
64. Paul J. Larkin Jr. and John-Michael Seibler, "Time to Prune the Tree: The
    Need to Repeal Unnecessary Criminal Laws," *Heritage Foundation Legal
    Memorandum* 173 (2016): 1, http://thf-reports.s3.amazonaws.com/2016
    /LM173.pdf.
65. *The Crimes on the Books and Committee Jurisdiction: Hearing before the
    Over-criminalization Task Force of 2014 of the H. Comm. on the Judiciary,*
    113th Cong. 2, 6 (2014) (statement of Rep. James Sensenbrenner, Chairman,
    Over-criminalization Task Force of 2014, H. Comm. on the Judiciary) (citing
    Alison M. Smith and Richard M. Thompson II, Cong. Research Serv.,
    Updated Criminal Offenses Enacted from 2008–2013 [2014]), https://
    judiciary.house.gov/wp-content/uploads/2016/02/113-102-88816.pdf; Sara
    Sun Beale, "Rethinking the Identity and Role of United States Attorneys,"
    Ohio State Journal of Criminal Law 6 (2009): 392, 399 (citing Task Force on
    Federalization of Criminal Law, American Bar Association, *The Federaliza-
    tion of Criminal Law* [1998], 7).
66. Jeff Welty, "Overcriminalization in North Carolina," *North Carolina Law
    Review* 92 (2014): 1939, 1954.
67. "Michigan's Absurd Laws Criminalize the Population," *American Legislative
    Exchange Council,* December 8, 2014, https://www.alec.org/article/michigans
    -absurd-laws-criminalize-population.
68. John Villasenor, "Over-criminalization and Mens Rea Reform: A Primer,"
    Brookings Institute, *FixGov Blog,* December 22, 2015, http://www.brookings
    .edu/blogs/fixgov/posts/2015/12/22-mens-rea-reform-villasenor.

69. John G. Malcolm, "The Pressing Need for Mens Rea Reform," *Heritage Foundation Legal Memorandum* 160 (2015): 7, http://thf_media.s3 .amazonaws.com/2015/pdf/LM160.pdf.

70. Malcolm, 7.

71. Malcolm, 7.

72. William J. Stuntz, "The Pathological Politics of Criminal Law," *Michigan Law Review* 100 (2001): 512–519.

73. *See The Adequacy of Criminal Intent Standards in Federal Prosecutions: Hearing before the S. Comm. on the Judiciary,* 114th Cong. 2 (2016) (statement of Leslie R. Caldwell, Assistant Attorney General), https://www .justice.gov/opa/file/814266/download; Samuel W. Buell, "The Upside of Overbreadth," *New York University Law Review* 83 (2008): 1491–1564.

74. *See* Paul H. Robinson and Markus D. Dubber, "The American Model Penal Code: A Brief Overview," *New Criminal Law Review* 10 (2007): 327–328.

75. *See, e.g.,* National Commission on Reform of the Federal Criminal Laws, *Final Report of the National Commission on Reform of Federal Criminal Laws* (1971), 28–30, 34, http://www.ndcourts.gov/court/resource /CriminalCode/FinalReport.pdf.

76. Tennessee v. Garner, 471 U.S. 1, 14 (1985).

77. Marie Gottschalk, "Bring It On: The Future of Penal Reform, the Carceral State, and American Politics," *Ohio State Journal of Criminal Law* 12 (2015): 559; Nicholas Eberstadt, "Why Is the American Government Ignoring 23 Million of Its Citizens?," *Washington Post,* March 31, 2016, https://www .washingtonpost.com/opinions/why-is-the-american-government-ignores-23 -million-of-its-citizens/2016/03/31/4da5d682-f428-11e5-a3ce-f06b5ba21f33 _story.html.

78. Michael Pinard, "An Integrated Perspective on the Collateral Consequences of Criminal Convictions and Reentry Issues Faced by Formerly Incarcerated Individuals," *Boston University Law Review* 86 (2006): 635–636.

79. Stephen J. Schulhofer, "Assessing the Federal Sentencing Process: The Problem Is Uniformity, Not Disparity," *American Criminal Law Review* 29 (1992): 847–848.

80. *See* Doris Layton Mackenzie, *Sentencing and Corrections in the 21st Century: Setting the Stage for the Future* (2001), 18, https://www.ncjrs .gov/pdffiles1/nij/189106-2.pdf; Naomi Murakawa, *The First Civil Right: How Liberals Built Prison America* (New York: Oxford University Press, 2014), 20.

81. Murakawa, *First Civil Right,* 20; Ewing v. California, 538 U.S. 11, 15 (2003).

82. Murakawa, *First Civil Right,* 116.

83. Eddings v. Oklahoma, 455 U.S. 104, 112 (1982).

84. *See* Pew Charitable Trusts, *Federal Drug Sentencing Laws Bring High Cost, Low Return* (2015), 2, http://www.pewtrusts.org/~/media/assets/2015/08 /pspp_feddrug_brief.pdf; Anti-Drug Abuse Act of 1986, Pub. L. No. 99–570, 100 Stat. 3207 (1986) (codified as amended in scattered sections of 26 U.S.C [2012]).

85. United States v. Dossie, 851 F. Supp. 2d 478, 479 (E.D.N.Y. 2012) (citing U.S. Sentencing Commission, *Mandatory Minimum Sentences*).
86. Colson Task Force, *Transforming Prisons,* 11, 12.
87. Colson Task Force, 21, 22.
88. 18 U.S.C. § 3553(f) (2012).
89. Families Against Mandatory Minimums, Safety Valves, http://famm.org /projects/federal/us-congress/safety-valves.
90. Families Against Mandatory Minimums, The Justice Safety Valve Act FAQ, http://famm.org/the-justice-safety-valve-act-faq.
91. Pesta, " The Accidental Sex Offender"; Stillman, "List."
92. "The Superpredator Myth, 20 Years Later," *Equal Justice Initiative,* April 7, 2014, http://www.eji.org/node/893.
93. Miller v. Alabama, 132 S. Ct. 2455, 2460 (2012).
94. Chris Christie, "Save Jail for the Dangerous," in *Solutions: American Leaders Speak Out on Criminal Justice,* ed. Inimai Chettiar and Michael Waldman (New York: Brennan Center for Justice, 2015), 19–20, https://www .brennancenter.org/analysis/save-jail-dangerous.
95. *See, e.g.,* Ryan J. Reilly and Julia Craven, "Lawyers Go after 'Dank and Dangerous' Conditions at Aging Baltimore Jail," *Huffington Post,* June 2, 2015, http://www.huffingtonpost.com/2015/06/02/baltimore-jail-lawsuit_n _7493962.html.
96. California Department of Corrections and Rehabilitation, Entering a California State Prison, http://www.cdcr.ca.gov/Ombuds/Entering_a_Prison _FAQs.html; Steven Raphael and Sarah Tahamont, *The Effect of Mandatory Minimum Punishments on the Efficiency of Criminal Justice Resource Allocation* 46 (Goldman School of Public Policy, Working Paper 2015), https://gspp.berkeley.edu/assets/uploads/research/pdf/draft_(classification _modeling)_04142015.pdf.
97. Pinard, "Integrated Perspective," 636; Legal Action Center, *After Prison: Roadblocks to Reentry: A Report on State Legal Barriers Facing People with Criminal Records* (2004), http://lac.org/roadblocks-to-reentry/upload /lacreport/LAC_PrintReport.pdf.

2. Senseless Sentencing

1. Brendan Farrington, "Legislature 2014: Florida Senate Passes Tougher Sexual Predator Bills," *Florida Times Union,* March 4, 2014, http://jacksonville.com /breaking-news/2014-03-04/story/senate-passes-tougher-sexual-predator-bills.
2. CBS and Associated Press, "Lawmaker Introduces Sex Offender Castration Bill in Alabama," CBS News, March 7, 2016, http://www.cbsnews.com/news /lawmaker-introduces-sex-offender-castration-bill-in-alabama.
3. Christopher Cousins, "Harsher Penalties for Drug Dealers Likely to Become Maine Law," *Bangor Daily News,* March 30, 2016, http://bangordailynews .com/2016/03/30/politics/state-house/harsher-penalties-for-drug-dealers-likely -to-become-maine-law.

4. Rick Green, "Oklahoma Lawmakers Struggle with How to Be Smart on Crime," *Oklahoman,* March 1, 2015, http://newsok.com/article/5397390.

5. Maurice Chammah, "American Sheriff," *Atlantic,* May 5, 2016, http://www.theatlantic.com/politics/archive/2016/05/american-sheriff/481131.

6. Paul H. Robinson, Geoffrey P. Goodwin, and Michael Reisig, "The Disutility of Injustice," *New York University Law Review* 85 (2010): 1961–1978; Paul H. Robinson and Robert Kurzban, "Concordance and Conflict in Intuitions of Justice," *Minnesota Law Review* 91 (2007): 1867.

7. U.S. Sentencing Commission, Quick Facts, Drug Trafficking Offenses 2013, http://www.ussc.gov/sites/default/files/pdf/research-and-publications/quick-facts/Quick_Facts_Drug_Trafficking_2013.pdf; Jessica Caruane, "Sex Offenders Have Shockingly Short Sentences," *Crime Wire,* October 15, 2012, https://instantcheckmate.com/crimewire/2012/10/15/sex-offenders-have-shockingly-short-sentences.

8. Joe Palazzolo, "Persuasive Judges Win Reduced Sentences for Some Convicts," *Wall Street Journal,* November 23, 2015, http://www.wsj.com/articles/persuasive-judges-win-reduced-sentences-for-some-convicts-1448324596.

9. United States v. Angelos, 345 F. Supp. 2d 1227, 1247 (D. Utah 2004). Angelos ultimately received a reduction in his sentence from a federal court only because of the enormous publicity generated by his case, but most individuals with disproportionate sentences languish in prison because there are few mechanisms for correction, as Chapter 4 explains. See, e.g., Ian Owens and Harlan Protass, "Felon: I Robbed Banks but I Should Get a Second Chance," *Detroit Free Press,* May 4, 2018, https://www.freep.com/story/opinion/contributors/2018/05/04/sentencing-laws-felon/525119002.

10. Claire Galofaro, "St. Tammany Courts Give Parish Nickname of 'St. Slammany,'" *Times-Picayune,* March 25, 2012, http://www.nola.com/crime/index.ssf/2012/03/st_tammany_courts_give_parish.html.

11. Lauren Krisai, "The Felony-Murder Rule Sends Non-killers to Prison and Doesn't Even Reduce Crime," *Reason,* March 23, 2016, http://reason.com/archives/2016/03/23/the-felony-murder-rule-sends-non-killers.

12. Cindy Chang, "Tough Sentencing Laws Keep Louisiana's Prisons Full," *Times-Picayune,* May 16, 2012, http://www.nola.com/crime/index.ssf/2012/05/tough_sentencing_laws_keep_lou.html.

13. Jacob Sullum, "Perverted Justice," *Reason,* July 2011, http://reason.com/archives/2011/06/14/perverted-justice/singlepage.

14. Sullum.

15. Sullum.

16. Stuart P. Green, *Thirteen Ways to Steal a Bicycle* (Cambridge, MA: Harvard University Press, 2012), 53.

17. Tom R. Tyler, "Procedural Justice, Legitimacy, and the Effective Rule of Law," *Crime and Justice* 30 (2003): 321–324.

18. Tom R. Tyler, "Can the Police Enhance Their Popular Legitimacy through Their Conduct? Using Empirical Research to Inform Law," *University of Illinois Law Review* (2017): 1972–1975, 1992; Tom R. Tyler, "Popular Legitimacy and the Exercise of Legal Authority: Motivating Compliance,

Cooperation and Engagement," *Psychology Public Policy and Law* 20 (2014): 78–95.

19. 114 Cong. Rec. 22,231–22,248 (1968) (Statement of Rep. Poff).

20. David M. Bartley and J. John Fox, "A Clamp on the Trigger Finger," *New York Times,* July 27, 1975, E17.

21. Stephen M. Saland, "Senator Saland's Sex Offense Training Bill Is Signed into Law," news release, October 4, 2011, https://www.nysenate.gov/newsroom /press-releases/stephen-m-saland/senator-saland%E2%80%99s-sex-offense -training-bill-signed-law.

22. Morgan Lee and Mary Hudetz, "Why New Mexico Is Bucking Criminal Justice Trends," *Christian Science Monitor,* January 25, 2016, http://www .csmonitor.com/USA/Justice/2016/0125/Why-New-Mexico-is-bucking -criminal-justice-trends-video.

23. Eliana Salzhauer and Clair Gordon, "Florida Becomes the Harshest State for Sex Offenders," Aljazeera America, April 5, 2014, http://america.aljazeera.com /watch/shows/america-tonight/articles/2014/4/5/florida-becomes -theharsheststateforsexoffenders.html.

24. Sullum, "Perverted Justice."

25. Republican Party Platform 2012, http://www.republicanviews.org/republican -views-on-crime.

26. Jamie Satterfield, "Knoxville Federal Prosecutor Battling in Congress against Sentencing Reform," *Knoxville News Sentinel,* April 22, 2016, http://www .knoxnews.com/news/crime-courts/knoxville-federal-prosecutor-battling-in -congress-against-sentencing-reform-3117e459-ec3e-1d89-e053-376797231 .html.

27. David Perdue, "Senator David Perdue Statement on Revised Criminal Leniency Bill," news release, April 28, 2016, http://www.perdue.senate.gov /news/press-releases/senator-david-perdue-statement-on-revised-criminal -leniency-bill.

28. Valerie Wright, *Deterrence in Criminal Justice* (Sentencing Project, 2010), 4, https://www.sentencingproject.org/wp-content/uploads/2016/01/Deterrence -in-Criminal-Justice.pdf (citing Patrick Langan and David Levin, Bureau of Justice Statistics, *Recidivism of Prisoners Released in 1994* [2002]); Charles Colson Task Force on Federal Corrections, *Transforming Prisons, Restoring Lives* (2016), 2.

29. "Fact Sheet: Prison Time Served and Recidivism," Pew Charitable Trusts, October 8, 2013, http://www.pewtrusts.org/en/research-and-analysis/fact -sheets/2013/10/08/prison-time-served-and-recidivism.

30. "Fact Sheet: Prison Time Served."

31. National Research Council, *The Growth of Incarceration in the United States: Exploring Causes and Consequences,* ed. Jeremy Travis and Bruce Western (Washington, DC: National Academies Press, 2014).

32. Council of Economic Advisers (CEA), *Economic Perspectives on Incarceration and the Justice System* (2016), 37.

33. CEA, 38.

34. Steven Durlauf and Daniel Nagin, "Imprisonment and Crime: Can Both Be Reduced?," *Criminology and Public Policy* 10 (2011): 13; Wright, *Deterrence in Criminal Justice,* 4; Paul J. Larkin Jr., "Swift, Certain, and Fair Punishment: 24/7 Sobriety and Hope; Creative Approaches to Alcohol- and Illicit Drug-Using Offenders," *Journal of Criminal Law and Criminology* 105 (2015): 39–40.

35. "Most States Cut Imprisonment and Crime," Pew Charitable Trusts, http://www.pewtrusts.org/en/multimedia/data-visualizations/2014 /imprisonment-and-crime.

36. "Most States Cut Imprisonment and Crime."

37. Eleanor Goldberg, "Here's Proof Mass Incarceration Doesn't Reduce Crime," *Huffington Post,* October 20, 2015, http://www.huffingtonpost.com/entry /proof-mass-incarceration-doesnt-reduce-crime_us _56255cfbe4b08589ef489a3d.

38. Reid Wilson, "Tough Texas Gets Results by Going Softer on Crime," *Washington Post,* November 27, 2014, https://www.washingtonpost.com /blogs/govbeat/wp/2014/11/27/tough-texas-gets-results-by-going-softer-on -crime.

39. Wilson.

40. Wilson.

41. U.S. Sentencing Commission, *Recidivism among Offenders Receiving Retroactive Sentence Reductions: The 2007 Crack Cocaine Amendment* (2014), http://www.ussc.gov/sites/default/files/pdf/research-and-publications /research-projects-and-surveys/miscellaneous/20140527_Recidivism_2007 _Crack_Cocaine_Amendment.pdf.

42. U.S. Sentencing Commission, 3.

43. U.S. Sentencing Commission, *Report to the Congress: Impact of the Fair Sentencing Act of 2010* (2015), 3, http://www.ussc.gov/sites/default/files/pdf /news/congressional-testimony-and-reports/drug-topics/201507_RtC_Fair -Sentencing-Act.pdf.

44. U.S. Sentencing Commission, *Recidivism among Federal Offenders Receiving Retroactive Sentence Reductions: The 2011 Fair Sentencing Act Guideline Amendment* (2018), 1, https://www.ussc.gov/sites/default/files/pdf/research -and-publications/research-publications/2018/20180328_Recidivism_FSA -Retroactivity.pdf.

45. Colson Task Force, *Transforming Prisons,* ix.

46. Colson Task Force, 15.

47. Colson Task Force, 296.

48. CEA, *Economic Perspectives,* 39 (citing Michael Mueller-Smith, *The Criminal Labor Market Impacts of Incarceration* [working paper, 2015]).

49. CEA, *Economic Perspectives,* 40.

50. Colson Task Force, *Transforming Prisons,* 17.

51. Colson Task Force, 29.

52. Joanna Shepherd, "The Imprisonment Puzzle, Understanding How Prison Growth Affects Crime," *Criminology and Public Policy* 5 (2006): 290.

53. B. B. Benda and T. J. Pavlak, "Aging out of Crime: A Neglected Area of Juvenile Delinquency Theory Research and Practice," *New Designs for Youth Development* 4, no. 6 (November/December 1983): 21–27.

54. Benda and Pavlak, 21–27.

55. Dana Goldstein, "Too Old to Commit Crime?," *New York Times,* March 20, 2015, https://www.nytimes.com/2015/03/22/sunday-review/too-old-to -commit-crime.html?emc=edit_tnt_20150320&nlid=21745381&tntemailo =y&_r=0.

56. Goldstein.

57. Goldstein.

58. Association of Certified Fraud Examiners, "Profiling a White Collar Criminal," news release, September 10, 2008, http://www.acfe.com/press-release .aspx?id=4294968561.

59. Association of Certified Fraud Examiners, "Profiling a White Collar Criminal."

60. Testimony of Kristen M. Zgoba, Ph.D., to the U.S. Sentencing Commission, March 13, 2014, 6, http://www.ussc.gov/sites/default/files/pdf/amendment -process/public-hearings-and-meetings/20140313/Testimony_Zgoba.pdf.

61. Testimony of Zgoba.

62. Jeffrey T. Ulmer and Darrell Steffersmeier, "The Age and Crime Relationship: Social Variation, Social Explanation," in *The Nurture versus Biosocial Debate in Criminology: On the Origins of Criminal Behavior and Criminality,* ed. Kevin M. Beaver, J. C. Barnes, and Brian B. Boutwell (Los Angeles: SAGE, 2013), 377, http://sk.sagepub.com/books/the-nurture-versus-biosocial -debate-in-criminology.

63. *See, e.g.,* Tomislav V. Kovandizic and Lynne M. Vieraitis, "The Effect of County-Level Prison Population Growth on Crime Rates," *Criminology and Public Policy* 5 (2006): 213–244; Shepherd, "Imprisonment Puzzle," 286.

64. Shepherd, "Imprisonment Puzzle," 292.

65. Shepherd, 291.

66. George Allen, Testimony before the House Government Reform Subcommittee on Criminal Justice, Drug Policy and Human Resources, May 11, 2000.

67. Timothy Hughes and Doris James Wilson, Bureau of Justice Statistics, *Reentry Trends in the United States,* http://www.bjs.gov/content/reentry /reentry.cfm.

68. E. Ann Carson and Daniela Golinelli, Bureau of Justice Statistics, NCJ 243920, *Prisoners in 2012: Trends in Admissions and Releases 1991–2012* (2013), 3.

69. David Roodman, *The Impacts of Incarceration on Crime* (2017), 98, http://files.openphilanthropy.org/files/Focus_Areas/Criminal_Justice_Reform /The_impacts_of_incarceration_on_crime_10.pdf.

70. Todd R. Clear et al., "Coercive Mobility and Crime: A Preliminary Examination of Concentrated Incarceration and Social Disorganization," *Justice Quarterly* 20 (2003): 57–58.

71. Wright, *Deterrence in Criminal Justice,* 1.

72. Daniel S. Nagin, "Deterrence in the Twenty-First Century," in *Crime and Justice in America,* ed. Joycelyn M. Pollock (New York: Routledge, 2013), 199.

73. Wesley Vaughn, "Does Putting More People in Prison Reduce Crime? Maybe Not Anymore," opinion, AL.com, September 15, 2014, http://www.al.com /opinion/index.ssf/2014/09/does_putting_more_people_in_pr.html.

74. CEA, *Economic Perspectives,* 34.

75. CEA, 34–35.

76. Donald Braman, "Families and Incarceration," in *Invisible Punishment: The Collateral Consequences of Mass Imprisonment,* ed. Marc Mauer and Meda Chesney-Lind (New York: New Press, 2002), 114.

77. Rucker Johnson, "Ever-Increasing Levels of Parental Incarceration and the Consequences for Children," in *Do Prisons Make Us Safer? The Benefits and Costs of the Prison,* ed. Steven Raphael and Michael Stoll (New York: Russell Sage Foundation, 2009), 177.

78. Ella Baker Center for Human Rights, *Who Pays? The True Cost of Incarceration* (2015), http://whopaysreport.org/executive-summary/pdf-executive -summary.

79. Office of the Assistant Secretary for Planning and Evaluation, U.S. Department of Health and Human Services, *The Oklahoma Marriage Initiative: Marriage and Relationship Skills Education as a Way to Prepare Prisoners for Reintegration* (2009), http://aspe.hhs.gov/hsp/06/omi/Reintegration/rb .shtml-2.

80. Mindi Herman-Stahl, Marni L. Kan, and Tasseli McKay, Office of the Assistant Secretary for Planning and Evaluation, U.S. Department of Health and Human Services, *Incarceration and the Family: A Review of Research and Promising Approaches for Serving Fathers and Families* (September 2008), https://aspe.hhs.gov/sites/default/files/pdf/75536/report.pdf.

81. Baker Center, *Who Pays?.*

82. Jeremy Travis, Elizabeth Cincotta McBride, and Amy L. Solomon, Urban Institute Justice Policy Center, *Families Left Behind: The Hidden Costs of Incarceration and Reentry* (2005), https://www.urban.org/sites/default/files /publication/50461/310882-Families-Left-Behind.PDF.

83. The fee in Arizona is $25. Tanzina Vega, "Costly Prison Fees Are Putting Inmates Deep in Debt," *CNN Money,* September 18, 2015, http://money.cnn .com/2015/09/18/news/economy/prison-fees-inmates-debt.

84. Mary Fainsod Katzenstein and Maureen Waller, "Phone Calls Won't Cost up to $14 a Minute Anymore but Here's How Prisoners' Families Are Still Being Fleeced," *Washington Post,* October 26, 2015, https://www.washingtonpost .com/news/monkey-cage/wp/2015/10/26/phone-calls-wont-cost-up-to-14-a -minute-anymore-but-heres-how-prisoners-families-are-still-being-fleeced.

85. Katzenstein and Waller, "Prisoners' Families."

86. Baker Center, *Who Pays?.*

87. Alicia Bannon, Mitali Negrecha, and Rebekah Diller, Brennan Center for Justice, *Criminal Justice Debt: A Barrier to Reentry* (2010), http://www .brennancenter.org/sites/default/files/legacy/Fees and Fines FINAL.pdf.

88. Pew Charitable Trusts, *Collateral Costs: Incarceration's Effects on Economic Mobility* (2010), http://www.pewtrusts.org/~/media/legacy/uploadedfiles/pcs_assets/2010/collateralcosts1pdf.pdf; Annie E. Casey Foundation, *A Shared Sentence* (2016), 1–2, http://www.aecf.org/m/resourcedoc/aecf-asharedsentence-2016.pdf.

89. Jeremy Travis, *But They All Come Back: Facing the Challenges of Prisoner Reentry* (Washington, DC: Urban Institute Press, 2005), 124, 130.

90. James Kilgore, *Understanding Mass Incarceration: A People's Guide to the Key Civil Rights Struggle of Our Time* (New York: New Press, 2015), 156.

91. Travis, *But They All Come Back,* 130.

92. Travis, 130.

93. S. D. Phillips et al., "Disentangling the Risks: Parent Criminal Justice Involvement and Children's Exposure to Family Risks," *Criminology and Public Policy* 5, no. 4 (2006): 677–702.

94. Casey Foundation, *Shared Sentence,* 3.

95. Yolanda Johnson-Peterkin, National Resource Center for Foster Care and Family Planning, *Information Packet: Children of Incarcerated Parents* (2003), http://www.hunter.cuny.edu/socwork/nrcfcpp/downloads/information_packets/children-of-incarcerated-parents.pdf.

96. Rivka Greenberg, "Mothers Who Are Incarcerated," *Women and Therapy* 29 (2007): 165.

97. CEA, *Economic Perspectives,* 51; Creasie Finney Hairston, *Focus on Children with Incarcerated Parents: An Overview of the Research Literature* (Annie E. Casey Foundation, October 2007), http://www.f2f.ca.gov/res/pdf/FocusOnChildrenWith.pdf.

98. Melinda D. Anderson, "How Mass Incarceration Pushes Black Children Further Behind in School," *Atlantic,* January 16, 2017, https://www.theatlantic.com/education/archive/2017/01/how-mass-incarceration-pushes-black-children-further-behind-in-school/513161.

99. Colson Task Force, *Transforming Prisons,* 15.

100. Shepherd, "Imprisonment Puzzle," 291.

101. Travis, *But They All Come Back,* 281.

102. Travis, 282.

103. Daniel Cooper and Ryan Lugalia-Hollon, "Million Dollar Blocks," Chicago's Million Dollar Blocks, http://chicagosmilliondollarblocks.com/#drug.

104. Cooper and Lugalia-Hollon.

105. Jennifer Gonnerman, "Million-Dollar Blocks," *Village Voice,* November 9, 2004, http://www.villagevoice.com/news/million-dollar-blocks-6398537.

106. James P. Lynch and William J. Sabol, "Assessing the Effects of Mass Incarceration on Informal Social Control in Communities," *Criminology and Public Policy* 3 (2004): 267.

107. Bruce Western, Becky Pettit, and Josh Guetzkow, "Black Economic Progress in the Era of Mass Imprisonment," in *Invisible Punishment,* ed. Mauer and Chesney-Lind, 170.

108. CEA, *Economic Perspectives,* 52.

109. CEA, 52.

110. Shelli B. Rossman et al., *The Multi-site Drug Court Evaluation: The Impact of Drug Courts* (Urban Institute Justice Policy Center, 2011), http://www .urban.org/sites/default/files/alfresco/publication-pdfs/412353-The-Multi -site-Adult-Drug-Court-Evaluation-Executive-Summary.pdf.

111. Shepherd, "Imprisonment Puzzle," 291; John J. DiIulio Jr., "Prisons Are a Bargain, by Any Measure," *New York Times,* January 16, 1996, A17; John DiIulio Jr., "Two Million Prisoners Are Enough," *Wall Street Journal,* March 12, 1999, A14.

112. Michael Tonry, "The Mostly Unintended Effects of Mandatory Penalties: Two Centuries of Consistent Findings," *Crime and Justice* 38 (2009): 95–98.

113. Chuck Grassley, "Tougher Sentences on Perpetrators of Sexual Assault and Domestic Violence," February 3, 2014, http://www.grassley.senate.gov/news /commentary/tougher-sentences-perpetrators-sexual-assault-and-domestic -violence.

114. Kevin Miller, "Lawmakers Consider Tougher Penalties for Bringing Heroin into Maine," *Portland Press Herald,* January 26, 2016, http://www .pressherald.com/2016/01/25/lawmakers-consider-tougher-penalties-for -bringing-heroin-into-maine.

115. Jordain Carney, "Rubio Backs Cruz on Tougher Penalties for Illegal Immigrants," *The Hill,* October 23, 2015, http://thehill.com/blogs/floor -action/senate/257867-rubio-backs-cruz-on-tougher-penalties-for-illegal -immigrants.

116. "New Data Reveals Devastating Impact of 'Kate's Law' on Federal Prisons, Public Safety," Families Against Mandatory Minimums, September 2, 2015, http://famm.org/new-data-reveals-devastating-impact-of-kates-law-on -federal-prisons-public-safety.

117. "Devastating Impact of 'Kate's Law.'"

118. Cousins, "Harsher Penalties."

119. Martin Kaste, "States Push for Prison Sentence Overhaul; Prosecutors Push Back," NPR, July 9, 2014, http://www.npr.org/2014/07/09/329587949 /states-push-for-prison-sentence-reform-and-prosecutors-push-back.

120. Associated Press, "Fatal Heroin Overdoses Spark Calls for Tougher Penalties," Wane.com, March 21, 2015, http://wane.com/2015/03/21/fatal -heroin-overdoses-spark-calls-for-tougher-penalties.

121. German Lopez, "The Opioid Painkiller and Heroin Epidemic, Explained," *Vox,* June 2, 2016, http://www.vox.com/2015/10/1/9433099/opioid -painkiller-heroin-epidemic.

122. "More Imprisonment Does Not Reduce State Drug Problems," Pew Charitable Trusts, March 8, 2018, http://www.pewtrusts.org/en/research -and-analysis/issue-briefs/2018/03/more-imprisonment-does-not-reduce -state-drug-problems.

123. Rob Kuznia, "Her Fiance Gave Her Heroin. She Overdosed. Does That Make Him a Murderer?," *Washington Post,* May 8, 2016, https://www

.washingtonpost.com/national/her-fiance-gave-her-heroin-she-overdosed
-does-that-make-him-a-murderer/2016/05/08/f9a9e79a-f29b-11e5-a2a3
-d4e9697917d1_story.html.

124. Kate Kilpatrick, "A Blurry Line Divides Addicts and Dealers in Heroin
Underworld," Aljazeera America, February 16, 2016, http://america
.aljazeera.com/articles/2016/2/16/a-blurry-line-divides-addicts-and-dealers
-in-heroin-underworld.html.

125. In response to this concern, 30 states have passed Good Samaritan laws
exempting those reporting an overdose. German Lopez, "Is Murder the
Right Charge for Drug Dealing? Some States Think So," *Vox,* May 10, 2016,
http://www.vox.com/2016/5/10/11643686/opioid-epidemic-tough-on-crime.

126. Andrew Forgotch, "'Pissed off' Lancaster County District Attorney Pushes
for Tougher Penalties for Heroin Dealers," ABC 27 News, June 7, 2016,
http://abc27.com/2016/06/07/pissed-off-lancaster-county-district-attorney
-pushes-for-tougher-penalties-for-heroin-dealers.

127. Franklin E. Zimring and Gordon Hawkins, *The Scale of Imprisonment*
(Chicago: University of Chicago Press, 1991), 140.

128. Human Rights Watch (HRW), *An Offer You Can't Refuse: How U.S.
Federal Prosecutors Force Drug Defendants to Plead Guilty* (2013),
114–117, https://www.hrw.org/report/2013/12/05/offer-you-cant-refuse/how
-us-federal-prosecutors-force-drug-defendants-plead.

129. Ari Shapiro, "New Orleans Man Faces 20 Years to Life for Candy Bar
Theft," *NPR,* April 4, 2016, http://www.npr.org/2016/04/04/473004950
/new-orleans-man-faces-20-years-to-life-for-candy-bar-theft.

130. Ken Daley, "Candy Thief Jacobia Grimes Faces Longer Sentence as DA Files
Enhancement," *Times-Picayune,* June 24, 2016, http://www.nola.com/crime
/index.ssf/2016/06/candy_thief_jacobia_grimes_hor.html.

131. His co-defendants were acquitted. Kenneth Jost, *Plea Bargaining: Does It
Promote Justice?* (CQ Researcher, February 12 1999), http://library.cqpress
.com/cqresearcher/document.php?id=cqresrre1999021200.

132. Jost.

133. HRW, *An Offer You Can't Refuse.*

134. Jacob Sullum, "Why Prosecutors Love Mandatory Minimums," *New York
Post,* August 9, 2014, http://nypost.com/2014/08/09/why-prosecutors-love
-mandatory-minimums.

135. Carrie Johnson, "Report: Threat of Mandatory Minimums Used to Coerce
Guilty Pleas," NPR, December 5, 2013, http://www.npr.org/sections/thetwo
-way/2013/12/05/248893775/report-threat-of-mandatory-minimums-used
-to-coerce-guilty-pleas.

136. Richard A. Oppel Jr., "Sentencing Shift Gives New Leverage to Prosecutors," *New York Times,* September 25, 2011, http://www.nytimes.com/2011
/09/26/us/tough-sentences-help-prosecutors-push-for-plea-bargains.html.

137. This number is based on data from 1994 to 1996. Linda Drazga Maxfield
and John H. Kramer, U.S. Sentencing Commission, *Substantial Assistance:
An Empirical Yardstick Gauging Equity in Current Federal Policy and
Practice* (1998), 4.

138. Brad Heath, "How Snitches Pay for Freedom," *USA Today*, December 14, 2012, http://www.usatoday.com/story/news/nation/2012/12/14/jailhouse-informants-for-sale/1762013.

139. Maxfield and Kramer, *Substantial Assistance*, 32, 35.

140. Frank Pompa, "USA Today Analysis of U.S. Sentencing Commission Data FY 2006 to FY 2011," *USA Today*, http://usatoday30.usatoday.com/news/_photos/2012/12/13/informants-chart.jpg.

141. Peter Elkind, "The Confessions of Andy Fastow," *Fortune*, July 1, 2013, http://fortune.com/2013/07/01/the-confessions-of-andy-fastow; Katharine Shilcutt, "Andrew Fastow Plots an Afterlife," *Houstonia*, January 4, 2015, http://www.houstoniamag.com/articles/2015/1/4/andrew-fastow-plots-an-afterlife-january-2015.

142. Alexandra Natapoff, "Secret Justice: Criminal Informants and America's Underground Legal System," *Prison Legal News*, June 2010, https://www.prisonlegalnews.org/news/2010/jun/15/secret-justice-criminal-informants-and-americas-underground-legal-system.

143. Stephen J. Schulhofer, "Rethinking Mandatory Minimums," *Wake Forest Law Review* 28 (1993): 212.

144. United States v. Jones, 145 F.3d 269, 966–967 (8th Cir. 1998).

145. HRW, *An Offer You Can't Refuse*.

146. HRW.

147. HRW.

148. Marie Gottschalk, "Bring It On: The Future of Penal Reform, the Carceral State, and American Politics," *Ohio State Journal of Criminal Law* 12 (2015): 575.

149. Department of Justice, "Attorney General Eric Holder Urges Congress to Pass Bipartisan 'Smarter Sentencing Act' to Reform Mandatory Minimum Sentences," news release, January 23, 2014, https://www.justice.gov/opa/pr/attorney-general-eric-holder-urges-congress-pass-bipartisan-smarter-sentencing-act-reform.

150. Letter from Robert Gay Guthrie, President, NAAUSA, to Senators Patrick Leahy and Charles Grassley, January 31, 2014, 2, http://www.naausa.org/2013/images/docs/MandMinSentencingLegOppose013114.pdf.

151. Ann E. Marimow, "Softening Sentences, Losing Leverage," *Washington Post*, October 31, 2015, http://www.washingtonpost.com/sf/national/2015/10/31/leverage.

152. Sari Horwitz, "Some Prosecutors Fighting Effort to Eliminate Mandatory Minimum Prison Sentences," *Washington Post*, March 13, 2014, https://www.washingtonpost.com/world/national-security/some-prosecutors-fighting-effort-to-eliminate-mandatory-minimum-prison-sentences/2014/03/13/f5426fc2-a60f-11e3-a5fa-55f0c77bf39c_story.html.

153. Marisa Lagos, "State's Prosecutors Oppose Gov. Brown's Proposal on Sentencing Reform," *KQED News*, February 11, 2016, https://www.kqed.org/news/10861549/states-prosecutors-oppose-gov-browns-proposal-on-sentencing-reform.

154. Lagos.

155. Steven Nelson, "Prosecutors Rally against Sentencing Reform, Say Build More Prisons," *U.S. News and World Report,* July 17, 2015, http://www.usnews.com/news/articles/2015/07/17/prosecutors-rally-against-sentencing-reform-say-build-more-prisons.

156. Ben Gutierrez, "City Prosecutor Suggests New Prison to Reduce Crime," *Hawaii News Now,* http://www.hawaiinewsnow.com/story/23607309/city-prosecutor-suggests-new-prison-to-reduce-crime.

3. Counterproductive Confinement

1. Jeremy Travis, *But They All Come Back: Facing the Challenges of Prisoner Reentry* (Washington, DC: Urban Institute Press, 2005), 43.

2. Beth Schwartzapfel, "Life without Parole," Marshall Project, July 10, 2015, https://www.themarshallproject.org/2015/07/10/life-without-parole; Joan Petersilia, *When Prisoners Come Home: Parole and Prisoner Reentry* (New York: Oxford University Press, 2003), 65–66, table 3.1.

3. Gerard E. Lynch, "Sentencing: Learning from, and Worrying about, the States," *Columbia Law Review* 105 (2005): 933.

4. *See, e.g.,* Francis T. Cullen and Paul Gendreau, "Assessing Correctional Rehabilitation: Policy, Practice, and Prospects," in *Criminal Justice 2000, Volume 3: Policies, Processes, and Decisions of the Criminal Justice System,* ed. Julie Horney (Rockville, MD: National Institute of Justice, 2000), 109–116, http://www.d.umn.edu/~jmaahs/Correctional Assessment/cullen and gendreau_CJ2000.pdf.

5. Williams v. New York, 337 U.S. 241, 247 (1949).

6. Rachel E. Barkow, "Administering Crime," *UCLA Law Review* 52 (2005): 738–740.

7. Travis, *But They All Come Back,* 42.

8. Schwartzapfel, "Life without Parole."

9. Robert Martinson, "What Works? Questions and Answers about Prison Reform," *Public Interest* 35 (1974): 22–54.

10. Travis, *But They All Come Back,* xvii.

11. Timothy Hughes and Doris Wilson, *Reentry Trends in the United States* (Bureau of Justice Statistics, 2004), 1, http://www.bjs.gov/content/pub/pdf/reentry.pdf. For statistics on life sentences; see Ashley Nellis, *Life Goes On: The Historic Rise of Life Sentences in America* (Sentencing Project, 2013), 5–6, http://www.sentencingproject.org/publications/life-goes-on-the-historic-rise-in-life-sentences-in-america.

12. Danielle Keeble and Lauren Glaze, *Correctional Populations in the United States, 2015* (Bureau of Justice Statistics, 2016), 2, table 1, https://www.bjs.gov/content/pub/pdf/cpus15.pdf.

13. In 2015, 434,600 people were imprisoned for offenses for which they had not been convicted. Todd D. Minton and Zhen Zeng, *Jail Inmates in 2015* (Bureau of Justice Statistics, 2016), 4, table 3. *See also* Peter Wagner and Bernadette Rabuy, *Mass Incarceration: The Whole Pie, 2017* (Prison Policy Institute, 2017), https://www.prisonpolicy.org/reports/pie2017.html.

14. *See* Emily Leslie and Nolan G. Pope, "The Unintended Impact of Pretrial Detention on Case Outcomes: Evidence from NYC Arraignments," *Journal of Law and Economics* 60 (2016): 530; Curtis E. A. Karnow, "Setting Bail for Public Safety," *Berkeley Journal of Criminal Law* 13 (2008): 1–30.

15. *See* New York City Criminal Justice Agency, *Annual Report 2015* (2016), 22, exhibit 14.

16. Lisa W. Foderaro, "New Jersey Alters Its Bail System and Upends Legal Landscape," *New York Times,* February 6, 2017, https://www.nytimes.com /2017/02/06/nyregion/new-jersey-bail-system.html.

17. Megan Stevenson, "Distortion of Justice: How the Inability to Pay Bail Affects Case Outcomes," SSRN, July 17, 2016, 5n8, https://papers.ssrn.com /sol3/Papers.cfm?abstract_id=2777615.

18. *See generally* Nick Pinto, "The Bail Trap," *New York Times Magazine,* August 13, 2015, http://nyti.ms/1INtghe.

19. Paul Heaton, Sandra Mayson, and Megan Stevenson, "The Downstream Consequences of Misdemeanor Pretrial Detention," *Stanford Law Review* 69 (2017): 724–729.

20. Christopher T. Lowenkamp, Marie VanNostrand and Alexander Holsinger, "Investigating the Impact of Pretrial Detention on Sentencing Outcomes," Laura and John Arnold Foundation, November 2013, 4, http://www .arnoldfoundation.org/wp-content/uploads/2014/02/LJAF_Report_state -sentencing_FNL.pdf.

21. Lowenkamp.

22. Heaton, Mayson, and Stevenson, "Downstream Consequences."

23. Christopher T. Lowenkamp, Marie VanNostrand, and Alexander Holsinger, "The Hidden Costs of Pretrial Detention," Laura and John Arnold Foundation, November 2013, 19, http://www.arnoldfoundation.org/wp-content /uploads/2014/02/LJAF_Report_hidden-costs_FNL.pdf.

24. "Developing a National Model for Pretrial Risk Assessment," Laura and John Arnold Foundation, 2, http://www.arnoldfoundation.org/wp-content /uploads/2014/02/LJAF-research-summary_PSA-Court_4_1.pdf.

25. The tool considers whether the current offense is violent, whether the person had a pending charge at the time of the current offense, whether the person has a prior misdemeanor conviction, whether the person has a prior felony conviction, whether the person has prior convictions for violent crimes, the person's age at the time of arrest, how many times the person has failed to appear at a pretrial hearing in the last two years, whether the person failed to appear at a pretrial hearing more than two years ago, and whether the person had previously been sentenced. "Public Safety Assessment," Laura and John Arnold Foundation, http://www.arnoldfoundation.org/initiative/criminal -justice/crime-prevention/public-safety-assessment.

26. Note, "Bail Reform and Risk Assessment: The Cautionary Tale of Federal Sentencing," *Harvard Law Review* 131 (2018): 1132.

27. *See* "Developing a National Model," 4.

28. Jon Schuppe, "Post Bail," NBC News, August 22, 2017, https://www.nbcnews .com/specials/bail-reform. While New Jersey uses the tool to provide a more objective measure by which judges can determine the need for bail, judges

still retain the right to override the tool's recommendation either to detain or release a defendant. Foderaro, "New Jersey Alters."

29. Issie Lapowski, "One State's Bail Reform Exposes the Promise and Pitfalls of Tech-Driven Justice," *Wired,* September 5, 2017, https://www.wired.com /story/bail-reform-tech-justice.

30. Lapowski.

31. New Jersey Courts, *Preliminary Statistical Report 2017,* https://www .judiciary.state.nj.us/courts/assets/criminal/cjrsummaryrpts.pdf; Lapowski, "One State's Bail Reform."

32. State of New Jersey, Department of Law and Public Safety, Division of State Police, Uniform Crime Reporting Unit, *Uniform Crime Reporting 2017 Current Crime Data* (2017), http://www.njsp.org/ucr/pdf/current/20171027 _crimetrend.pdf.

33. Shaila Dewan, "Judges Replacing Conjecture with Formula for Bail," *New York Times,* June 26, 2015, https://www.nytimes.com/2015/06/27/us/turning -the-granting-of-bail-into-a-science.html.

34. Frank Main, "Cook County Judges Not Following Bail Recommendations: Study," *Chicago Sun Times,* July 3, 2016, https://chicago.suntimes.com /chicago-politics/cook-county-judges-not-following-bail-recommendations -study-find; Megan Crepeau, "Bond Court Gets Underway in Cook County with Different Judges, New Guidelines," *Chicago Tribune,* September 18, 2017, http://www.chicagotribune.com/news/local/breaking/ct-met-cook -county-cash-bond-20170918-story.html.

35. Donna Lyons, "Criminal Justice Policy Is Using Science to Predict Risk, Helping Courts Make Decisions about the Conditions of Pretrial Release," NCSL, February 1, 2014, http://www.ncsl.org/research/civil-and-criminal -justice/predicting-pretrial-success635260723.aspx; "Results from the First Six Months of the Public Safety Assessment—Court™ in Kentucky," Laura and John Arnold Foundation, July 2014, 2, http://www.arnoldfoundation.org /wp-content/uploads/2014/02/PSA-Court-Kentucky-6-Month-Report.pdf.

36. Megan T. Stevenson, "Assessing Risk Assessment in Action," *Minnesota Law Review* 103 (forthcoming), https://ssrn.com/abstract=3016088.

37. Meagan Flynn, "Ogg Outlines Plans for 'More Diversion, Less Jail' for Small-Time Offenders," *Houston Press,* October 18, 2017, http://www .houstonpress.com/news/oggs-transition-team-wants-more-diversion-less-jail -for-mentally-ill-substance-abusers-9885201.

38. Megan Crepeau, "Bail Reform in Cook County Gains Momentum," *Chicago Tribune*, June 12, 2017, http://www.chicagotribune.com/news/local/breaking /ct-cook-county-prosecutors-bail-policy-20170612-story.html.

39. "Groups Begin Bailing out Strangers to Free Poor from Jail," *Chicago Tribune,* January 30, 2017, http://www.chicagotribune.com/news /nationworld/ct-cash-bail-out-20170130-story.html; *see also* Alysia Santo, "Bail Reformers Aren't Waiting for Bail Reform," Marshall Project, August 23, 2016, https://www.themarshallproject.org/2016/08/23/bail-reformers -aren-t-waiting-for-bail-reform; Chicago Community Bond Fund, https://www.chicagobond.org.

40. Bronx Freedom Fund, http://www.thebronxfreedomfund.org; Brooklyn Community Bail Fund, https://brooklynbailfund.org.

41. "Community Bail Funds Reclaim Bail Decision Power," Pretrial Justice Institute, January 19, 2017, http://www.pretrial.org/community-bail-funds -reclaim-bail-decision-power; "Mama's Bail Out," Pretrial Justice Institute, May 2, 2017, http://www.pretrial.org/mamas-bail-out.

42. Alan Feuer, "Bronx Charity Founder Wants to Pay Bail for Poor Defendants Nationwide," *New York Times,* November 13, 2017, https://www.nytimes .com/2017/11/13/nyregion/bail-project-fund-poor-defendants.html.

43. For a table of their current cost-benefit findings for dozens of prison programs, see Stephanie Lee et al., *What Works and What Does Not? Benefit-Cost Findings From WSIPP* (Washington State Institute for Public Policy, 2015), 5–6, http://www.wsipp.wa.gov/ReportFile/1602/Wsipp_What-Works -and-What-Does-Not-Benefit-Cost-Findings-from-WSIPP_Report.pdf.

44. Mark W. Lipsey et al., "Effects of Cognitive-Behavioral Programs for Criminal Offenders," *Campbell Systematic Reviews* 6 (2007): 22.

45. Lipsey, 22.

46. Minnesota Department of Corrections, *An Outcome Evaluation of Minncor's EMPLOY Program* (2011), 27–28, http://www.doc.state.mn.us/pages/files /large-files/Publications/03–11EMPLOYEvaluation.pdf.

47. Minnesota Department of Corrections, 22, 24; *see also* Grant Duwe, "The Benefits of Keeping Idle Hands Busy: An Outcome Evaluation of a Prisoner Reentry Employment Program," *Crime and Delinquency* 61 (2015): 559–586.

48. Jeffrey D. Hopper, "Benefits of Inmate Employment Programs: Evidence from the Prison Industry Enhancement Certification Program," *Journal of Business and Economic Research* 11 (2013), 213–214, 220.

49. John M. Nalley et al., "Post-release Recidivism and Employment among Different Types of Released Offenders: A 5-Year Follow-up Study in the United States," *International Journal of Criminal Justice Sciences* 9, no. 1 (January–June 2014): 29.

50. Nalley, 29.

51. Ojmarrh Mitchell et al., "The Effectiveness of Incarceration-Based Drug Treatment on Criminal Behavior: A Systematic Review," *Campbell Systemic Reviews* 18 (2012): 6.

52. Michael Prendergast, *Report to the National Institute of Justice, Outcome Evaluation of the Forever Free Substance Abuse Treatment Program: One-Year Post-release Outcomes* (2003), vi–ix, 25, https://www.ncjrs.gov /pdffiles1/nij/grants/199685.pdf.

53. Travis, *But They All Come Back,* 107.

54. Travis, *But They All Come Back,* 161.

55. National Research Council, *The Growth of Incarceration in the United States: Exploring Causes and Consequences,* ed. Jeremy Travis et al. (Washington, DC: National Academies Press, 2014), 191.

56. Federal Bureau of Prisons, "UNICOR: Program Details," https://www.bop .gov/inmates/custody_and_care/unicor_about.jsp.

57. Caroline W. Harlow, *Education and Correctional Populations* (Bureau of Justice Statistics, 2003), 1, http://www.bjs.gov/content/pub/pdf/ecp.pdf.

58. Jennifer Bronson, Laura M. Maruschak, and Marcus Berzofsky, *Disabilities among Prison and Jail Inmates, 2011–12* (Bureau of Justice Statistics, December 2015), 3, http://www.bjs.gov/content/pub/pdf/dpji1112.pdf.

59. Margaret E. Shippen et al., "An Examination of the Basic Reading Skills of Incarcerated Males," *Adult Learning* (Summer–Fall 2010): 4, 7.

60. Shippen, 9.

61. James Kilgore, *Understanding Mass Incarceration: A People's Guide to the Key Civil Rights Struggle of Our Time* (New York: New Press, 2015), 93.

62. National Research Council, *Growth of Incarceration,* 191.

63. Richard J. Coley and Paul E. Barton, *Locked Up and Locked Out: An Educational Perspective on the U.S. Prison Population* (Educational Testing Service, 2006), 16.

64. Matt Clarke, "Prison Education Programs Threatened," *Prison Legal News,* May 19, 2014, https://www.prisonlegalnews.org/news/2014/may/19/prison -education-programs-threatened.

65. Lois M. Davis et al., *How Effective Is Correctional Education, and Where Do We Go from Here? The Results of a Comprehensive Evaluation* (RAND Corporation, 2014), 77.

66. Davis, 77.

67. Tracey Kyckelhahn, *State Corrections Expenditures, FY 1982—2010* (Bureau of Justice Statistics, 2012), 1, http://www.bjs.gov/content/pub/pdf/scefy8210 .pdf.

68. Lois M. Davis et al., *Evaluating the Effectiveness of Correctional Education: A Meta-analysis of Programs That Provide Education to Incarcerated Adults* (RAND Corporation, 2013), 40, http://www.rand.org/content/dam/rand/pubs /research_reports/RR200/RR266/RAND_RR266.sum.pdf.

69. Davis, xvi; *see also* Laura Winterfield et al., *The Effects of Postsecondary Correctional Education: Final Report* (Urban Institute, Justice Policy Center, 2009), v, http://www.urban.org/sites/default/files/alfresco/publication-pdfs /411954-The-Effects-of-Postsecondary-Correctional-Education.pdf.

70. Violent Crime Control and Law Enforcement Act, Pub. L. No. 103–322, § 20411 (1994).

71. Kilgore, *Understanding Mass Incarceration,* 93.

72. U.S. Department of Education, "12,000 Incarcerated Students to Enroll in Postsecondary Educational and Training Programs through Education Department's New Second Chance Pell Pilot Program," news release, June 24, 2016, http://www.ed.gov/news/press-releases/12000-incarcerated-students -enroll-postsecondary-educational-and-training-programs-through-education -departments-new-second-chance-pell-pilot-program.

73. Council of Economic Advisers (CEA), *Economic Perspectives on Incarceration and the Justice System* (2016), 32.

74. National Center on Addiction and Substance Abuse at Columbia University, *Behind Bars II: Substance Abuse and America's Prison Population* (2010), ii.

75. Redonna K. Chandler et al., "Treating Drug Abuse and Addiction in the Criminal Justice System: Improving Public Health and Safety," *JAMA* 301 (2009): 185.

76. Chandler, 183.

77. David Sack, "We Can't Afford to Ignore Drug Addiction in Prison," *Washington Post*, August 14, 2014, https://www.washingtonpost.com/news/to-your-health/wp/2014/08/14/we-cant-afford-to-ignore-drug-addiction-in-prison.

78. Federal Bureau of Prisons, *A Directory of Bureau of Prisons' National Programs* (2015), 15.

79. Federal Bureau of Prisons, Office of Research and Evaluation, *TRIAD Drug Treatment Evaluation Project Final Report of Three-Year Outcomes: Part 1* (2000), 4; 74 Fed. Reg. 1892, 1893 (January 14, 2009).

80. Travis, *But They All Come Back,* 203–204; Federal Bureau of Prisons, *TRIAD;* Ojmarrh Mitchell et al., "Does Incarceration-Based Drug Treatment Reduce Recidivism? A Meta-analytic Synthesis of the Research," *Journal of Experimental Criminology* 3 (2007): 353–375.

81. CEA, *Economic Perspectives,* 33.

82. Anasseril E. Daniel, "Care of the Mentally Ill in Prisons: Challenges and Solutions," *Journal of the American Academy of Psychiatry and the Law* 35 (2007): 406–410.

83. Travis, *But They All Come Back,* 202; *see also* Treatment Advocacy Center, *The Treatment of Persons with Mental Illness in Prisons and Jails* (2014), 4–5.

84. KiDeuk Kim, Miriam Becker-Cohen, and Maria Serakos, *The Processing and Treatment of Mentally Ill Persons in the Criminal Justice System* (Urban Institute, March 2015), 32.

85. National Institute for Corrections, *Corrections Agency Collaboration with Public Health* (2003); *see also* Jacques Baillargeon, Stephen K. Hoge, and Joseph V. Penn, "Addressing the Challenge of Community Reentry among Released Inmates with Serious Mental Illness," *American Journal of Community Psychology* 46 (December 2010): 361–375.

86. Charles Colson Task Force on Federal Corrections, *Transforming Prisons, Restoring Lives* (2016), 35.

87. Robert T. Muller, "Prisons Perpetuate Trauma in Female Inmates," *Psychology Today,* January 27, 2016; Doris James Wilson and Lauren E. Glaze, *Special Report: Mental Health Problems of Prison and Jail Inmates* (Bureau of Justice Statistics, 2006).

88. Richard P. Seiter and Karen R. Kadela, "Prisoner Reentry: What Works, What Does Not, and What Is Promising," *Crime and Delinquency* 49 (2003): 373–374, 378.

89. Massachusetts Department of Correction, *1986 Annual Statistical Report of the Furlough Program* (1987), 4, http://www.mass.gov/eopss/docs/doc/research-reports/furlough/316-furlough.pdf.

90. Kilgore, *Understanding Mass Incarceration,* 34.

91. Travis, *But They All Come Back,* 89–91.

92. "Work-Release Is Suspended after Inmate Shoots Officer," *New York Times,* April 6, 1994, http://www.nytimes.com/1994/04/06/us/work-release-is -suspended-after-inmate-shoots-officer.html.

93. Adam Doster, "'Setting the Record Straight' on Quinn's Early Release Program," Progress Illinois, October 28, 2010, http://www.progressillinois .com/posts/content/2010/10/28/inside-early-release-scandal. Four years later, Quinn was once again up for reelection, and his new opponent once again ran attack ads on the subject; Quinn lost the election. Monique Garcia and Rick Pearson, "Rauner Talks Crime, Pivots from Nursing Home Trial," *Chicago Tribune,* September 23, 2014, http://www.chicagotribune.com /news/local/politics/chi-rauner-talks-crime-to-pivot-from-nursing-home-trial -20140923-story.html.

94. Matthew R. Durose, Alexia D. Cooper, and Howard N. Snyder, *Recidivism of Prisoners Released in 30 States in 2005: Patterns from 2005 to 2010* (U.S. Department of Justice, Office of Justice Programs, April 2014), http://www.bjs.gov/content/pub/pdf/rprts05p0510.pdf; CEA, *Economic Perspectives,* 26, 39.

95. Travis, *But They All Come Back,* 92–93.

96. Durose et al., *Recidivism.*

97. Colson Task Force, *Transforming Prisons,* 32, 34.

98. Bernadette Rabuy and Daniel Kopf, "Separation by Bars and Miles: Visitation in State Prisons," Prison Policy Initiative, October 20, 2015, https://www.prisonpolicy.org/reports/prisonvisits.html.

99. Rabuy and Kopf.

100. William D. Bales and Daniel P. Mears, "Inmate Social Ties and the Transition to Society: Does Visitation Reduce Recidivism?," *Journal of Research in Crime and Delinquency* 45 (2008): 304–305.

101. *See* Overton v. Bazzetta, 539 U.S. 126, 132 (2003).

102. The Liman Progam, Yale Law School, and Association of State Correctional Administrators, *Time-in-Cell: The ASCA-Liman 2014 National Survey of Administrative Segregation in Prison* (2015), 44, https://www.law.yale.edu /system/files/documents/pdf/asca-liman_administrative_segregation_report _sep_2_2015.pdf.

103. Chesa Boudin, Trevor Stutz, and Aaron Littman, "Prison Visitation Policies: A Fifty-State Survey," *Yale Law and Policy Review* 32 (2013): 161.

104. Boudin, Stutz, and Littman, 161.

105. Grant Duwe and Valerie Clark, "Blessed Be the Social Tie That Binds: The Effects of Prison Visitation on Offender Recidivism," *Criminal Justice Policy Review* 24 (2011): 271; Bales and Mears, "Inmate Social Ties," 287.

106. Bernadette Rabuy and Peter Wagner, *Screening Out Family Time: The For Profit Video Visitation Industry in Prisons and Jails* (Prison Policy Institute, 2015), 3–4, 7.

107. *See generally* Center on the Administration of Criminal Law, "Comment on Proposed Rule for Rates for Interstate Inmate Calling," December 24, 2012, http://www.law.nyu.edu/sites/default/files/ecm_pro_075270.pdf; Michel

Martin and Cecilia Kang, "FCC Decides to Cap Prices of In-State Phone Calls by Prison Inmates," NPR, June 18, 2017, http://www.npr.org/2017/06/18/533438857/fcc-decides-to-cap-prices-of-in-state-phone-calls-by-prison-inmates.

108. Martin and Kang, "FCC Decides to Cap Prices."
109. Timothy Williams, "The High Cost of Calling the Imprisoned," *New York Times,* March 30, 2015, https://www.nytimes.com/2015/03/31/us/steep-costs-of-inmate-phone-calls-are-under-scrutiny.html.
110. Cecilia Kang, "Court Strikes Obama-Era Rule Capping Cost of Phone Calls from Prison," *New York Times,* June 13, 2017, https://www.nytimes.com/2017/06/13/technology/fcc-prison-phone-calls-regulations.html?mcubz=1&_r=0.
111. CEA, *Economic Perspectives,* 64.
112. Barack Obama, "The President's Role in Advancing Criminal Justice Reform," *Harvard Law Review* 130 (2017): 830.
113. Craig Haney, "Mental Health Issues in Long-Term Solitary and 'Supermax' Confinement," *Crime and Delinquency* 49 (2003): 124–156; Daniel P. Mears and William D. Bales, "Supermax Incarceration and Recidivism," *Criminology* 47 (2009): 1131, 1149–1151.
114. Alison Shames, Jessa Wilcox, and Ram Subramanian, *Solitary Confinement: Common Misconceptions and Emerging Safe Alternatives* (Vera Institute of Justice, 2015), 13–14.
115. Emily Bazelon, "The Shame of Solitary Confinement," *New York Times Magazine,* February 19, 2015, http://www.nytimes.com/2015/02/19/magazine/the-shame-of-solitary-confinement.html.
116. Bazelon.
117. David Cole, "Justice Breyer v. the Death Penalty," *New Yorker,* June 30, 2015.
118. Mark Binelli, "Inside America's Toughest Prison," *New York Times Magazine,* March 26, 2015, http://www.nytimes.com/2015/03/29/magazine/inside-americas-toughest-federal-prison.html.

4. Obsolete Outcomes

1. *See* 132 Cong. Rec. H6578 (daily ed. Sept. 10, 1986) (statement of Rep. Florio); U.S. Sentencing Commission (USSC), *Special Report to the Congress: Cocaine and Federal Sentencing Policy* (1995), 122–123, http://www.ussc.gov/Legislative_and_Public_Affairs/Congressional_Testimony_and_Reports/Drug_Topics/199502_RtC_Cocaine_Sentencing_Policy/CHAP6.HTM.
2. Naomi Murakawa, *The First Civil Right: How Liberals Built Prison America* (New York: Oxford University Press, 2014), 125.
3. *See* Craig Reinarman, "5 Myths about That Demon Crack," *Washington Post,* October 14, 2007, http://www.washingtonpost.com/wp-dyn/content/article/2007/10/09/AR2007100900751.html; USSC, *Special Report.*

4. U.S. Sentencing Commission, *Quick Facts: Crack Cocaine Trafficking* (2014), 1, http://www.ussc.gov/sites/default/files/pdf/research-and-publications/quick -facts/Quick_Facts_Crack_Cocaine.pdf.

5. U.S. Sentencing Commission, *Quick Facts: Powder Cocaine Trafficking* (2014), 1, http://www.ussc.gov/sites/default/files/pdf/research-and -publications/quick-facts/Quick_Facts_Powder_Cocaine.pdf.

6. Fair Sentencing Act of 2010, Pub. L. 111–220, 124 Stat. 2372; 156 Cong. Rec. E1665–05 (2010) (statement of Rep. Inglis).

7. Steffen Huck, Georg Kirchsteiger, and Jörg Oechssler, "Learning to Like What You Have: Explaining the Endowment Effect," *Economic Journal* 115 (July 2005): 689–702.

8. Maurice Chammah, "American Sheriff," *Atlantic,* May 5, 2016, http://www .theatlantic.com/politics/archive/2016/05/american-sheriff/481131.

9. George Skelton, "A Father's Crusade Born from Pain," *Los Angeles Times,* December 9, 1993, http://articles.latimes.com/1993–12–09/news/mn-65402 _1_mike-reynolds; CA Assem. B. Hist., 1993–1994 A.B. 971.

10. Michael Vitiello, "Three Strikes and the Romero Case: The Supreme Court Restores Democracy," *Loyola of Los Angeles Law Review* 30 (1997): 1605n5.

11. Ewing v. California, 538 U.S. 11 (2003).

12. *See* Cal. Penal Code § 667(c)(5) (West 1999).

13. Jonathan Saltzman, "Patrick Overhauls Parole," *Boston Globe,* January 14, 2011, http://archive.boston.com/news/politics/articles/2011/01/14/five_out_as _governor_overhauls_parole_board/?page=1; Brian R. Ballou, "'Melissa's Bill' Signed in Nearly Private Ceremony," *Boston Globe,* August 3, 2012, https://www.bostonglobe.com/metro/2012/08/02/quiet-ceremony-governor -signs-melissa-law-legislation/31AsmuWaaZqEESAKwFwRqL/story.html.

14. Eric Bedner, "Prison Early Release Program Called into Question," *Journal Inquirer,* October 13, 2016, http://www.journalinquirer.com/politics_and _government/prison-early-release-program-called-into-question/article _b197a098–9159–11e6–8b2b-db62557ba335.html; Len Suzio, "Letter: Sen. Suzio Seek Signatures for End Early Release Bill," *Middletown Press,* March 24, 2017, http://www.middletownpress.com/opinion/20170324/letter -sen-suzio-seek-signatures-for-end-early-release-bill.

15. Michael A. Fletcher, "Virginia Attacks Crime by Abolishing Parole, Lengthening Prison Sentences," *Baltimore Sun,* October 2, 1994, http://articles .baltimoresun.com/1994–10–02/news/1994275041_1_abolishing-parole -parole-after-serving-eligible-for-parole.

16. Lindsey Millar, "Arkansas's Prison Population, and Related Expense, Is Exploding," *Arkansas Times,* July 23, 2015, http://www.arktimes.com /arkansas/arkansass-prison-population-and-related-expense-is-exploding /Content?oid=3973297.

17. Rob Moritz, "Lawmakers to Take Up Parole System," *Arkansas News,* July 8, 2013, http://arkansasnews.com/sections/news/arkansas/lawmakers-take -parole-system.html.

18. Millar, "Arkansas's Prison Population."

19. Moritz, "Lawmakers."
20. Millar, "Arkansas's Prison Population."
21. Lindsey Millar, "More Reminders of How Bad Arkansas's Prison, Parole, and Probation Systems Are," *Arkansas Times,* June 22, 2016, http://www .arktimes.com/ArkansasBlog/archives/2016/06/22/more-reminders-of-how -bad-arkansass-prison-parole-and-probation-systems-are.
22. Millar, "Arkansas's Prison Population."
23. Millar, "Arkansas's Prison Population."
24. Andy Barbee et al., *Justice Reinvestment in Arkansas: 2nd Presentation to the Legislative Criminal Justice Oversight Task Force* (Justice Center, 2016), 9, 12, https://csgjusticecenter.org/wp-content/uploads/2016/03 /ARSecondPresentation.pdf.
25. Barbee, 12.
26. Barbee, 8.
27. Barbee, 10–11.
28. Patrick A. Langan and David Levin, *Recidivism of Prisoners Released in 1994* (Bureau of Justice Statistics, 2002), http://www.bjs.gov/content/pub/pdf /rpr94.pdf; Pew Charitable Trusts, *Time Served: The High Cost, Low Return of Longer Prison Terms* (2012), http://www.pewtrusts.org/~/media/assets /2012/06/06/time_served_report.pdf.
29. Jeremy Travis, *But They All Come Back: Facing the Challenge of Prisoner Reentry* (Washington, DC: Urban Institute Press, 2005), 106.
30. ABA Commission on Effective Criminal Sanctions, *Sentence Reduction Mechanisms in a Determinate Sentencing System: Report of the Second Look Roundtable,* 21 Fed. Sent'g Rep. 217 (2009) (Margaret C. Love, Reporter) (quoting Professor Douglas Berman).
31. Joan Petersilia, *When Prisoners Come Home: Parole and Prisoner Reentry* (New York: Oxford University Press, 2009), 65.
32. Bureau of Justice Statistics, *Reentry Trends in the United States* (2000), https://www.bjs.gov/content/reentry/releases.cfm; Pub. L. No. 98–473, 98 Stat. 1987 (codified at 18 U.S.C. § 3551 (2012)).
33. Sentencing Project, *Trends in US Corrections* (2017), 8, https://www .sentencingproject.org/publications/trends-in-u-s-corrections. While life sentences increase, violent crime rates are decreasing, and there is little evidence that longer sentences have a substantial impact on public safety. Sentencing project, 8.
34. Doris Layton Mackenzie, *Sentencing and Corrections in the 21st Century: Setting the Stage for the Future* (National Criminal Justice Reference Service, 2001), https://www.ncjrs.gov/pdffiles1/nij/189106-2.pdf.
35. This figure applies only to persons serving one year or more in prison. Pew Charitable Trusts, *Max Out: The Rise in Prison Inmates Released without Supervision* (2014), 2, http://www.pewtrusts.org/~/media/assets/2014/06/04 /maxout_report.pdf.
36. Leslie Walker et al., *White Paper: The Current State of Parole in Massachusetts* (Prisoners' Legal Services, 2013), 1, http://www.cjpc.org/uploads/1/0/4/9 /104972649/white-paper-addendum-2.25.13.pdf.

37. Walker et al., 2–3.
38. New York Department of Corrections and Community Supervision, *Earned Eligibility Program Summary Semiannual Report: April 2014–September 2014* (2014), 5, http://www.doccs.ny.gov/Research /Reports/2014/EEP_Report_Apr14-Sep14.pdf.
39. Jennifer Palmer, "Parole Is Not Likely for Violent Offenders in Oklahoma," *Oklahoman*, January 19, 2016, http://newsok.com/article/5473072. *See also* Clifton Adcock, "Growth in Prison Population Persists," Oklahoma Watch, January 7, 2016, http://oklahomawatch.org/2016/01/07/number-of-prison -inmates-surges-again.
40. Nazgol Ghandnoosh, *Delaying a Second Chance: The Declining Prospects for Parole on Life Sentences* (Sentencing Project, 2013), 7, https://www .sentencingproject.org/publications/delaying-second-chance-declining -prospects-parole-life-sentences.
41. ACLU, *False Hope: How Parole Systems Fail Youth Serving Extreme Sentences* (2016), 39, https://www.aclu.org/issues/juvenile-justice/youth -incarceration/false-hope-how-parole-systems-fail-youth-serving-extreme.
42. ACLU, 39.
43. Christine S. Scott-Hayward, "The Failure of Parole: Rethinking the Role of the State in Reentry," *New Mexico Law Review* 41 (2011): 439; Mona Lynch, "Rehabilitation as Rhetoric: The Ideal of Reformation in Contemporary Parole Discourse and Practices," *Punishment and Society* 2 (2000): 40–65.
44. Marie Gottschalk, *Caught: The Prison State and the Lockdown of American Politics* (Princeton, NJ: Princeton University Press, 2016), 96.
45. Mario A. Paparozzi and Paul Gendreau, "An Intensive Supervision Program That Worked: Service Delivery, Professional Orientation, and Organizational Supportiveness," *Prison Journal,* December 2005, 445, 458. Even more important than the orientation of the office might be whether they use a risks / needs assessment. A 2011 analysis of the American Probation and Parole Associate's data found that, regardless of whether parole officers embody a social work or a law enforcement attitude, parole strategies that utilize risks and needs assessments of individuals are the most effective. *See generally* Matthew T. Demichele, Brian K. Payne, and Adam K. Matz, "Probation Philosophies and Workload Considerations," *American Journal of Criminal Justice* 36 (2011): 29–43.
46. Pew, *Max Out,* 1–3.
47. James B. Jacobs, "Sentencing by Prison Personnel: Good Time," *UCLA Law Review* 30 (1982): 221.
48. Todd Edwards, *Correctional Good-Time Credits in Southern States* (Council of State Governments, 2001), 6, 7.
49. Michigan Department of Corrections, *Truth in Sentencing Information* (2017), http://www.michigan.gov/corrections/0,4551,7-119-9741_12798– 208276—,00.html.
50. Paul J. Larkin, "Clemency, Parole, Good-Time Credits, and Crowded Prisons: Reconsidering Early Release," *Georgetown Journal of Law and Public Policy* 11 (2013): 41.

51. In 2016, 38 states had some form of earned time credit policy. Pew Charitable Trusts, *Missouri Policy Shortens Probation and Parole Terms, Protects Public Safety* (2016), 3, figure 2, http://www.pewtrusts.org/~/media/assets /2016/08/missouri_policy_shortens_probation_and_parole_terms_protects _public_safety.pdf; Allison Lawrence, *Cutting Corrections Costs, Earned Time for State Prisoners* (National Conference of State Legislatures, 2009), 1.

52. S. 467, 114th Cong. (2015).

53. Sentencing Reform and Corrections Act of 2015, S. 2123, 114th Cong. (2015).

54. Michael M. O'Hear, "Solving the Good-Time Puzzle: Why Following the Rules Should Get You Out of Prison Early," *Wisconsin Law Review* (2012): 200–201.

55. Lawrence, *Cutting Corrections Costs;* California Department of Corrections and Rehabilitation, *Proposition 57: Credit Earning for Inmates, Frequently Asked Questions* (updated July 2017), 2.

56. Charles Colson Task Force on Federal Corrections, *Transforming Prisons, Restoring Lives* (2016), 45.

57. Michael Massoglia and Christopher Uggen, "Settling Down and Aging Out: Toward an Interactionist Theory of Desistance and the Transition to Adulthood," *American Journal of Sociology* 116 (2010): 544; National Institute of Justice, *From Juvenile Delinquency to Young Adult Offending* (2014), 1, figure 1, https://www.nij.gov/topics/crime/Pages/delinquency-to-adult -offending.aspx-note1. The age/crime curve is slightly adjusted for gender, type of crime, and the socioeconomic makeup of a neighborhood. Girls tend to peak earlier than boys, property crime tends to peak earlier than violent crime, and the curve is higher and wider in lower socioeconomic areas. National Institute of Justice, 1.

58. Joshua A. Markman et al., *Recidivism of Offenders Placed on Federal Community Supervision in 2005: Patterns from 2005 to 2010* (Bureau of Justice Statistics, June 2016), 6, table 8, https://www.bjs.gov/content/pub/pdf /ropfcs05p0510.pdf.

59. Colson Task Force, *Transforming Prisons,* 46.

60. Model Penal Code: Sentencing 570, 575 (Am. Law Inst., Proposed Final Draft, 2017).

61. Alexander Hamilton, *Federalist* No. 74, in *The Federalist Papers,* ed. Clinton Rossiter (New York: New American Library, 1961), 447.

62. James Iredell, "Address at the North Carolina Ratifying Convention (July 28, 1788)," in *The Founders' Constitution,* vol. 4, ed. Philip B. Kurland and Ralph Lerner (Indianapolis, IN: Liberty Fund, 1987), 18.

63. U.S. Const. art. II, § 2.

64. Kathleen Ridolfi and Seth Gordon, "Gubernatorial Clemency Powers: Justice or Mercy?," *Criminal Justice* 24, no. 3 (Fall 2009): 26–41.

65. *See* A. Keith Bottomley, "Parole in Transition: A Comparative Study of Origins, Developments, and Prospects for the 1990s," *Crime and Justice* 12 (1990): 324; Rachel E. Barkow, "Clemency and Presidential Administration of Criminal Law," *New York University Law Review* 90 (2015): 813.

66. Margaret Colgate Love, "Freedom in Decline: The Twilight of Pardon Power," *Journal of Criminal Law and Criminology* 100 (2010): 1186; Ridolfi and Gordon, "Gubernatorial Clemency Powers," 33.

67. Bottomley, "Parole in Transition," 325; Joan Petersilia, "Parole and Prisoner Reentry in the United States," *Crime and Justice* 26 (1999): 479–529.

68. Rachel E. Barkow, "The Politics of Forgiveness: Reconceptualizing Clemency," *Federal Sentencing Reporter* 21 (2009): 153.

69. U.S. Sentencing Commission, *Life Sentences in the Federal System* (2015), 4, 16.

70. Families against Mandatory Minimums (FAMM), "Ricky Minor," http://famm.org/ricky-minor. Minor's sentence was commuted by President Obama in 2016. FAMM.

71. "State Marijuana Laws in 2018 Map," Governing, updated March 23, 2017, http://www.governing.com/gov-data/state-marijuana-laws-map-medical-recreational.html.

72. U.S. Sentencing Commission, *Frequently Asked Questions: Retroactive Application of the 2014 Drug Guidelines Amendment* (2014), 1–3.

73. Barkow, "Clemency," 816–824.

74. Rachel E. Barkow, "Prosecutorial Administration: Prosecutor Bias and the Department of Justice," *Virginia Law Review* 99 (2013): 288.

75. Mike Huckabee, "Why I Commuted Maurice Clemmons' Sentence," *Washington Post*, December 7, 2009, http://www.washingtonpost.com/wp-dyn/content/article/2009/12/07/AR2009120702333.html.

76. "Mike Huckabee's Clemency under Scrutiny," Fox News, December 10, 2007, http://www.foxnews.com/story/2007/12/10/mike-huckabee-clemency-record-is-under-scrutiny.html.

77. *See, e.g.,* Jay Carney, "Huckabee's Willie Horton," *Time*, December 5, 2007, http://swampland.time.com/2007/12/05/huckabees_willie_horton; Ben Smith, "A Huckabee Clemency Gone Awry?," *Politico*, November 29, 2009, http://www.politico.com/blogs/ben-smith/2009/11/a-huckabee-clemency-gone-awry-023100.

78. P. S. Ruckman Jr., "Hat Tip to the Old Man," *Pardon Power* (blog), December 2, 2009, http://www.pardonpower.com/2009/12/hat-tip-to-old-man.html; Perry Bacon Jr. and Garance Franke-Ruta, "After Police Killings, Huckabee Defends Clemency for Suspect," *Washington Post*, December 1, 2009, http://www.washingtonpost.com/wp-dyn/content/article/2009/12/01/AR2009120102601.html.

79. Office of the Pardon Attorney, U.S. Department of Justice, Clemency Statistics, https://www.justice.gov/pardon/clemency-statistics.

80. Mark W. Osler, "Clemency for the 21st Century: A Systemic Reform of the Federal Clemency Process," SSRN, April 15, 2013, 1, http://ssrn.com/abstract=2248361.

81. "Governors' Pardons Are Becoming a Rarity," Governing, February 8, 2013, http://www.governing.com/news/state/sl-governors-balance-politics-with-pardons.html; *see also* Margaret Colgate Love, "Fear of Forgiving: Rule and Discretion in the Theory and Practice of Pardoning," *Federal Sentencing Reporter* 13 (2001): 125–133.

82. Rachel Barkow and Mark Osler, "Designed to Fail: The President's Deference to the Department of Justice in Advancing Criminal Justice Reform," *Williams and Mary Law Review* 59 (2017): 437.

83. U.S. Sentencing Commission, *An Analysis of the Implementation of the 2014 Clemency Initiative* (2017), 2.

84. U.S. Sentencing Commission, 9.

85. B. Jaye Anno et al., *Correctional Health Care: Addressing the Needs of Elderly, Chronically Ill, and Terminally Ill Inmates* (U.S. Department of Justice, National Institute of Corrections, 2004), 13, https://s3.amazonaws.com/static.nicic.gov/Library/018735.pdf.

86. U.S. Department of Justice, Office of the Inspector General (OIG), *The Impact of an Aging Inmate Population on the Federal Bureau of Prisons* (2016), 37–40, https://oig.justice.gov/reports/2015/e1505.pdf.

87. *See* U.S. Department of Justice, Office of the Inspector General, *The Federal Bureau of Prisons' Compassionate Release Program* (2013), 49–50, https://oig.justice.gov/reports/2013/e1306.pdf.

88. U.S. Department of Justice, 40.

89. Tina Chiu, *It's About Time: Aging Prisoners, Increasing Costs, and Geriatric Release* (Vera Institute of Justice, 2010), 5, https://www.vera.org/publications/its-about-time-aging-prisoners-increasing-costs-and-geriatric-release.

90. U.S. Sentencing Commission, *Public Hearing on Compassionate Release and Conditions of Supervision before the U.S. Sentencing Commission* (2016), 65, http://www.ussc.gov/sites/default/files/Transcript_6.pdf (statement of Michael E. Horowitz, Inspector General, U.S. Department of Justice).

91. OIG, *Aging Inmate Population*, i, 10.

92. Chiu, *It's About Time*, 5.

93. OIG, *Aging Inmate Population*, 18, 21, 32.

94. OIG, *Aging Inmate Population*; Sari Horwitz, "The Painful Price of Aging in Prison," *Washington Post*, May 2, 2015, http://www.washingtonpost.com/sf/national/2015/05/02/the-painful-price-of-aging-in-prison.

95. Tina Maschi, "The State of Aging Prisoners and Compassionate Release Programs," *Huffington Post*, October 23, 2012, http://www.huffingtonpost.com/tina-maschi/the-state-of-aging-prisoners_b_1825811.html; Colorado Department of Corrections, *Statistical Report: Fiscal Year 2008* (2009), 1, https://drive.google.com/file/d/0B8WLSXAboMg8bE5yLUxSVTBodkU/view.

96. Chiu, *It's About Time*, 6–8.

97. Maschi, "Aging Prisoners."

98. OIG, *Compassionate Release*, 1.

99. Chiu, *It's About Time*, 4.

100. USSC, *Public Hearing on Compassionate Release*, 65 (statement of Michael E. Horowitz, Inspector General, U.S. Department of Justice); OIG, *Aging Inmate Population*, i.

101. U.S. Sentencing Commission, *Testimony of Brie Williams, MD, MS, before the United States Sentencing Commission, Public Hearing on Compassionate Release and Conditions of Supervision*, February 17, 2016, 2,

http://www.ussc.gov/sites/default/files/pdf/amendment-process/public
-hearings-and-meetings/20160217/williams.pdf.

102. U.S. Sentencing Commission, (testimony of Williams).

103. Chiu, *It's About Time*, 6, 9; National Conference of State Legislatures, *The Bulletin: Online Sentencing and Corrections Policy Updates* (2010), 4–6, http://www.ncsl.org/portals/1/Documents/cj/bulletinJune-2010.pdf.

104. NCSL, *The Bulletin*, 5; OIG, *Aging Inmate Population*, 7.

105. Human Rights Watch (HRW) and FAMM, *The Answer Is No: Too Little Compassionate Release in US Federal Prisons* (2012), 43, 57, https://www .hrw.org/sites/default/files/reports/us1112ForUploadSm.pdf.

106. OIG, *Compassionate Release*, 3, 27–29.

107. OIG, 12, 17–18; USSC, *Public Hearing on Compassionate Release*, 138–140, 154–160 (testimony of Dr. Brie Williams, University of California San Francisco, School of Medicine).

108. Prior to April 2013, a request had to go through a regional director as well. *See* 28 C.F.R § 571.62 (2013).

109. U.S. Department of Justice, Federal Bureau of Prisons, *No. 5050.49, Program Statement, Compassionate Release/Reduction in Sentence: Procedures for Implementation of 18 U.S.C. §§ 3582(c)(1)(A) and 4205(g) 18* (2013), https://www.bop.gov/policy/progstat/5050_049_CN-1.pdf.

110. OIG, *Compassionate Release*, 5.

111. OIG, *Compassionate Release*, 29, 39.

112. USSC, *Public Hearing on Compassionate Release*, 37.

113. USSC, 127 (testimony of Mary Price, Families Against Mandatory Minimums).

114. HRW and FAMM, *Answer Is No*, 1.

115. HRW and FAMM, 14.

5. Collateral Calamities

1. Matthew R. Durose, Alexia D. Cooper, and Howard N. Snyder, *Recidivism of Prisoners Released in 30 States in 2005: Patterns from 2005 to 2010* (Bureau of Justice Statistics, 2014); Council of Economic Advisers, *Economic Perspectives on Incarceration and the Justice System* (2016), 26, 39.

2. Jeremy Travis, *But They All Come Back: Facing the Challenges of Prisoner Reentry* (Washington, DC: Urban Institute Press, 2005), 66–67; Margaret Colgate Love, Jenny Roberts, and Cecelia M. Klingele, *Collateral Consequences of Criminal Convictions: Law, Policy and Practice* (Minneapolis, MN: Thomson West, 2013), § 1.4.

3. Velmer S. Burton, Jr., Francis T. Cullen, and Lawrence F. Travis III, "The Collateral Consequences of a Felony Conviction: A National Study of State Statutes," *Federal Probation* 51 (1987): 52–60.

4. Kathleen M. Olivares, Velmer S. Burton Jr., and Francis T. Cullen, "The Collateral Consequences of a Felony Conviction: A National Study of State Legal Codes 10 Years Later," *Federal Probation* 60 (1996): 10–17.

5. Sandra G. Mayson, "Collateral Consequences and the Preventive State," *Notre Dame Law Review* 91 (2015): 309.

6. Ram Subramanian, Rebecka Moreno, and Sophia Gebreselassie, *Relief in Sight? States Rethink the Collateral Consequences of Criminal Conviction, 2009–2014* (Vera Institute of Justice, 2014), 11, 14, 28, 29; Margaret Colgate Love, "States 'Rethinking' Collateral Consequences? Vera Institute Jumps the Gun," Collateral Consequences Resource Center, January 7, 2015, http:// ccresourcecenter.org/2015/01/07/states-rethinking-collateral-consequences -not-fast-vera-institute.

7. Travis, *But They All Come Back*, 227.

8. Travis, 239.

9. Bruce Western et al., "Stress and Hardship after Prison," *American Journal of Sociology* 120 (2015): 1526.

10. 42 U.S.C. § 13662(c).

11. Department of Housing and Urban Development v. Rucker, 535 U.S. 125 (2002); 42 U.S.C. §§ 13662(c); 1437d(1)(6).

12. 24 C.F.R. § 966.4(l)(5)(i)(B), § 966.4(l)(5)(iii)(A).

13. Rucker v. Davis, No. C 98–00781 CRB, 1998 WL 345403, at *2 (N.D. Cal. June 19, 1998).

14. Arin Greenwood, "'One Strike' Public Housing Policy Hits Virginia Woman Who Needs Kidney Transplant," *Huffington Post*, December 22, 2011, http://www.huffingtonpost.com/2011/12/22/one-strike-policy-housing -alexandria-virginia-kidney-transplant_n_1151639.html.

15. Housing Authority of New Orleans v. Green, 657 So. 2d 552, 552 (La. App. 4 Cir. 1995).

16. Travis, *But They All Come Back*, 232.

17. Travis.

18. Marah Curtis et al., "Alcohol, Drug, and Criminal History Restrictions in Public Housing," *Cityscape: A Journal of Policy Development and Research* 15 (2013): 43.

19. Curtis et al., 48.

20. 42 U.S.C. § 13664(a); 24 C.F.R. § 960.204(a)(4).

21. Human Rights Watch (HRW), *Raised on the Registry: The Irreparable Harm of Placing Children on Sex Offender Registries in the US* (2013), 21, 49, 81, https://www.hrw.org/report/2013/05/01/raised-registry/irreparable-harm -placing-children-sex-offender-registries-us.

22. Sidney Butler, "'Untouchable' Questions the Unspeakable Truth," *Washington Square News*, April 22, 2016, http://www.nyunews.com/2016/04/22 /untouchable-questions-the-unspeakable-truth.

23. Marie Claire Tran Leung, *When Discretion Means Denial: A National Perspective on Criminal Records Barriers to Federally Subsidized Housing* (Sargent Shriver National Center on Poverty Law, 2015), 2.

24. Travis, *But They All Come Back*, 234.

25. HRW, *No Second Chance: People with Criminal Records Denied Access to Public Housing* (2004), 21, 37, https://www.hrw.org/reports/2004/usa1104 /usa1104.pdf.

26. 42 U.S.C. § 862a.
27. Rebecca Reitsch, "States Rethink Restrictions on Food Stamps, Welfare for Drug Felons," Pew Charitable Trusts, July 30, 2015, http://www.pewtrusts .org/en/research-and-analysis/blogs/stateline/2015/07/30/states-rethink -restrictions-on-food-stamps-welfare-for-drug-felons.
28. Cody Tuttle, "Snapping Back: Food Stamp Bans and Recidivism," March 29, 2018, https://ssrn.com/abstract=2845435.
29. Reitsch, "States Rethink Restrictions."
30. Marie French, "Missouri Considers Lifting Lifetime Food Stamp Ban for Drug Felons," *St. Louis Post-Dispatch,* April 8, 2014, http://www.stltoday .com/news/local/govt-and-politics/missouri-considers-lifting-lifetime-food -stamp-ban-for-drug-felons/article_1c8dc38e-e970–5d36-be1b -f51dcae58624.html.
31. Erin Edgemon, "Alabama Drug Felons to Get Welfare Benefits after 2 Decade Ban," Alabama.com, June 24, 2015, http://www.al.com/news/index.ssf/2015 /06/alabama_drug_felons_wait_for_n.html.
32. A survey of formerly incarcerated people and their related communities in 14 states found that 60% of formerly incarcerated individuals were unemployed 1 year after release, with 67% still unemployed or underemployed 5 years after release. *See* Saneta deVuono-powell et al., *Who Pays? The True Coast of Incarceration on Families* (Ella Baker Center, 2015), 20.
33. Travis, *But They All Come Back,* 292.
34. 20 U.S.C. § 1091(r)(1).
35. DeVuono-powell et al., *Who Pays?,* 20.
36. DeVuono-powell et al., 20; 20 U.S.C. §1091(r)(2).
37. Thomas D. Snyder, Cristobal de Brey, and Sally A. Dillow, *Digest of Education Statistics 2014* (National Center for Education Statistics, 2016), 411; U.S. Government Accountability Office, GAO-05–238, *Drug Offenders: Various Factors May Limit the Impacts of Federal Laws That Provide for Denial of Selected Benefits* (2005), 12–13.
38. GAO, *Drug Offenders,* 59.
39. Drug Policy Alliance, *The Drug War, Mass Incarceration and Race* (2016), 1, https://www.drugpolicy.org/sites/default/files/DPA%20Fact%20Sheet _Drug%20War%20Mass%20Incarceration%20and%20Race_%28Feb.%20 2016%29_0.pdf.
40. National Center for Education Statistics, *Digest of Education Statistics* (2015), table 302.60; Jamie Fellner, "Race, Drugs, and Law Enforcement in the United States," *Stanford Law and Policy Review* 20 (2009): 271.
41. 23 U.S.C. § 159.
42. Joshua Aikin, "Reinstating Common Sense: How Driver's License Suspensions for Drug Offenses Unrelated to Driving Are Falling Out of Favor," Prison Policy Initiative, December 12, 2016, https://www.prisonpolicy.org /driving/national.html; Molly Davis, "Driver Licenses to No Longer Be Suspended for Drug Users," Libertas Institute, March 15, 2018, https:// libertasutah.org/2018-bills/driver-licenses-to-no-longer-be-suspended-for-drug -users/; Mary Wolfe, "New Laws Will Ease Some Driving Restrictions," *Clinton Herald,* June 12, 2018, http://www.clintonherald.com/opinion

/columns/new-laws-will-ease-some-driving-restrictions/article_f834c3d4-367c
-5c6c-bedf-fo4c1258cab2.html.

43. Oliver Hinds, Jacob Kang-Brown, and Olive Lu, "For the Record: People in
Prison in 2017," Vera Institute of Justice, May 2018, https://storage
.googleapis.com/vera-web-assets/downloads/Publications/people-in-prison
-2017/legacy_downloads/people-in-prison-2017.pdf.

44. Adie Tomer et al., "Missed Opportunities: Transit and Jobs in Metropolitan
America," The Brookings Policy Program, May 2011, https://www.brookings
.edu/wp-content/uploads/2016/06/0512_jobs_transit.pdf.

45. Alana Samuels, "No Driver's License, No Job," *The Atlantic,* June 15, 2016,
https://www.theatlantic.com/business/archive/2016/06/no-drivers-license-no
-job/486653/.

46. Brentin Mock, "Why Is Pennsylvania Still Suspending Driver's Licenses for
Drug Offenses?," CityLab, January 18, 2018, https://www.citylab.com/equity
/2018/01/taking-the-high-road-on-drivers-license-suspensions/550688/.

47. Jon A. Carnegie, "Driver's License Suspensions, Impacts and Fairness Study,"
Alan M. Voorhees Transportation Center at Rutgers University, August 2007,
https://www.nj.gov/transportation/refdata/research/reports/FHWA-NJ-2007
-020-V1.pdf.

48. Shaila Dewan, "Driver's License Suspensions Create Cycle of Debt," *New
York Times,* April 14, 2015, https://www.nytimes.com/2015/04/15/us/with
-drivers-license-suspensions-a-cycle-of-debt.html.

49. Clifton Adcock, "Ex-offenders Face Steep Price to Reinstate Driver's Licenses,"
Oklahoma Watch, February 23, 2015, http://oklahomawatch.org/2015/02/23
/for-released-offenders-a-steep-price-to-drive-again.

50. Adcock.

51. HRW, *No Easy Answers: Sex Offender Laws in the US* (2007), 35–36,
https://www.hrw.org/sites/default/files/reports/us0907webwcover.pdf.

52. Pub. L. No. 109–248, 120 Stat. 587.

53. Pub. L.

54. National Conference of State Legislatures, "Adam Walsh Child Protection
and Safety Act," May 7, 2014, http://www.ncsl.org/research/civil-and
-criminal-justice/adam-walsh-child-protection-and-safety-act.aspx; Emanuella
Grinberg, "5 Years Later, States Struggle to Comply with Federal Sex
Offender Law," CNN, July 28, 2011, http://www.cnn.com/2011/CRIME/07
/28/sex.offender.adam.walsh.act.

55. Olivares et al., "Collateral Consequences of a Felony Conviction," 16.

56. Darren Wheelock, Christopher Uggen, and Heather Hlavka, "Employment
Restrictions for Individuals with Felon Status and Racial Inequality in the
Labor Market," in *Global Perspectives on Re-entry,* ed. Ikponwosa Ekunwe
and Richard S. Jones (Tampere, Finland: Tampere University Press, 2011),
283, http://epublications.marquette.edu/cgi/viewcontent.cgi?article
=1044&context=socs_fac.

57. National Association of Criminal Defense Lawyers, *America's Failure to
Forgive or Forget in the War on Crime: A Roadmap to Restore Rights and
Status after Arrest or Conviction* (2014), 32, http://www.nacdl.org/WorkArea
/DownloadAsset.aspx?id=33203.

58. Shawn D. Bushway and Gary Sweeten, "Abolish Lifetime Bans for Ex-felons," *Criminology and Public Policy* 6 (2007): 698, http://www.albany.edu /bushway_research/publications/Bushway_Sweeten_2007.pdf.

59. Margaret Colgate Love, "Managing Collateral Consequences in the Sentencing Process: The Revised Sentencing Articles of the Model Penal Code," *Wisconsin Law Review* (2015): 250.

60. Michael Pinard, "Reflections and Perspectives on Reentry and Collateral Consequences," *Journal of Criminal Law and Criminology* 100 (2010): 1218n30, http://digitalcommons.law.umaryland.edu/cgi/viewcontent.cgi ?article=2040&context=fac_pubs; Gwen Rubinstein and Debbie Mukamal, "Welfare and Housing: Denial of Benefits to Drug Offenders," in *Invisible Punishment: The Collateral Consequences of Mass Imprisonment,* ed. Marc Mauer and Meda Chesney-Link (New York: New Press, 2002), 50–52.

61. Center for Sex Offender Management (CSOM), *Sex Offender Registration: Policy Overview and Comprehensive Practices* (1999), 2, http://www.csom .org/pubs/sexreg.pdf.

62. Jane Shim, "Listed for Life," *Slate,* August 13, 2014, http://www.slate.com /articles/news_and_politics/jurisprudence/2014/08/sex_offender_registry _laws_by_state_mapped.html; Collateral Consequences Resource Center (CCRC), "50-State Comparison: Relief from Sex Offender Registration Obligations," http://ccresourcecenter.org/resources-2/restoration-of -rights/50-state-comparison-relief-from-sex-offender-registration -obligations.

63. S.C. Code Ann. § 23-3-460(A), § 23-3-430 (2015); CCRC, "50-State Comparison."

64. Wayne A. Logan, "Database Infamia: Exit from the Sex Offender Registries," *Wisconsin Law Review* (2015): 225.

65. Collateral Consequences Resource Center, "Relief from Sex Offender Registration and Notification Requirements," December 4, 2014, http:// ccresourcecenter.org/2014/12/04/relief-sex-offender-registration-notification -requirements; Va. Code § 9.1–910 (2008); Haw. Rev. Stat. § 846E-10(e).

66. CSOM, *Sex Offender Registration,* 5.

67. Chanakya Sethi, "The Ridiculous Laws That Put People on the Sex Offender List," *Slate,* August 12, 2014, http://www.slate.com/articles/news_and _politics/jurisprudence/2014/08/mapped_sex_offender_registry_laws_on _statutory_rape_public_urination_and.html.

68. Melody Gutierrez, "Calls for Limiting Sex-Offender Registry Will Be Tough to Act On," *San Francisco Chronicle,* March 25, 2016, http://www.sfchronicle .com/politics/article/Calls-for-limiting-sex-offender-registry-will-be-7123214 .php; HRW, *No Easy Answers,* 36; CSOM, *Sex Offender Registration,* 2.

69. Miami-Dade County, Fla., Art. XVII, Code of Ordinances §§ 21-277 to 21-285 (2015).

70. Kelly K. Bonnar-Kidd, "Sexual Offender Laws and Prevention of Sexual Violence or Recidivism," *American Journal of Public Health* 100 (2010): 415, http://www.ncbi.nlm.nih.gov/pmc/articles/PMC2820068/pdf/412.pdf.

71. Bonnar-Kidd, 415; La. Stat. Ann. § 32:412 (2015) (amended 2016).

72. HRW, *Raised on the Registry,* 63.

73. Hanna Kozlowska, "How America Treats Its Sex Offenders Is Deeply, Morally Complex," *Quartz,* April 29, 2016, http://qz.com/671413/how-america-treats-its-sex-offenders-is-deeply-morally-complex.

74. Naomi Murakawa, *The First Civil Right: How Liberals Built Prison America* (2014), 130.

75. Murakawa, 130.

76. Subramanian et al., *Relief in Sight?,* 4; Jeremy Travis, "Invisible Punishment: An Instrument of Social Exclusion," in *Invisible Punishment,* ed. Mauer and Chesney-Link, 15–17.

77. Travis, *But They All Come Back,* 64–65.

78. Travis, 70.

79. Curtis et al., "Alcohol, Drug, and Criminal History Restrictions," 43, 45.

80. Michelle N. Rodriguez and Beth Avery, *Unlicensed and Untapped: Removing Barriers to State Occupational Licenses for People with Records* (National Employment Law Project, 2016), 1.

81. Mike Ward, "Second Chances Blocked by State Licensing Rules," *Houston Chronicle,* December 26, 2014, http://www.houstonchronicle.com/news/politics/texas/article/Second-chances-blocked-by-state-licensing-rules-5980367.php.

82. HRW, *Raised on the Registry,* 7, 21.

83. INA § 237(a), 8 U.S.C. § 1227.

84. HRW, *A Price Too High: US Families Torn Apart by Deportations for Drug Offenses* (2015), https://www.hrw.org/report/2015/06/16/price-too-high/us-families-torn-apart-deportations-drug-offenses; Immigration Policy Center, American Immigration Council, *Aggravated Felonies: An Overview* (2012), http://www.immigrationpolicy.org/just-facts/aggravated-felonies-overview.

85. Department of Homeland Security, *ICE Enforcement and Removal Operations Report: Fiscal Year 2015* (2015), 3, https://www.ice.gov/sites/default/files/documents/Report/2016/fy2015removalStats.pdf.

86. Marshall Project, "Six States Where Felons Can't Get Food Stamps," February 4, 2016, https://www.themarshallproject.org/2016/02/04/six-states-where-felons-can-t-get-food-stamps.

87. 42 U.S.C. § 13664(a); 24 C.F.R. § 960.204(a)(4).

88. Dara Lind, "Ban the Box: President Obama's Plan to Help Ex-prisoners Get Jobs, Explained," *Vox,* April 29, 2016, https://www.vox.com/2015/11/2/9660282/obama-ban-the-box.

89. James Dennin, "'Banning the Box' May Have Unintended Consequences, Thanks to Racist Employers," *Mic,* August 22, 2016, https://mic.com/articles/152252/banning-the-box-may-have-unintended-consequences-thanks-to-racist-employers-.V9wUtgmm4.

90. Amanda Agan and Sonja Starr, "Ban the Box, Criminal Records, and Statistical Discrimination: A Field Experiment" (University of Michigan Law and Economics Research Paper Series, Paper No. 16–012, 2016); Jennifer L. Doleac and Benjamin Hansen, "Does 'Ban the Box' Help or Hurt Low-Skilled Workers? Statistical Discrimination and Employment Outcomes When Criminal Histories Are Hidden" (National Bureau of Economic Research Working Paper No. 22469, July 2016), http://www.nber.org/papers/w22469.pdf.

91. Jennifer L. Doleac, "'Ban the Box' Does More Harm than Good," Brookings, May 31, 2016, https://www.brookings.edu/opinions/ban-the-box-does-more-harm-than-good.

92. N.Y. Correct. Law §§ 750 to 755 (McKinney 2007).

93. Subramanian et al., *Relief in Sight?*, 33–34.

94. Margaret Colgate Love and April Frazier, *Certificates of Rehabilitation and Other Forms of Relief from the Collateral Consequences of Conviction: A Survey of State Laws* (American Bar Association, 2006), 2, http://www.wnyschoolofrealestate.org/certificate of relief facts2.pdf.

95. CCRC, "50-State Comparison."

96. Love, "Managing Collateral Consequences in the Sentencing Process, 256.

97. "Pardons Become Very Rare during Governor Patrick's Tenure," CBS Boston, July 7, 2012, http://boston.cbslocal.com/2012/07/07/pardons-become-very-rare-during-governor-patricks-tenure.

98. Collateral Consequences Resource Center, "Massachusetts Restoration of Rights, Pardon, Expungement and Sealing," http://ccresourcecenter.org/state-restoration-profiles/massachusetts-restoration-of-rights-pardon-expungement-sealing; Maria Cramer, "As 2 Felons Earn Pardons, Time for Others Runs Short," *Boston Globe,* January 2, 2015, https://www.bostonglobe.com/metro/2015/01/02/true-see-allah-granted-pardon-vote-governor-council/yO6t9mXHlGwIfNGgKA70AK/story.html.

99. Collateral Consequences Resource Center, "West Virginia Restoration of Rights, Pardon, Expungement and Sealing," http://ccresourcecenter.org/state-restoration-profiles/west-virginia-restoration-of-rights-pardon-expungement-sealing.

100. U.S. Department of Justice, "Clemency Statistics," https://www.justice.gov/pardon/clemency-statistics.

101. Subramanian et al., *Relief in Sight?*, 18.

102. Mass. Gen. Laws Ann. ch. 276, § 100A (West 2012); Wash. Rev. Code Ann. § 9.94A.640 (West 2012); Minn. Stat. Ann. §§ 332.70(3)(a), 364.04, 609A.01, 609A.02 (West 2015); N.Y. Crim. Proc. Law § 160.59 (McKinney 2017).

103. N.Y. Crim. Proc. Law § 160.59.

104. Wash. Rev. Code Ann. § 9.64A.640(3); Mass. Gen. Laws Ann. ch. 276, § 100A (West 2012).

105. Subramanian et al., *Relief in Sight?*, 17–18, 34.

106. Subramanian et al., 33.

107. Margaret Colgate Love, *Relief from the Collateral Consequences of a Criminal Conviction: A State-by-State Resource Guide* (2006), 6; N.M. Stat. Ann. § 30–31–28(D); N.C. Gen. Stat. §§ 15A-145 et seq.; W. Va. Code § 61–11–26 (2009); Wis. Stat. § 973.015 (2016); National Association of Criminal Defense Lawyers, *America's Failure,* 58.

108. Margaret Love, "Indiana's New Expungement Law the Product of 'Many, Many Compromises,'" Collateral Consequences Resource Center, December 15, 2014, http://ccresourcecenter.org/2014/12/15/indianas-new-expungement-law-product-many-many-compromises.

109. Rebecca Beitsch, "Here's Why Many Americans Don't Clear Their Criminal Records," *PBS NewsHour,* June 8, 2016, http://www.pbs.org/newshour /rundown/heres-why-many-americans-dont-clear-their-criminal-records.

110. Subramanian et al., *Relief in Sight?,* 18; Love, "Managing Collateral Consequences," 256; James B. Jacobs, *The Eternal Criminal Record* (Cambridge, MA: Harvard University Press, 2015).

111. Eli Hager, "Forgiving v. Forgetting," Marshall Project, March 17, 2015, https://www.themarshallproject.org/2015/03/17/forgiving-vs-forgetting# .4SGtbQAxz.

112. Collateral Consequences Resource Center, "Washington Enacts Certificate of Restoration of Opportunity," July 6, 2016, http://ccresourcecenter.org /2016/07/06/washington-enacts-certificate-of-restoration-of-opportunity /-more-10417; Subramanian et al., *Relief in Sight?,* 18–19.

113. Subramanian et al., *Relief in Sight?,* 33.

114. Hager, "Forgiving v. Forgetting."

115. Subramanian et al., *Relief in Sight?,* 20–21.

116. Sarah Parvini et al., "San Francisco Will Wipe out Thousands of Marijuana Convictions Dating to 1975," *Los Angeles Times,* January 31, 2018, http://www.latimes.com/local/lanow/la-me-san-francisco-marijuana -20180131-story.html.

117. Timothy Williams and Thomas Fuller, "San Francisco Will Clear Thousands of Marijuana Convictions," *New York Times,* January 31, 2018, https://www .nytimes.com/2018/01/31/us/california-marijuana-san-francisco.html.

118. Williams and Fuller.

119. Daniel Beekman and Christine Clarridge, "Seattle to Vacate Hundreds of Misdemeanor Marijuana Convictions, Dismiss Charges," *Seattle Times,* February 8, 2018, https://www.seattletimes.com/seattle-news/seattle-to -vacate-misdemeanor-marijuana-convictions-dismiss-charges.

120. Williams and Fuller, "San Francisco."

121. Love, *Relief from the Collateral Consequences,* 5.

122. Joan Petersilia, *When Prisoners Come Home: Parole and Prisoner Reentry* (New York: Oxford University Press, 2003), 216; Marie Gottschalk, *Caught: The Prison State and the Lockdown of American Politics* (Princeton, NJ: Princeton University Press, 2016), 96.

123. Summary and indictable offenses are the equivalent of misdemeanor and felony offenses in the United States. *See* Michael Pinard, "Collateral Consequences of Criminal Convictions: Confronting Issues of Race and Dignity," *New York University Law Review* 85 (2010): 503; Margaret Love, "Canada Stiffens Policy on Sealing of Criminal Records—But It Still Looks Pretty Liberal from Here," Collateral Consequences Resource Center, November 23, 2014, http://ccresourcecenter.org/2014/11/23/canada-stiffens -policy-sealing-criminal-records-still-looks-pretty-liberal.

124. Love, "Canada Stiffens Policy"; Criminal Records Act, R.S.C. 1985, c. C-47, http://laws-lois.justice.gc.ca/PDF/C-47.pdf.

125. NACRO, *Rehabilitation of Offenders Act 1974: A Nacro Guide* (2015), 3, https://3bx16p38bch132soe12dio3h-wpengine.netdna-ssl.com/wp-content

/uploads/2014/05/rehabilitation-of-offenders-act-1974-guide.pdf; Legal Aid, Sentencing and Punishment of Offenders Act 2012, c. 10 (Eng.), http://www .legislation.gov.uk/ukpga/2012/10/section/139/enacted.

6. Populist Politics

1. Lauren-Brooke Eisen and Oliver Roeder, *America's Faulty Perception of Crime Rates* (Brennan Center for Justice, 2015), https://www.brennancenter .org/blog/americas-faulty-perception-crime-rates. For explorations of the larger cultural forces prompting the political shift, see Michelle Alexander, *The New Jim Crow* (New York: New Press, 2010); David Garland, *The Culture of Control* (Chicago: University of Chicago Press, 2001); Jonathan Simon, *Governing through Crime* (New York: Oxford University Press, 2007); William Stuntz, *The Collapse of American Criminal Justice* (Cambridge, MA: Harvard University Press, 2011).
2. Naomi Murakawa, *The First Civil Right: How Liberals Built Prison America* (New York: Oxford University Press, 2014), 72.
3. Peter K. Enns, *Incarceration Nation: How the United States Became the Most Punitive Democracy in the World* (New York: Cambridge University Press, 2016), 60–64; Hazel Erskine, "The Polls: Fear of Violence and Crime," *Public Opinion Quarterly* 38 (1974): 131.
4. Murakawa, *First Civil Right*, 7–8, 16; Alexander, *New Jim Crow*, 44–45.
5. Jeremy Travis, *But They All Come Back: Facing the Challenges of Prisoner Reentry* (Washington, DC: Urban Institute Press, 2005), 22.
6. Murakawa, *First Civil Right*, 75.
7. Murakawa, 113.
8. National Research Council, *The Growth of Incarceration in the United States: Exploring Causes and Consequences*, ed. Jeremy Travis, Bruce Western, and Steve Redburn (Washington, DC: National Academies Press, 2014), 104–129.
9. Melissa S. Kearney et al., *Ten Economic Facts about Crime and Incarceration in the United States* (Hamilton Project/Brookings, May 2014), 4, figure 1, https://www.brookings.edu/research/ten-economic-facts-about -crime-and-incarceration-in-the-united-states/.
10. Travis, *But They All Come Back*, 23.
11. Francis T. Cullen, Bonnie S. Fisher, and Brandon K. Applegate, "Public Opinion about Punishment and Corrections," *Crime and Justice* 27 (2000): 3; Ilya Somin, *Democracy and Political Ignorance: Why Smaller Government Is Smarter* (Stanford, CA: Stanford University Press, 2013).
12. Lincoln Quillian and Devah Pager, "Estimating Risk: Stereotype Amplification and the Perceived Risk of Criminal Victimization, *Social Psychology Quarterly* 73 (2010): 79–104.
13. *See generally* Amos Tversky and Daniel Kahneman, "Judgments of and by Representativeness," in *Judgment under Uncertainty: Heuristics and Biases,* ed. Daniel Kahneman, Paul Slovic, and Amos Tversky (New York: Oxford University Press 1982), 84.

14. Bryan Stevenson, *Just Mercy: A Story of Justice and Redemption* 14 (New York: Spiegel and Grau, 2014).

15. Katherine Beckett, *Making Crime Pay: Law and Order in Contemporary American Politics* 62 (New York: Oxford University Press, 1997), 62; Willard M. Oliver, "The Power to Persuade: Presidential Influence over Congress on Crime Control Policy," *Criminal Justice Review* 28 (2003): 120.

16. James Kilgore, *Understanding Mass Incarceration: A People's Guide to the Key Civil Rights Struggle of Our Time* (New York: New Press, 2015), 113.

17. Gregg Barak, "Between the Waves: Mass-Mediated Themes of Crime and Justice," in *Politics, Crime Control and Culture,* ed. Stuart A. Scheingold (New York: Routledge, 1997), 135–136; Sarah Eschholz, "The Media and Fear of Crime: A Survey of the Research," *Florida Journal of Law and Public Policy* 9 (1997): 38; Marc Mauer, "Why Are Tough on Crime Policies So Popular?," *Stanford Law and Policy Review* 11 (1999): 15; Rachel E. Barkow, "The Criminal Regulatory State," in *The New Criminal Justice Thinking,* ed. Sharon Dolovich and Alexandra Natapoff (New York: New York University Press, 2015), 33–52 and n. 13.

18. Center for Media and Public Affairs, "Network News in the Nineties: The Top Topics and Trends of the Decade," *Media Monitor,* July/August 1997, 2–3; Mauer, "Tough on Crime Policies," 15.

19. S. Robert Litcher and Linda S. Litcher, "The Media at the Millennium: The Networks' Top Topics, Trends, and Joke Targets of the 1990s," *Media Monitor* 14 (2000): 2; Federal Bureau of Investigation, *Crime in the United States, Uniform Crime Reports 1999* (2000), 64, table 1.

20. See, e.g., Lori Dorfman and Vincent Schiraldi, *Off Balance: Youth, Race and Crime in the News* (Justice Policy Institute, 2001), 10, http://www .justicepolicy.org/research/2060; Nazgol Ghandnoosh, *Race and Punishment: Racial Perceptions of Crime and Support for Punitive Policies* (Sentencing Project, 2014), 22–23, https://www.sentencingproject.org/wp-content/uploads /2015/11/Race-and-Punishment.pdf.

21. Eisen and Roeder, *America's Faulty Perception.*

22. Aamer Madhani, "Chicago Hits Grim Milestone of 700 Murders for 2016 and the Year's Not Over," *USA Today,* December 1, 2016, https://www .usatoday.com/story/news/2016/12/01/chicago-700-murders-2016/94732276; "Why the Public Perception of Crime Exceeds the Reality," NPR, July 26, 2016, http://www.npr.org/2016/07/26/487522807/why-the-public-perception -of-crime-exceeds-the-reality.

23. John J. Donohue, "A Critical Look at Crime and Policing in the United States: Comey, Trump, and the Puzzling Pattern of Crime in 2015 and Beyond," *Columbia Law Review* 117 (2017): 1307.

24. Karen Tumulty and David Nakamara, "Trump's Rallying Cry: Fear Itself," *Washington Post,* February 3, 2017, https://www.washingtonpost.com /politics/trumps-rallying-cry-fear-itself/2017/02/03/7d2a0432-ea4a-11e6-bf6f -301b6b443624_story.html.

25. Ames C. Grawert and Natasha Camhi, *Criminal Justice in President Trump's First 100 Days* (Brennan Center for Justice, 2017), https://www

.brennancenter.org/sites/default/files/publications/Criminal_Justice_in
_President_Trumps_First_100_Days.pdf.; Alex Altman, "No President Has
Spread Fear Like Donald Trump," *Time,* February 9, 2017, http://time.com
/4665755/donald-trump-fear; Molly Ball, "Donald Trump and the Politics of
Fear," *Atlantic,* September 2, 2016, https://www.theatlantic.com/politics
/archive/2016/09/donald-trump-and-the-politics-of-fear/498116.

26. Altman, "No President Has Spread Fear."

27. David W. Moore, "As Confidence in Police Rises, Americans' Fear of Crime
Diminishes," Gallup, http://www.gallup.com/poll/4132/Confidence-Police
-Rises-Americans-Fear-Crime-Diminishes.aspx; FBI, *Uniform Crime Reports
1999,* 64, table 1.

28. Eisen and Roeder, *America's Faulty Perception.*

29. Eisen and Roeder.

30. John Gramlich, "Voters' Perceptions of Crime Continue to Conflict with
Reality," Pew Research Center, November 16, 2016, http://www.pewresearch
.org/fact-tank/2016/11/16/voters-perceptions-of-crime-continue-to-conflict
-with-reality.

31. Marie Gottschalk, *Caught: The Prison State and the Lockdown of American
Politics* (Princeton, NJ: Princeton University Press, 2016), 29; Josh Sanburn,
"Why Americans Are Worrying More about Crime," *Time,* April 7, 2016,
http://time.com/4285848/crime-violence-gallup-poll-2016.

32. Gary Kleck and Dylan Baker Jackson, "Does Crime Cause Punitiveness?,"
Crime and Delinquency 63 (2017): 1584.

33. Kleck and Jackson, 1584.

34. Kleck and Jackson, 1591.

35. Sean Patrick Roche et al., "The Scary World of Online News? Internet News
Exposure and Public Attitudes toward Crime and Justice," *Journal of
Quantitative Criminology* 32 (2016): 215–236.

36. Dorfman and Schiraldi, *Off Balance,* 3; Travis L. Dixon and Daniel Linz,
"Overrepresentation and Underrepresentation of African Americans and
Latinos as Lawbreakers on Television News," *Journal of Communication* 50
(2000): 143–144; Travis L. Dixon and Daniel Linz, "Race and Misrepresen-
tation of Victimization on Local Television News," *Communication Research*
27 (2000): 560–561; Daniel Romer et al., "The Treatment of Persons of
Color in Local Television News: Ethnic Blame Discourse or Realistic Group
Conflict?," *Communications Research* 25 (1998): 297.

37. Romer et al., 295; Richard J. Lundman, "The Newsworthiness and Selection
Bias in News about Murder: Comparative and Relative Effects of Novelty
and Race and Gender Typifications on Newspaper Coverage of Homicide,"
Sociological Forum 18 (2003): 377.

38. Steven Chermak, "Crime in the News Media: A Refined Understanding of
How Crimes Become News," in *Media, Process and the Social Construction
of Crime: Studies in Newsmaking Criminology,* ed. Gregg Barak (New York:
Routledge, 1995), 111, table 4.4.

39. Beckett, *Making Crime Pay,* 75–77.

40. Beckett, 56–58.

41. Dorfman and Schiraldi, *Off Balance,* 29.
42. *See* Kevin H. Wozniak, "American Public Opinion about Prisons," *Criminal Justice Review* 39 (2014): 317–319.
43. Hugo Hopenhayn and Susanne Lohmann, "Fire-Alarm Signals and the Political Oversight of Regulatory Agencies," *Journal of Law, Economics, and Organization* 12 (1996): 210; Chermak, "Crime in the News Media," 115.
44. Murakawa, *First Civil Right,* 152.
45. Beckett, *Making Crime Pay,* 108.
46. Brandon K. Applegate et al., "Assessing Public Support for Three-Strikes-and-You're-Out Laws: Global versus Specific Attitudes," *Crime and Delinquency* 42 (1996): 528–530.
47. Julian V. Roberts, "Public Opinion, Crime, and Criminal Justice," *Crime and Justice* 16 (1992): 101, 150, 152.
48. Memo from the Mellman Group and Public Opinion Strategies to the Public Safety Performance Project of the Pew Charitable Trusts, Re: National Survey Key Findings (February 10, 2016), 2, http://www.pewtrusts.org/~/media /assets/2016/02/national_survey_key_findings_federal_sentencing_prisons .pdf.
49. *See* Roberts, "Public Opinion," 158.
50. Memo from the Mellman Group, 4.
51. Timothy J. Flanagan and Dennis R. Longmire, *Americans View Crime and Justice: A National Public Opinion Survey* (Thousand Oaks, CA: SAGE, 1996), 69.
52. Mark A. Cohen, Roland T. Rust, and Sara Steen, *Measuring Public Perception of Appropriate Sentences* (U.S. Department of Justice, 2003), 20–21, https://www.ncjrs.gov/pdffiles1/nij/grants/199365.pdf.
53. Garland, *Culture of Control,* 201–203.
54. Lord Windlesham, *Politics, Punishment, and Populism* (New York: Oxford University Press, 1998), 77.
55. Albert W. Alschuler, "The Failure of Sentencing Guidelines: A Plea for Less Aggregation," *University of Chicago Law Review* 58 (1991): 932.
56. Barkow, "Criminal Regulatory State."
57. Douglas A. Berman, "A Common Law for This Age of Federal Sentencing: The Opportunity and Need for Judicial Lawmaking," *Stanford Law and Public Policy Review* 11 (1999): 107; *see also* Stephen J. Schulhofer and Ilene H. Nagel, "Plea Negotiations under the Federal Sentencing Guidelines: Guideline Circumvention and Its Dynamics in the Post-*Mistretta* Period," *Northwestern University Law Review* 91 (1997): 1298.
58. Beckett, *Making Crime Pay,* 15.
59. Donohue, "A Critical Look," 1299.
60. Ian Haney López, *Dog Whistle Politics: How Coded Racial Appeals Have Reinvented Racism and Wrecked the Middle Class* (New York: Oxford University Press, 2015), 51; Sentencing Project, *Race and Punishment: Racial Perceptions of Crime and Support for Punitive Policies* (2014), 24, https://www.sentencingproject.org/wp-content/uploads/2015/11/Race-and -Punishment.pdf.

61. *See* J. D., "Joe Arpaio Is No Longer America's Toughest Sheriff," *Economist,* January 6, 2017, https://www.economist.com/blogs/democracyinamerica /2017/01/new-sheriff-town; Melissa Etehad, "Joe Arpaio, Former Sheriff in Arizona, Is Found Guilty of Criminal Contempt," *Los Angeles Times,* July 31, 2017, http://www.latimes.com/nation/la-na-joe-arpaio-verdict -20170706-story.html; Julie Hirschfield Davis and Maggie Haberman, "Trump Pardons Arpaio, Who Became Face of Crackdown on Illegal Immigration," *New York Times,* August 25, 2017, https://www.nytimes.com /2017/08/25/us/politics/joe-arpaio-trump-pardon-sheriff-arizona.html.

62. Fernanda Santos, "Sheriff Joe Arpaio Loses Bid for 7th Term in Arizona," *New York Times,* November 9, 2016, https://www.nytimes.com/2016/11/09 /us/joe-arpaio-arizona-sheriff.html.

63. Jessica Autumn Brown, "Running on Fear: Immigration, Race and Crime Framings in Contemporary GOP Presidential Debate Discourse," *Critical Criminology* 24 (2016): 315–331.

64. Ball, "Donald Trump and the Politics of Fear," 34.

65. Murakawa, *First Civil Right,* 45.

66. Jessica Pishko, "Prosecutors Are Banding Together to Prevent Criminal-Justice Reform," *Nation,* October 18, 2017, https://www.thenation.com /article/prosecutors-are-banding-together-to-prevent-criminal-justice-reform.

67. Pishko.

68. *See* Rachel E. Barkow, "Recharging the Jury: The Criminal Jury's Constitutional Role in an Era of Mandatory Sentencing," *University of Pennsylvania Law Review* 152 (2003): 97–100; *Reevaluating the Effectiveness of Federal Mandatory Minimum Sentences: Hearings before the S. Comm. on the Judiciary,* 113th Cong. 3 (2013) (statement of Scott Burns, Executive Director, National District Attorneys' Association).

69. *See, e.g.,* Letter from Robert Gay Guthrie, President, NAAUSA, to Senators Patrick Leahy and Charles Grassley, January 31, 2014, 2, http://www.naausa .org/2013/images/docs/MandMinSentencingLegOppose013114.pdf; *Child Abduction Prevention Act and the Child Obscenity and Pornography Protection Act of 2003: Hearings before the Subcomm. on Crime, Terrorism and Homeland Security of the House Comm. on the Judiciary,* 108th Cong. 15–17 (2003) (statement of Daniel P. Collins, Associate Deputy Attorney General, Department of Justice); *Federal Cocaine Sentencing Policy: Hearing before the Subcomm. on Crime and Drugs of the Senate Comm. on the Judiciary,* 107th Cong. 16–33 (2002) (statement of Roscoe C. Howard, U.S. Attorney for the District of Columbia); *Penalties for White Collar Crime: Hearings before the Subcomm. on Crime and Drugs of the Senate Comm. on the Judiciary,* 107th Cong. 102 (2002) (statement of James B. Comey Jr., U.S. Attorney, Southern District of New York).

70. *See, e.g.,* John Pfaff, "The Perverse Power of the Prosecutor," *Democracy Journal,* February 22, 2018, https://democracyjournal.org/arguments/the -perverse-power-of-the-prosecutor; Daniel F. Conley, "DA: Time for Mandatory Minimum Myth-Busting," *Massachusetts Lawyers Weekly,* March 23, 2015, http://masslawyersweekly.com/2015/03/23/da-time-for-mandatory

-minimum-myth-busting; Alex Rose, "A Mandatory Debate: Report Recommends Changes to the State's Sentencing Guidelines," *Delaware County Daily Times,* December 7, 2009, http://www.delcotimes.com/article/DC/20091207/NEWS/312079997; Kevin Deutsch, "Acting Nassau DA Proposes Tougher Penalties against Heroin Dealers," *Newsday,* September 4, 2015, http://www.newsday.com/long-island/nassau/madeline-singas-acting-nassau-da-wants-to-charge-heroin-dealers-with-homicide-if-customers-od-1.10808915; Martha Stolley, Leslie R. Caldwell, and Kelly A. Moore, "Manhattan District Attorney Promises Broader Use of the Martin Act in Combating Financial Fraud and Vows to Fight for Tougher Penalties," Mondaq, February 2, 2011, http://www.mondaq.com/unitedstates/x/121368/White+Collar+Crime+Fraud/Manhattan+District+Attorney+Promises+Broader+Use+of+the+Martin+Act+in+Combating+Financial+Fraud+and+Vows+to+Fight+for+Tougher+Penalties; Amy Leigh Womack, "Georgia AG Pushes for Tougher State Laws," *Macon Telegraph,* April 19, 2011, http://www.macon.com/news/local/community/houston-peach/article28608742.html; Christian Schiavone, "Massachusetts AG Seeking Tougher Penalties for Traffickers of Overdose-Linked Painkiller Fentanyl," *Patriot Ledger,* August 18, 2015, http://www.patriotledger.com/article/20150817/NEWS/150817102; David Alan Sklansky, "The Changing Political Landscape for Elected Prosecutors," *Ohio State Journal of Criminal Law* 14 (2017): 647–674.

71. Pfaff, "Perverse Power."

72. Beckett, *Making Crime Pay,* 98–101; "Developments in the Law: The Law of Prisons," *Harvard Law Review* 115 (2002): 1872–1873; Murakawa, *First Civil Right,* 16; Kilgore, *Understanding Mass Incarceration,* 36, 188.

73. Rebecca U. Thorpe, "Perverse Politics: The Persistence of Mass Imprisonment in the Twenty-First Century," *Perspectives on Politics* 13 (2015): 627.

74. Ted Gest, "The Evolution of Crime and Politics in America," *McGeorge Law Review* 33 (2002): 764, 766; *see* Lord Windlesham, *Politics, Punishment, and Populism,* 142; Franklin E. Zimring, "Populism, Democratic Government, and the Decline of Expert Authority: Some Reflections on 'Three Strikes' in California," *Pacific Law Journal* 28 (1996): 246; Robert E. Freeman-Longo, *Revisiting Megan's Law and Sex Offender Registration: Prevention or Problem* (American Probation and Parole Association, n.d.), https://www.appa-net.org/eweb/docs/appa/pubs/RML.pdf.

75. *See, e.g.,* Kent Scheidegger, "Retro Parole Bill Killed in Arizona," Crime and Consequences, January 29, 2010, http://www.crimeandconsequences.com/crimblog/2010/01/retro-parole-bill-killed-in-ar.html.

76. Mark T. Berg et al., "Victim-Offender Overlap in Context: Examining the Role of Neighborhood Street Culture," *Criminology* 50 (2012): 359–390; Simon I. Singer, "Victims of Serious Violence and Their Criminal Behavior: Subcultural Theory and Beyond," *Violence and Victims* 1, no. 1 (February 1986): 61–70; Vik Kanwar, "Capital Punishment as 'Closure': The Limits of a Victim-Centered Jurisprudence," *New York University Review of Law and Social Change* 27 (2007): 231.

77. Marie Gottschalk, "Bring It On: The Future of Penal Reform, the Carceral State, and American Politics," *Ohio State Journal of Criminal Law* 12 (2015): 593.

78. Ghandnoosh, *Race and Punishment,* 10.

79. Ghandnoosh, 10.

80. Andrew V. Papachristos and Christopher Wildeman, "Network Exposure and Homicide Victimization in an African American Community," *American Journal of Public Health* 104 (2014): 143.

81. Kanwar, "Capital Punishment," 232.

82. Simon, *Governing through Crime,* 89–106.

83. Clifford Atiyeh, "Senate Wants to Send Automaker Employees to Prison—for Up to Life—for Vehicle Defects," *Car and Driver,* August 6, 2014, http://blog .caranddriver.com/senate-wants-to-send-automaker-employees-to-prison-for -up-to-life-for-vehicle-defects.

84. Richard A. Oppel Jr., "Taping of Farm Cruelty Is Becoming the Crime," *New York Times,* April 6, 2013, http://www.nytimes.com/2013/04/07/us/taping-of -farm-cruelty-is-becoming-the-crime.html.

85. Victoria F. Nourse and Jane S. Schacter, "The Politics of Legislative Drafting: A Congressional Case Study," *New York University Law Review* 77 (2002): 587–588.

86. John Malcom, *The Pressing Need for Mens Rea Reform* (Heritage Foundation, September 1, 2015), http://www.heritage.org/research/reports/2015/09 /the-pressing-need-for-mens-rea-reform; Zach Carter, "Kochs Embedded in Major Rift on Bipartisan Criminal Justice Reform," *Huffington Post,* November 25, 2015, http://www.huffingtonpost.com/entry/criminal-justice -reform-koch_us_56560fb0e4b079b2818a13fe.

87. Xander Landen, "More Cities across the U.S. Consider Homelessness a Crime," PBS, July 19, 2014, http://www.pbs.org/newshour/rundown /homelessness-now-crime-cities-throughout-u-s.

88. Jamie Fellner and Marc Mauer, *Losing the Vote: The Impact of Felony Disenfranchisement Laws in the United States* (Human Rights Watch, Sentencing Project, 1998), 1, http://www.hrw.org/reports98/vote.

89. Gottschalk, "Bring It On," 560.

90. Marc Meredith and Michael Morse, "Do Voting Rights Notification Laws Increase Ex-Felon Turnout?," *Annals of the American Academy of Political Science* 651 (2014): 220–221; Michael V. Haselswerdt, "Con Job: An Estimate of Ex-felon Voter Turnout Using Document-Based Data," *Social Science Quarterly* 90 (2009): 262–273.

91. *See* Pew Charitable Trusts, *Collateral Costs: Incarceration's Effect on Economic Mobility* (2010), http://www.pewtrusts.org/~/media/legacy /uploadedfiles/pcs_assets/2010/collateralcosts1pdf.pdf; Devah Pager, "The Mark of a Criminal Record," *American Journal of Sociology* 108 (2003): 937.

92. Christy Visher, Jennifer Yahner, and Nancy La Vigne, *Life after Prison: Tracking the Experiences of Male Prisoners Returning to Chicago, Cleveland, and Houston* (Urban Institute, 2010), 3; Christy Visher, Nancy La Vigne, and Jeremy Travis, *Returning Home: Understanding the Challenges of Prisoner Reentry* (Urban Institute, 2004), 6.

93. J. David Goodman, "Mayor Backs Plan to Close Rikers and Open Jails Elsewhere," *New York Times,* March 31, 2017, https://www.nytimes.com /2017/03/31/nyregion/mayor-de-blasio-is-said-to-back-plan-to-close-jails-on -rikers-island.html; Juleyka Lantigua-Williams, "Can a Notorious New York City Jail Be Closed?," *Atlantic,* April 26, 2016, https://www.theatlantic .com/politics/archive/2016/04/will-rikers-island-be-closed/479790.

94. Jennifer Gonnerman, "Million-Dollar Blocks," *Village Voice,* November 9, 2004, http://www.villagevoice.com/2004-11-09/news/million-dollar-blocks.

95. James Forman Jr., "Racial Critiques of Mass Incarceration: Beyond the New Jim Crow," *New York University Law Review* 87 (2012): 36–45; James Forman Jr., *Locking Up Our Own: Crime and Punishment in Black America* (New York: Farrar, Strauss, and Giroux, 2017).

96. *See* Thomas Giovanni and Roopal Patel, *Gideon at 50: Three Reforms to Revive the Right to Counsel* (Brennan Center for Justice, 2003), 4–5, https://www.brennancenter.org/publication/gideon-50-three-reforms-revive -right-counsel.

97. New York City Bar Association, *Mass Incarceration: Seizing the Moment for Reform* (2015); American Bar Association, "Experts Examine Conse- quences of Mass Incarceration at ABA Annual Meeting," news release, August 3, 2015, http://www.americanbar.org/news/abanews/aba-news -archives/2015/08/legal_experts_examin.html.

98. Jed S. Rakoff, "Judge Rakoff Speaks Out at Harvard Conference: Full Speech," Big Law Business, April 13, 2015, https://biglawbusiness.com/judge -rakoff-speaks-out-at-harvard-conference-full-speech.

99. Sanford C. Gordon and Gregory Huber, "The Effect of Electoral Competi- tiveness on Incumbent Behavior," *Quarterly Journal of Political Science* 2 (2007): 107–138; Kate Berry, *How Judicial Elections Impact Criminal Cases* (Brennan Center for Justice, 2015), 2, https://www.brennancenter.org /publication/how-judicial-elections-impact-criminal-cases; Carlos Berdejó and Noam Yuchtman, *Crime, Punishment, and Politics: An Analysis of Political Cycles in Criminal Sentencing* (Loyola Los Angeles Law School Legal Studies Paper No. 2012–50, 2012), https://papers.ssrn.com/so13 /papers.cfm?abstract_id=2194605.

100. United States v. Kupa, 976 F. Supp. 2d 417 (E.D.N.Y. 2013); United States v. Diaz, No. 11-CR-821, 2013 WL 322243 (E.D.N.Y. Jan. 28, 2013).

101. Colby Hamilton, "Holder Praises Prison-Alternatives in Brooklyn," *Politico,* October 30, 2014, https://www.politico.com/states/new-york/city-hall/story /2014/10/holder-praises-prison-alternatives-in-brooklyn-017069; Jesse Wegman, "A Federal Judge's New Model for Forgiveness," opinion, *New York Times,* March 16, 2016, A22.

102. Jed S. Rakoff, "Mass Incarceration: The Silence of the Judges," *New York Review of Books,* May 21, 2015; Rakoff, "Judge Rakoff Speaks Out."

103. *See, e.g.,* Nancy Gertner, "Undoing the Damage of Mass Incarceration," *Boston Globe,* November 4, 2015, https://www.bostonglobe.com/opinion /2015/11/04/undoing-damage-mass-incarceration/9Ww80SKxQm9 EbdHxmZG5sM/story.html.

104. Alex Stamm, "States' Top Jurists Call for Criminal Justice Reform," ACLU, March 12, 2012, https://www.aclu.org/blog/states-top-jurists-call-criminal -justice-reform.

105. Alliance for Justice, *Broadening the Bench: Professional Diversity and Judicial Nominations* (2016), 6, https://www.afj.org/reports/professional -diversity-report; Gregory L. Acquaviva and John D. Castiglione, "Judicial Diversity on State Supreme Courts," *Seton Hall Law Review* 39 (2009): 1235, table 10.

106. Alexander, *New Jim Crow,* 54, 211–217.

107. Alexander, 211–217.

108. *See, e.g.,* NAACP Legal Defense Fund, *Police Violence—Rapid Response Fund Report* (2015), http://www.naacpldf.org/publication/police-violence -rapid-response-fund-report-2015; NAACP, *Invest to Educate, Not Incarcerate* (2013), http://naacp.3cdn.net/a7d13b90509eca30f1_mlbrzfaq8 .pdf; Leadership Conference Education Fund, *A Second Chance: Charting a New Course for Re-entry and Criminal Justice Reform* (2013), http:// civilrightsdocs.info/pdf/reports/A_Second_Chance_Re-Entry_Report.pdf.

109. NAACP Legal Defense Fund, "LDF Statement on Bipartisan Sentencing Reform Bill," news release, October 22, 2015, http://www.naacpldf.org /press-release/ldf-statement-bipartisan-sentencing-reform-bill.

110. Leadership Conference on Civil and Human Rights, "The Leadership Conference on Civil and Human Rights 2016 Legislative Priorities (Senate)," January 19, 2016, https://civilrights.org/the-leadership-conference -on-civil-and-human-rights-2016-legislative-priorities-senate/.

111. ACLU, "ACLU Awarded $50 Million by Open Society Foundations to End Mass Incarceration," news release, November 7, 2014, https://www.aclu.org /news/aclu-awarded-50-million-open-society-foundations-end-mass -incarceration.

112. ACLU, "Campaign for Smart Justice," https://www.aclu.org/smart-justice -fair-justice.

113. Neil King Jr., "As Prisons Squeeze Budgets, GOP Rethinks Crime Focus," *Wall Street Journal,* June 20, 2013, http://online.wsj.com/article/SB1000142 4127887323836504578551902602217018.html.

114. Coalition for Public Safety, "About the Coalition," http://www .coalitionforpublicsafety.org/about.

115. George Will, "Leahy and Paul Plan on Mandatory Sentencing Makes Sense," opinion, *Washington Post,* June 5, 2013, http://www.washingtonpost.com /opinions/george-will-leahy-and-paul-plan-on-prison-sentences-makes-sense /2013/06/05/9731afba-cdfc-11e2-8845-d970ccb04497_story.html; Richard A. Viguerie, "A Conservative Case for Prison Reform," opinion, *New York Times,* June 10, 2013, A23; Justice Safety Valve Act of 2013, S. 619, 113th Cong. (2013).

116. Gottschalk, "Bring It On," 565.

117. Sentencing Project, *U.S. Prison Population Trends: 1999–2014: Broad Variation among States in Recent Years* (n.d.), http://sentencingproject.org /doc/publications/inc_US_Prison_Population_Trends_1999-2014.pdf.

118. Nazgol Ghandnoosh, *Can We Wait 75 Years to Cut the Prison Population in Half?* (Sentencing Project, 2018), 1, https://www.sentencingproject.org/publications/can-wait-75-years-cut-prison-population-half/.

119. Gottschalk, "Bring It On," 565; Brown v. Plata, 563 U.S. 493 (2011).

120. U.S. Sentencing Commission, *Annual Report: Fiscal Year 2014* (2014), A-2 to A-3, http://www.ussc.gov/sites/default/files/pdf/research-and-publications/annual-reports-and-sourcebooks/2014/2014-Annual-Report.pdf.

121. U.S. Sentencing Commission, *2014 Drug Guidelines Amendment Retroactivity Data Report* (2017), tables 3, 7.

122. U.S. Sentencing Commission, *Sensible Sentencing Reform: The 2014 Reduction of Drug Sentences* (2015), 1.

123. Sentencing Project, *Trends: 1999–2014;* Matthew Friedman, "Just Facts: The U.S. Prison Population Is Down (a Little)," Brennan Center for Justice, October 29, 2015, https://www.brennancenter.org/blog/us-prison-population-down-little.

124. Gottschalk, "Bring It On," 563; Gottschalk, *Caught,* 165.

125. *See* E. Ann Carson, *Prisoners in 2014* (Bureau of Justice Statistics, 2015), 16–17, tables 16–17 (totaling state and federal inmates sentenced for drug offenses, immigration offenses, "other" public offender offenses, fraud, "other property offenses," and "other/unspecified offenses").

126. Oklahoma State Senate, "Senate Approves Criminal Justice Reforms," news release, April 20, 2016, http://www.oksenate.gov/news/press_releases/press_releases_2016/pr20160420a.htm.

127. "Gov. Fallin Signs Four Criminal Justice Reform Bills," news release, April 27, 2016, http://services.ok.gov/triton/modules/newsroom/newsroom_article.php?id=223&article_id=20542; Michael Haugen, "Oklahoma Adopts Comprehensive Criminal Justice Reforms to Right-Size Prison System," Right on Crime, April 29, 2016, http://rightoncrime.com/2016/04/oklahoma-adopts-comprehensive-criminal-justice-reforms-rightsize-prison-system.

128. Associated Press, "Oklahoma Unseats Louisiana for Highest U.S. Incarceration Rate," *Times-Picayune,* June 9, 2018, https://www.nola.com/politics/index.ssf/2018/06/louisiana_incarceration_rate_1.html.

129. Haugen, "Oklahoma Adopts Comprehensive Criminal Justice Reforms."

130. Oklahoman Editorial Board, "Allbaugh Actively Seeking Ways to Help Oklahoma Corrections," *Oklahoman,* April 11, 2016, http://newsok.com/article/5490444.

131. Oklahoman Editorial Board.

132. Oklahoman Editorial Board.

133. Rory Carroll, "Oklahoma Budget Crisis Opens Door to Criminal Justice Reform," Reuters, April 8, 2016, http://www.reuters.com/article/us-oklahoma-prisons-reform-idUSKCN0X514O.

134. "Historic Criminal Justice Reforms Approved by Louisiana Lawmakers," ACLU, June 8, 2017, https://www.aclu.org/news/historic-criminal-justice-reforms-approved-louisiana-lawmakers; Julie O'Donoghue, "Louisiana Criminal Justice Reform Passed by Legislature," *Times-Picayune,* June 8, 2017, http://www.nola.com/politics/index.ssf/2017/06/louisiana_criminal_justice_ove

.html; Julie O'Donoghue, "Louisiana Criminal Justice Reform: What You Need to Know about the Changes," *Times-Picayune,* June 29, 2017, http://www.nola .com/politics/index.ssf/2017/06/louisiana_criminal_justice_ref_1.html.

135. Associated Press, "Oklahoma Unseats Louisiana," https://www.apnews.com/ 6b1daf378e4d48269e0506d159c42e03.

136. *See* O'Donoghue, "Louisiana Criminal Justice Reform Passed by Legislature."

137. E. Ann Carson, *Prisoners in 2013* (Bureau of Justice Statistics, 2014), https://www.bjs.gov/content/pub/pdf/p13.pdf.

138. Adam Gelb, Terry Schuster, and Emily Levett, "Louisiana Adopts Landmark Criminal Justice Reforms," Pew Charitable Trusts, June 22, 2017, http://www.pewtrusts.org/en/research-and-analysis/analysis/2017/06/22 /louisiana-adopts-landmark-criminal-justice-reforms; E. Ann Carson, *Prisoners in 2015* (Bureau of Justice Statistics, 2016), table 6., https://www .bjs.gov/content/pub/pdf/p15.pdf.

139. Naomi Shavan, "A Republican Governor Is Leading the Country's Most Successful Prison Reform," *New Republic,* March 31, 2015, https:// newrepublic.com/article/121425/gop-governor-nathan-deal-leading-us -prison-reform.

140. Greg Bluestein, "Georgia to Embark on New Phase of Criminal Justice Reform," *Atlanta Journal-Constitution,* April 27, 2016, http://politics.blog .ajc.com/2016/04/27/georgia-to-embark-on-new-phase-of-criminal-justice -reform.

141. From the end of 2009 to the end of 2010, all before Governor Deal took office, Georgia's population declined slightly, from 56,986 to 56,432. Paul Guerino, Paige M. Harrison, and William J. Sabol, *Prisoners in 2010* (Bureau of Justice Statistics, 2011), 14, http://www.bjs.gov/content/pub/pdf /p10.pdf. At the end of 2014, after Deal's first four years in office, the population had declined to 52,719, a decrease of 6.57%. E. Ann Carson, *Prisoners in 2014* (Bureau of Justice Statistics, 2015), 8, 12, http://www.bjs .gov/content/pub/pdf/p14.pdf.

142. Carrie Teegardin, "Georgia's Bold Step: Rethinking Prison Sentences," *Atlanta Journal-Constitution,* August 22, 2015, https://www.myajc.com /news/crime--law/georgia-bold-step-rethinking-prison-sentences /uBqNDm3pmoGwMVcMp8vkPP/.

143. Teegardin.

144. Southern Center for Human Rights, *2015 Revisions to Georgia's Drug Recidivist Law: House Bill 328's Parole Eligibility Provisions* (2015), 1, https://www.schr.org/files/post/HB 328 fact sheet and text.pdf.

145. Teegardin, "Georgia's Bold Step"; Deb Belt, "Georgia Incarceration Rate: See How It Stacks Up to Other States," *Atlanta Patch,* January 23, 2018, https://patch.com/georgia/atlanta/georgia-incarceration-rate-see-how-it -stacks-other-states.

146. Sentencing Project, *The State of Sentencing 2015: Developments in Policy and Practice* (2016), 5, http://sentencingproject.org/doc/publications/State-of -Sentencing-2015.pdf.

147. Sentencing Project.

148. *See, e.g.,* Sentencing Project, "South Dakota Bans Life-Without-Parole Sentences for Youth," Newscenter1, March 14, 2016, http://www.newscenter1.tv/story/31497823/south-dakota-bans-life-without-parole-sentences-for-youth.

149. Sentencing Project, *The State of Sentencing 2014: Developments in Policy and Practice* (2015), 2, http://sentencingproject.org/doc/publications/sen_State_of_Sentencing_2014.pdf (presenting table of state reforms in 2014).

150. 21 U.S.C. §§ 841(b)(1), 960(b).

151. Rachel E. Barkow and Mark Osler, "Designed to Fail: The President's Deference to the Department of Justice in Advancing Criminal Justice Reform," *William and Mary Law Review* 59 (2017): 387–474.

152. Memorandum from Attorney General Holder to Heads of Department of Justice Components and United States Attorneys, August 12, 2013, https://www.justice.gov/sites/default/files/ag/legacy/2014/04/11/ag-memo-substantial-federal-interest.pdf.

153. Department of Education, *Federal Student Aid Eligibility for Students Confined in Adult Correctional or Juvenile Justice Facilities* (December 2014), https://studentaid.ed.gov/sa/sites/default/files/aid-info-for-incarcerated-individuals.pdf.

154. U.S. Sentencing Commission, *An Analysis of the Implementation of the 2014 Clemency Initiative* (2017).

155. Barack Obama, "The President's Role in Advancing Criminal Justice Reform," *Harvard Law Review* 130 (2017): 811–866.

156. Barkow and Osler, "Designed to Fail," 437–438.

157. U.S. Sentencing Commission, *Implementation of the 2014 Clemency Initiative,* 2.

158. Barkow and Osler, "Designed to Fail," 442.

159. U.S. Department of Justice, Office of the Inspector General, *I-2013–006, The Federal Bureau of Prisons' Compassionate Release Program* (2013), i, https://oig.justice.gov/reports/2013/e1306.pdf; U.S. Department of Justice, Office of the Inspector General, *The Impact of an Aging Inmate Population on the Federal Bureau of Prisons* (2016), 2, https://oig.justice.gov/reports/2015/e1505.pdf.

160. Barkow and Osler, "Designed to Fail," 416–417.

161. Lee Fang, "Maryland Gov. Larry Hogan Vetoes Major Criminal Justice Reform Bills," Intercept, May 22, 2015, https://theintercept.com/2015/05/22/maryland-gov-larry-hogan-vetoes-major-criminal-justice-reform-bills.

162. Niki Kelly, "Local Corrections Funds in Doubt," *Journal Gazette,* March 22, 2015, http://www.journalgazette.net/news/local/indiana/Local-corrections-funds-in-doubt-5663150.

163. "Criminal Justice Reform Accomplishments from the 84th Texas Legislature," *Grits for Breakfast* (blog), July 1, 2015, http://gritsforbreakfast.blogspot.com/2015/07/criminal-justice-reform-accomplishments.html.

164. Sentencing Project, *Trends: 1999–2014.*

165. Emily Lane, "Bobby Jindal Signs into Law Bill Increasing Heroin Penalties for Dealers to 99 Years," Nola.com, May 31, 2014, http://www.nola.com

/politics/index.ssf/2014/05/bobby_jindal_heroin_penalties.html; Ally
Marotti, "Punishments Increasing for Dealers of Deadly Heroin," *Cincinnati
Enquirer,* September 11, 2014, http://www.cincinnati.com/story/news/crime
/2014/09/09/punishments-increasing-dealers-deadly-heroin/15347165;
Kevin Miller, "Maine Attorney General, Advocates Clash over Heroin
Penalties," *Portland Press Herald,* February 3, 2016, https://www
.pressherald.com/2016/02/03/maine-attorney-general-says-stiffer-heroin
-penalties-could-prod-addicts-into-treatment.
166. Fla. Stat. § 794.0115(2)(e) (2014).
167. *See, e.g.,* Mass. Gen. Laws ch. 6, § 167A (2014).
168. Memorandum from Deputy Attorney General Sally Quillian Yates to All
United States Attorneys, September 9, 2015, https://www.justice.gov/dag/file
/769036/download; Shahien Nasiripour, "The Obama Administration
Could Repeat Its Biggest Mistake of the Financial Crisis," *Huffington Post,*
January 6, 2016, https://www.huffingtonpost.com/entry/department-of
-justice-volkswagen_us_568a0b8e4b06fa688831b99; Department of
Justice, "Statement by U.S. Attorney John W. Huber on Kate's Law and the
No Sanctuary for Criminals Act," news release, June 28, 2017, https://www
.justice.gov/opa/pr/statement-us-attorney-john-w-huber-kate-s-law-and-no
-sanctuary-criminals-act; Letter from Kenneth A. Blanco, Assistant Attorney
General (Acting), Criminal Division, U.S. Department of Justice, to Judge
William H. Pryor Jr., Acting Chair, U.S. Sentencing Commission, July 31,
2017, 7–8, https://www.ussc.gov/sites/default/files/pdf/amendment-process
/public-comment/20170731/DOJ.pdf; Mike Riggs, "The Justice Department
Wants to Put Small-Time Fentanyl Dealers in Federal Prison," *Hit and Run*
(blog), Reason, August 12, 2017, http://reason.com/blog/2017/08/12/the
-justice-department-wants-to-put-smal.
169. Seung Min Kim, "Cotton Leads Effort to Sink Sentencing Overhaul,"
Politico, January 25, 2016, http://www.politico.com/story/2016/01/criminal
-justice-tom-cotton-218121.
170. Joey Peters, "NM Swims against Criminal Justice Reform Tide," NM
Political Report, July 9, 2015, http://nmpoliticalreport.com/6149/nm-swims
-against-criminal-justice-reform-tide.
171. *See, e.g.,* Jim Geraghty, "Homicides Spike, Complicating the Republicans'
Push for Criminal-Justice Reform," *National Review,* August 25, 2015,
http://www.nationalreview.com/article/423012/homicides-spike
-complicating-republicans-push-criminal-justice-reform-jim-geraghty.

7. Institutional Intransigence

1. Lawrence M. Friedman, *A History of American Law,* 3rd ed. (New York:
Simon and Schuster, 2005), 434–462, 567–575; William J. Stuntz, *The
Collapse of American Criminal Justice* (Cambridge, MA: Harvard University
Press, 2011), 1–60.
2. Alexander Hamilton, *Federalist* No. 74, in *The Federalist,* ed. Jacob E. Cooke
(Middletown, CT: Wesleyan University Press, 1961), 501.

3. Jeremy Bentham, "Principles of Penal Law, pt. II, bk. 1, ch. 6," in *The Works of Jeremy Bentham,* ed. John Bowring (1843; repr., Indianapolis: Liberty Fund, 1962), 401.

4. James Madison, *Federalist* No. 47, in Cooke, *The Federalist,* 324.

5. Rachel E. Barkow, "Separation of Powers and the Criminal Law," *Stanford Law Review* 58 (2006): 992, 1012–1020.

6. U.S. Const. art. I, § 9, cl. 3; U.S. Const. § 10, cl. 1.

7. United States v. Brown, 381 U.S. 437, 442 (1965).

8. Weaver v. Graham, 450 U.S. 24, 29 (1981) (citations omitted).

9. Weaver v. Graham, 29n10.

10. U.S. Const. art. I, § 9, cl. 2; Alexander Hamilton, *Federalist* No. 84, in Cooke, *The Federalist,* 444.

11. U.S. Const. art. II, § 2, cl. 1.

12. United States v. Klein, 80 U.S. 128, 147 (1871).

13. James Iredell, "Address at the North Carolina Ratifying Convention (July 28, 1788)," in *The Founders' Constitution,* vol. 4, ed. Philip B. Kurland and Ralph Lerner (Indianapolis: Liberty Fund 1987), 17.

14. John H. Langbein, "Albion's Fatal Flaws," *Past and Present* 98 (1983): 118; Rachel E. Barkow, "Clemency and Presidential Administration," *New York University Law Review* 90 (2015): 832.

15. Hamilton, *Federalist* No. 74, 500–501.

16. *Ex parte* Grossman, 267 U.S. 87, 120–121 (1925) (emphasis added).

17. Barkow, "Clemency and Presidential Administration," 829–840.

18. United States *ex rel.* McCann v. Adams, 126 F.2d 774, 775–776 (2nd Cir.), rev'd on other grounds, 317 U.S. 269 (1942).

19. Rachel E. Barkow, "Recharging the Jury: The Criminal Jury's Constitutional Role in an Era of Mandatory Sentencing," *University of Pennsylvania Law Review* 152 (2003): 48–51.

20. Roscoe Pound, "Law in Books and Law in Action," *American Law Review* 44 (1910): 18.

21. Antonin Scalia, "The Rule of Law as a Law of Rules," *University of Chicago Law Review* 56 (1989): 1180.

22. Barkow, "Separation of Powers," 1016.

23. Hurtado v. California, 110 U.S. 516 (1884); Duncan v. Louisiana, 391 U.S. 145 (1968); Apodaca v. Oregon, 406 U.S. 404 (1972).

24. U.S. Const. art. I, § 10, cl. 1.

25. Kathleen (Cookie) Ridolfi and Seth Gordon, "Gubernatorial Clemency Powers: Justice or Mercy?," *Criminal Justice* 24 (2009): 26–41.

26. Joan Petersilia, "Parole and Prisoner Reentry in the United States," *Crime and Justice* (1999): 488.

27. M. Elizabeth Magill, "The Real Separation of Powers in Separation of Powers Law," *Virginia Law Review* 86 (2000): 1193.

28. George Fisher, *Plea Bargaining's Triumph: A History of Plea Bargaining in America* (Palo Alto, CA: Stanford University Press, 2003); Santobello v. New York, 404 U.S. 257, 260 (1971).

29. Blackledge v. Allison, 431 U.S. 63, 76 (1977).

30. Barkow, "Separation of Powers," 1045–1046 and n. 303.

31. Rachel E. Barkow, "The Court of Life and Death: The Two Tracks of Constitutional Sentencing Law and the Case for Uniformity," *Michigan Law Review* 107 (2009): 1145–1205.

32. Barkow, 1159–1160.

33. Ewing v. California, 538 U.S. 11, 20 (2003) (plurality opinion).

34. Barkow, "Court of Life and Death," 1156–1157.

35. Rummel v. Estelle, 445 U.S. 263 (1980).

36. Harmelin v. Michigan, 501 U.S. 957, 961 (1991).

37. Ewing v. California, 18.

38. Lockyer v. Andrade, 538 U.S. 63, 66 (2003).

39. Graham v. Florida, 560 U.S. 48 (2010); Miller v. Alabama, 567 U.S. 460 (2012); Jackson v. Hobbs, 567 U.S. 460 (2012).

40. Rachel E. Barkow, "Institutional Design and the Policing of Prosecutors: Lessons from Administrative Law," *Stanford Law Review* 61 (2009): 880–881.

41. U.S. Sentencing Commission, *2014 Sourcebook of Federal Sentencing Statistics,* figure C, http://www.ussc.gov/sites/default/files/pdf/research-and -publications/annual-reports-and-sourcebooks/2014/FigureC.pdf.

42. Sean Rosenmerkel et al., *NCJ 226846, Felony Sentences in State Courts, 2006—Statistical Tables* (Bureau of Justice Statistics, 2009), tables 4.1, 4.3, https://www.bjs.gov/content/pub/pdf/fssco6st.pdf.

43. Stephanos Bibas, "Plea Bargaining outside the Shadow of Trial," *Harvard Law Review* 117 (2008): 2464.

44. Gerard E. Lynch, "Screening versus Plea Bargaining: Exactly What Are We Trading Off?," *Stanford Law Review* 55 (2003): 1403–1404.

45. John Pfaff, *Locked In: The True Causes of Mass Incarceration—and How to Achieve Real Reform* (New York: Basic Books, 2017), 74. Pfaff makes the bold claim that this is *the* driver of mass incarceration, as opposed to sentencing increases, and others have questioned whether his data support that view. *See* Jeffrey Bellin, "Reassessing Prosecutorial Power through the Lens of Mass Incarceration," *Michigan Law Review* 116 (2018): 837–852. Regardless of how much of the current increase in incarceration is the result of sentencing increases in statutes and guidelines versus prosecutorial charging decisions, the important point is that the two dynamics work in tandem to create the system we have now. Thus any solution needs to address both aspects.

46. Memorandum from Jeff Sessions, Attorney General of the United States, to All Federal Prosecutors, May 10, 2017, 1, https://www.justice.gov/opa/press -release/file/965896/download; Memorandum from John Ashcroft, Attorney General of the United States, to All Federal Prosecutors, September 22, 2003, 2, http://www.justice.gov/opa/pr/2003/September/03_ag_516.htm; Memo-randum from Eric H. Holder Jr., Attorney General of the United States, to All Federal Prosecutors, May 19, 2010, 2, http://www.justice.gov/oip/holder -memo-charging-sentencing.pdf.

47. Barkow, "Clemency and Presidential Administration," 856, 860.

48. Rachel Barkow, "Overseeing Agency Enforcement: A Foreword to the Annual Review of Administrative Law," *George Washington Law Review* 84 (2016): 1149.

49. Nicholas Bagley and Richard L. Revesz, "Centralized Oversight of the Regulatory State," *Columbia Law Review* 106 (2006): 1286–1289.
50. Rachel E. Barkow, "Insulating Agencies: Avoiding Capture through Institutional Design," *Texas Law Review* 89 (2010): 22.
51. William J. Stuntz, "The Pathological Politics of Criminal Law," *Michigan Law Review* 100 (2001): 547–549.
52. Barkow, "Clemency and Presidential Administration," 859.
53. Josie Duffy Rice, "Prosecutors Aren't Just Enforcing the Law—They're Making It," In Justice Today, April 20, 2018, https://injusticetoday.com/prosecutors-arent-just-enforcing-the-law-they-re-making-it-d83e6e59f97a.
54. 5 U.S.C. §§ 554(d), 556(b).
55. 5 U.S.C. § 554(b), (c); § 557(c), § 557(d)(1).
56. 5 U.S.C. § 557(c).
57. Issa Kohler-Hausmann, *Misdemeanorland: Criminal Courts and Social Control in an Age of Broken Windows Policing* (Princeton, NJ: Princeton University Press, 2018).
58. Gerard E. Lynch, "Our Administrative System of Criminal Justice," *Fordham Law Review* 66 (1998): 2128–2129, 2132.
59. United States v. Armstrong, 517 U.S. 456, 464 (1996) (quoting Bordenkircher v. Hayes, 434 U.S. 357, 364 (1978)).
60. Lynch, "Our Administrative System," 2122.
61. Blackledge v. Perry, 417 U.S. 21, 27 (1974); United States v. Armstrong, 464; Barkow, "Separation of Powers," 1025; Stuntz, *Collapse of American Criminal Justice,* 119–120.
62. Barkow, "Separation of Powers," 1027, 1049.
63. Jason A. Schwartz, *52 Experiments with Regulatory Review: The Political and Economic Inputs into State Rulemaking* (Institute for Policy Integrity Report No. 6, 2010), http://policyintegrity.org/files/publications/52_Experiments_with_Regulatory_Review.pdf.
64. Exec. Order No. 12,866; Exec. Order No. 13,563.
65. 47 U.S.C. § 307(a) (2012).
66. Edward M. Kennedy, "Toward a New System of Criminal Sentencing: Law with Order," *American Criminal Law Review* 16 (1979): 380.
67. Kenneth R. Feinberg, "Federal Criminal Sentencing Reform: Congress and the United States Sentencing Commission," *Wake Forest Law Review* 28 (1993): 297.
68. Shadd Maruna et al., "Ex-Offender Reintegration: Theory and Practice," in *After Crime and Punishment: Pathways to Offender Reintegration,* ed. Shadd Maruna and Russ Immarigeon (Portland, OR: Willan, 2011), 7–8.
69. Petersilia, "Parole and Prisoner Reentry," 491.
70. David Rothman, *Conscience and Convenience: The Asylum and Its Alternatives in Progressive America* (New York: Routledge, 1980), 173.
71. Edward E. Rhine et al., "The Future of Parole Release," *Crime and Justice* 46 (2017): 287.
72. Beth Schwartzapfel, "Life without Parole," Marshall Project, July 10, 2015, https://www.themarshallproject.org/2015/07/10/life-without-parole-.gvgVE2eVe.

73. Sharon Dolovich, "Forms of Deference in Prison Law," *Federal Sentencing Reporter* 24 (2012): 245–259.
74. Silmon v. Travis, 95 N.E.2d 501, 504 (N.Y. 2000) (citations omitted).
75. *In re* Rosenkrantz, 59 F.3d 174 (Cal. 2002).

Part Three

1. Steven W. Perry and Duren Banks, *Prosecutors in State Courts, 2007—Statistical Tables* (Bureau of Justice Statistics, 2011), https://www.bjs .gov/content/pub/pdf/psc07st.pdf.
2. Peter Wagner and Wendy Sawyer, "States of Incarceration: The Global Context 2018" (Prison Policy Initiative, June 2018), https://www .prisonpolicy.org/global/2018.html.
3. *See* Richard C. Dieter, *The 2% Death Penalty: How a Minority of Counties Produce Most Death Cases at Enormous Costs to All* (Death Penalty Information Center, 2013), https://deathpenaltyinfo.org/documents /TwoPercentReport.pdf.
4. Noelle E. Fearn, "A Multilevel Analysis of Community Effects on Criminal Sentencing," *Justice Quarterly* 22 (2005): 452–487; Iain Pardoe and Robert R. Weidner, "Sentencing Convicted Felons in the United States: A Bayesian Analysis Using Multilevel Covariates," *Journal of Statistical Planning and Inference* 136 (2006): 1433–1455.
5. Wagner and Sawyer, "States of Incarceration."

8. Policing Prosecutors

1. Rachel E. Barkow, "Prosecutorial Administration: Prosecutor Bias and the Department of Justice," *Virginia Law Review* 99 (2013): 271–342.
2. Margaret Colgate Love, "Time for a Really New Broom at the Federal Bureau of Prisons," Crime Report, April 17, 2011, https://thecrimereport.org /2011/04/18/2011-04-time-for-a-really-new-broom-at-the-federal-bureau-of.
3. Barkow, "Prosecutorial Administration," 298 (internal quotation and citation omitted).
4. Barkow, 301–302.
5. Rachel E. Barkow, "Insulating Agencies: Avoiding Capture through Institutional Design," *Texas Law Review* 89 (2010): 72–73.
6. Barkow, "Prosecutorial Administration," 309–319.
7. Barkow, 336–341.
8. Adam M. Gershowitz, "Consolidating Local Criminal Justice: Should Prosecutors Control the Jails?," *Wake Forest Law Review* 51 (2016): 677–703; W. David Ball, "Defunding State Prisons," *Criminal Law Bulletin* 50 (2014): 1060–1090; W. David Ball, "Tough on Crime (on the State's Dime): How Violent Crime Does Not Drive California Counties' Incarceration Rates—and Why It Should," *Georgia State University Law Review* 28

(2012): 987–1083; Robert L. Misner, "Recasting Prosecutorial Discretion," *Journal of Criminal Law and Criminology* 86 (1996): 717–777.

9. Washington State Institute of Public Policy, http://www.wsipp.wa.gov/topic .asp?cat=10&subcat=0&dteSlct=0.

10. Imbler v. Pachtman, 424 U.S. 409, 430 (1976).

11. Rachel E. Barkow, "Organizational Guidelines for the Prosecutor's Office," *Cardozo Law Review* 31 (2010): 2094–2097.

12. Rachel E. Barkow, "Institutional Design and the Policing of Prosecutors: Lessons from Administrative Law," *Stanford Law Review* 61 (2009): 889.

13. 5 U.S.C. § 554(d).

14. Barkow, "Policing of Prosecutors," 898–900.

15. Barkow, 915–917.

16. Pretrial Justice Institute, Early Screening by an Experienced Prosecutor: Recommendation, http://www.pretrial.org/solutions/early-screening; NYU Center on the Administration of Criminal Law (CACL), *Disrupting the Cycle: Reimaging the Prosecutor's Role in Reentry* (2017), 13, http://www .law.nyu.edu/sites/default/files/upload_documents/CACL Report.pdf.

17. Memorandum from Michael E. Horowitz, Inspector General, U.S. Department of Justice, to the Attorney General and the Deputy Attorney General, December 11, 2013, reissued December 20, 2013, https://oig.justice.gov /challenges/2013.htm [https://perma.cc/5YRW-Z9VH]; see also *Oversight of the Department of Justice: Hearing on Appropriations for 2014 before the Subcomm. on Commerce, Justice, Science and Related Agencies of the H. Comm. on Appropriations,* 113th Cong., 131–132 (2013) (statement of Michael E. Horowitz, Inspector General, U.S. Department of Justice).

18. Rachel E. Barkow and Mark Osler, "Designed to Fail: The President's Deference to the Department of Justice in Advancing Criminal Justice Reform," *William and Mary Law Review* 59 (2017): 470–471.

19. U.S. Sentencing Commission, *U.S. Sentencing Guideline Manual,* § 8B2.1(a)(2).

20. Barkow, "Organizational Guidelines," 2106.

21. NYU Center on the Administration of Criminal Law, Conviction Integrity Project, *Establishing Conviction Integrity Programs in Prosecutors' Offices* (2012), 8, http://www.law.nyu.edu/sites/default/files/upload_documents /Establishing_Conviction_Integrity_Programs_FinalReport_ecm_pro _073583.pdf.

22. Ronald F. Wright, "Beyond Prosecutor Elections," *Southern Methodist University Law Review* 67 (2014): 599–604; Ronald F. Wright, "How Prosecutor Elections Fail Us," *Ohio State Journal of Criminal Law* 6 (2009): 582–583, 589, 592–593, 600–606.

23. Leon Neyfakh, "How to Run against a Tough-on-Crime District Attorney—and Win," *Slate,* November 12, 2015, http://www.slate.com/articles /news_and_politics/crime/2015/11/district_attorneys_scott_colom_proves _you_can_run_against_a_tough_on_crime.html.

24. Wesley Lowery, "How Civil Rights Groups Are Using the Election [to] Create Black Political Power," *Washington Post,* November 8, 2016, https://www.washingtonpost.com/news/post-nation/wp/2016/11/08/black

-political-power-how-civil-rights-groups-are-using-the-election-to-drive
-criminal-justice-reform; David Alan Sklansky, "The Changing Political
Landscape for Elected Prosecutors," *Ohio State Journal of Criminal Law* 14
(2017): 647–674.

25. *See, e.g.*, John Woodrow Cox, Keith L. Alexander, and Ovetta Wiggins, "Who
Is Baltimore State's Attorney Marilyn J. Mosby?," *Washington Post*, May 1,
2015, https://www.washingtonpost.com/local/who-is-baltimore-states
-attorney-marilyn-j-mosby/2015/05/01/12be80e2-f013-11e4-8abc
-d6aa3bad79dd_story.html; Sklansky, "Changing Political Landscape,"
654–656, 661–663, 665–666.

26. Sklansky, "Changing Political Landscape," 664–665.

27. Tom Beres, "Why Mike O'Malley Will Replace Tim McGinty as Cuyahoga
County Prosecutor," WKYC.com, March 16, 2016, http://www.wkyc.com
/news/politics/why-is-mike-omalley-going-to-replace-tim-mcginty-as
-cuyahoga-co-prosecutor/85609823.

28. Brandon Ellington Patterson, "Black Lives Matter Notches Wins in Chicago
and Cleveland," *Mother Jones,* March 15, 2016, http://www.motherjones
.com/politics/2016/03/chicago-primary-black-lives-matter.

29. John Byrne and Hal Dardick, "Foxx: Cook County State's Attorney Win Is
about 'Turning the Page,'" *Chicago Tribune,* March 16, 2016, http://www
.chicagotribune.com/news/local/politics/ct-cook-county-states-attorney-anita
-alvarez-kim-foxx-met-0316-20160315-story.html; Annie Sweeney and Jason
Meisner, "A Moment-by-Moment Account of What the Laquan McDonald
Video Shows," *Chicago Tribune,* November 25, 2015, http://www
.chicagotribune.com/news/ct-chicago-cop-shooting-video-release-laquan
-mcdonald-20151124-story.html.

30. Ben Austen, "Chicago after Laquan McDonald," *New York Times Magazine,*
April 20, 2016, http://www.nytimes.com/2016/04/24/magazine/chicago-after
-laquan-mcdonald.html.

31. Maurice Chammah, "These Prosecutors Campaigned for Less Jail Time—and
Won," Marshall Project, November 9, 2016, https://www.themarshallproject
.org/2016/11/09/these-prosecutors-campaigned-for-less-jail-time-and-won.

32. Carol Felsenthal, "Why Kim Foxx Is Challenging Anita Alvarez for State's
Attorney," *Chicago Magazine,* October 28, 2015, http://www.chicagomag
.com/Chicago-Magazine/Felsenthal-Files/October-2015/Kim-Foxx.

33. BYP100, "Statement on the Defeat of Cook County State's Attorney Anita
Alvarez," March 16, 2016, http://byp100.org/byp100-statement-on-the
-defeat-of-cook-county-states-attorney-anita-alvarez.

34. Dana Liebelson and Ryan J. Reilly, "Sandra Bland Died One Year Ago,"
Huffington Post, July 13, 2016, http://highline.huffingtonpost.com/articles/en
/sandra-bland-jail-deaths.

35. Dan Frosch, "Jailed Rape Victim Case Takes Focus in Texas District Attorney
Race," *Wall Street Journal,* November 7, 2016, http://www.wsj.com/articles
/jailed-rape-victim-case-takes-focus-in-texas-district-attorney-race
-1478534712; Gillian Mohney, "Activists Reject Claims That Black Lives

Matter Led to Shooting of Houston Deputy," *Vice News,* August 30, 2015, https://news.vice.com/article/activists-reject-claims-that-black-lives-matter-led -to-shooting-of-houston-deputy; Jessica Pishko, "This Texas Prosecutor Jailed a Rape Victim—Could It Cost Devon Anderson Her Election?," *The Nation,* November 7, 2016, https://www.thenation.com/article/this-texas-prosecutor -jailed-a-rape-victim-could-she-lose-her-election.

36. Michael Barajas, "Looks Like Pot Could Be a Major Issue in the District Attorney's Race. Again," *Houston Press,* January 22, 2016, http://www .houstonpress.com/news/looks-like-pot-could-be-a-major-issue-in-the-district -attorney-s-race-again-8093192.

37. Kim Ogg for Harris County District Attorney, "Bail Reform," http://www .kimogg.com/bail_reform.

38. Joel Currier, "Former Prosecutor Turned State Rep Takes St. Louis Circuit Attorney Primary," *St. Louis Post-Dispatch,* August 3, 2016, http://www .stltoday.com/news/local/crime-and-courts/former-prosecutor-turned-state-rep -takes-st-louis-circuit-attorney/article_3f31a308-d84f-52bd-8d9e -f19e3dfb4ea3.html.

39. Kim Gardner: Circuit Attorney, City of St. Louis, http://www.kimgardnerforstlouis.com.

40. Vivian Yee, "Thompson Defeats Hynes, Again, for Brooklyn District Attorney," *New York Times,* November 5, 2013, http://www.nytimes.com/2013 /11/06/nyregion/thompson-claims-victory-over-hynes-again-for-brooklyn -district-attorney.html.

41. Yee, "Thompson Defeats Hynes."

42. Sklansky, "Changing Political Landscape," 656–657; Neyfakh, "How to Run."

43. Christopher Hooks, "Is the Best Offense a Good Defense Lawyer?," *Texas Monthly,* November 2016, http://www.texasmonthly.com/politics/best -offense-good-defense-lawyer.

44. Hooks.

45. Sklansky, "Changing Political Landscape," 661.

46. Dan Sullivan, "Mother of Victim in Sex Case Criticizes Ober amid Contentious State Attorney Race," *Tampa Bay Times,* September 9, 2016, http://www.tbo.com/news/politics/mother-of-victim-in-sex-case-criticizes-ober -amid-contentious-state-attorney-race-20160909; Maurice Chammah, "The Battle for Criminal-Justice Reform Is Being Fought in Local District Attorney Races," *Business Insider,* October 19, 2016, http://www.businessinsider.com /the-battle-for-criminal-justice-reform-is-being-fought-in-local-district -attorney-races-2016-10.

47. Steven Lemongello, "Jeff Ashton Scandal: Former Casey Anthony Prosecutor Admits Using Ashley Madison," *Orlando Sentinel,* August 23, 2015, http://www.orlandosentinel.com/news/breaking-news/os-jeff-ashton-ashley -madison-20150823-story.html.

48. Brandon Ellington Patterson, "Black Lives Matter Was a Game Changer in These Six Races," *Mother Jones,* November 8, 2016, http://www

.motherjones.com/politics/2016/11/prosecutor-races-black-lives-matter
-election-day.

49. Yamiche Alcindor, "After High-Profile Shootings, Blacks Seek Prosecutor
Seats," *New York Times,* November 5, 2016, http://www.nytimes.com/2016
/11/06/us/politics/black-prosecutors.html.

50. "Pattillo to Try Again for Henry County District Attorney Seat," *Henry
Herald,* January 20, 2016, http://www.henryherald.com/news/pattillo-to-try
-again-for-henry-county-district-attorney-seat/article_fce6c9b4-8d48-5fcc
-891a-daddc368ff79.html.

51. Edmund "Ed" Perea for District Attorney of Bernalillo County ABQ NM
2016, Facebook, https://www.facebook.com/pg/ed4da/about; Raul Torrez,
"Raul Torrez for District Attorney—'Smart,' " YouTube, May 17, 2016,
https://www.youtube.com/watch?v=JG4pDPDMk7c.

52. Sarah Willets, "Incumbents Out in Durham Sheriff, District Attorney Races,"
INDY Week, May 8, 2018, https://www.indyweek.com/news/archives/2018
/05/08/incumbents-out-in-durham-sheriff-district-attorney-races.

53. Alan Feuer, "He Sued Police 75 Times. Democrats Want Him as Philadelphia's Top Prosecutor," *New York Times,* June 17, 2017, https://www.nytimes
.com/2017/06/17/us/philadelphia-krasner-district-attorney-police.html.

54. Harrison Jacobs, "Our Exclusive Interview with New Philadelphia District
Attorney Larry Krasner, Who Blew Out the Competition with an Ultra
Progressive Platform," *Business Insider,* http://www.businessinsider.com/larry
-krasner-philadelphia-district-attorney-interview-platform-2017-11/-krasner
-says-he-may-have-spent-his-career-defending-protesters-but-he-wont-be
-defending-nazis-1.

55. Jake Lilly for District Attorney, http://jakelilly.com.

56. Jacobs, "Our Exclusive Interview"; Ciara McCarthy, "Chicago-Area Prosecutor Election Race Shows Impact of Black Lives Matter," *Guardian,*
March 11, 2016, https://www.theguardian.com/us-news/2016/mar/11
/chicago-prosecutor-election-anita-alvarez-cook-county-black-lives-matter
-laquan-mcdonald; Janell Ross, "Black Lives Matter Won on Tuesday.
Prosecutors Lost," *Washington Post,* March 16, 2016, https://www
.washingtonpost.com/news/the-fix/wp/2016/03/16/black-lives-matter-won-on
-tuesday-prosecutors-lost.

57. Lowery, "How Civil Rights Groups."

58. Zusha Elinson and Joe Palazzolo, "Billionaire Soros Funds Local Prosecutor
Races," *Wall Street Journal,* November 3, 2016, http://www.wsj.com/articles
/billionaire-soros-funds-local-prosecutor-races-1478194109.

59. Elinson and Palazzolo; Andy Lyman, "Kubiak Drops Out of BernCo DA
Race," *New Mexico Political Report,* June 23, 2016, http://nmpoliticalreport
.com/54139/kubiak-drops-out-of-bernco-da-race.

60. He supported the following candidates as of November 2016: Scott Colom
(Mississippi); James Stewart (Louisiana); Kim Foxx (Chicago); Jake Lilly
(Denver); Morris Overstreet (Houston); Kim Ogg (Houston); Aramis Ayala
(Orlando); Kim Gardner (St. Louis); Darius Pattillo (Georgia); Raúl Torrez

(New Mexico). Pattillo denied any knowledge of Soros's contributions, and Pattillo's opponents dropped out of the race before any known Soros-funded advertising was released. Of these, Ogg and Lilly lost; Soros went on to support Ogg's opponent, Morris Overstreet, in the Houston race against the incumbent.

61. Byrne and Dardick, "Foxx"; Melissa Harris, "Attention-Shy Democratic Donor Fred Eychaner Opens Up," *Chicago Tribune,* May 1, 2014, http:// articles.chicagotribune.com/2014-05-01/business/ct-eychaner-lockett -confidential-0501-biz-20140501_1_pflag-donor-ed-burke.

62. Blake Paterson, "Soros Again Pumps Money into Harris County District Attorney's Race," *Houston Chronicle,* October 13, 2016, http://www .houstonchronicle.com/news/politics/houston/article/Soros-again-pumps -money-into-Harris-County-9970308.php.

63. Matt Ferner, "George Soros, Progressive Groups to Spend Millions to Elect Reformist Prosecutors," *Huffington Post,* March 12, 2018, https://www .huffingtonpost.com/entry/george-soros-prosecutors-reform_us _5af2100ae4b0a0d601e76f06.

64. David Alan Sklansky, "The Progressive Prosecutor's Handbook," *UC Davis Law Review Online* 50 (2017): 28–29.

65. Angela Davis, ed., *Policing the Black Man: Arrest, Prosecution and Imprisonment* (New York: Pantheon, 2017); Wright, "Beyond Prosecutor Elections," 604.

66. Lauren-Brooke Eisen, Nicole Fortier, and Inimai M. Chettiar, *Federal Prosecution for the 21st Century* (Brennan Center for Justice, 2014).

67. Wright, "Beyond Prosecutor Elections," 612.

68. Federal Bureau of Investigation, *Uniform Crime Report, 2016 Crime in the United States: Offenses Cleared* (2017), 2, https://ucr.fbi.gov/crime-in-the-u.s /2016/crime-in-the-u.s.-2016/topic-pages/clearances.pdf.

69. Aamer Madhani, "At End of Bloody Year in Chicago, Too Few Murders Solved," *USA Today,* December 30, 2016, https://www.usatoday.com/story /news/2016/12/30/chicago-murders-clearance-rate-2016/96009878.

70. Wesley Lowery, Kimbriell Kelly, and Steven Rich, "An Unequal Justice," *Washington Post,* July 25, 2018, https://www.washingtonpost.com/graphics /2018/investigations/black-homicides-arrests/?utm_term=.42c5d408d20b.

71. See generally CACL, *Disrupting the Cycle.*

72. Laura and John Arnold Foundation, "New Data: Pretrial Risk Assessment Tool Works to Reduce Court Appearances," news release, August 8, 2016, http://www.arnoldfoundation.org/new-data-pretrial-risk-assessment-tool -works-reduce-crime-increase-court-appearances; Laura and John Arnold Foundation, *Results from the First Six Months of the Public Safety Assessment—Court in Kentucky* (2014), 1, 3, http://www.arnoldfoundation .org/wp-content/uploads/2014/02/PSA-Court-Kentucky-6-Month-Report.pdf.

73. New Jersey Courts, *Criminal Justice Reform: Report to the Governor and Legislature* (2016), 1.

9. Engaging Experts

1. Steven W. Perry and Duren Banks, *Prosecutors in State Courts, 2007—Statistical Tables* (Bureau of Justice Statistics, 2011), https://www.bjs.gov/content/pub/pdf/psco7st.pdf.
2. Rachel E. Barkow and Mark Osler, "Designed to Fail: The President's Deference to the Department of Justice in Advancing Criminal Justice Reform," *William and Mary Law Review* 59 (2017): 392–393.
3. W. David Ball, "Why State Prisons?," *Yale Law and Policy Review* 33 (2014): 75–117.
4. Franklin E. Zimring and Gordon Hawkins, *The Scale of Imprisonment* (Chicago: University of Chicago Press, 1991), 140.
5. W. David Ball, "Tough on Crime (on the State's Dime): How Violent Crime Does Not Drive California Counties' Incarceration Rates—and Why It Should," *Georgia State University Law Review* 28 (2012): 1014.
6. W. David Ball, "Defunding State Prisons," *Criminal Law Bulletin* 50 (2014): 1060–1090; Robert L. Misner, "Recasting Prosecutorial Discretion," *Criminal Law and Criminology* 86 (1996): 717–777; Adam M. Gershowitz, "Consolidating Local Criminal Justice: Should Prosecutors Control the Jails?," *Wake Forest Law Review* 51 (2016): 677–703.
7. Sarah K. S. Shannon et al., "The Growth, Scope, and Spatial Distribution of People with Felony Records in the United States, 1948–2010," *Demography* 54 (2017): 1814.
8. Malcolm M. Feeley and Jonathan Simon, "Actuarial Justice: The Emerging New Criminal Law," in *Crime and the Risk Society,* ed. Pat O'Malley (New York: Ashgate, 1998), 449.
9. Feely and Simon, 457.
10. Carol S. Steiker, "Foreword: The Limits of the Preventive State," *Journal of Criminal Law and Criminology* 88 (1998): 771–808.
11. Issa Kohler-Hausmann, "Managerial Justice and Mass Misdemeanors," *Stanford Law Review* 66 (2014): 611; Bernard E. Harcourt, *Against Prediction: Profiling, Policing, and Punishing in an Actuarial Age* (Chicago: University of Chicago Press, 2007).
12. University of Minnesota, Robina Institute of Criminal Law and Criminal Justice, *The Composition of Sentencing Commissions* (2016), https://sentencing.umn.edu/content/composition-sentencing-commissions-footnote1_detu2c7.
13. For a more detailed discussion, see Rachel E. Barkow, "Administering Crime," *UCLA Law Review* 52 (2005): 743–754.
14. Barkow, 768–770.
15. Federal Bureau of Prisons, Population Statistics, https://www.bop.gov/about/statistics/population_statistics.jsp.
16. Pew Charitable Trusts, "Prison Time Surges for Federal Inmates," November 18, 2015, http://www.pewtrusts.org/en/research-and-analysis/issue-briefs/2015/11/prison-time-surges-for-federal-inmates.

17. U.S. Sentencing Commission, *Preliminary Crack Cocaine Retroactivity Data Report* (2011), tables 1, 8.
18. U.S. Sentencing Commission, *2014 Drug Guidelines Amendment Retroactivity Data Report* (2017), tables 3, 7.
19. Marcia Shein, "U.S. Sentencing Commission Votes to Change 'Crimes of Violence' Definition," Federal Criminal Law Center News, January 12, 2016, https://federalcriminallawcenter.com/2016/01/u-s-sentencing-commission-votes-to-change-crimes-of-violence-definition; U.S. Sentencing Commission, "U.S. Sentencing Commission Approves Significant Changes to the Federal Sentencing Guidelines," news release, April 15, 2016, https://www.ussc.gov/about/news/press-releases/april-15-2016.
20. E. Ann Carson, *Prisoners in 2016* (Bureau of Justice Statistics, 2018), https://www.bjs.gov/content/pub/pdf/p16.pdf.
21. Rachel E. Barkow, "Administering Crime," 775.
22. Barkow, 781, 787.
23. Rachel E. Barkow and Kathleen M. O'Neill, "Delegating Punitive Power: The Political Economy of Sentencing Commission and Guideline Formation," *Texas Law Review* 84 (2006): 1976.
24. Barkow and O'Neill, 2008.
25. Barkow, "Administering Crime," 780–782, 784–787, 804–812.
26. Barkow, 780–782, 784–787, 804–812.
27. Barkow, 780–782, 784–787, 804–812.
28. Jeremy Travis, *But They All Come Back: Facing the Challenges of Prisoner Reentry* (Washington, DC: Urban Institute Press, 2005), 25.
29. Travis, *But They All Come Back*, 25.
30. Barkow, "Administering Crime," 811.
31. Barkow and O'Neill, "Delegating Punitive Power," 2009.
32. Sari Horwitz, "Justice Department Set to Free 6,000 Prisoners, Largest One-Time Release," *Washington Post*, October 6, 2015, https://www.washingtonpost.com/world/national-security/justice-department-about-to-free-6000-prisoners-largest-one-time-release/2015/10/06/961f4c9a-6ba2-11e5-aa5b-f78a98956699_story.html; Nancy La Vigne and Julie Samuels, *The Growth and Increasing Cost of the Federal Prison System: Drivers and Potential Solutions* (Urban Institute, 2012), https://www.urban.org/sites/default/files/publication/26191/412693-The-Growth-amp-Increasing-Cost-of-the-Federal-Prison-System-Drivers-and-Potential-Solutions.PDF; Horwitz, "Justice Department Set to Free 6,000 Prisoners."
33. Barkow, "Administering Crime," 802–804.
34. Barkow, 783.
35. S. Rep. No. 98–225, at 38 (1983).
36. Rachel E. Barkow and Mark Osler, "Restructuring Clemency: The Cost of Ignoring Clemency and a Plan for Renewal," *University of Chicago Law Review* 82 (2015): 22.
37. Barkow, "Administering Crime," 761–762, 772.
38. Giovanna Shay, "Ad Law Incarcerated," *Berkeley Journal of Criminal Law* 14 (2009): 346.

39. Sandra G. Mayson, "Collateral Consequences and the Preventive State," *Notre Dame Law Review* 91 (2015): 311.

40. Mayson, 335.

41. 538 U.S. 84, 105 (2003).

42. 363 U.S. 144, 160 (1960).

43. Does #1–5 v. Snyder, 834 F.3d 696, 704 (6th Cir. 2016).

44. *See, e.g.,* David Schoenbrod, *Power without Responsibility: How Congress Abuses the People through Delegation* (New Haven, CT: Yale University Press, 1993), 56–57; Neomi Rao, "Administrative Collusion: How Delegation Diminishes the Collective Congress," *New York University Law Review* 90 (2015): 1478.

45. Exec. Order No. 12,866 § 6, 3 C.F.R. 638, 644–648 (1994), *reprinted in* 5 U.S.C. § 601 (2012); Exec. Order No. 13,563 § 1, 3 C.F.R. 215, 215–216 (2012), *reprinted in* 5 U.S.C. § 601 (2012).

46. Christopher C. DeMuth and Douglas H. Ginsburg, "White House Review of Agency Rulemaking," *Harvard Law Review* 99 (1986): 1081.

47. Barkow and Osler, "Designed to Fail," 463–465.

48. Edward Glaeser and Cass R. Sunstein, "Regulatory Review for the States," *National Affairs,* Summer 2014, https://www.nationalaffairs.com/publications/detail/regulatory-review-for-the-states.

49. Pew Charitable Trusts, "Pew-MacArthur Results First Initiative," http://www.pewtrusts.org/en/projects/pew-macarthur-results-first-initiative; Christian Henrichson, "Cost-Benefit Knowledge Bank for Criminal Justice," Vera Institute of Justice, https://www.vera.org/projects/cost-benefit-knowledge-bank-for-criminal-justice.

50. Rachel E. Barkow, "Overseeing Agency Enforcement," *George Washington Law Review* 84 (2016): 1176.

51. Barkow, 1178–1179; Barkow and Osler, "Designed to Fail," 469–471.

52. Barkow and Osler, "Designed to Fail," 470–471.

53. Barkow, "Overseeing Agency Enforcement," 1151–1152.

54. Washington adopted an appropriations bill in December 2016 to introduce a pilot racial and ethnic impact statement program, H.B. 2376, 64th Leg., 1st Spec. Sess. (Wash. 2016). Minnesota's sentencing commission has also produced such information even though it is not required to as a matter of law. Minnesota Sentencing Guidelines Commission, "Reports," https://mn.gov/sentencing-guidelines/reports.

55. Ryan J. Foley, "Racial-Impact Law Has Modest Effect in Iowa," *Journal Sentinel,* January 21, 2015, http://www.jsonline.com/story/news/politics/2015/01/21/racial-impact-law-effect-iowa-legislature/22138465.

56. Jonathan Lippman, "How One State Reduced Both Crime and Incarceration," *Hofstra Law Review,* 38 (2010): 1077.

57. Travis, *But They All Come Back,* 243–244; *see also* Nino Rodriguez and Brenner Brown, *Preventing Homelessness among People Leaving Prison* (Vera Institute of Justice, 2003), https://www.vera.org/publications/preventing-homelessness-among-people-leaving-prison; Carrie A. Pettus and Margaret Severson, "Paving the Way for Effective Reentry Practice: The

Critical Role and Function of the Boundary Spanner," *Prison Journal* 86 (2006): 206–229.

58. Anthony C. Thompson, "Navigating the Hidden Obstacles to Ex-Offender Reentry," *Boston College Law Review* 45 (2004): 255–306; Michael Pinard, "Broadening the Holistic Mindset: Incorporating Collateral Consequences and Reentry into Criminal Defense Lawyering," *Fordham Urban Law Journal* 31 (2004): 1067–1095.

59. Naomi Murakawa, *The First Civil Right: How Liberals Built Prison America* (New York: Oxford University Press, 2014), 17.

60. Charles Colson Task Force on Federal Corrections, *Transforming Prisons, Restoring Lives* (2016), 58.

61. Nancy LaVigne et al., *Justice Reinvestment Initiative Report* (Urban Institute, 2014), https://www.urban.org/sites/default/files/publication/22211/412994 -Justice-Reinvestment-Initiative-State-Assessment-Report.PDF.

62. Georgia Department of Community Supervision, Georgia Council on Criminal Justice Reform, https://dcs.georgia.gov/georgia-council-criminal -justice-reform.

63. Michael P. Boggs and W. Thomas Worthy, *Report of the Georgia Council on Criminal Justice Reform* (Georgia Council on Criminal Justice Reform, 2014), 3, https://dcs.georgia.gov/sites/dcs.georgia.gov/files/related_files/site _page/2013-GA-Council-on-Criminal-Justice-Reform.pdf.

64. Casey Tolan, "How Republican-Controlled Georgia Became a National Leader in Criminal Justice Reform," Splinter, January 28, 2016, https:// splinternews.com/how-republican-controlled-georgia-became-a-national-lea -1793854362.

10. Catalyzing Courts

1. Marie Gottschalk, "Bring It On: The Future of Penal Reform, the Carceral State, and American Politics," *Ohio State Journal of Criminal Law* 12 (2015): 565.

2. Brown v. Plata, 563 U.S. 493 (2011).

3. Joan Petersilia, "California Prison Downsizing and Its Impact on Local Criminal Justice Systems," *Harvard Law and Policy Review* 8 (2014): 327.

4. Richard J. Couzens and Tricia A. Bigelow, *Felony Sentencing after Realignment* (2014), 58, www.courts.ca.gov/partners/documents/felony_sentencing .pdf; Cal. Penal Code § 1170 (h); Cal. Penal Code § 17.5.

5. California Legislative Analyst's Office, *The 2012–13 Budget: The 2011 Realignment of Adult Offenders—An Update* (2012), 11, http://www.cdcr.ca .gov/Reports/docs/External-Reports/Refocusing-CDCR-After-2011 -Realignment-022312.pdf; Petersilia, "California Prison Downsizing," 327.

6. Petersilia, "California Prison Downsizing"; Magnus Lofstrom and Steven Raphael, *Realignment, Incarceration, and Crime Trends in California* (Public Policy Institute of California, 2015), 1–2.

7. Lofstrom and Raphael, 7.

8. U.S. Const. art. III, § 2; U.S. Const. amend. VI.
9. *See generally* Richard E. Epstein, "Unconstitutional Conditions, State Power, and the Limits of Consent," *Harvard Law Review* 102 (1988): 6–7; Phillip Hamburger, "Unconstitutional Conditions: The Irrelevance of Consent," *Virginia Law Review* 98 (2012): 491; Rachel E. Barkow, "Separation of Powers and the Criminal Law," *Stanford Law Review* 58 (2006): 1045–1056.
10. Bordenkircher v. Hayes, 434 U.S. 357, 358–359 (1978).
11. Brady v. United States, 397 U.S. 742, 743–744 (1970).
12. United States v. Angelos, 345 F. Supp. 2d 1227 (2004).
13. Rachel E. Barkow, "The Court of Life and Death: The Two Tracks of Constitutional Sentencing Law and the Case for Uniformity," *Michigan Law Review* 107 (2009): 1145–1205.
14. United States v. Beverly, 369 F.3d 516, 536 (6th Cir. 2004).
15. Bell v. United States, 349 U.S. 81, 83 (1955).
16. United States v. Bass, 404 U.S. 336, 348 (1971).
17. United States v. Santos, 553 U.S. 507, 514 (2008) (Scalia, J., dissenting).
18. McBoyle v. United States, 283 U.S. 25, 27 (1985).
19. Joseph E. Bauerschmidt, Note, "Mother of Mercy—Is This the End of RICO—Justice Scalia Invites Constitutional Void-for-Vagueness Challenge to RICO Pattern," *Notre Dame Law Review* 65 (1990): 1118–1119.
20. Anthony G. Amsterdam, Note, "The Void-for-Vagueness Doctrine in the Supreme Court," *University of Pennsylvania Law Review* 109 (1960): 72.
21. Imbler v. Pachtman, 424 U.S. 409 (1976); Buckley v. Fitzsimmons, 509 U.S. 259 (1993).
22. William Baude, "Is Qualified Immunity Unlawful?," *California Law Review* 106 (2018): 49–77; Margaret Z. Johns, "Unsupportable and Unjustified: A Critique of Absolute Prosecutorial Immunity," *Fordham Law Review* 80 (2011): 521–527.
23. Monell v. New York City Dept. of Social Servs., 436 U.S. 658, 691 (1978).
24. 563 U.S. 51 (2011).
25. Joseph Shapiro, "As Court Fees Rise, the Poor Are Paying the Price," NPR, May 19, 2014, https://www.npr.org/2014/05/19/312158516/increasing-court-fees-punish-the-poor; Lauren-Brooke Eisen, "Paying for Your Time: How Charging Inmates Fees behind Bars May Violate the Excessive Fines Clause," Brennan Center for Justice, July 31, 2014, https://www.brennancenter.org/analysis/paying-your-time-how-charging-inmates-fees-behind-bars-may-violate-excessive-fines-clause.
26. U.S. Department of Justice (DOJ), Civil Rights Division, *Investigation of the Ferguson Police Department* (2015), 56; Cain v. City of New Orleans, No. CV 15-4479, 2016 WL 2962912 (E.D. La. May 23, 2016); *see also* Tate v. Short, 401 U.S. 395 (1971).
27. Bearden v. Georgia, 416 U.S. 660, 665 (1983).
28. Bearden v. Georgia, 671; Tate v. Short, 401 U.S. 395 (1971), Williams v. Illinois, 399 U.S. 235 (1970).

29. *See generally* Alicia Bannon, Mitali Nagrecha, and Rebekah Diller, *Criminal Justice Debt: A Barrier to Reentry* (Brennan Center for Justice, 2010), 20, http://www.brennancenter.org/sites/default/files/legacy/Fees%20and%20 Fines%20FINAL.pdf; Council of Economic Advisers, *Fines, Fees, and Bail: Payments in the Criminal Justice System That Disproportionately Impact the Poor* (2015), https://obamawhitehouse.archives.gov/sites/default/files/page /files/1215_cea_fine_fee_bail_issue_brief.pdf.

30. DOJ, *Ferguson Police Department,* 58; *see also* DOJ, 57 (quoting Bearden v. Georgia, 671).

31. Bannon et al., *Criminal Justice Debt,* 20.

32. Joseph Shapiro, "Supreme Court Ruling Not Enough to Prevent Debtors Prisons," NPR, May 21, 2014, https://www.npr.org/2014/05/21/313118629 /supreme-court-ruling-not-enough-to-prevent-debtors-prisons.

33. Apprendi v. New Jersey, 530 U.S. 466 (2000); United States v. Booker, 543 U.S. 220 (2005).

34. Blakely v. Washington, 542 U.S. 296 (2004); United States v. Booker, 543 U.S. 220 (2005).

35. Alleyne v. United States, 133 S. Ct. 2151 (2013).

36. Crystal S. Yang, "Free at Last? Judicial Discretion and Racial Disparities in Federal Sentencing," *Journal of Legal Studies* 44 (2015): app. Table A4.

37. U.S. Sentencing Commission, *Overview of Mandatory Minimum Penalties in the Federal Criminal Justice System* (2017), https://www.ussc.gov/sites/default /files/pdf/research-and-publications/research-publications/2017/20170711 _Mand-Min.pdf.

38. Rachel E. Barkow, "Recharging the Jury: The Criminal Jury's Constitutional Role in an Era of Mandatory Sentencing," *University of Pennsylvania Law Review* 152 (2003): 33.

39. *See* Rachel E. Barkow, "Originalists, Politics, and Criminal Law on the Rehnquist Court," *George Washington Law Review* 74 (2006): 1046.

40. Rachel E. Barkow, "Federalism and the Politics of Sentencing," *Columbia Law Review* 105 (2005): 1283.

41. Lafler v. Cooper, 132 S. Ct. 1376 (2012); Missouri v. Frye, 132 S.Ct. 1399 (2012).

42. Lafler v. Cooper, 166.

43. Lafler v Cooper, 169–170.

44. Buffey v. Ballard, 236 W. Va. 509 (2015).

45. Buffey v. Ballard, 513.

46. Buffey v. Ballard, 523.

47. 397 U.S. 742, 751 n.8 (1970).

48. James Vorenberg, "Decent Restraint of Prosecutorial Power," *Harvard Law Review* 94 (1981): 1560–1561; Maximo Langer, "Rethinking Plea Bargaining," *American Journal of Criminal Law* 33 (2006): 277–286.

49. Ewing v. California, 28.

50. 560 U.S. 48, 61, 76 (2010).

51. 567 U.S. 460, 465 (2012).

52. Woodson v. North Carolina, 428 U.S. 280, 304 (1976) (plurality opinion) (citation omitted).

53. Barkow, "Court of Life and Death," 1178.

54. Cain v. City of New Orleans, No. CV 15–4479, 2016 WL 2962912 (E.D. La. May 23, 2016); Fant v. City of Ferguson, No. 4:15-CV-00254-AGF, 2015 WL 4232917 (E.D. Mo. July 13, 2015).

55. Mitchell v. City of Montgomery, No. 2:14-CV-186-MHT, 2014 WL 11099432 (M.D. Ala. Nov. 17, 2014); McCullogh v. City of Montgomery, No. 2:15-CV-463 (RCL), 2017 WL 956362, at *1 (M.D. Ala. Mar. 10, 2017); *see also* Carter v. City of Montgomery, No. 2:15-CV-555 (RCL), 2017 WL 957540 (M.D. Ala. Mar. 10, 2017); Rudolph v. City of Montgomery, No. 2:16-CV-57 (RCL), 2017 WL 956359 (M.D. Ala. Mar. 10, 2017).

56. Rodriguez v. Providence Community Corrections, Inc., 155 F. Supp. 3d 758 (M.D. Tenn. 2015).

57. Noel v. State, 191 So. 3d 370 (Fla. 2016); State v. Sleater, 378 P. 3d 218 (Wash. Ct. App. 2016); *see also* Cain v. City of New Orleans, No. CV 15–4479, 2016 WL 2962912, at *5, *7 (E.D. La. May 23, 2016).

58. 135 S. Ct. 2551 (2015).

59. Lyle Denniston, "Court to Decide *Johnson* Retroactivity," *SCOTUSblog,* January 8, 2016, http://www.scotusblog.com/2016/01/court-to-decide -johnson-retroactivity; Dara Lind, "*Johnson v. United States:* Part of Armed Career Criminal Act Struck Down by Supreme Court," *Vox,* June 26, 2015, https://www.vox.com/2015/6/26/8845183/johnson-united-states; "How Many Hundreds (or Thousands?) of ACCA Prisoners Could Be Impacted by a Big Ruling in *Johnson,*" *Sentencing Law and Policy Blog,* June 13, 2015, http://sentencing.typepad.com/sentencing_law_and_policy/2015/06/how -many-hundreds-or-thousands-of-acca-prisoners-could-be-impacted-by-a-big -ruling-in-johnson.html (citing U.S. Sentencing Commission, *Quick Facts: Felon in Possession of Firearm* [2014], https://www.ussc.gov/sites/default/files /pdf/research-and-publications/quick-facts/Quick_Facts_Felon_in_Possession _FY14.pdf); Libby Nelson, "*Welch v. US:* A Surprise Supreme Court Decision Will Let Some Federal Prisoners Out Early," *Vox,* April 18, 2016, https://www.vox.com/2016/4/18/11450368/supreme-court-sentencing-welch -us. *See generally* Leah M. Litman, "Residual Impact: Resentencing Implica- tions of *Johnson*'s Potential Ruling on ACCA's Constitutionality," *Columbia Law Review Sidebar* 115 (2015): 55–78.

60. U.S. Sentencing Commission, *Supplement to the 2015 Guidelines Manual* (2016), https://www.ussc.gov/sites/default/files/pdf/guidelines-manual/2015 /GLMSupplement.pdf; Caroline Grueskin, "13 Words That Could Mean Freedom for Many," Marshall Project, October 19, 2015, https://www .themarshallproject.org/2015/10/19/13-words-that-could-mean-freedom-for -many.

61. William T. Pizzi, "A Comparative Perspective on the Sentencing Chaos in the U.S.," *Global Jurist Topics* 6, no. 2 (2006): 1; William T. Pizzi, "Lessons from Reforming Inquisitorial Systems," *Federal Sentencing Reporter* 8 (1995): 42–43.

62. United States v. Nesbeth, 188 F. Supp. 3d 179 (E.D.N.Y. 2016).

63. United States v. Holloway, 68 F.Supp. 3d 310, 311 (E.D.N.Y. 2014).

64. United States v. Holloway, 311.

65. United States v. Young, 960 F. Supp. 2d 881 (N.D. Iowa 2013); United States v. Kupa, 976 F. Supp. 2d 417 (E.D.N.Y. 2013); United States v. Dossie, 851 F. Supp. 2d 478 (E.D.N.Y. 2012).

66. Rachel E. Barkow, "Organizational Guidelines for the Prosecutor's Office," *Cardozo Law Review* 31 (2010): 2112.

67. Alex Kozinski, "Preface: Criminal Law 2.0," *Georgetown Law Journal Annual Review of Criminal Procedure* 44 (2015): iii.

68. Barkow, "Organizational Guidelines," 2112–2113.

69. Barkow, 2113–2114.

70. Jessica A. Roth, "The 'New' District Court Activism in Criminal Justice Reform," *New York University Annual Survey of American Law* 73 (2017): 187–273.

71. Rachel Barkow, "Overseeing Agency Enforcement: A Foreword to the Annual Review of Administrative Law," *George Washington Law Review* 84 (2016): 1167–1169.

72. Allegra McLeod, "Decarceration Courts: Possibilities and Perils of a Shifting Criminal Law," *Georgetown Law Journal* 100 (2012): 1606.

73. Daniel M. Fetsco, "Reentry Courts: An Emerging Use of Judicial Resources in the Struggle to Reduce the Recidivism of Released Offenders," *Wyoming Law Review* 13 (2013): 603; Christine Lindquist et al., *The National Institute of Justice's Evaluation of Second Chance Act Adult Reentry Courts: Program Characteristics and Preliminary Themes from Year 1* (2013), 8, https://www.ncjrs.gov/pdffiles1/nij/grants/241400.pdf.

74. U.S. Sentencing Commission, *Federal Alternative-to-Incarceration Court Programs* (2017), 8–9, 17.

75. Anthony M. Kennedy, "Speech at the American Bar Association Annual Meeting," August 9, 2003, https://www.supremecourt.gov/publicinfo/speeches/sp_08–09–03.html; Liz Mineo, "Kennedy Assails Prison Shortcomings," *Harvard Gazette,* October 22, 2015; Editorial, "Justice Kennedy's Plea to Congress," *New York Times,* April 4, 2015, https://www.nytimes.com/2015/04/05/opinion/sunday/justice-kennedys-plea-to-congress.html.

76. Jed S. Rakoff, "Mass Incarceration: The Silence of the Judges," *New York Review of Books,* May 21, 2015, http://www.nybooks.com/articles/2015/05/21/mass-incarceration-silence-judges; Jed S. Rakoff, "Why Prosecutors Rule the Criminal Justice System—And What Can Be Done about It," *Northwestern University Law Review* 111 (2017): 1436.

77. Jon Schuppe, "Bail Reform Movement Gets Powerful Ally: California's Top Judge," NBC, October 24, 2017, https://www.nbcnews.com/news/us-news/bail-reform-movement-gets-powerful-ally-california-s-top-judge-n813906.

78. Richard A. Oppel Jr., "Defendants Can't Be Jailed Solely Because of Inability to Pay, Judge Says," *New York Times,* July 17, 2017, https://www.nytimes.com/2017/07/17/us/chicago-bail-reform.html.

79. Rachel E. Barkow, "Tribute to Justice Antonin Scalia," *New York University Annual Survey of American Law* 62 (2006): 15.
80. Robert Batey, "The Vagueness Doctrine in the Roberts Court: Constitutional Orphan," *UMKC Law Review* 80 (2011): 128; Barkow, "Tribute to Justice Scalia," 17–18; Peter W. Low and Joel S. Johnson, "Changing the Vocabulary of the Vagueness Doctrine," *Virginia Law Review* 101 (2015): 2051–2116; Sarah Newland, Note, "The Mercy of Scalia: Statutory Construction and the Rule of Lenity," *Harvard Civil Rights-Civil Liberties Law Review* 29 (1994): 197; Bar of the Supreme Court of the United States, *Resolutions in Gratitude and Appreciation for the Life, Work and Service of Justice Antonin Scalia* (2016), 19, https://www.supremecourt.gov /pdf/Scalia_Resolution.pdf.
81. Crawford v. Washington, 541 U.S. 36 (2004); Ohio v. Clark, 135 S. Ct. 2173, 2185 (2015) (Scalia, J., concurring in the judgment); Carella v. California, 491 U.S. 263, 269 (1989) (Scalia, J., concurring in the judgment); Neder v. United States, 527 U.S. 1, 30 (Scalia, J., concurring in part and dissenting in part); Apprendi v. New Jersey, 530 U.S. 466, 498 (2000) (Scalia, J., concurring); United States v. Booker, 543 U.S. 220 (2005).
82. Harmelin v. Michigan, 501 U.S. 951, 977–978 (1991).
83. For example, President Obama reportedly considered two women who have experience as federal public defenders: Jane Kelly, a judge on the U.S. Court of Appeals for the 8th Circuit, and Ketanji Brown Jackson, a judge on the U.S. District Court for the District of Columbia. Eric Beech, "Federal Judge Being Considered for U.S. Supreme Court Nomination," Reuters, February 26, 2016, http://www.reuters.com/article/us-usa-court-obama-jackson -idUSKCN0W003J; Grant Rodgers, "Iowa Judge Jane Kelly Possible U.S. Supreme Court Pick," *Des Moines Register,* February 20, 2016, http://www .desmoinesregister.com/story/news/crime-and-courts/2016/02/20/iowa-judge -would-bring-unique-background-high-court/80602170.
84. *See, e.g.,* United States v. Burwell, 690 F.3d 500 (D.C. Cir. 2012); United States v. Riley, 376 F.3d 1160 (D.C. Cir. 2004); United States v. Watson, 171 F.3d 695, 703 (D.C. Cir. 1999) (Garland, J., dissenting); United States v. Spinner, 152 F.3d 950, 962 (D.C. Cir. 1998) (Garland, J., dissenting); David A. Graham, "How Did the Oklahoma City Bombing Shape Merrick Garland?," *Atlantic,* March 17, 2016, https://www.theatlantic.com/politics /archive/2016/03/merrick-garland-oklahoma-city-bombing-supreme-court /474090/.
85. *See, e.g.,* Sessions v. Dimaya, 138 S.Ct. 1204 (2018); United States v. Carloss, 818 F.3d 988, 1005–1006 (10th Cir. 2016) (Gorsuch, J., dissenting); United States v. Rentz, 777 F.3d 1105, 1113 (10th Cir. 2015) (en banc).
86. Eliza Relman, "Reproductive Rights Groups Help Pressure Democrats into Filibuster on Trump's Supreme Court Nominee," *Business Insider,* April 6, 2017, http://www.businessinsider.com/gorsuch-on-repro-rights-tktktk-2017-3.
87. Timothy M. Phelps, "Liberal Groups Urge Senate to Block Obama Judicial Nominees," *Los Angeles Times,* May 12, 2014, http://www.latimes.com /nation/la-na-senate-judges-20140512-story.html.

88. Thomas Hopson, "Potential Nominee: Judge Sri Srinivasan, Appellate Veteran," *SCOTUSblog,* March 11, 2016, http://www.scotusblog.com/2016 /03/potential-nominee-judge-sri-srinivasan-appellate-veteran.
89. Rachel E. Barkow and Mark Osler, "Designed to Fail: The President's Deference to the Department of Justice in Advancing Criminal Justice Reform," *William and Mary Law Review* 59 (2017): 472.
90. Barkow and Osler, 472.
91. The seven judges are G. Steven Agee, Bernice Donald, Jane Kelly, Edward Prado, Luis Restrepo, Robert Wilkins, and James Wynn.
92. Gregory L. Acquaviva and John D. Castiglione, "Judicial Diversity on State Supreme Courts," *Seton Hall Law Review* 39 (2010): 1225; Casey Tolan, "Why Federal Defenders Are Less Likely to Become Judges—and Why That Matters," Splinter, March 18, 2016, https://splinternews.com/why-public -defenders-are-less-likely-to-become-judges-a-1793855687.
93. *See, e.g.,* James M. Anderson and Eric Helland, "How Much Should Judges Be Paid? An Empirical Study on the Effect of Judicial Pay on the State Bench," *Stanford Law Review* 64 (2012): 1308; Nick Gorny, "Pipeline to the Bench: New Judges Often Former Prosecutors," *Ocala,* November 14, 2015, http://www.ocala.com/news/20151114/pipeline-to-the-bench-new-judges -often-former-prosecutors; A. Young, "Nomination of Another Prosecutor as Judge a Concern for Governor's Councilors," *Enterprise News,* June 29, 2016, http://www.enterprisenews.com/news/20160629/nomination-of -another-prosecutor-as-judge-concern-for-governors-councilors.
94. Gorny, "Pipeline."
95. Martha Myers, "Social Background and the Sentencing Behavior of Judges," *Criminology* 26 (1988): 649–676; Stuart S. Nagel, "Political Party Affiliation and Judges' Decision," *American Political Science Review* 55 (1961): 843–850; Donald R. Songer and Susan J. Tabrizi, "The Religious Right in Court: The Decision Making of Christian Evangelicals in State Supreme Courts," *Journal of Politics* 61 (1999): 507–526.
96. Barkow and Osler, "Designed to Fail," 473.

Conclusion

1. Rachel E. Barkow, "Administering Crime," *UCLA Law Review* 52 (2005): 751.
2. Howard Shelanski, "Will Today's Politics Upend Sound Regulation?," *Marquette Lawyer,* Fall 2017, 29–30.
3. Evan McMullin, "Trump's Rise Proves How Dangerous Populism Is for Democracy," opinion, NBC News, October 13, 2017, https://www.nbcnews .com/think/opinion/trump-s-rise-proves-populism-democracy-s-greatest -threat-ncna809521.
4. Harrison Jacobs, "Our Exclusive Interview with New Philadelphia District Attorney Larry Krasner, Who Blew Out the Competition with an Ultra-Progressive Platform," *Business Insider,* November 8, 2017, http://www

.businessinsider.com/larry-krasner-philadelphia-district-attorney-interview
-platform-2017-11/-krasner-says-he-may-have-spent-his-career-defending
-protesters-but-he-wont-be-defending-nazis-1.

5. *See also* Paul H. Robinson and John M. Darley, "The Utility of Desert,"
Northwestern University Law Review 91 (1997): 453–499.

Acknowledgments

This book is the product of more than sixteen years of work on these issues, and I owe a debt of gratitude to everyone who has helped me along the way.

I am grateful to my generous colleagues at NYU School of Law who have read countless articles of mine with the seeds of the ideas in this book and who have talked me through many of the book's chapters and issues. Thanks especially to Barry Friedman, David Garland, Jim Jacobs, Daryl Levinson, Erin Murphy, Rick Pildes, and Steve Schulhofer, who have given me so much of their time over the years and invaluable advice. Thanks to my two wonderful assistants, Lara Maraziti and Janou Hooykaas, who helped proofread and format the manuscript. I am also grateful to have had two deans who have been tremendously supportive of me and my scholarship, Ricky Revesz and Trevor Morrison. I cannot think of a more encouraging environment to work than NYU.

My students have been extraordinary as well, and I am thankful for wonderful and robust class discussions over the years and for the many great questions that helped spark much of the research in the book. I am particularly indebted to the following students for providing me with first-class research assistance and help producing this book: Beth Caldwell, Patrick Cordova, Stephanie Damon-Moore, Cassandra Deskus, Destiny Dike, Tyler Domino, Abe Dyk, Katrina Feldkamp, Isabela Garcez, Connor Haynes, Stephen Hylas, Elizabeth Janszky, Grace Li, Daniel Loehr, Steve Marcus, Samantha Reiser, Ravinder Singh, Jarmonique Smith, Matthew Smith, Molly Stein, Samuel Steinbock-Pratt, Michael Taintor, Ben Wylly, and Amy Zimmerman.

I presented chapters of the book over the past couple of years at workshops, and the attendees were enormously helpful to me in shaping the ideas. Many thanks to the workshop participants at the Center for the Study of Law and Society Speaker Series at the University of California, Berkeley, School of Law; the Public Law and Legal Theory Workshop at the University of Chicago Law School; the faculty workshop at Washington University School of Law; and to the audience members at the Barrock Lecture at Marquette University Law School.

I owe special thanks to the participants at the Criminal Justice Roundtable at Stanford Law School who helped me conceptualize and frame the project when it was at an early stage and to the participants at other Criminal Justice Roundtables who have been such supportive colleagues over the years as I pursued many of the ideas and arguments in the book. In particular, I am thankful to Paul Butler, Sharon Dolovich, Jeff Fagan, James Forman Jr., Bernard Harcourt, Christopher Kutz, Maximo Langer, Tracey Meares, Dan Richman, David Sklansky, Carol Steiker, and Jordan Steiker. William Stuntz, one of the founders of the Criminal Justice Roundtable, was an early supporter of my scholarship, and his work in the field remains a lodestar for my own.

Many of my ideas are the outgrowth of my time working on criminal justice reform in the trenches, either at the United States Sentencing Commission, the Center on the Administration of Criminal Law, or with colleagues on clemency reform. I am grateful to them for inspiration and for showing me that reform is possible with dedicated people working toward it. My fellow commissioners and the staff at the commission represent the best in public service, and it has been a privilege to work with them. A big thanks to Deb Gramiccioni, Nancy Hoppock, Anne Milgram, and Courtney Oliva at the Center on the Administration of Criminal Law for their tireless work on reforming the ways that prosecutors do their jobs and for finding so many ways to improve how criminal laws are administered. My partner in clemency reform, Mark Osler, is a perfect example of what one person committed to justice can achieve. I am thankful to call him both a friend and a coauthor. Paul J. Larkin, Jr., at Heritage has also been a valued partner on clemency reform, and I am grateful for his comments on an earlier draft of the introduction.

The team at Harvard University Press has been terrific, and I want to give special thanks to Thomas LeBien for his guidance. As I was negotiating the process of finding a publisher, I could not have asked for better advice than what I received from Noah Feldman and Mehrsa Baradaran. Noah, in particular, suffered through more than one draft of a proposal, and I owe him enormous thanks for all the help.

I can never repay my friends and family for their unflinching love and support through the years and for never (okay, rarely) mocking my pie-in-the-sky hopes of making the world a better place. My mom has always told me she is proud of me no matter what I have worked on, and I am grateful for her unconditional love and encouragement, as well as the love of my siblings. I have the best nieces and nephews in the world, and I am thankful to them for always at least appearing interested in what I am doing. I am lucky to have in-laws who have felt like family from the beginning. I wish my mother-in-law, Barbara Barkow, were alive to see this book, which I know she would proudly display. I have the best friends in the world, who are there for me in good times and bad, and I count them among the greatest blessings in my life. There are too many to list, but if you're not sure you would have made the cut, that probably means you owe me a phone call.

An author should probably not admit that it is hard to find words to describe something, but I am struggling to find the right way to capture how grateful I am for my husband, Tony Barkow. I give thanks each day that we are still a team on life's journey. No one gave me better feedback on this book or offered more support as I wrote it, and we have had too many conversations to count over the years about the issues within it. Thanks for never tiring of my ideas and for always supporting my work. I am glad that Nate gets to see a model of what a supportive spouse should look like.

The book is dedicated to my son, Nate, who is the light of my life and was a little rock as I wrote this. On days when I got discouraged or stressed, he was the first person to tell me how proud he was that I was writing it. Raising such a kind and loving son will always be my proudest accomplishment.

Index